Theories of
Organization

Dedicated to Grace . . .

Theories of Organization

Henry L. Tosi

University of Florida

Los Angeles • London • New Delhi • Singapore • Washington DC

For information:

SAGE Publications, Inc.
2455 Teller Road
Thousand Oaks, California 91320
E-mail: order@sagepub.com

SAGE Publications India Pvt. Ltd.
B 1/I 1 Mohan Cooperative Industrial Area
Mathura Road, New Delhi 110 044
India

SAGE Publications Ltd.
1 Oliver's Yard
55 City Road
London EC1Y 1SP
United Kingdom

SAGE Publications Asia-Pacific Pte. Ltd.
33 Pekin Street #02-01
Far East Square
Singapore 048763

Printed in the United States of America

Library of Congress Cataloging-in-Publication Data

Theories of organization / [compiled by] Henry L. Tosi.
       p. cm.
Includes bibliographical references and index.
ISBN 978-1-4129-2499-3
    1. Organization. 2. Industrial organization. 3. Industrial sociology. I. Tosi, Henry L.

HD31.T486 2009
302.3'5—dc22   2008020269

08   09   10   11   12   10   9   8   7   6   5   4   3   2   1

Acquisitions Editor:	Al Bruckner
Editorial Assistant:	MaryAnn Vail
Copy Editor:	Tony Moore
Typesetter:	C&M Digitals (P) Ltd.
Proofreader:	Taryn Bigelow
Indexers:	Henry L. Tosi and Kathy Paparchontis
Cover Designer:	Candice Harman
Marketing Manager:	Jennifer Reed Banando

Contents

Contingency Theories

Economic Approaches

PART I

Overture

A book like this, of course, is never complete for the user—or for me, for that matter—because there are models that are not here that others would like to have been included. But what is here is a matter of taste, for which I take full responsibility. But then that is why some of us prefer Brunnello to Bordeaux or Monet to Michelangelo.

These summaries, extracts, and reviews have been gathered from a number of sources. In them are presented the major variables and relationships in the various points of view about organizations. The premise is straightforward: If a theory is a set of systematically related concepts that abstract observed reality, then to understand the theory it is important to understand the comprehensive scheme of the main variables of a theory, rather than its fragmentary elements. Of course, the elegance and the logic of the original models may have been lost, but not the substance of the theory. In this way the reader gets an abbreviated view of the whole theory that is presented without evaluative comment.

The purpose of this collection is to expose the student quickly to a broad range of theories. It is not meant to substitute for the complete works themselves. Students have much to learn by immersing themselves in the original works. I would have it no other way.

— Henry L. Tosi

CHAPTER 1

About Theories of Organization

Henry L. Tosi

What This Book Is About

There are two disciplines that constitute the field of organization studies: organizational theory and organizational behavior. Each has a relatively unique perspective and each consists of different variables and conceptual schemes that address organizational issues. The major difference between these two fields is the unit of analysis on which they focus. Organizational behavior is the study of individual and group behavior within organizations and the application of such knowledge. The concepts are primarily psychological—for example, attitudes, personality, motivation, and psychological aspects of decision making. The organization is usually treated, both empirically and theoretically, as an independent variable that affects individual- and group-dependent variables and is generally construed as the concept "organizational structure."

In organization theory, it is organization, not the individuals or groups in it, that is the unit of analysis. The discipline is very broad, catholic in many ways. It draws from diverse disciplines such as sociology, economics, the classic theory of bureaucracy, and, more recently, postmodern approaches. Common constructs are organization structure, organizational environments, formalization, technology, authority, groups, and departments, among other variables.

This book presents a selection of different organizational theories that, with few exceptions, are positivist approaches, used as meant by Burrell and Morgan (1979). These models seek to "explain or predict what happens in the social world by searching for regularities and causal relationships between . . . constituent elements" (p. 5). They take the natural sciences and their methodologies as their model. However, there are other views that are also of interest to some students of organization—for example, critical theory (see Chapter 18, by Jermier) and postmodernism (Calas & Smircich, 1999; see Chapter 19).

The approach here differs from the more conventional treatments of organizational theory by others. For example, Scott (2003), Hall and Tolbert (2005), Daft (2004), and Grandori (1987) tend to take a topical approach that offers an analysis and comparison of conceptual domains such as formalization, authority, or bureaucracy and then discuss how these concepts are treated in different theories. Or they may examine different schools of thought such as administrative theory, institutional approaches, or economic approaches to the study of organizations and then provide useful analytical and critical commentary about these theoretical schemes and how they differ.

Here, each theory is presented in its skeletal form, to include the range of important theoretical concepts and how they are related to each other. Thus the reader gets an abbreviated view of the whole theory that is set forth in as descriptive a way as possible, without evaluative comment. The premise is straightforward: If a theory is a set of systematically related concepts that abstract observed reality, then to understand the theory it is important to understand the comprehensive scheme of the main variables of a theory, rather than its fragmentary elements

Without such an overall theoretical perspective, it is easy to misconstrue a particular theory and its concepts. Take, for example, agency theory, an economic approach to organizations that has been the target of some criticism. Once the reader understands the basic constructs from the agency approach, it can be seen as the economists' attempt to introduce a set of well-developed concepts from their literature into the study of internal organizational processes, such as how to ensure that managers of firms act in the interests of the owners. Further, understanding this sets forth the theory as an innovative attempt by economists to broaden the theoretical base of their own discipline. Instead, much of the criticism of agency theory emanates from the fact that it is one more competitive theoretical model of organization to which can be applied some very rigorous standard theoretical and empirical tools from the economists' armamentarium (Hirsch, Friedman, & Koza, 1990). However, close attention to the theory will show that there is some important conceptual overlap with other approaches—for example, with administrative theory (the basis for authority in organizations is the right of private property), population ecology (the survival of organizations in their environments), and institutional models (how organizations take their form).

This conceptual overlap between many of these theories is perfectly reasonable; all are about the same phenomena—organizations—and they take, for the most part, a positivist approach. What differentiates them is that each theorist uses a different set of concepts to explain organization. For example, Williamson and Ouchi (1981) draw heavily from economics (particularly transaction cost analysis) and sociology to explain why particular forms of organization structures exist, while Burns and Stalker (1961), as well as Woodward (1965), draw from the administrative theory school in building their contingency approach to organizational design.

These theories, like all in the social sciences, have a normative bias. That is, there are implicit, systematic dogmatic predispositions beneath the surface of the models of different schools of thought. So, to say a theory is biased or that its scope does not include certain important concepts and relationships is only to say that it was constructed by a person who builds a theoretical system by defining, with some degree of precision, the variables that are to be included that are a result of his or her socialization, both professional and cultural. So it should come as no surprise that there are theory wars—the "mine is better than yours" arguments that are frequently encountered in the discussion of different theoretical schools.

The theories are also different because those who formulate them are interested in different things, and different writers seek to explain these things from their own perspectives, and with tools and concepts with which they are familiar.

The values, beliefs, and background of the theorist determine not only the variables and concepts that make up the theory but also the manner in which a theory may be used to predict and explain organizational phenomena. Whether a given phenomenon may be studied in the laboratory, in a field experiment, or simply by observation is largely a function of the extent to which the researcher is capable of operationalizing concepts from a theory and/or the degree to which one is willing to interpret results from a "controlled" experiment into generalized effects that would occur in a "real world" environment. It remains, finally, the responsibility of the student of organization to examine theories in detail so to be aware of the bases for relationships as developed by the theorist.

What Is Organization?

Conceptually, there are only slight differences in the various terms used in the theories to define organizations. Barnard (1938) calls an organization a "system of consciously coordinated personal activities or forces" and a "system of interrelated activities" (p. 72) and Davis (1951) calls it "group(s) of people working together, under a leader, to accomplish an objective" (p. 18). And, in general, most models would include, implicitly or explicitly, the following concepts:

1. *Impersonal relationships.* The size of complex organizations makes it impossible to maintain close interpersonal relationships with a large number of the members, relative to the total membership.

2. *Formalization.* Formalization refers to written, documented guides for action and behavior of members and is common to all bureaucracies. Formalization simply means that ways of doing things, such as procedures and policies, are written and stated in such a way that they become stable, quasi-permanent directions, ranging from very general to very specific, for interaction and decisions. This is necessary because formalization provides a basis for the different types of interactions required of members, since the size of the organization makes it extremely difficult for members to work these out among themselves any other way. Formalization also provides a degree of stability to interaction patterns, regardless of the incumbent of the position in the organization. Thus, when an individual newly arrives in an organization, there are specified actions and interactions that facilitate the person's accommodation to the organization.

3. *Rationality.* Rationality is another characteristic attributed to large organizations, meaning that they are goal-directed systems of activities. If activities

are goal directed, then resources can be more effectively utilized. Rationality is partially achieved by "goal factoring." The organization has a general goal. This goal is factored, or broken down into subgoals. These are assigned to lower-level units. If these units achieve their purpose, or goal, the general organization goal will be attained. Individuals in lower-level units essentially "assume" the goal of the unit when they accept a position. They have an obligation to achieve their goals. Their obligations may be viewed as responsibilities of the position. In addition to the obligation, an incumbent will have certain prerogatives to allocate organization resources to accomplish these subunit goals. These prerogatives are called "authority."

4. *Hierarchical structure.* This refers to the presence of different degrees of authority at the various levels and in different positions of the organization. It is the chain of formal authority relationships from the top of the structure to its bottom, tying different levels of the organization together. It is through the authority structure that the various activities of the organization are integrated in order to achieve coordination in attaining goals. The degree of authority at a particular level may be defined in terms of the range of discretion an individual has over resource allocation, both physical and human. In general, positions at higher organizational levels are allocated greater discretion and are accorded more status and deference than those at lower levels.

5. *Specialization.* Specialization refers to the particular configuration of activities performed by an individual. The activities assigned to a particular position, or an individual, should be "rationally" grouped in such a way as to make sense in terms of effectiveness and efficiency.

    Specialization can be viewed as a continuum. At one end is the *division of labor.* This is called task specialization, and it occurs when the particular task is analyzed and broken down into relatively well-defined and narrow routine subtasks. An individual then is assigned to perform these subtasks, which are simpler and more repetitive than the total task requirements. The individual is able to learn the tasks and their concomitant skills quickly. This results in both increased "efficiency" and less dependence by the organization on the skills of a particular person.

    The other end of the specialization continuum is called *social specialization* (Thompson, 1961). This occurs when the broader task requirements cannot be easily subdivided and routinized, either because of their complexity and intensive development or because they are not needed to as great an extent as other more routine tasks. Thus, the *person,* not the work, is specialized in that the individual is assigned a task that requires a broader range of skills that are organizationally necessary. In this case, there is less "efficiency" and more dependence by the organization on the skills of a particular person than in the case of task specialization.

It's obvious that organizations in different industries or sectors will vary on these dimensions (e.g., high-technology electronics firms may have fewer hierarchical levels and less formalization than a similarly sized machine tool company). It is also possible that organizations of the same type (e.g., that are in the same environments or industries, such as hospitals or automobile manufacturing firms) may also vary substantially with respect to these characteristics. The most obvious difference is probably organization size; some hospitals are very large, others much smaller. But there may also be important differences in the number of levels, the level of formalization, and how organizational rationality is reflected in organizational objectives, policies, and procedures.

These differences often result from strategic decisions and organizational design decisions made by the organization's dominant coalition. For example, the management of some organizations may have implemented policies and practices that are much less formalized (e.g., rules and policies governing employee behavior) and with fewer hierarchical levels, while other firms in the same sector might be more hierarchical, with more vertical levels.

They may also reflect cross-cultural differences. Differences across countries in similar organizations (say, steel manufacturing companies in Japan and Italy) may also be a result of cultural preferences about appropriate power relationships. For instance, Hofstede (1980) has argued that organizations in high power-distance cultures (such as Spain and Argentina) may have more organizational levels than those in lower power-distance cultures (such as the United States and Australia).

The Elements of Theory

A theory is a special case of language, a way to communicate meaning about some phenomenon. Like a language, every theory has a vocabulary and a grammar; the vocabulary defines what the words mean (concepts and variables), and the grammar defines how words are related (relationships) to other words, can be combined with other words, and how the language is used to create meaning. As you will see when you read the selections, different languages are used: the languages of economics, sociology, and administrative theory, for example. So, like languages, a theory is an invented, abstract way to describe reality by defining a set of systematically interrelated concepts, definitions, and propositions about tentative relationships between the concepts that characterize the reality that is the object of the theory.

Theory aids in understanding reality and in predicting what will occur under different conditions. For example, consider what population ecology theory and contingency theory tell us about organizations. Population ecology (Hannan & Freeman, 1977) predicts that those organizations in a population that have adapted to changing environments will survive. Contingency theory (Burns & Stalker, 1961) shows how some organizational designs will adapt to the environment, depending on the nature of the environment. It posits that in a relatively stable environment, a mechanistic (or bureaucratic) structure may be more effective than one that approaches a more loosely structured form. However, in a highly variable or volatile environment, more flexible forms, which they call "organic," would be appropriate.

Theoretical Concepts. The set of concepts make up the vocabulary of a theory. A concept, sometimes called a variable or a construct, is like a word; it is a human invention to provide and convey meaning for different observed elements, both objective and subjective, that the theory seeks to describe. Some constructs, or variables, describe things or activities (the nouns) and some describe actions (the verbs). Some concepts may be very specific; some more general. Labels are then associated with a concept to convey the concept's meaning to others.

Variables in a theory may take on a range of values. For example, the concept "organization structure" may range from the state of relatively loose (organic) to relatively rigid (mechanistic). According to Burns and Stalker (1961), the organic organization exists when

1. There is adjustment and continual redefinition of tasks through interaction.
2. There is a network structure of control, authority, and communication.
3. There is lateral, not vertical, communication.

A mechanistic organization state exists when

1. There is precise definition of rights and objections and methods into the functional responsibilities of a position.
2. There is a hierarchical structure of control.
3. There are vertical communication patterns.

Theoretical Relationships. As with any language, it is necessary to understand not only what specific words mean but also to know how they are related to each other. This is the function of the grammar of the theory: the set of rules that determines whether a particular combination of concepts is appropriate and how specific concepts are related to each other. These rules may be very precise, as they are in agency theory, or they may be more general, as they are in Mintzberg's (1979) theory of organizational structures.

The grammar is stated in terms of different types of relationships between constructs. Some statements describe a *causal sequence* between variables (Schwab, 1999). An example of a causal theoretical statement is "an increase in the level of formalization in an organization will result in higher productivity and lower member satisfaction." This statement is clear and unequivocal about what causes what. Other statements will describe simple, non-causal associations about how concepts exist together in a particular way. Such an associative statement about organizations is "personal specialization and social specialization occur in complex organizations." This simply tells us that these two types of specialization will be found in complex organizations and implies no causal sequence between the concepts.

Some relationships have, or are assumed to have, law-like properties with respect to the concepts in a theory. Such statements constitute "givens" that are attributed high truth value. These statements are either widely accepted because of convention or because there is convincing empirical evidence.

Other relationships will be stated in the form of a proposition or a hypothesis. *Propositions* state relationships that are logical conclusions deduced from the theory. They may be an idea or hunch that is presented in the form of a scientific statement. A *hypothesis* is the translation of concepts in a proposition into empirical measures and then applying an analytical or statistical procedure to determine whether the hypothesis is to be rejected or to be retained as a theoretical deduction.

Testing the Theory. Because theories are abstractions of reality, they must be tested to assess how closely they approximate the observed reality. This requires operational definitions of the construct (see Schwab, 1999). An operational definition is the application of a quantitative or qualitative indicator to a concept, and this is necessary to measure it to test for its presence, its level, and how concepts are related to others in the theoretical domain. It is, in the strictest sense, the hypothesis (which has been constructed with empirical indicators) that is subjected to empirical test and not the concepts themselves. When a hypothesis has been confirmed by research such that scientists accept it as a fundamental truth, it then becomes a "law-like generalization." Construct validation is the process of ensuring that the operational measure is, in fact, a useful representation of the concept that purports to measure. This step of validation is one of the more important tasks of the researcher.

The Boundaries of a Theory. The concepts and the nature of the relationships that circumscribe the theory determine its *boundaries*, or the observational field to which the theory is limited and is expected to hold. The general boundary of the theories in this book is the complex organization. Yet, while theories may have similar boundaries, they may differ because the unit of analysis (in our case, the organization) may be constructed from different concepts (because of the bias of the theorists). For example, Barnard (1938) and Davis (1951) are both concerned with organization structure and managerial processes. Davis uses concepts that describe formal organization phenomena while Barnard emphasizes the informal *and* the formal structure of organizations. Etzioni's (1961) boundaries contain the power structure of organizations, the motivational orientations of the members, and a taxonomy of organizational types. Williamson and Ouchi (1981) use similar concepts of organizational types but show how they are related to the market environment and the transaction costs that are incurred that determine the particular organization form. And for a final example, the boundaries of population ecology include populations of organizations, or groups of organizations in similar environments, and the process of adapting to those environments.

The Use of Theory—Explanation, Prediction, Control, and Research. There is much truth to the statement that "there is nothing as useful as a good theory." Theories are ways of organizing reality, and good theories can be used to explain and predict behavior, as a basis for the control of events and as a guide for research.

Explanation and Prediction. The difference between explanation and prediction depends on where one is located in time with respect to the event. Three conditions are necessary for explanation or prediction. First, there must be a description of an outcome (O) or theoretical concept that can be thought of as a dependent variable. For example, the outcome that is the focus of agency theory is the maximization of firm performance, or firm profitability ($O_{profitability}$). Second, there must be independent, causal variables ($C_1 \ldots C_n$) that describe the circumstances leading to the outcome. In agency theory, that would be the interests of the principals ($C_{principals}$) and the interests of the agents (C_{agents}). Third, there must be relational statements (R's) that state how the independent variables (the C's) are related to the outcome (O). In the agency model, this relational statement would appear as

$$\text{When } [(C_{principals}) = (C_{agents})] \rightarrow (O_{profitability})$$

That is, the relational statement (R) is: When the interests of the principal and the agent are equal, there is incentive alignment and profitability will be maximized.

If the observer is located before the outcome, as

$$[(C_{principals}) = (C_{agents})] \text{ (Observer)} \rightarrow (O_{profitability})],$$

the theory has predicted. So that if one observes the situation in a firm and finds that $[(C_{principals}) = (C_{agents})]$, then it can be said that future profitability will be maximized. If the relationship is otherwise, as $[(C_{principals}) < (C_{agents})]$, then one would predict from the theory that the interests of the agent will be satisfied at a greater level than the principals, and therefore profitability will not be maximized. If the observer is located after the outcome, as

$$[(C_{principals}) = (C_{agents})] \rightarrow (O_{profitability})] \text{ (Observer)},$$

then theory has explained the event.

Control. To use a theory for control, it is necessary to have casual antecedents $(C_1 \ldots C_n)$ for an outcome (O) and the relational statements (R) that specify how C's are related to O's. But there is one more condition: The C's must be subject to manipulation. In other words, we must be able to act on C in such a way that we can change its level or its state to achieve the intended event, O. Thus, if we have $[(C_{principals}) < (C_{agents})]$ that would lead to lower levels of O according to the model, then we could increase O by changing the level or the condition of (C_{agents}) by, for example, making the compensation of the agent contingent on achieving a certain level of the outcome, O.

There can be concern that if a theory is able to be used for control, then it opens the possibility that the control of casual factors (the C's) will fall into the hands of undesirable actors. Thus, if malevolent agents learn how to use theory to control the behavior of others, considerable freedom may be lost. Such a fear underlies much criticism of the power elites in a society who are able, through wealth and personal relationships, to drive important social values that become the basis for social norms in the culture, thus imposing sometimes very subtle but powerful control over people. This issue is one that appears to be at the root of the critical theory approach to organizations, as set forth by Jermier (Chapter 18, this volume) in his contribution to this book. It is also an important issue for postmodern approaches to organization, which also focus on how the language and the concepts used to formulate theory may result in subordinating certain groups in the society (Calas & Smircich, 1999).

Yet another concern about the control issue is that a casual factor (C_1) or a set of factors $(C_1 \ldots C_n)$ may result in several outcomes $(O_1 \ldots O_n)$ and that there is a different preference ordering for different O's by different constituencies (e.g., that O_1 is more preferred than O_3 by some in power, while O_3 is preferred by others). This may lead to conflict over whether O_1 or O_3 should be the maximization criterion. For instance, suppose we have a predictive statement as follows.

An increase (R) in the specificity (C_1) of organizational goals (C_2) will be followed by an increase in organization efficiency (O_1).

There may be other outcomes ($O_1 \ldots O_n$) that are stated or unstated in the theory, such as increased stress on employees (O_s) or increased unemployment (O_e). Neither of the outcomes, stress or unemployment, would be desirable to employees, while organization efficiency may be more preferred by the dominant managerial coalition. Thus, each group may wish to have its O receive the highest priority and may exert pressures to have it that way. Disagreement about preferred outcomes is a basis for conflict in organizations.

Research. Theory should also serve as the basis for research. The propositions and hypotheses that are explicit and implicit in theory provide guides for empirical efforts toward verification or rejection of the theory itself, or will serve to sharpen the explanatory and predictive capacity of theory.

An Organizing Theme for This Book

This book contains a range of theoretical approaches to organizations, mostly positivist, that represent the particular view of the theorist. These theories are set into an organizing taxonomy, shown in Figure 1.1, that has both a historical tone and an epistemological theme (both of which will be more fully articulated in the selections by Burrell & Morgan, 1979 [Chapter 2], and Scott, 2003 [Chapter 17]).

One dimension is whether the theory more strongly presents organizations as a predominantly rational model or a predominantly natural model (see Figure 1.1). *Rational models* are the things of management theory, essentially approaches to the design of an organization. Once goals of the organization have been determined, or specified, then the development of organization structure, the flow of authority, and the other relationships clearly follow and the organization can be designed in a logical fashion. *Natural models* tend to be the things of organizational sociologists. These theories recognize that individuals in organizations do not operate with the strictures of rules and policies: They modify them and adapt them and then adapt.

The second dimension is whether the theory emphasizes organizations as a closed system or an open system (see Figure 1.1). A *closed system approach* treats an organization as a determinate system (Thompson, 1967). Therefore, organizations are seen as tools to achieve their predetermined goals (Scott, 2003). This approach assumes the organization's environment is relatively fixed, or has been determined, and the resources are in place to move the organization to its next state (Thompson, 1967). An *open system approach* assumes that the internal structure and processes of an organization are affected by the environment in which the organization exists. "Open systems are capable of self-maintenance on the basis of throughput of resources from the environment" (Scott, 2003, p. 89). The underlying assumption

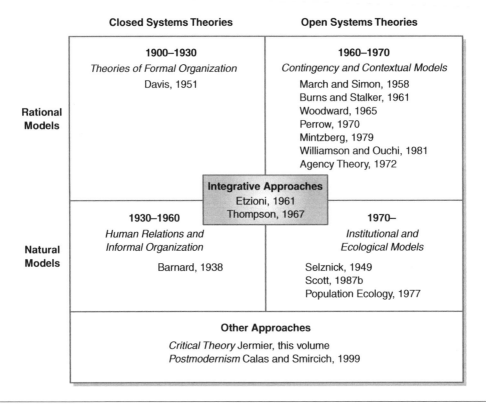

Figure 1.1   Classes of Organization Theories

of open system models is the interdependence of the organization and the context, or the environments in which it is located. Thus, the environment is a condition, or a set of conditions, that goes far in determining what happens with respect to organization form, structure, and behavior of members and, as well, is not under complete control of the organization so that the organization must adapt and/or cope with it (Thompson, 1967).

Closed System Rational Models

Closed system rational models tend to be *theories of formal organization* (see Figure 1.1). They focus on the design of formal organization, or how to organize and manage people and take a top-down approach, in that they imply that organizations can be designed by top managers in ways that increase organizational performance. In this cluster, Scott (2003) includes the work in scientific management, bureaucratic theory (Weber, 1947), and administrative theory (Fayol, 1949).

The early history of organization theory is marked by models that often carry the label *classical management theory.* The *scientific management approach* focused on the lowest level of organization: the worker and the boss. The basic question it addressed was, "How can work be designed most efficiently?" Many people were associated with the beginnings of scientific management, but the most prominent was Frederick W. Taylor, and he was to become the "father of scientific management." Taylor developed many ideas to increase efficiency, and his ideas, when applied, resulted in significant productivity increases. The analysis and redesign of work from methods that Taylor initiated were so widely applied in industry that one social historian wrote,

> The prophet of modern work was Frederick W. Taylor, and the stopwatch was his rod. If any social upheaval can ever be attributed to one man, the logic of efficiency as a mode of life is due to Taylor. With "scientific management," as formulated by Taylor in 1893, we pass far beyond the old, rough computations of the division of labor and move into the division of time itself. (Bell, 1970, p. 5)

By the early 1920s, another perspective emerged. A number of writers began to analyze the work of managers. Their ideas concerned understanding the basic functions of management and developing guidelines, or principles, about how to manage effectively. This came to be called *administrative theory.* They focused on two things. One was the *functions of management* (planning, organizing, and controlling), activities that all executives perform in whole or in part. The second was *principles of management,* general guides that tell a manager what to do when faced with problems of designing an organization, making decisions, or dealing with people. I have included the administrative theory of Davis (1951), a management theorist in the fashion of Fayol (trans., 1949), in this book.

A similar view is reflected in the work of Max Weber (trans., 1947), a German sociologist who was an important influence on writing and theory about the study of organization. Weber developed a theory of *bureaucracy,* and his analysis considered organizations as part of a broader society. Weber felt that bureaucracies could be effectively designed and that predictability of behavior and results and showed greater stability over time. He suggested that organizations naturally evolved toward this rational form.

Open System Rational Models

Open system rational models are also "management models," in that they focus on how organizations should be designed, but they recognize that differences in the environment will drive different forms of organization. They generally are *contingency* or *contextual models of organization* that emerged as a result of three major criticisms of classical management approaches (Lawrence & Lorsch, 1967; March & Simon, 1958). The classical models, it was argued,

1. Assumed that there was "one best way" to design an organization in a way that would maximize organization performance

2. Did not adequately take into account human factors and individual differences

3. Were not empirically evaluated

One important response to these criticisms is March and Simon's book *Organizations* (1958). Based on the work of Barnard (1938), they developed a set of propositions, supported by research and theory, about organizations. They set forth a model that argued that while organizations may develop routine programs of action of the sort implied in the classical management theory, they must also develop more general problem-solving routines to deal with unforeseen circumstances (Scott, 2003).

Another important idea from Barnard and March and Simon, the concept of "satisficing," dealt with the maximizing implication of the classical models. Organizations cannot maximize, they posited, because to do so would mean that a decision maker would have to know all the available alternatives. This isn't possible, because rationality is "bounde," in the sense that one cannot know these alternatives and therefore will make a decision within the constrained set of which he or she is aware.

A second important response to these criticisms is *contingency theory*. These contingency theories not only correctly argued that the best way to manage "all depended," but they advanced models that specified on what it depended. They tended to describe how the structure of an organization is affected by the external environment—and this would lead not only to survival but to better economic performance. For example, Lawrence and Lorsch (1967) studied how organizational structure was affected by the rate of technological change for the products produced, the production methods used, and environmental uncertainty. In general, they concluded that organizations in a stable environment are more effective if they have more detailed procedures and a more centralized decision-making process; organizations in an unstable environment should be decentralized, have less emphasis on rules and standard procedures, and use participative strategies to be effective.

In this book are contingency theories by Burns and Stalker (1961), Woodward (1965), Perrow (1970), and Mintzberg (1979). Burns and Stalker specified more precisely than ever before what the organizational structure should look like, given a certain kind of environment: When the technological and market environments were uncertain and prone to rapid change, there was a loose, organic organization; when the environment was more predictable and stable, a traditional bureaucracy seemed to be more effective.

Joan Woodward's book *Industrial Organization* (1965) reports the results of nearly a decade of empirical study of British industry located in South Essex in which she and her colleagues examined firms as complex social systems and line-staff relationships as parts of a whole rather than in isolation. Perrow (1970) concludes that the organizational structure depends on the state of the art in each organization function and the changes required by the environment. Mintzberg (1979) says that organizations are driven toward a particular natural cluster based on the strength of different parts of the organization, the ways in which the parts of the organization coordinate their work, the structural design parameters, and contingency factors such as age, size, and environment.

Finally, an important theoretical development in the 1970s was from the field of economics. Two economic approaches are described in this book. One is the transaction cost approach by Williamson (1975; see Chapter 14), which shows how transaction costs, environmental certainty, and opportunism explain how hierarchies (organizations) emerge to manage conditions where markets are not efficient regulating mechanisms. Another is agency theory (see Chapter 12), which applies classical economic thinking to problems of organizational control and design.

Closed System Natural Models

Closed system natural models are derived from the schools of *human relations* and *informal organization.* Like other closed system approaches, they treat the environment as well-defined or fixed. They also say that the organization design and structure may be intended to achieve maximum performance, but the dominant theme of these models is that through social processes and conflict processes, persons within organizations do modify the designed organization structure and policies. According to Scott (2003), models of this type are articulated by Whyte (1959), Barnard (1938), Mayo (1945), and Gouldner (1954).

One of the first set of ideas developed in the human relations perspective was identified in the classic Hawthorne studies (Roethlisberger & Dickson, 1939). These were carried out in the Hawthorne plant of Western Electric, an AT&T subsidiary in Cicero, Illinois. The studies, between 1924 and 1927, were prompted by an experiment that was carried out by the company's engineers. In the best tradition of scientific management, they were seeking the answers to industrial questions through research. In perhaps the most famous of the studies, two groups of workers were observed to determine the effects of different levels of illumination on worker performance. In one group, the level of illumination was changed; in the other, it was not. They found that when illumination was increased, the level of performance increased. However, productivity also increased when the level of illumination decreased, even down to the level of moonlight. Moreover, productivity also increased in the control group. These results seemed contrary to reason, so the engineers examined other factors that might have affected the results. The researchers concluded that how people were treated made an important difference in performance and that the workers were responding in a way that they thought the experimenters wanted and because they were the center of attention. Obviously, the subjects were responding not to the level of light but to the experiment itself and to their involvement in it. Since that time, this effect in research has been known as the *Hawthorne Effect.* Other studies followed and continued to demonstrate the importance of leadership practices and workgroup pressures on employee satisfaction and performance. They showed that the importance of economic incentives in worker motivation was overrated, and they stressed the importance of recognizing that employees react to a wide set of complex forces, rather than to one factor alone

The exemplar for closed system natural models in this book is Chester Barnard's *The Functions of the Executive* (1938). His explanation of the nature of the "informal organization" demonstrated how it, as well as formal structures, existed in the organizational context. His explanation of "the zone of indifference" and "the acceptance theory of authority" expanded the thinking about the nature of compliance processes in organizations beyond what might be expected to result from the formal authority structure in an organization.

Open System Natural Models

By the end of the 1960s, rationality as a theme in the design of organizations was confronted by the emergence of *institutional* and *ecological models.* These are open system natural models that, like their open rational counterparts, acknowledge the importance of the environment, but not in quite the same way. While the assumption of open system rational models *appears* to suggest what seems to be a unidirectional causality (i.e., environment → structure), the open system natural models imply an interactive process (i.e., environment ↔ structure). In this cluster of approaches are Weick's (1969) organizing model, the sociotechnical systems view (Miller & Rice, 1967), the resource dependence view (Pfeffer & Salancik, 1978), organizational ecology (Hannan & Freeman, 1977), and the institutional approaches of Selznick (1949), Meyer and Rowan (1977), and DiMaggio and Powell (1983).

I have included three selections from this class of models. The first is the institutional approach of Phillip Selznick (1949). In his study of the development of the Tennessee Valley Authority that was reported in *TVA and the Grass Roots*, he described how the structure of an organization is affected by outside restraints, so that the organization develops both formal and informal systems that help it to adapt to the outside environment and thus to survive.

A second piece by Scott (1987b; see Chapter 17) elaborates on the more recent developments in institutional theory. In it, he discusses different institutional approaches and their strengths and weaknesses, providing a very useful overview of the state of the field.

The third selection is the classic paper on organization ecology by Hannan and Freeman (1977; see Chapter 16) in which they set forth a Darwinist perspective on the survival of organizations. The central idea of ecological models is that a natural selection process operates such that "environments differentially select organizations for survival on the basis of fit between organizational forms and environmental characteristics" (Scott, 2003, p. 117).

Other Approaches

There are some approaches that do not fall neatly into the four main quadrants of Figure 1.1. Scott (2003) pointed to approaches by Etzioni (1964) and Thompson (1967) that integrate what are ostensibly contradicting perspectives. Other views, such as critical theory and postmodern approaches to organization, take a different tack, both focusing on the alienating, deleterious, and insidious effects of organizations as mechanisms of social control. Further, they raise serious questions about the utility and validity of the more conventional approaches.

Integrative Approaches. Two integrative approaches are included in this book. One is by Etzioni (1964), who developed a typology of organizations and examined how individual involvement with an organization and the type of power predominant in the various forms interact to explain compliance. This is a "structuralist" perspective that seeks a synthesis between the rational schools and the natural schools (Scott, 2003). It is *rational* in that it addresses how authority and power are structured in terms of the formal hierarchy. It is *natural* in the way that he focused on the idea that the type of power that will result in compliance is contingent on the nature of the organization and the motivation of people who are there. One of the key points is that

Organizations are under pressure to be effective. Hence to the degree that the environment allows, organizations tend to shift their compliance structures from incongruent to congruent types and organizations which have congruent compliance of structures tend to resist factors pushing them toward incongruent structures. (Etzioni, 1961, p. 13)

The second is James Thompson's (1967) *Organizations in Action*. He discussed the inherent conflict between the "closed system" and "open system" models: Closed system models cannot accommodate environmental influences, and open system models overstate adaptability to the neglect of more controllable factors. His synthesis considered complex organizations as open systems that may be faced with uncertainty but at the same time are subject to criteria of rationality. He said, for instance, that

if the closed-system aspects of organizations are seen most clearly at the technical level, and the open-system qualities appear most vividly at the institutional level, it would suggest that a significant function of the managerial level is to mediate between the two extremes and the emphasis they exhibit. (p. 12)

Critical Theory Approaches to Organization. Critical theory is a normative theory that has its roots in the work of Karl Marx (Burrell & Morgan, 1979). Its proponents seek to reveal society for what it is, to unmask its essence and mode of operation, and to lay the foundations for emancipation through deep-seated social change. It is an overtly political philosophy (Burrell and Morgan, p. 284). This is clear in Jermier's paper (this volume; see Chapter 18), as he argues that "no knowledge is neutral" and the dominant theme of more conventional organization theorizing is the domination of the working class by disguising control "in the rhetoric of emancipation."

Postmodernist Approaches to Organization. The paper by Calas and Smircich (1999; see Chapter 19) describes a postmodern approach to organizations and its implications for the field of organization studies. Postmodernists in the field of organization studies argue that since conceptions of the world, and in our case theories organizations, are socially constructed, then the theoretical models themselves must be a function of cultural and symbolic elements that the theorist (as well as others who are part of the discipline) has experienced. As such, a person with different experiences would have a different view of the world, which may be equally valid, though significantly different. Thus, you can't really be sure what the theorist means, but rather the meaning is what the reader interprets it to be—which becomes the basis for the reader's meaning. This is what the term *deconstructionism*, a key concept of postmodernism, means.

Summary

This book presents a selection of different theories of organization, from different schools of thought, and delineates their skeletal structure in the hope that the points of similarity and dissimilarity may clearly emerge. The theories in this book were selected because they are representative of certain approaches, have been widely used as points of reference, and/or present formulations that are of particular interest to me.

The models here are by no means exhaustive of theoretical approaches extant. One writer (Stogdill, 1966) has categorized no less than 18 different ways to theorize about organizations. Among these are viewing organizations as a cultural product, as an exchange agent with the environment, as an independent agency, as a structure in action over time, or as an input–output system. Each of the orientations presents a legitimate point of departure for inquiry, each has a different set of biases and value judgments that affect the manner in which the theory is developed, yet each focuses on organized behavior.

The approaches have been condensed, summarized, or presented in some other brief form to show the relationship between the various concepts of each theory. However, the student is urged not to rely on these summaries but to examine the theories in more detail in the original work of the authors.

CHAPTER 2

Assumptions About the Nature of Social Science and Society*

Gibson Burrell and Gareth Morgan

Central to our thesis is the idea that "all theories of organization are based upon a philosophy of science and a theory of society." [Here we] wish to address ourselves to the first aspect of this thesis and to examine some of the philosophical assumptions which underwrite different approaches to social science. We shall argue that it is convenient to conceptualise social science in terms of four sets of assumptions related to ontology, epistemology, human nature, and methodology.

All social scientists approach their subject via explicit or implicit assumptions about the nature of the social world and the way in which it may be investigated. First, there are assumptions of an *ontological* nature—assumptions which concern the very essence of the phenomena under investigation. Social scientists, for example, are faced with a basic ontological question: whether the "reality" to be investigated is external to the individual—imposing itself on individual consciousness from without—or the product of individual consciousness; whether "reality" is of an "objective" nature, or the product of individual cognition; whether "reality" is a given "out there" in the world, or the product of one's mind.

Associated with this ontological issue is a second set of assumptions of an *epistemological* nature. These are assumptions about the grounds of knowledge—about how one might begin to understand the world and communicate this as knowledge to fellow human beings. These assumptions entail ideas, for example, about what

---

*From *Sociological Paradigms and Organizational Analysis: Elements of the Sociology of Corporate Life* (Chapters 2 and 3), by G. Burrell and G. Morgan, 1979, London: Heinemann.

forms of knowledge can be obtained, and how one can sort out what is to be regarded as "true" from what is to be regarded as "false." Indeed, this dichotomy of "true" and "false" itself presupposes a certain epistemological stance. It is predicated upon a view of the nature of knowledge itself: whether, for example, it is possible to identify and communicate the nature of knowledge as being hard, real and capable of being transmitted in tangible form, or whether "knowledge" is of a softer, more subjective, spiritual or even transcendental kind, based on experience and insight of a unique and essentially personal nature. The epistemological assumptions in these instances determine extreme positions on the issue of whether knowledge is something which can be acquired on the one hand, or is something which has to be personally experienced on the other.

Associated with the ontological and epistemological issues, but conceptually separate from them, is a third set of assumptions concerning *human nature* and, in particular, the relationship between human beings and their environment. All social science, clearly, must be predicated upon this type of assumption, since human life is essentially the subject and object of enquiry. Thus, we can identify perspectives in social science which entail a view of human beings responding in a mechanistic or even deterministic fashion to the situations encountered in their external world. This view tends to be one in which human beings and their experiences are regarded as products of the environment; one in which humans are conditioned by their external circumstances. This extreme perspective can be contrasted with one which attributes to human beings a much more creative role: with a perspective where "free will" occupies the centre of the stage; where man is regarded as the creator of his environment, the controller as opposed to the controlled, the master rather than the marionette. In these two extreme views of the relationship between human beings and their environment we are identifying a great philosophical debate between the advocates of determinism on the one hand and voluntarism on the other. Whilst there are social theories which adhere to each of these extremes, as we shall see, the assumptions of many social scientists are pitched somewhere in the range between.

The three sets of assumptions outlined above have direct implications of a *methodological* nature. Each one has important consequences for the way in which one attempts to investigate and obtain "knowledge" about the social world. Different ontologies, epistemologies and models of human nature are likely to incline social scientists towards different methodologies. The possible range of choice is indeed so large that what is regarded as science by the traditional "natural scientist" covers but a small range of options. It is possible, for example, to identify methodologies employed in social science research which treat the social world like the natural world, as being hard, real and external to the individual and others which view it as being of a much softer, personal and more subjective quality.

If one subscribes to a view of the former kind, which treats the social world as if it were a hard, external, objective reality, then the scientific endeavour is likely to focus upon an analysis of relationships and regularities between the various elements which it comprises. The concern, therefore, is with the identification and definition of these elements and with the discovery of ways in which these relationships can be expressed. The methodological issues of importance are thus the concepts themselves, their measurement and the identification of underlying themes. This perspective expresses itself most forcefully in a search for universal laws which explain and govern the reality which is being observed.

If one subscribes to the alternative view of social reality, which stresses the importance of the subjective experience of individuals in the creation of the social world, then the search for understanding focuses upon different issues and approaches them in different ways. The principal concern is with an understanding of the way in which the individual creates, modifies and interprets the world in which he or she finds himself. The emphasis in extreme cases tends to be placed upon the explanation and understanding of what is unique and particular to the individual rather than of what is general and universal. This approach questions whether there exists an external reality worthy of study. In methodological terms it is an approach which emphasises the relativistic nature of the social world to such an extent that it may be perceived as "anti-scientific" by reference to the ground rules commonly applied in the natural sciences.

In this brief sketch of various ontological, epistemological, human and methodological standpoints which characterise approaches to social sciences, we have sought to illustrate two broad and somewhat polarised perspectives. Figure 2.1 seeks to depict these in a more rigorous fashion in terms of what we shall describe as the subjective-objective dimension. It identifies the four sets of assumptions relevant to our understanding of social science, characterising each by the descriptive labels under which they have been debated in the literature on social philosophy. In the following section of this chapter we will review each of the four debates in necessarily brief but more systematic terms.

The Strands of Debate

Nominalism-realism: the ontological debate.[1] These terms have been the subject of much discussion in the literature and there are great areas of controversy

The Subjectivist-Objectivist Dimension

The Subjectivist Approach to Social Science		The Objectivist Approach to Social Science
Nominalism	←—— Ontology ——→	Realism
Anti-positivism	←—— Epistemology ——→	Positivism
Voluntarism	←—— Human nature ——→	Determinism
Ideographic	←—— Methodology ——→	Nomothetic

Figure 2.1   A Scheme for Analysing Assumptions About the Nature of Social Science

surrounding them. The nominalist position revolves around the assumption that the social world external to individual cognition is made up of nothing more than names, concepts and labels which are used to structure reality. The nominalist does not admit to there being any "real" structure to the world which these concepts are used to describe. The "names" used are regarded as artificial creations whose utility is based upon their convenience as tools for describing, making sense of and negotiating the external world. Nominalism is often equated with conventionalism, and we will make no distinction between them.[2]

Realism, on the other hand, postulates that the social world external to individual cognition is a real world made up of hard, tangible and relatively immutable structures. Whether or not we label and perceive these structures, the realists maintain, they still exist as empirical entities. We may not even be aware of the existence of certain crucial structures and therefore have no "names" or concepts to articulate them. For the realist, the social world exists independently of an individual's appreciation of it. The individual is seen as being born into and living within a social world which has a reality of its own. It is not something which the individual creates—it exists "out there"; ontologically it is prior to the existence and consciousness of any single human being. For the realist, the social world has an existence which is as hard and concrete as the natural world.[3]

Anti-positivism: the epistemological debate.[4] It has been maintained that "the word 'positivist' like the word 'bourgeois,' has become more of a derogatory epithet than a useful descriptive concept."[5] We intend to use it in the latter sense, as a descriptive concept which can be used to characterise a particular type of epistemology. Most of the descriptions of positivism in current usage refer to one or more of the ontological, epistemological dimensions of our scheme for analysing assumptions with regard to social science. Positivism is also sometimes mistakenly equated with empiricism. Such conflations cloud basic issues and contribute to the use of the term in a derogatory sense.

We use "positivist" here to characterise epistemologies which seek to explain and predict what happens in the social world by searching for regularities and causal relationships between its constituent elements. Positivist epistemology is in essence based upon the traditional approaches which dominate the natural sciences. Positivist may differ in terms of detailed approach. Some would claim, for example, that hypothesised regularities can be verified by an adequate experimental research programme. Others would maintain that hypothesis can only be falsified and never demonstrated to be "true."[6] However, both "verificationists" and "falsificationists" would accept that the growth of knowledge is essentially a cumulative process in which new insights are added to the existing stock of knowledge and false hypotheses eliminated.

The epistemology of anti-positivism may take various forms but is firmly set against the utility of a search for laws or underlying regularities in the world of social affairs. For the anti-positivist, the social world is essentially relativistic and can only be understood from the point of view of the individuals who are directly involved in the activities which are to be studied. Anti-positivists reject the standpoint of the "observer," which characterises positivist epistemology as a valid vantage point for understanding human activities. They maintain that one can only "understand" by occupying the frame of reference of the participant in action. One has to understand from the inside rather than the outside. From this point of view social science is seen as being essentially a subjective rather than an objective enterprise. Anti-positivists tend to reject the notion that science can generate objective knowledge of any kind.[7]

Voluntarism-determinism: the "human nature" debate. This debate revolves around the issue of what model of man is reflected in any given social-scientific theory. At one extreme we can identify a determinist view which regards man and his activities as being completely determined by the situation or "environment" in which he is located. At another extreme we can identify the voluntarist view that man is completely autonomous and free-willed. Insofar as social science theories are concerned to understand human activities, they must incline implicitly or explicitly to one or the other of these points of view, or adopt an intermediate standpoint which allows for the influence of both situational and voluntary factors in accounting for the activities of human beings. Such assumptions are essential elements in social-scientific theories, since they define in broad terms the nature of the relationships between man and the society in which he lives.[8]

Ideographic-nomothetic theory: the methodological debate. The ideographic approach to social science is based on the view that one can only understand the social world by obtaining firsthand knowledge of the subject under investigation. It thus places considerable stress upon getting close to one's subject and exploring its detailed background and life history. The ideographic approach emphasises the analysis of the subjective accounts which one generates by "getting inside" situations and involving oneself in the everyday flow of life—the detailed analysis of the insights generated by such encounters with one's subject and the insights revealed in impressionistic accounts found in diaries, biographies and journalistic records. The ideographic method stresses the importance of letting one's subject unfold its nature and characteristics during the process of investigation.[9]

The nomothetic approach to social science lays emphasis on the importance of basing research upon systematic protocol and technique. It is epitomised in the approach and methods employed in the natural sciences, which focus upon the process of testing hypotheses in accordance with the canons of scientific rigour. It is preoccupied with the construction of scientific tests and the use of quantitative techniques for the analysis of data. Surveys, personality tests and standardised research instruments of all kinds are prominent among the tools which comprise nomothetic methodology.[10]

Analysing Assumptions About the Nature of Social Science

These four sets of assumptions with regard to the nature of social science provide an extremely powerful tool for the analysis of social theory. In much of the literature there is a tendency to conflate the issues which are involved. We wish to argue here that considerable advantages accrue from treating these four strands of debate as analytically distinct. While in practice there is often a strong relationship between the positions adopted by our strands, assumptions about each can in fact vary quite considerably. It is worth examining this point in more detail.

The extreme positions on each of the four strands are reflected in the two major intellectual traditions which have dominated social science over the last two hundred years. The first of these is usually described as "sociological positivism." In essence this reflects the attempt to apply models and methods derived from the natural sciences to the study of human affairs. It treats the social world as if it were the natural world, adopting a "realist" approach to ontology. This is backed up by a "positivist" epistemology, relatively "deterministic" views of human nature and the use of "nomothetic" methodologies. The second intellectual tradition, that of "German idealism," stands in complete opposition to this. In essence it is based upon the premise that the ultimate reality of the "spirit" or "idea" rather than in the data of sense is essentially "nominalist" in its approach to social reality. In contrast to the natural sciences, it stresses the essentially subjective nature of human affairs, denying the utility and relevance of the models and methods of natural science to studies in this realm. It is "anti-positivist" in epistemology, "voluntarist" with regard to human nature and it favours ideographic methods as a foundation for social analysis. Sociological positivism and German idealism thus define the objective and subjective extremes of our model.

Many sociologists and organisation theorists have been brought up within the tradition of sociological positivism, without exposure to the basic tenets of German idealism. Social science for them is seen as consonant with the configuration of assumptions which characterise the objective extreme of our model. However, over the last seventy years or so there has been an increasing interaction between these two traditions, particularly at a socio-philosophical level. As a result intermediate points of view have emerged, each with its own distinctive configuration of assumptions about the nature of social science. They have all spawned theories, ideas and approaches characteristic of their intermediate position. As we shall argue in later chapters, developments in phenomenology, ethnomethodology and the action frame of reference are to be understood in these terms. These perspectives, whilst offering their own special brand of insight, have also often been used as launching pads for attacks on sociological positivism and have generated a considerable amount of debate between rival schools of thought. The nature of this debate can only be fully understood by grasping and appreciating the different assumptions which underwrite the competing points of view.

It is our contention that the analytical scheme offered here enables one to do precisely this. It is offered not as a mere classificatory device, but as an important tool for negotiating social theory. It draws attention to key assumptions. It allows one to focus on precise issues which differentiate socio-scientific approaches. It draws attention to the degree of congruency between the four sets of assumptions about social science which characterise any given theorist's point of view. We offer it here as the first principal dimension of our theoretical scheme for analysing theory in general and organisational theory in particular. For the sake of convenience we shall normally refer to it as the "subjective-objective" dimension, two descriptive labels which perhaps capture the points of commonality between the four analytical strands.

Assumptions About the Nature of Society

All approaches to the study of society are located in a frame of reference of one kind or another. Different theories tend to reflect different perspectives, issues and problems worthy of study, and are generally based upon a whole set of assumptions which reflect a particular view of the nature of the subject under investigation. The last twenty years or so have witnessed a number of attempts on the part of sociologists to delineate the differences which separate various schools of thought and the meta-sociological assumptions which they reflect.

The Order-Conflict Debate

Dahrendorf (1959) and Lockwood (1956), for example, have sought to distinguish between those approaches to sociology which concentrated upon explaining the nature of social order and equilibrium on the one hand, and those which were more concerned with problems of change, conflict and coercion in social structures on the other. This distinction has received a great deal of attention and has come to be known as the "order-conflict debate." The "order theorists" have greatly outnumbered the "conflict theorists," and as Dawe has observed, "the thesis that sociology is centrally concerned with the problem of social order has become one of the discipline's few orthodoxies. It is common as a basic premise to many accounts of sociological theory which otherwise differ considerably in purpose and perspective" (1970, p. 207).[11]

Many sociologists now regard this debate as dead or as having been a somewhat spurious non-debate in the first place (Cohen, 1968; Silverman, 1970; van den Berghe, 1969). Influenced by the work of writers such as Coser (1965), who pointed to the functional aspects of social conflict, sociologists have been able to incorporate conflict as a variable within the bounds of theories which are primarily geared towards an explanation of social order. The approach advocated by Cohen, for example, clearly illustrates this. He takes his point of departure from the work of Dahrendorf and elaborates some of the central ideas in the order-conflict debate to present two models of society, which are characterised in terms of competing sets of assumptions which attribute to social systems the characteristics of *commitment, cohesion, solidarity, consensus, reciprocity, co-operation, integration, stability* and *persistence* on the one hand, and the characteristics of *coercion, division, hostility, dissensus, conflict, malintegration* and *change* on the other (Cohen, 1968, pp. 166–167).

Cohen's central criticism is that Dahrendorf is mistaken in treating the order and conflict models as being entirely separate. He in effect suggests that it is possible for theories to involve elements of both models and that one need not necessarily incline to one or the other. From this point of view, the order and conflict views of society are but two sides of the same coin; they are not mutually exclusive and thus do not need to be reconciled. The force of this sort of argument has been very powerful in diverting attention away from the order-conflict debate. In the wake of the so-called counter-culture movement of the late 1960s and the failure of the 1968 revolution in France, orthodox sociologists have become much more interested in and concerned with the problems of the "individual" as opposed to those of the "structure" of society in general. The influence of "subjectivist" movements such as phenomenology, ethnomethodology and action theory, . . . have tended to become much more attractive and more worthy of attention. As a result, interest in continuing the order-conflict debate has subsided under the influence of issues relating to the philosophy and methods of social science.

Our contention here is that if one reviews the intellectual source and foundations of the order-conflict debate, one is forced to conclude that it has met a premature death. Dahrendorf and Lockwood sought to revitalise the work of Marx through their writings and to restore it to a central place in sociological theory. For the most part Marx had been largely ignored by leading sociologists, the influence of theorists such as Durkheim, Weber, and Pareto having been paramount. Interestingly enough, these sociologists are all very much concerned with the problem of social order; it is Marx who is preoccupied with the role of conflict as the driving force behind social change. Stated in this way, therefore, the order-conflict debate is underwritten by a difference between the perspectives and concerns of leading social theorists of the nineteenth and early twentieth centuries. Modern sociology has done little more than articulate and develop the basic themes initiated by these pioneers of social analysis. To state that the order-conflict debate is "dead" or a "non-debate" is thus to underplay, if not ignore, substantial differences between the work of Marx and, for example, Durkheim, Weber, and Pareto. Anyone familiar with the work of these theorists and aware of the deep division which exists between Marxism and sociology is forced to admit that there are fundamental differences, which are far from being reconciled.[12] In this chapter, therefore, we wish to reevaluate the order-conflict issue with a view to identifying a key dimension for analysing the assumptions about the nature of society reflected in different social theories. In order to do so, let us return to the work of Dahrendorf, who seeks to set out the opposing issues in the following terms:

The integration theory of society, as displayed by the work of Parsons and other structural-functionalists, is founded on a number of assumptions of the following type:

1. Every society is a relatively persistent, stable structure of elements.

2. Every society is a well integrated structure of elements.

3. Every element in a society has a function, i.e., renders a contribution to its maintenance as a system.

4. Every functioning social structure is based on a consensus of values among its members. . . .

. . . What I have called the coercion theory of society can also be reduced to a small number of basic tenets, although here again these assumptions oversimplify and overstate the case:

1. Every society is at every point subject to processes of change; social change is ubiquitous.

2. Every society displays at every point dissensus and conflict; social conflict is ubiquitous.

3. Every element in a society renders a contribution to its disintegration and change.

4. Every society is based on the coercion of some of its members by others. (Dahrendorf, 1959, pp. 160–162)

The opposing adjectives which Dahrendorf's schema suggest for distinguishing approaches to the study of society can be conveniently brought together in the form of a table, as shown in Table 2.1. As Dahrendorf admits, this conceptualisation is something of an oversimplification, and whilst providing a very useful tool for coming to grips with the differences between the two standpoints, it is open to the possibility of misinterpretation, in that the different adjectives mean different things to different people. Nowhere is this more evident than in the way in which the notion of *conflict* has been treated in the sociological literature. Since Coser's demonstration of the functions of social conflict, for example, the role of conflict as an integrating mechanism has received a great deal of attention. In effect, the whole notion of "conflict" has often been incorporated within the notion of integration. Dahrendorf's integration/conflict dimension has been conveniently telescoped so that it is brought within the bounds of sociology's traditional concern for the explanation of order. The fallacy of this position becomes clear if one considers certain extreme forms of conflict, such as class conflict, revolution and war, which can only be incorporated in the integrationist model by the wildest stretch of one's imagination. Examples such as these suggest that it is misleading to equate this type of macrostructural conflict with the functional conflict identified by Coser. There is an important question of degree involved here, which emphasises the dangers of the dichotomisation of integration and conflict; realistically the distinction between the two is much more of a continuum than the majority of writers have recognised.

Another strand of the Dahrendorf scheme which can be regarded as somewhat problematic lies in the distinction between *consensus* and *coercion*. At first sight the distinction appears obvious and clear-cut, focusing upon shared values on the one hand and the imposition of some sort of force on the other. On closer inspection there is a certain ambiguity. Where do the shared values come from? Are they acquired autonomously or imposed on some members of society by others? This question identifies the possibility that consensus may be a product of the use of some form of coercive force. For example, C. Wright Mills has pointed out, "What Parsons and others call 'value orientations' and 'normative structure' has mainly to do with master symbols of legitimation" (1959, p. 46).

Table 2.1   Theories of Society: "Order" and "Conflict"

The "order" or "integrationist" view of society emphasises	The "conflict" or "coercion" view of society emphasises
Stability	Change
Integration	Conflict
Functional coordination	Disintegration
Consensus	Coercion

A normative structure here—what Dahrendorf would view as elements consensus—is treated as a system legitimising the power structure. From Mills's point of view, it reflects the fact of domination. In other words, shared values may be regarded not so much as an index of the degree of integration which characterises a society as one which reflects the success of the forces of domination in a society prone to disintegration. From one point of view, extant shared ideas, values and norms are something to be preserved; from another, they represent a mode of domination from which man needs to be released. The consensus/coercion points dimension can thus be seen as focusing upon the issue of social control. Consensus—however it may arise—is identified in Dahrendorf's scheme as something independent of coercion. This we believe to be a mistaken view since, as suggested above, it ignores the possibility of a form of coercion which arises through the control of value systems.

In distinguishing between *stability* and *change* as respective features of the order and conflict models Dahrendorf is again open to misinterpretation, even though he explicitly states that he does not intend to imply that the theory of order assumes that societies are static. His concern is to show how functional theories are essentially concerned with those processes which serve to maintain the patterns of the system as a whole. In other words, functional theories are regarded as static in the sense that they are concerned with explaining the *status quo*. In this respect conflict theories are clearly of a different nature; they are committed to, and seek to explain, the process and nature of deep-seated structural change in society as opposed to change of a more superficial and ephemeral kind. The fact that all functional theories recognise change, and that change is an obvious empirical reality in everyday life, has led Dahrendorf's categorisation in relation to stability and change to lose its potential radical force and influence. It can be argued that different labels are required to identify Dahrendorf's two paramount concerns: first, that the order view of society is primarily *status quo* orientated; second, that it deals with change of a fundamentally different nature from that with which conflict theorists are concerned. [13]

Dahrendorf's notions of *functional coordination* and *disintegration* can be seen as constituting one of the most powerful strands of thought which distinguish the order and conflict perspectives. Here again, however, there is room for misinterpretation. The concept of integration in Dahrendorf's work derives from the functionalists' concern with the contribution which constituent elements of a system make to the whole. In many respects this is an oversimplification. Merton (1948) introduced the idea of manifest and latent functions, some of which may be dysfunctional for the integration of society. [14] Again, Gouldner (1959), writing shortly after the publication of the German edition of Dahrendorf's work, suggests that various parts of a system may have a high degree of autonomy and may contribute very little by way of integration to the system as a whole. The term "functional coordination" is thus something of an oversimplification and, given the existence of the points of view expressed above within the functionalist camp itself, it is not surprising that the concept of "disintegration" should be seen as relevant and capable of being used from a functional standpoint. "Disintegration" can be very easily viewed as an integrationist concept and, as with other aspects of Dahrendorf's scheme, this dimension has often been telescoped and brought within the theories of order. For this reason it may well have been clearer if the position of conflict theory on this dimension had been presented in more radical and distinctive terms. There is much in Marxian theory, for example, which refers to the notion of "contradiction" and the basic incompatibility between different elements of social structure. Contradiction implies heterogeneity imbalance and essentially antagonistic and divergent social forces. It thus stands at the opposite pole to the concept of "functional coordination," which must presuppose a basic compatibility between the elements of any given system. To argue that the concept of contradiction can be embraced within functional analysis requires either an act of faith or at least a considerable leap of imagination.

Dahrendorf's work has clearly served a very useful purpose in identifying a number of important strands of thought distinguishing theorists of order from theorists of conflict. However, as will be apparent from the above discussion, in many respects the distinctions which have been drawn between the two meta-theories do not go far enough. In particular, the insights of some twenty years of debate suggest that the characterisation of the conflict perspective has not been sufficiently radical to avoid confusion with the "integrationist" perspective. This has allowed theorists of order to meet the challenge which Dahrendorf's scheme presents to their frame of reference within the context of their order-oriented mode of thought. In order to illustrate this point, let us return to the work of Cohen (1968) referred to earlier.

In advocating his viewpoint Cohen appears to be misinterpreting the distinction between the two models. His interpretation of concepts telescopes the different variables into a form in which they can be seen as consistent with each other. In effect his whole analysis reflects an attempt to incorporate the conflict model within the bounds of the contemporary theory of order. He thus loses the radical essence of the conflict perspective and is able to conclude that the two models are not mutually exclusive and do not need to be reconciled. He argues that the two models are not genuine alternatives and in effect suggests that each is no more than the reciprocal of the other. He is therefore able to leave Dahrendorf's analysis with the central concern of his book—the problem of order—largely intact. The incorporation of conflict into the bounds of the model of order de-emphasises its importance.[15]

In line with the analysis which we presented earlier, we argue that the attempt to reduce the two models to a common base ignores the fundamental differences which exist between them. A conflict theory based on deep-seated structural conflict and concerned with radical transformations of society is not consistent with a functionalist perspective. The differences between them, therefore, are important and worthy of distinction in any attempt to analyse social theory. With the benefit of hindsight, it is possible to see that many of the misinterpretations which have arisen have done so because the models in Dahrendorf's analysis were not sufficiently differentiated. We wish to propose, therefore, that certain modifications be made in order to articulate the differences in a more explicit and radical form. Since much of the confusion has arisen because of the ambiguity of the descriptions associated with the two models we wish to suggest the use of a somewhat different terminology.

"Regulation" and "Radical Change"

Our analysis has shown that the order-conflict distinction is in many senses the most problematic. We suggest, therefore, that it should be replaced as a central theme by the notions of "regulation" and "radical change."

We introduce the term *"sociology of regulation"* to refer to the writings of theorists who are primarily concerned to provide explanations of society in terms which emphasise its underlying unity and cohesiveness. It is a sociology which is essentially concerned with the need for regulation in human affairs; the basic questions which it asks tend to focus upon the need to understand why society is maintained as an entity. It attempts to explain why society tends to hold together rather than fall apart. It is interested in understanding the social forces which prevent the Hobbesian vision of "war of all against all" becoming a reality. The work of Durkheim [1947] with its emphasis upon the nature of social cohesion and solidarity, for example, provides a clear and comprehensive illustration of a concern for the sociology of regulation.

The *"sociology of radical change"* stands in stark contrast to the "sociology of regulation," in that its basic concern is to find explanations for the radical change, deep-seated structural conflict, modes of domination and structural conflict, and modes of domination and structural contradiction which its theorists see as characterising modern society. It is a sociology which is essentially concerned with man's emancipation from the structures which limit and stunt his potential for development. The basic questions which it asks focus upon the deprivation of man, both material and psychic. It is often visionary and Utopian, in that it looks towards potentiality as much as actuality; it is concerned with what is possible rather than with what is; with alternatives rather than with acceptance of the *status quo*. In these respects it is as widely separate and distant from the sociology of regulation as the sociology of Marx is separate and distant from the sociology of Durkheim.

The distinction between these two sociologies can perhaps be best illustrated in schematic form; extreme points of view are counter-posed in order to highlight the essential differences between them. Table 2.2 summarises the situation.

We offer this regulation-radical change distinction as the second principal dimension of our scheme for analysing social theories. Along with the subjective-objective dimension developed in the previous chapter, we present it as a powerful means for identifying and analysing the assumptions which underlie social theories in general.

The notions of "regulation" and "radical change" have thus far been presented in a very rough and extreme form. The two models illustrated in Table 2.2 should be regarded as ideal-typical formulations. The seven elements which we have identified lend themselves to much more rigorous and systematic treatment in which their overall form and nature [can be] spelt out in detail, [but here] we wish to address ourselves to the broad relationships which exist between the sociologies of regulation and radical change. We maintain that they present fundamentally different views and interpretations of the nature of society. They reflect fundamentally different frames of reference. They present themselves, therefore, as *alternative* models for the analysis of social processes.

Table 2.2   The Regulation-Radical Change Dimension

The sociology of REGULATION is concerned with	The sociology of RADICAL CHANGE is concerned with
(a) The status quo	(a) Radical change
(b) Social order	(b) Structural conflict
(c) Consensus*	(c) Modes of domination
(d) Social integration and cohesion	(d) Contradiction
(e) Solidarity	(e) Emancipation
(f) Need satisfaction**	(f) Deprivation
(g) Actuality	(g) Potentiality

Notes

* By "consensus" we mean voluntary and "spontaneous" agreement of opinion.

** The term *need satisfaction* is used to refer to the focus upon satisfaction of individual or system "needs." The sociology of regulation tends to presume that various social characteristics can be explained in relation to these needs. It presumes that it is possible to identify and satisfy human needs within the context of existing social systems, and that society reflects these needs. The concept of "deprivation," on the other hand, is rooted in the notion that the social "system" prevents human fulfillment; indeed, that "deprivation" is created as the result of the status quo. The social "system" is not seen as satisfying needs but as eroding the possibilities for human fulfillment. It is rooted in the notion that society has resulted in deprivation rather than in gain.

To present the models in this way is to invite criticism along the lines of that levelled at Dahrendorf's work. For example, it could be suggested that the two models are the reciprocals of each other—no more than two sides of the same coin—and that relationships between the subelements of each model need not be congruent, that is, an analysis may pay attention to elements of both.

The answer to both criticisms follows our defence of Dahrendorf's work. To conflate the two models and treat them as variations on a single theme is to ignore or at least to underplay the fundamental differences which exist between them. Whilst it may be possible to use each model in a diluted form and thus obtain two analyses of the middle ground which approximate each other, they must remain essentially separate, since they are based upon opposing assumptions. Thus, as we have illustrated, to discuss the "functions" of social conflict is to commit oneself to the sociology of regulation as opposed to that of radical change. However close one's position might be to the middle ground, it would seem that one must be committed to one side more than another. The fundamental distinctions between the sociologies of regulation and radical change will become clear from our analysis of their intellectual development and constituent schools of thought in later chapters. We conceptualise these two broad sociological perspectives in the form of a polarised dimension, recognising that while variations within the context of each are possible, the perspectives are necessarily separate and distinct from each other.

Notes

1. For a further discussion of the nominalism-realism debate, see Kolakowski (1972), pp. 15–16.

2. Kolakowski (1972), pp. 158–159. In its most extreme form nominalism does not recognise the existence of any world outside the realm of individual consciousness. . . . This is the solipsist position. . . .

3. For a comprehensive review of "realism," see Keat and Urry [1975], 27–45. They make much of the distinction between "positivism" and "realism" but, as they admit, these terms are used in a somewhat unconventional way.

4. For further discussion of positivism—anti-positivism, for example, [see] Giddens (1974) and Walsh (1972).

5. Giddens (1974), p. 1.

6. See, for example, Popper (1963).

7. For a good illustration of an anti-positivist view of science, Douglas (1970), pp. 3–44.

8. The human nature debate in its widest sense involves many to whom we have not referred here. The precise model of man to be employed in any analytical scheme, underwritten by assumptions which reflect the voluntarism-determinism issue in one way or another. We have isolated this element of the debate here as a way of treating at its most basic level a necessary assumption of all social-scientific theories which purport to account for human activities. Detailed propositions with regard to the precise explanation of human activities elaborate in one way or another this basic theme.

9. For an excellent discussion of the nature of the ideographic social science, see Blumer (1969), ch. 1.

10. It is important to emphasise here that both nomothetic and ideographic methodologies can be employed in a deductive and inductive sense. Whilst the inductive-deductive debate in science is a subject of considerable interest and importance, we do not see it as being central to the four suggested here as a means of distinguishing between the *nature* of social science theories. That notwithstanding, it remains an important methodological issue, of relevance to both sociology and organisational analysis, within the context of the assumptions explored here.

11. Among the numerous theorists primarily concerned with the problem of order, Dawe cites Parsons (1949), Nisbet (1967), Bramson (1961), Cohen (1968), and Aron (1968).

12. For a discussion of the Marxism versus social science debate, see Shaw (1975). The division between Marxist theorists and orthodox sociologists is now so deep that they either ignore each other completely, or indulge in an exchange of abuse and accusation regarding the political conservatism or subversiveness commonly associated with their points of view. Debate about the intellectual strengths and weaknesses of their opposing standpoints is conspicuous by its absence.

13. Later in this chapter we suggest that the descriptions of "*concern with the status quo*" and "*concern for radical change*" provide more accurate views of the issues involved here.

14. Dahrendorf acknowledges Merton's distinction between latent and manifest functions but does not pursue the consequence of "dysfunctions" for the concept of integration (Dahrendorf, 1959, pp. 173–179).

15. Other "order" theorists who have addressed themselves to Dahrendorf's model tend to follow a similar path in the attempt to embrace conflict theory within their perspective. See, for example, van den Berghe (1969).

PART II

Closed System
Rational Models

The early history of organization theory is marked by models that often carry the label *classical management theory*. They focus on the design of formal organization, or how to organize and manage people and take a top-down approach, in that they imply organizations can be designed by top managers in ways that increase organizational performance.

Although there was earlier writing and thinking about organizing people (otherwise, how could the empires of Egypt, Rome, and Alexander the Great be managed?), the focus of this work tended toward managing government, military, and political organization. The writing and thinking about what most think of as modern organization and management theory started at the end of the 19th and the beginning of the 20th century with the work of Frederick W. Taylor and his colleagues in scientific management.

The Scientific Management Approach

Around 1900, managers began to experiment with ways to use raw materials, men, and equipment more efficiently. When their experiments met with success, their ideas were sought out by others who had similar problems. Scientific management emerged from such a way of thinking and was focused on the lowest level of the organization: the worker and his boss. The basic question to which most management research was addressed was, "How can the job be designed most efficiently?" These issues were taken up by a number of writers, including Henry L. Gantt, Frank and Lillian Gilbreth, and Dexter Kimball.

However, the most influential of these was Frederick Taylor. He was born to a well-to-do Philadelphia family but was unable to complete college because of poor eyesight. He took a job in industry as an apprentice at the Midvale Steel Company in

1878 and quickly rose through the ranks to become chief engineer in 1884, at the age of 28. Based on his experiences and studies, Taylor developed many ideas to increase management efficiency and became widely sought as a consultant to other firms.

Some of the more important ideas of scientific management are that:

1. Current management practice was inefficient.

2. Management must adopt the scientific method in industry.

3. Specialization should be practiced.

4. Planning and scheduling were essential.

5. Proper selection, the right person for each job, should be done.

6. The standard method, the best way to perform a task, should be found.

7. Standard times for each task should be established.

8. Wage incentives should be utilized.

The application of these principles resulted in significant productivity increases. In his most famous case, Taylor significantly improved productivity of the loading of pig iron bars into railroad cars. In the well-known shoveling experiment, Taylor was able to increase productivity from 16 to 59 tons of material shoveled per day, while the number of shovelers needed per day was decreased from 500 to 140. Others, like the Gilbreths, in a number of applications of their work redesign methods, also demonstrated spectacular increases in productivity. For example, Frank Gilbreth was able to increase the average productivity of bricklayers from 120 to 350 bricks per hour. Such results were typical when scientific management was applied, and they led to a strong advocacy of scientific management methods that were widely applied.

Administrative Theory

In the mid 1920s, a group of managers had begun to write about the job of the administrator. They sought to analyze the basic task of management. They were also concerned with the development of principles of management guides for designing and managing an organization. Most of these writers worked independently of the others but nevertheless came to similar conclusions about management.

Henri Fayol, a Frenchman, had the most impact of these writers with his book *General and Industrial Management in France* (trans., 1949). He and these other writers distinguished management activities from technical activities, pointing out that managerial activities increased in importance and technical activities decreased in importance as one moves from the lowest to the highest level of an organization. He proposed 14 principles of management, stressing the importance of specialization of labor to make the best use of human resources, although he warned that this could be carried too far. He was concerned about the use of human resources as well. Equality of treatment was to him very important. To facilitate motivation, the wage payment system, he believed, must fit the type of work.

A similar view could also be found in the work of Max Weber (trans., 1947). This German sociologist, whose emphasis was on bureaucracy, was an important influence on writing and theory about the study of organization. Max Weber's analysis considered organizations as part of broader society. He described the characteristics of the bureaucracy, which he viewed as the most efficient form for large complex organizations such as business, government, and the military. The bureaucratic form of organization, as described by Weber, uses extensive formal rules and procedures to govern the job behavior of organizational members. Organizational positions are arrayed in a hierarchy, each with a particular established amount of authority and responsibility. Promotion to higher positions is based on technical competence, objectively judged. Weber felt that this type of organization emphasized predictability of behavior and results and showed great stability over time. He suggested that organizations naturally evolved toward this rational form.

However, Weber also was concerned with the form of bureaucratic rationality that took a negative turn and was reflected in the dark side of this form of organization (Jermier, this volume, Chapter 18 personal correspondence). This aspect of his work, for some, made Weber a "critical" theorist and less so one that would be lumped into the classical management tradition.

In Chapter 3 the work of Ralph C. Davis (1951) is presented. Davis's work falls into the school of thought called "administrative management," part of the closed system strategy for studying organization. This is a "rational" approach to organization. Once goals of the organization have been determined, the development of structure, the flow of authority, and the other relationships clearly follow in a logical fashion.

CHAPTER 3

The Classical Approach

The Fundamentals of Top Management*

Ralph C. Davis

Management is the function of executive leadership. Its organic subfunctions are the creative planning, organizing, and controlling of the organizational activities for which the executive is responsible. They have to do with the accomplishment of the group and project objectives of the organization.

Creative planning provides the answers to such questions as what should be done, how and where it should be done, who should do it, what physical and human resources are necessary for the accomplishment of the particular mission, and other questions of a similar nature. Its purpose is to determine an effective, economical basis for the accomplishment of designated objectives.

Organizing sets up the common basic conditions that underlie effective, economical execution by a particular group over a period of time. They must be created before work starts on the kinds of activities for which they are a prerequisite. These general conditions are specified in the plan, or derived from it.

Controlling constrains and regulates action in accordance with the requirements of the plan. Business standards are criteria that enable us to measure, proportion, and maintain business factors, forces, and effects in proper condition and relation to one another. They are necessary for the satisfactory performance of all management functions. Effective economical execution requires these conditions and relationships to be adequately standardized.

---

*From *The Fundamentals of Top Management* (Chapter 21), by R. C. Davis, 1951, New York: Harper Brothers.

There must be and is a body of related knowledge that concerns the solution of management problems. The pioneers in the field recognized this fact clearly at the turn of the [twentieth] century. They saw the need for a science of management. The term science seems to perturb some people unnecessarily. It may refer to any classified body of fundamental facts, principles, and techniques that explains certain basic phenomena. It supplies a basis for the solution of problems associated with these phenomena.

Scientific management attempts to apply the logic of effective thinking to the solution of business problems. It depends on and leads to a further development of a philosophy of management. The latter is any system of thought that explains basic business problems. It is based on logical relationships between business factors, forces, effects, and principles. It must supply the basis for an intelligent approach to the solution of these problems. The principal problems have to do with business objectives, standards of business conduct, executive leadership, business policy, business functions, personnel, physical performance factors, organization structure, business procedure, and organization morale.

The consuming public does not exist to serve the owners and employees of business organizations. Business exists to serve the public. The sanctions that enable the owners of business establishments to engage in private enterprise rest on the individual's right of private property in his capital. This right is the basis of free enterprise. The sanctions that enable either executive or operative employees to engage in individual or collective bargaining are based on the individual's right of private property in his services. The right is the basis of free labor. The right of private property is delegated by the body politic through its elected representatives. It can be modified if it is abused by either labor or capital. It has been so abused in the past. Such modifications move in the direction of state capitalism and socialism, even though they may be necessary.

There are certain obligations that are a condition of the granting of the right of private property for the performance of economic functions. They have to do basically with the obligation to provide the public with the goods and services it requires in the quantities and qualities it desires, when and where it wants them and at a competitive price. They require the maintenance of free competition and free markets for both capital and labor, subject to such a minimum of government regulation as may be necessary in the public interest. They require the maintenance of the customer's right of freedom of choice in the market to the maximum degree that is practicable.

An objective is any value or values that are needed or desired by an individual or group, provided that the person or group is willing to make some sacrifice or effort to obtain them. An economic value is any satisfaction of need or a desire for which an individual or group is willing to exchange other values. These values may or may not be tangible. The primary objective of the business organization is necessarily its service objectives. They are customer satisfactions, in terms of business' basic obligation to supply goods and services as required. The desire or need of owners for a profit and of employees for a wage are collateral objectives. They are earned to the extent that the public is well served. The business organization also has certain secondary objectives. They have to do with economy and effectiveness in the performance of business functions. They are set up by the obligation to serve the public at a competitive price.

The general relations between business objectives may be summarized as follows: The primary objective of the business organization is an economic service. A profit is a personal objective of owners. Wages, salaries, bonuses, and related benefits are the personal objectives of executive and operative employees. Any personal objectives are necessarily collateral business objectives. There are many subclasses of these objectives. The accomplishment of any objectives must conform to accepted standards of business conduct.

Values must be created by work. Business objectives condition accordingly the work of the organization. They are the starting points of business thought and action. The determination and analysis of objectives involve forecasting. Many techniques for estimating and specifying the objective have been developed. Their importance suggests that further development of them may be expected.

An organization basically is any group of individuals who are cooperating to a common end under the guidance of leadership. A particular organization may be good, bad, or indifferent from the standpoint of objectives, policies, or any other criterion. A leader is anyone who accepts responsibility for the accomplishment of group objectives. He must usually discharge this responsibility to the satisfaction of the group. Otherwise, there may be a loss of morale and organizational effectiveness that may cost him his position. He is expected to motivate, coordinate, and direct the organization, or some element of it, in the achievement of its objectives.

Satisfactory accomplishment implies an effective, economical performance of both managerial and operative functions. The requirements and conditions of such accomplishment change as our society develops and our economy changes accordingly. There have been and are various kinds, grades, and conditions of executive leadership in business organizations. A great business leader who was successful in one era might not be successful in the next. The conditions of executive leadership under a war economy are different from those in peacetime. The founder of a business often lacks the executive ability to lead it successfully from its pioneer stage through the stage of exploitation to the stage of relative stabilization. Leadership that is successful during a period of inflation may be unable to lead the organization successfully through a period of depression. Positive leadership is usually more effective than negative leadership in the long run. There are times, however, when negative leadership is necessary for the successful handling of disciplinary cases or emergency situations. The leadership responsibilities of the administrative executive are related to but different from those of the operative executive. It is evident that any formula for continuing executive success must be open to question. There are principles of effective executive leadership. They are the principles of good management.

Administrative management is chiefly group management. Operative management is chiefly project management. The former is concerned largely with long-time projections of the activities of organizational groups. Operative management is concerned largely with short-time action in the execution of specific projects. Usually they must be accomplished with reference to time objectives in the immediate future. Other fundamental distinctions between administrative and operative management . . . account partly for the fact that many capable operative executives are unable to rise to top business leadership.

The big financial rewards are found in the echelon of top administrative management. They supply much of the incentives that induce bright, ambitious young men to strive for advancement in an organization. There is no easy road to success, however. These rewards are usually paid for inspiration rather than for perspiration. There is a high rate of obsolescence among executives who are too "practical" to keep abreast of the developing science of management.

Policy is a basic factor in business organization. A business policy is essentially a principle or group of related principles, and their consequent rules of action. They condition and govern the successful achievement of certain business objectives toward which they are directed. A principle is an expression of the relationships between cause and effect in a particular problem. It is a statement of these relationships that is accepted as a significant truth. A good statement of sound policy supplies, therefore, a cogent relationship between business objectives and ideals on the one hand, and organizational functions, physical factors, and personnel on the other. Sound policy is obviously a requisite for sound planning. A statement of policy, express or implied, is often found in the statement of a plan. Nevertheless, a policy is not a plan.

The policy-making function breaks down into certain definite phases. They are policy formulation, promulgation, education, acceptance, application, interpretation, and control. They are part of any executive job in some degree. Much of the top executive's time is spent on problems of general administrative policy. Such policies enter into long-range planning and the subsequent work of organizing. Rules, on the other hand, are restrictive. They enter into control. Even a minor operative executive occasionally makes rules for the guidance of operatives under his supervision. If not, he must interpret rules that have been made by his superior. These rules must be made within the framework of the broader policies that are originated on higher levels.

The intelligence with which policies are made and applied can stimulate or depress the morale of the organization. Unity of action depends on unity of thought. Effective accomplishment depends on unity of action. A common body of principle is an important factor in the development of unity of thought. There appears, in consequence, to be a growing tendency to commit important policies to writing in the form of policy manuals and rule books. There is also a tendency to link management's policy-making responsibilities more closely with the lower echelons of the business organization in which they are applied. Executives on operative levels are included in the work of policy formulation to a greater degree, through application of the Principle of Participation. Policy control in large organizations tends to be decentralized.

Business functions are the work of accomplishing the various objectives of the business organization. The nature and amount of this work depend on the characteristics and requirements of these objectives. Business is an economic institution. Its objectives are primarily economic. The mission of the business organization is to supply the portion of the public which it serves with certain goods and services.

Structural and procedural planning for an organization rests necessarily on some theory of functionalization. Any such theory in business organization must rest on the concept of economic utility. Such utility may be defined as the ability of an economic good or service to supply the customer with the satisfactions of his needs or desires for which he spends his money. He may transfer his patronage to a competitor if he does not get these satisfactions in satisfactory amounts. The customer still has the right of freedom of choice in the marketplace. The attributes of the product or service that give it the required utilities are its quality attributes. They are so recognized in industry by marketing experts, engineering executives, and quality managers.

The organic functions of a business establishment are, therefore, the creation of economic utilities, the distribution of these utilities, and the provision of the capital that is necessary for the performance of the first two functions. They are the functions of production, distribution, and finance in a manufacturing establishment. They are different in other basic types of economic institutions, except for the common function of finance.

All chains of command within a business organization stem originally from one of its organic functions. They develop, by the processes of functional differentiation, with increasing business volume and consequent organizational growth. The devolution of a line organization leads directly downward to a division of operative work and specialization in the creation of primary service values. Finance is an exception to this statement. . . . A staff organization evolves from a line organization. It makes possible a division of managerial work and specialization in the creation of collateral or secondary service values. It may be appended to a line organization at any level where such managerial service is needed. It cannot be part of the line organization, however. Both line and staff functions have their executive and operative phases. There are no distinctions between them in this respect. There are various distinguishing characteristics, of course. One simple test of a staff function is this: Does its devolution lead directly to specialization in the creation or distribution of salable values? If it does not, it is probably staff.

Functions must be grouped on a logical basis as they are differentiated from one another. This basis should permit the development of good cooperation, coordination, and leadership. There are various principles of functionalization that underlie structural and procedural planning. They have these objectives in view. Some functions are similar to one another. They have similar objectives, factors, and difficulties. They require for their performance personnel having similar background, training, experience, personality, and other attributes. We may group functions in accordance with these similarities. We may relate these groups by lines of responsibility and authority. The result is some form of organization structure. Some functions are complementary to one another. They produce values that are a prerequisite for other values that must be produced subsequently in accomplishing the mission. These functions may be grouped in steps in its accomplishment. They may be related to one another on the basis of their complementary nature, but with due regard for organizational lines. The result is some form of business procedure. All business functions have complementary and similar characteristics with respect to other related functions.

The complexity of functionalization necessarily increases as the volume of business grows. There is some evidence that this complexity tends to increase in geometric progression. Much of it is a result of staff organization growth. Staff contributes necessary collateral and secondary values. Otherwise the staff personnel would not be retained on the payroll. It is overhead expense, nevertheless. This suggests that there is an optimum size for a business establishment. Yet a rising standard of living requires increasing aggregations of capital and labor in some industries. "Bigness" in business organizations is not bad *per se*. If it were, the difficulty could not be cured by bigger state trusts that are run by governmental functionaries. The answer in business organization is usually some form and degree of economic integration and decentralization. It is not necessarily dissolution.

The problems of business functionalization are not simple. The design of organization structure and procedure has become, in consequence, an increasingly important part of the work of administrative planning in large organizations. Some good techniques for functional investigation and analysis have been developed. Some sound principles of functionalization have been established. Nevertheless, the subject can benefit from more research.

Effective performance, in any organized activity, requires a delegation of responsibility and authority. This is true for both executive and operative performance. Responsibility is an individual rather than a group phenomenon. It is the obligation that an individual acquires in any organization when he accepts an assignment of certain objectives, functions, and duties. An executive responsibility is an obligation to perform leadership functions under certain conditions. It necessarily involves the direction and supervision of others. An operative responsibility is an obligation to perform, to the best of one's ability, certain assigned duties, under executive direction, in the accomplishment of a particular project. An operative responsibility does not involve direction and supervision of the work of others. Authority is the term for the rights that are necessary for the satisfactory discharge of one's organizational obligations. Executive authority includes, therefore, the rights of decision and command with respect to the organizational activities of one's subordinates. Operative authority includes such rights of decision as are necessary for the proper performance of assigned operative duties.

Accountability is a condition of membership in an organization. It requires that each member must render a report of his discharge of responsibilities, and be judged fairly on the basis of his record of accomplishment. Such judgments rest on qualitative and quantitative evaluations of individual and group performance. These evaluations result chiefly from the performance of the control functions of supervision and comparison. They determine the extent to which the individual has accomplished the assigned objectives. The operative employee is accountable for the accomplishment of operative objectives that have been assigned to him. The executive employee is accountable for the results accomplished by the individuals and groups who are working under his direction. The principal phases of the problem are (1) analysis of objectives, (2) functional analysis with respect to the requirements for the accomplishment of these objectives, (3) functional grouping and the division of responsibility as a basis for structural and procedural design, (4) determination of the authority required for each allocation of functions and responsibility, (5) the delegation of responsibility and authority, (6) the establishment of control, and (7) the development of accountability. Many problems are involved. The economy and effectiveness with which the organization accomplishes its mission depend on how well they are solved.

The division, allocation, and delegation of responsibility rest on whatever groupings of functions have been made. They may be line or staff. The ultimate unit function, in any case, is a single, simple act of operative performance, either mental or physical. It must have definite points of starting and stopping. This concept enters directly into the techniques of motion and time study. The motion principles associated with it enter directly into the design of organization structure, however. The ultimate unit of operative responsibility is the obligation of an operative employee to perform assigned duties within his job classification. It is based on the general work assignment that is set up in his job specification. The ultimate unit of executive responsibility is the unit of operative supervision. It is the number of units of operative responsibility that is suitable for direction and the exercise of face-to-face leadership by a first-level supervisory executive. Experience indicates that the size of this supervisory unit tends to range from ten to thirty operatives. The reasons have to do with the economy and effectiveness of supervisory leadership. There is also an effective, economical unit of executive supervision. Experience indicates that its size tends to range from three to eight or nine subordinate executives. The relations in organization structure between these units of operative and executive supervision have an important influence on the success of the organization.

The value of the contribution that an individual is required to make increases with the service level on which he works. There is some good evidence that it tends to increase in geometric progression. A given job is and should be worth more in a big concern than in a small one. The importance of the individual in organization success tends to vary inversely with organization size, nevertheless. The "indispensable men" are more likely to be found in small concerns than in large ones. The division and allocation of responsibility may be made in the former with respect to the individual ability and know-how of the present executive personnel. The supply of leadership material may be quite limited in the small organization. In the big concern, it may be made largely with respect to the requirements of functions for proper performance. Any modifications of sound organizational relationships to suit the inadequacies of present personnel are likely to be temporary. The large organization tends to have greater stability and permanence for these and other reasons.

A delegate is a person who is appointed to represent and act for another. Any subordinate, whether executive or operative, is in a sense a delegate of the superior executive to whom he reports directly. The process of delegation is one whereby certain of the executive's functions, responsibilities, and authorities are released and committed to designated subordinate positions. Responsibility and authority are attributes of the job. Delegation enables an executive to extend his abilities beyond the limits of his personal powers. It makes possible a division of labor and the development of specialization, whether executive or operative. It may stimulate or depress organization morale, depending on how well it is done. It has other effects on the organization. It is, accordingly, an important managerial problem. There are various principles of delegation. An understanding of them is an important part of an executive's know-how.

Decentralization takes place when a higher central source of responsibility and authority assigns certain functions to subordinate individuals and groups. These functions may be managerial or operative, line or staff. Their decentralization is accomplished through delegation. Any assignment of functions to subordinates should be accompanied by adequate delegation of responsibility and authority. Otherwise the individual cannot justly be held accountable for results. There are various advantages and disadvantages of decentralization. There are various principles and conditions that govern the extent to which it is practicable. This extent tends to vary directly with the size of the organization. There are some obvious limitations, however. Delegation cannot result in the abdication of one's responsibilities and authorities. There is no direct relation between processes of delegation and the democratic process. The latter is a political concept. The business organization is an economic institution, under a condition of free enterprise and the right of private property.

Organization structure is the structure of relationships between groups of similar functions, physical factors, and personnel. These relationships have to do largely with responsibility, authority, and accountability. They affect organizational morale. It is possible, therefore, to have a good organization structure, a beautiful organization chart, and a poor organization. An effective, economical accomplishment of assigned objectives is not characteristic of poor organizations.

There are only two basic forms of organization structure: line and staff. All other forms are variants of them. The "line" is the primary form. It is the backbone of the organization. A primary hierarchy of functions leads directly from an organic business function to a division of primary operative labor. It is an effect of functional differentiation. It results directly in specialization in the creation and distribution of salable values. A primary chain of command is the hierarchy of responsibility, authority, and accountability that is related directly to the primary functional hierarchy. A primary line organization is the present hierarchy of individuals, both managerial and operative, who perform line functions. The necessary responsibility and authority for such performance should be delegated to their job assignments. All staff groups exist to serve the line organizations, or other staff groups, for this reason. The tendency in most business concerns has been to resist the transfer of line authority to staff groups. Such transfer tends to break down the line organization. It leads to the defeat of the enterprise in the battle of competition, as it approaches a condition of complete functionalization.

The growth and devolution of the line organization begins, theoretically, with the owner-manager. Some concerns have actually started from this point. It results increasingly in the grouping of primary operative functions on one or more of the following bases: (1) product, commodity, or service, (2) process or method, (3) equipment or other dominant physical factors, and (4) the physical dispersion of business activities on a geographical basis.

These functions must be grouped in units of operative and executive supervision. The relationships that should exist between these units are primary determinants of line organization form. The basic relationships between them can be expressed mathematically. Such relationships assist in the provisional determination of the number of major service levels or echelons that are needed by an organization. They help in determining general criteria of the number of line executives required by the organization at various levels. They underlie the solution of other organizational problems. An application of these relationships results in some interesting conclusions. Very few major echelons are required to command a very large organization. The percentage of line executives to primary operatives should increase very little with organization growth. Top executive payroll is and should be insignificant, relative to the total payroll of the organization and the contributions of effective top leadership. Other significant conclusions may be drawn. It should of course be remembered that there is no mathematical substitute for executive judgment. A concern does not manage by formulas.

The structural form of the small organization is predominately line. The characteristics of line organization make its use particularly advantageous in the small business. Its advantages may be lost with organizational growth. This will take place unless the line is supplemented increasingly with staff organization. Management must be decentralized increasingly without loss of control of the organization's activities. Lack of organizational know-how may limit the growth of the small business as much as the competition of big business, and possibly more.

Staff organization structure is an evolution from a primary functional hierarchy. It is made necessary chiefly by increases in the load of managerial work and increasing requirements for specialized background, training, experience, and ability. Hence it has to do with a division and specialization of managerial labor. It takes place necessarily above the level of operative performance. A staff organization, accordingly, assists the line and other staff organizations in the performance of some phase of an organic managerial function. It usually performs some facilitative services in addition. The nature, extent, and degree of staff performance are determined and limited by delegation.

The basic classification of staff functions must rest, therefore, on the classification of organic managerial functions. These functions are the creative planning, organizing, and controlling of the activities of organizational members in the accomplishment of a common objective. Technical staff functions assist the organization in planning. They may assist it by performing certain specialized functions that are purely facilitative. They may do both. They require a certain specialized background, training, and experience for their performance. They may or may not be professional, however. Coordinative staff functions assist the organization in control. They too may perform certain facilitative functions. Successful performance of staff control functions usually requires breadth of background, training, and experience, rather than intensity. There are no staff groups that specialize solely in organizing.

All managerial functions, whether line or staff, have their operative phases. This is evident, since all functional devolution leads to operative specialization, either primary or secondary. Staff objectives are principally secondary. Staff organizations supply values that the line organization must have for the accomplishment or primary objectives. The latter are certain utilities in goods or services. They enable the customer to enjoy the values for which he pays his money. It is evident that staff objectives and functions are necessarily secondary in incidence of service to the public. They are not necessarily secondary in the importance and value of their contributions, however.

Organizational growth, whether line or staff, tends to follow a typical structural pattern. It is helpful in analyzing structural problems, if it does not result in a formulistic approach to organizational planning. Any general pattern must be modified and adjusted to fit the realities of the particular situation. We saw, during the discussion of organization structure, that the assigned mission of a staff group, and the conditions under which it must be accomplished, govern the detailed form that this pattern tends to take. It is evident that the devolution of a technical staff function must lead to professional or other operative specialization in planning, when the principal objective of the staff group is certain types of plans. The engineering department is a classic example. The devolution of a technical staff function must lead to professional or other operative specialization in facilitation, when the principal objective of the staff group is facilitative assistance. The devolution of a coordinative staff function must lead to operative specialization in control. Such specialization must be based on the organic staff phases of control. Any supporting planning services or associated services of facilitation for any staff organization must be placed in a secondary technical staff function in business organization, regardless of how vitally important it may be and how great its development is in the particular concern. Any supporting control services also must be placed in a secondary coordinative staff position. Such a position means that the particular function is attached directly to a secondary chain of command in a staff relationship.

Any staff organization is overhead. There is nothing scientific about an elaborate, complicated, and expensive staff organization that is not needed. It is not good business on the other hand to refuse to spend money for staff organization that is needed.

The development and growth of staff organization results from the growth in the demand for the company's services. It is both a cause and an effect of business success. The development of staff services has to do largely with the development and expansion of the basic staff duties. These duties are (1) investigation, including research, (2) analysis of facts and information, (3) interpretation, including services of information, (4) recommendation, including the formulation of plans, (5) coordination, including assistance in control, and (6) facilitation, including assistance in organizing and executing plans. Such development often requires continuing staff evolution with business growth. The principal stages of staff evolution are (1) line integration, (2) distinct staff differentiation, (3) complete staff differentiation, (4) staff integration, (5) staff elevation, (6) staff decentralization, and (7) complete staff separation. It is not necessary that all staff development begin with the first stage. It is not necessary either that the development of all staff functions be carried through to the final stage. It is helpful in diagnosing present staff difficulties to be able to recognize the stage of development of the particular staff organization. One must of course know the basic requirements for staff economy and effectiveness that are associated with this stage. It is helpful in organizational planning for staff growth to know the subsequent stages and their requirements. Such knowledge should be part of the professional background of the modern executive. In too many cases, it is not.

There has been increasing interest, in recent years, in top administrative management. The importance of top leadership in rapidly changing situations is apparent. The desirability of relieving top executives of some of the burden of administrative management has been realized. Some interesting developments in the field of top administrative staff organization have taken place as a result.

A staff organization that assists the chief executive in administrative planning is concerned with interdivisional coordination of thought. It is concerned, therefore, with problems of top administrative organization structure, procedure, general policies and objectives, and the general condition of organizational morale. It has close relations necessarily with financial planning. It does not do the work of any major technical staff division. Such divisions are still responsible for the development of plans and policies for activities within their fields of specialization. A vice-president in charge of personnel and industrial relations, for example, is still responsible for developing and recommending personnel plans and policies. A staff executive for administrative planning merely achieves a meeting of minds between the immediate line and staff subordinates of the chief executive. Any resulting plans are subject to the latter's approval.

A staff organization that assists the chief executive in administrative control is concerned largely with the interdivisional coordination. Much of the work at this level has to do with long-range planning. Accordingly, it is concerned with progress in the accomplishment of planning projects. It is concerned subsequently with the progress of the major divisions of the business in organizing for the execution of plans. It must evaluate divisional performance in the accomplishment of assigned objectives. Administrative control deals with the constraint and regulation of group action in the completion of administrative projects. These projects may extend over considerable time periods—a month, a quarter, a year, or longer. It is not concerned directly with the current execution of operative projects and their schedules. General administrative control performs its functions at the top administrative level of the organization.

There are a great many structural problems, such as the difficulties associated with functional emergence; the location of dissimilar staff functions; the duties, responsibilities, and authority of headquarters staff executives; the development of staff parallelism; the use and limitations of committees; and many others. They greatly affect the development of top administrative organization. Much more information concerning their characteristics and requirements would be helpful. The literature of business management deals largely with the discussion of technical and coordinative staff problems at the various levels of operative management. . . .

[M]ajor organizational problems within the business establishment [must be understood by business executives. Their] responsibilities require executives to understand the attributes of business organization that are required for growth. They are, in general, the attributes of good organization anywhere. The principal ones are (1) effective executive leadership, (2) sound business objectives and policies, (3) sound functional relationships as determined by objectives, (4) adequate physical implementation that will make possible an economical, effective accomplishment of objectives, (5) a complement of abilities, both executive and operative, to handle present business problems economically and effectively, (6) organizational stability, (7) organizational flexibility, (8) organizational capacity for growth, (9) organizational balance, and (10) good organizational morale.

The first five of these attributes were discussed earlier in this chapter. The remaining five require further comment. Organizational stability is the quality that enables an organization to adjust itself promptly to personnel losses without serious losses of economy or effectiveness. Organizational flexibility is the quality that enables it to adjust itself to temporary changes in business volume and conditions without serious losses of economy or effectiveness. Many concerns have done a good job of developing these organizational attributes. Most concerns appear to have done a poor job of developing capacity for growth. The exceptions are found usually among large, successful corporations. This attribute may be defined as the ability of an organization to adjust its personnel and structure to permanent changes in business volume, without serious losses of economy or effectiveness. It is concerned usually with the permanent expansion and development of the organization. This is likely to be a continuing problem, as long as our economy is expanding. Growth is a requirement, in some industries, for the maintenance of competitive effectiveness. Many concerns do not conform to the requirements of this definition, because they handle growth problems on the basis of short-range planning, trial and error, and expediency. Their weaknesses show up quickly when they are forced to expand to a large size quickly during a war emergency.

Some of the greatest failures of executive leadership have been in the field of morale. It has appeared, at times, as though anyone could take away from the executive the leadership of his employees by the simple expedient of offering something for nothing. It is possible that this has been another effect of too many business mechanics and too few professional executives who are capable of exercising economic statesmanship.

Morale is a mental condition of individuals and organizations. It determines their attitudes. As a result, it conditions the degree of acceptance of executive leadership by organization members. It governs the quality of their cooperation in the accomplishment of organizational objectives. Good organizational morale is a condition in which individuals and groups voluntarily make a reasonable subordination of their personal objectives to the service objectives of their organization. An industrial society can be overthrown by the destruction of the morale of its industrial organizations. There is an organizational Principle of the Primacy of the Service Objective. It says that an organization may fail when any important individuals or groups in it succeed in placing their personal interests ahead of its interests for any considerable period of time.

The morale-building process is, accordingly, a process of integrating interests. It is any process that develops and maintains identities and interdependencies between the organization's service objectives and the personal objectives of its members. The interests of individuals are most acute with respect to the values they desire for themselves and for those immediately dependent on them. The process has to do, therefore, with creating the conditions that will assure an adequate satisfaction of personal objectives. It must do this in a manner that is compatible with competitive effectiveness.

Confidence in the integrity and ability of executive leadership is an important condition for the successful operation of the morale-building process. There must exist some belief that the present subordination of personal interests to organizational interests will result in worthwhile future benefits for the individual or group. The desired benefits may be tangible or intangible, or both. Surveys of employee interests have indicated, for example, that wages, hours, and working conditions are not always the principal considerations of operatives. This may happen when employees in a particular organization generally regard the benefits associated with such considerations to be fair and adequate. Such surveys suggest that a feeling of worthwhileness, a feeling of belonging to an organization in which one can take pride, a feeling of security, or some other intangible value may be the thing that is desired.

The morale problem, like any other, must be broken down into its principal elements before a general method of approach to its solution can be devised. The following are the principal functions in the morale-building process: (1) analyses of individual and group interests and objectives and of their relation to organizational service objectives, (2) establishment of common concepts and yardsticks of value, (3) provision of values that are desired by individuals and groups in the organization in adequate and proper amounts, (4) prompt, equitable adjustments of conflicts between personal and organizational interests as they develop, [and] (5) morale maintenance, including continuous identification of organizational and personal objectives.

No problems can be solved without adequate facts that are reasonably accurate. Various techniques for getting morale facts have been devised. They involve some form of intermittent or continuous morale surveys. The former are usually a statistical approach, based on the use of questionnaires. The latter are usually a qualitative approach, based on the use of trained observers. The most effective observers should be line supervisors, provided that they have been trained to do the job and have the ability. The most effective method for getting morale facts is likely to involve a combination of statistical and qualitative techniques.

A distinction between morale factors and morale effects should be made in applying any survey method. The attitudes of individuals and groups toward the organization and its leaders are obviously effects of their state of mind. They directly affect the economy and effectiveness with which the organization accomplishes its mission. Some of the more important effects of good morale are willing cooperation, loyalty to the organization and its leadership, good discipline, and organizational initiative. There are others. A morale index is a relative measure of the attitudes that indicate morale effects.

A morale factor is anything within or outside the organization that affects the personal interests of its members in relation to its own. We saw above that these interests include more than money. A morale stimulant is any factor that tends to produce favorable attitudes toward the organization and its leadership. A morale depressant is a factor that tends to produce unfavorable attitudes. It is possible for a particular morale factor to be a stimulant and a depressant at different times and under different circumstances. Some of the more common factors in good morale are worthwhile organizational and personal objectives, good leadership based on a sound philosophy of management, homogeneity of group characteristics and interests, decentralization, indoctrination, satisfactory physical work environment, and many others. They should be determined and specified clearly, concisely, and in as much detail as is practicable.

The scale of values that individuals and groups in an organization apply to their interests is obviously an important factor in morale development and maintenance. It is an effect of their philosophy. It affects morale directly, insofar as it bears on the activities of the organization and its leadership. An outside agency has an opportunity to substitute a scale that suits its purposes when the organization's members have no philosophy of their own.

A philosophy is a body of doctrine. The latter term refers to any formal statement, either express or implied, of objectives, ideals, principles, points of view, and general modes of procedure. A doctrine is laid down for the guidance of others, either with or without the authority to compel its acceptance. It can relate to physical or psychical phenomena, or both. The purpose of a managerial philosophy is to make clear the significance of business concepts. It underlies the mission of rendering an economic service for producers and consumers. Proper indoctrination of its members is a leadership responsibility in any type of organization. Business organization is no exception. Complete indoctrination in a business organization is not proper, of course. It is practically impossible, so long as we retain the rights underlying freedom of press, freedom of speech, and freedom of assembly. It is not in the long-term interests of business executives in a competitive society. The process in the business organization is one of self-indoctrination. It is a process of education. . . .

Poor morale cannot be blamed successfully on professional labor leaders. Organizational morale is a responsibility of the organization's leadership. This is not an argument against collective bargaining. Free enterprise, collective bargaining, and individual liberty rest squarely on the right of private property. The destruction of any one of them tends to destroy the right of private property. The destruction of the right of private property tends to destroy them all.

Voluntary cooperation, an intelligent exercise of initiative, self-coordination, and similar values are effects of good morale. They reduce the degree and extent of control that is necessary. Good morale cannot be a substitute for good control, however, even in small organizations. Self-control breaks down quickly with increasing organization size. Increasing executive control must be developed with organizational growth. Otherwise, paradoxically, an organization may fail in accomplishing its mission as a result of its success.

It was noted earlier that the organic functions of management are the creative planning, organizing, and controlling of the activities of the organization's members in the execution of their assigned tasks. They are the functions of executive leadership. The function of control is the work of constraining and regulating such actions in accordance with plans for the accomplishment of specified objectives. The economy and effectiveness of execution and control depend directly on creative planning and organizing. The ultimate objectives of control are, of course, the ultimate service objectives of business. They are, therefore, better customer values. Control coordinates and correlates action in accordance with a plan for the accomplishment of such objectives. The immediate objectives of control are derived from the objectives of the particular plan. They are, in general, (1) assurance of correct performance as specified by the plan, (2) a well-coordinated condition of action, and (3) a minimum of losses due to interferences with the proper execution of the plan.

The two grand divisions of the work of executive leadership are administrative management and operative management. Each division has its line and staff phases. They may be completely differentiated and highly developed in large organizations.

Staff functions may exist only potentially in the very small organization. A distinction must be made accordingly between operative control and administrative control. Operative control is chiefly project control. Administrative control is chiefly group control. It is the function of constraining and regulating group action in the completion of assigned programs. The latter summarize the results that are anticipated from the completion of assigned projects during a designated period of time. The cumulation of values resulting from the completion of these projects during this period provides a measure of the degree of accomplishment of organizational objectives. The latter were set up when the program was planned. The facts that are necessary for the operation of a system of administrative control come, then, from the reports originated by the system of operative control on the lower echelons.

Control on any echelon tends to break down into eight basic subfunctions. They are the organic phases of control. They are (1) routine planning, (2) scheduling, (3) preparation, (4) dispatching, (5) direction, (6) supervision, (7) comparison, and (8) corrective action. . . . [The] eight control functions tend to be performed in the order indicated. This temporal order is not mandatory, of course. However, it provides a useful basis for the analysis of control procedure. The line phases of control are direction, supervision, and corrective action. They cannot be differentiated from the line organization and assigned to staff groups, except to a very limited degree with respect to their most routine aspects. The reasons are found in their direct relations to line leadership responsibilities. The remaining five control functions may be assigned to staff control groups in a very high degree.

The extent to which control is exercised by subordinates is governed by the extent to which control responsibilities have been delegated and decentralized. Supervisory executives are responsible only for the line phases of control when the staff phases are highly centralized. They have certain responsibilities for morale maintenance that are inherent in the relation of face-to-face leadership. They have no control responsibilities if they have no obligations and rights with respect to direction, supervision, and corrective action. Their leadership position is undermined. They are not likely to discharge their morale responsibilities satisfactorily in such case. A centralized staff control sets up a completely functionalized relationship. It tends to concentrate responsibility and authority in the hands of higher line executives.

Differing degrees of centralized control may exist within one organization for the same function. The administrative control of production is highly decentralized down to the plant level in large concerns engaged in continuous manufacturing. It is highly centralized within the plant, down to and including plant stores and the production lines. The reasons are found in the principles of decentralization that have been discussed.

Just as morale conditions the quality of control, so control conditions the quality of morale. Disciplinary action, for example, is a phase of corrective action. Good discipline is an effect of good morale. It is a condition of voluntary conformity with policies, rules, and regulations. The latter are necessary for coordinated and cooperative action in the accomplishment of group objectives. Good discipline is related to other morale effects such as willing acceptance of executive decisions, voluntary cooperation, and organizational pride. Disciplinary action is a managerial process for conditioning individual and group behavior. Its objectives are the inhibition of improper behavior, the integration of personal and organizational interests, and the assurance of correct action in the future. It accomplishes these objectives by means of penalties or rewards. Disciplinary action has to do, therefore, with the addition or subtraction of certain values in the situation of an individual or a small group. It may be taken with respect to a person, but it should not be personal. The intent is usually to condition the quality of future action by the group of which the individual is a part.

Control may have other important effects. Their implications may go far beyond the limits of the particular undertaking that is being controlled. An understanding of the basic principles and significances of control is an important part of the background of the professional executive.

Business procedure is a basic factor in the performance of organizational functions. It is a relationship of complementary functions that is set up as a basis for the execution of a project. The latter may be managerial or operative. It may be line or staff. It must be planned, in any event, with regard for the requirements for the successful accomplishment of project objectives. It must consider the requirements for human and physical factors in performance, and the limitations of their use that must be observed. The specified procedure is an important part of a project plan, since it supplies a basis of action. The installation of standard procedures is often an important part of the work of organizing.

A procedure specifies, among other things, the order in which the various steps in the accomplishment of the project must be performed. It states the quantitative time requirements for the performance of each step, or indicates where such information may be obtained. A procedure necessarily cuts across organizational lines, because of the complementary nature of its functions. Coordination of action is a control responsibility. It has to do largely with the time and order in which the steps or phases of an undertaking are performed. Business procedure is therefore a basic factor in control.

The economy and effectiveness with which project and organizational objectives are accomplished depend greatly on the quality of procedural planning. The executive head of each group is responsible for developing and using the best methods for the accomplishment of his objectives. A mark of a good executive is ability to make effective use of staff, whether his own or others. No one usually cares, within reason, how he develops the best methods, provided that he uses them. This concept brings up some interesting problems in line and staff relationships as the organization grows. They must be solved, if the organization is to enjoy continued success.

The objectives of procedural development are secondary values. The principal values are (1) orderliness in the execution of business undertakings, (2) consequent uniformity of results, (3) facilitation of specialization, (4) a more effective and economical utilization of personnel, (5) conservation of executive ability, time, and health, (6) facilitation of executive and self-coordination, and (7) economy and effectiveness in the performance of managerial and operative functions. Responsibility for developing a particular type of business procedure is often delegated to the staff group in whose special field the problem falls. It would be impractical for top line executives, for example, to concern themselves personally with the details of planning a top administrative procedure. This is too important, on the other hand, to be delegated to people with limited ability and then forgotten. The result of such action may be ineffectiveness, high cost, and red tape. A top staff executive for administrative planning can be given staff responsibility for coordinating thought concerning structural planning, procedural planning, and other problems of administrative planning. The scope of his responsibility must be limited to the top administrative echelons. He should be available for consultation when executives on lower echelons are unable to achieve a meeting of minds on their procedural problems. This may be an intelligent compromise. There is some evidence of a trend in this direction.

A profit is a legitimate reward of capital for the successful acceptance of business risk in rendering an economic service. It is necessary for the formation of private capital and the continuation of the free enterprise system. It is necessary for the maintenance of the right of private property, and in consequence the freedom of the individual. Ability to operate a business at a profit should not be the sole criterion of managerial excellence; however, a profit may be a legitimate objective of businessmen. It should not be the primary objective of a business organization. The objective of the latter is an economic service. There are collateral business objectives. Business operations vitally affect the public interest. The sum total of all goods and services produced and distributed by all business enterprises everywhere, great and small, approximates the total national income. It represents the material benefits that support a high standard of living in an industrial economy.

Management is a principal form of economic leadership. Accordingly, the executive in private business has a great public responsibility. This has been recognized increasingly by organized business. One effect has been the development of more professional executives. Their numbers are still too few, however. Their development has been limited by the evolution of a sound philosophy of management. This evolution has been taking place, of course. Such a philosophy ... will be needed for the preservation of our democratic institutions when the subsequent contraction of business activities takes place. It will be necessary for a further, sound development of our economy. . . .

PART III

Closed System Natural Models

C losed system natural models represent the second wave of organization and management thinking and are represented in works by Barnard (1938), Mayo (1945), Whyte (1959), and Gouldner (1954). These approaches, beginning in about 1930, recognize that, even given the closed nature of the organization in terms of environment–organization interaction, persons within organizations can and do modify the designed structure and policies (Scott, 2003).

In the early years of the scientific management movement, behavioral scientists were deeply involved, but their concern was with problems such as worker fatigue, boredom, and job design so that work could be designed more efficiently. Quite a different perspective emerged in the late 1920s after the Hawthorne studies at Western Electric, an AT&T subsidiary in Cicero, Illinois (Roethlisberger & Dickson, 1939). The Hawthorne studies, carried out between 1924 and 1927, were prompted by the best tradition of scientific management to find answers to industrial questions through research. The most famous study was of two groups to determine the effects of different levels of illumination on worker performance. In one group the level of illumination was changed, while in the other it was not. The researchers found that when illumination was increased, the level of performance increased. But productivity also increased when the level of illumination decreased, even down to the level of moonlight. Moreover, productivity also increased in the control group.

The studies that followed the original experiment were conducted by a team of researchers headed by Elton Mayo and F. J. Roethlisberger from Harvard. These were

1. The First Relay Assembly Group

2. The Second Relay Assembly Group

3. The Mica-Splitting Test Room

4. The Interviewing Program

5. The Bank Wiring Observation Room

The Hawthorne studies pointed to the importance of leadership practices and workgroup pressures on employee satisfaction and performance. They downgraded the importance of economic incentives in worker motivation. They also stressed the importance of examining the effect of any one factor, such as pay, in terms of a whole social system, pointing out that employees react to a whole complex of forces together, rather than to one factor alone.

This work had a significant impact on thinking about organization and management problems. The studies provided the impetus for later critics of the scientific management movement to argue that any effort to develop a science of management without taking the human factor into account would be fruitless.

Chester Barnard was the president of New Jersey Bell Telephone company when he presented a series of lectures at Harvard that were published as *The Functions of the Executive* (1938), a work from this school of thought. An important influence on these lectures was his contact with those sociologists at Harvard who were involved in the Hawthorne studies (Burrell & Morgan, 1979). Like Fayol and other classical theorists, Barnard was aware of the formal, designated structure of organization, but he recognized that what really occurred in the context of any organization was different from the charts, job specifications, and procedures specified by management. He made it clear in his analysis that there were informal organizations that existed along with the formal. These resulted from different human needs that could not be dealt with by the formal system. He saw organizations evolving out of the attempt to reconcile organizational needs with individual needs. Organizations, to Barnard, are systems of cooperative effort and coordinated activities. They are formed, or develop, to overcome the inherent limitations of an individual's capacity; that is, when the task to be done requires more than one person, organized effort is necessary.

Barnard provided the groundwork for much analysis of organizations to follow him, especially the work of Herbert Simon (1976; March & Simon, 1958). He developed in some detail, for example, such concepts as the "linking pin," "the zone of indifference," and "the acceptance theory of authority." The "linking pin" concept is a way of considering organizational relationships between superiors and subordinates in organizations. The executives of several unit organizations, as a group, usually with at least one other person as a superior, form an executive organization. Accordingly, persons specializing in executive functions are "members of" or contributors to two units of organization in one complex organization—first, the so-called working unit, and second, the executive unit (Barnard, 1938). The "zone of indifference" and the "acceptance theory of authority" contributed substantially to the view of how compliance was obtained. In the administrative school's view, authority was seen as the right of a superior. Barnard maintained that authority works when it is accepted, and that it is accepted often because communication from a superior falls within the recipient's "zone of indifference," which means substantially that the person is willing to comply.

CHAPTER 4

The Functions
of the Executive*

Chester Barnard

The individual possesses certain properties which are comprehended in the word "person." Usually it will be most convenient if we use the noun "individual" to mean *one* person" and reserve the adjectival form "personal" to indicate the emphasis on the properties. These are (a) activities or behavior arising from (b) psychological factors, to which are added (c) the limited power of choice, which results in (d) purpose.

(a) An important characteristic of individuals is activity; and this in its gross and readily observed aspects is called behavior. Without it there is no individual person.

(b) The behaviors of individuals we shall say are the result of psychological factors. The phrase "psychological factors" means the combination, resultants, or residues of the physical, biological, and social factors which have determined the history and the present state of the individual in relation to his present environment.

(c) Almost universally in practical affairs, and also for most scientific purposes, we grant to persons the power of choice, the capacity of determination, the

---

*The materials in this section generally are drawn from opening statements of passages that are carefully developed and explained in the original work. The purpose of the excerpt is to highlight main themes. The development of these themes can be found in the original work. Excerpted by permission of the publishers from *The Functions of the Executive,* by C. L. Barnard, 1938, Cambridge, MA: Harvard University Press. Copyright 1938, 1968 by the President and Fellows of Harvard College; 1966 by Grace F. Noera Barnard.

possession of free will. By our ordinary behavior it is evident that nearly all of us believe in the power of choice as necessary to normal, sane conduct. Hence the idea of free will is inculcated in doctrines of personal responsibility, of moral responsibility, and of legal responsibility. This seems necessary to preserve a sense of personal integrity. It is an induction from experience that the destruction of the sense of personal integrity is the destruction of the power of adaptation, especially to the social aspects of living. We observe that persons who have no sense of ego, who are lacking in self-respect, who believe that what they do or think is unimportant, who have no initiative whatsoever, are problems, pathological cases, insane, not of this world, are *unfitted for cooperation.*

This power of choice, however, is limited. This is necessarily true if what has already been stated is true, namely, that the individual is a region of activities which are the combined effect of physical, biological, and social factors. Free will is limited also, it appears, because the power of choice is paralyzed in human beings if the number of equal opportunities is large. This is an induction from experience. For example, a man set adrift while sleeping in a boat, awaking in a fog in the open sea, free to go in any direction, would be unable at once to choose a direction. Limitation of possibilities is necessary to choice. Finding a reason why something should *not* be done is a common method of deciding what should be done. The processes of decision as we shall see are largely techniques for narrowing choice.

(d) The attempt to limit the conditions of choice, so that it is practicable to exercise the capacity of will, is called making or arriving at a "purpose." It is implied usually in the verbs "to try," "to attempt." . . . We are greatly concerned with purposes in relation to organized activities.

It is necessary to impress upon the reader the importance of this statement of the properties of persons. . . . It will be evident as we proceed, I think, that no construction of the theory of cooperative systems or of organizations, nor any significant interpretation of the behavior of organizations, executives, or others whose efforts are organized, can be made that is not based on *some* position as to the psychological forces of human behavior [pp. 13–14]. . . . The individual human being possesses a limited power of choice. At the same time he is a resultant of, and is narrowly limited by, the factors of the total situation. He has motives, arrives at purposes, and wills to accomplish them. His method is to select a particular factor or set of factors in the total situation and to change the situation by operations on these factors. These are, from the viewpoint of purpose, the limiting factors, and are the strategic points of attack.

1. Among the most important limiting factors in the situation of each individual are his own biological limitations. The most effective method of overcoming these limitations has been that of cooperation. This requires the adoption of a group, or non-personal, purpose. The situation with reference to such a purpose is composed of innumerable factors, which must be discriminated as limiting or nonlimiting factors.

2. Cooperation is a social aspect of the total situation and social factors arise from it. These factors may be in turn the limiting factors of any situation. This arises from two considerations: (a) the processes of interaction must be discovered or invented, just as a physical operation must be discovered or invented; (b) the interaction changes the motives and interest of those participating in the cooperation.

3. The persistence of cooperation depends upon two conditions: (a) its effectiveness, and (b) its efficiency. Effectiveness relates to the accomplishment of the cooperative purpose, which is social and non-personal in character. Efficiency relates to the satisfaction of individual motives, and is personal in character. The test of effectiveness is the accomplishment of a common purpose or purposes; effectiveness can be measured. The test of efficiency is the eliciting of sufficient individual wills to cooperate.

4. The survival of cooperation, therefore, depends upon two interrelated and interdependent classes of processes: (a) those which relate to the system of cooperation as a whole in relation to the environment, and (b) those which relate to the creation or distribution of satisfactions among individuals.

5. The instability and failures of cooperation arise from defects in each of these classes of processes separately, and from defects in their combination. The functions of the executive are those of securing the effective adaptation of these processes [pp. 60–61]...

6. It is [a] central hypothesis ... that the most useful concept for the analysis of experience of cooperative systems is embodied in the definition of a formal organization as a *system of consciously coordinated activities or forces of two or more persons* [p. 73]....

The system, then, to which we give the name "organization" is a system composed of the activities of human beings. What makes these activities a system is that the efforts of different persons are here coordinated [p. 77]....

[a] If organizations are systems, it follows that the general characteristics of systems are also those of organizations. For our purposes we may say that a system is something which must be treated as a whole because each part is related to every other part included in it in a significant way. What is significant is determined by order as defined for a particular purpose, or from a particular point of view, such that if there is a change in the relationship of one part to any or all of the others, there is a change in the system. It then either becomes a new system or a new state of the same system.

Usually, if the parts are numerous, they group themselves into subsidiary or partial systems. Where this is the case, each partial system consists of relationships between its own parts which can change, creating a new state of the partial system, without altering the system as a whole in significant degree. But this is true only when the system is viewed from a single or special point of view and the changes of the subsidiary system are within limits. When this is the case we may disregard the larger systems, treating them as constants or the subsidiary system as if it were isolated. Thus the whole physical universe is the single and fundamental system, consisting of parts—which, let us say, are electrons, neutrons, and protons—and relationship between them; but in practice, if our interest is narrow enough, we can deal with the solar system, or the sun, or the earth, or a piece of iron, or a molecule, or an atom, as if each were a complete and final system. This we can do if we do not exceed certain limits. These are determined by whether or not exceeding these limits involves important changes in, or important reactions from, the larger system.

This is similarly true of the systems called organizations. First of all each organization is a component of a larger system which we have called a "cooperative system," the other components of which are physical systems, social systems, biological systems, persons, etc. Moreover, most formal organizations are partial systems included within larger organization systems. The most comprehensive formal organizations are included in an informal, indefinite, nebulous, and undirected system usually named a "society." . . .

[b] But we must now refer to one question about systems in general, and about organization systems in particular, the answer to which is of fundamental importance. I refer to the question as to whether the whole is more than the sum of the parts; whether a system should be considered as merely an aggregate of its components; whether a system of cooperative efforts, that is, an organization, is something more or less than or different from its constituent efforts; whether there emerge from the system properties which are not inherent in the parts.

The opinion that governs [here] is that when, for example, the efforts of five men become coordinated in a system, that is, an organization, there is created something new in the world that is more or less than or different in quantity and quality from anything present in the sum of the efforts of the five men [pp. 77–79]. . .

[c] It remains to present a few remarks on the dimensional characteristics of the system of cooperative interactions which we define as organizations. It perhaps has impressed many executives how indefinitely organizations are located in space. The sense of being "nowhere" is commonly felt. With the great extension of the means of electrical communication this vagueness has increased. To be sure, since the material of organizations is acts of persons, and since they relate in some degree to physical objects or are fixed in some physical environment, they have some degree of physical location. This is especially true of organizations in factories, or connected with railroad or communication systems. But even in these cases location is indirect, by attachment to a system of physical things; and in the case of political and religious organizations even mere location is only feebly conceivable. The notion of spatial dimensions of these systems is hardly applicable.

On the other hand, the dimension of time is of prime importance. Temporal relationship and continuity are primary aspects of organizations. When and how long are the first items of description. . . . The persons whose acts are the components of these systems are continually changing, yet the organization persists [p. 80].

The Theory of Formal Organization

An organization comes into being when (1) there are persons able to communicate with each other, (2) who are willing to contribute action, and (3) to accomplish a common purpose. The elements of an organization are therefore (1) communication,

(2) willingness to serve, and (3) common purpose. These elements are necessary and sufficient conditions initially, and they are found in all such organizations. The third element, purpose, is implicit in the definition. Willingness to serve, and communication, and the interdependence of the three elements in general, and their mutual dependence in specific cooperative systems, are matters of experience and observation.

For the continued existence of an organization either *effectiveness* or *efficiency* is necessary; and the longer the life, the more necessary both are. The vitality of organizations lies in the willingness of individuals to contribute forces to the cooperative system. This willingness requires the belief that the purpose can be carried out, a faith that diminishes to the vanishing point as it appears that it is not in fact in process of being attained. Hence, when effectiveness ceases, willingness to contribute disappears. The continuance of willingness also depends upon the satisfactions that are secured by individual contributors in the process of carrying out the purpose. If the satisfactions do not exceed the sacrifices required, willingness disappears, and the condition is one of organization inefficiency. If the satisfactions exceed the sacrifices, willingness persists, and the condition is one of efficiency of organization.

In summary, then, the initial existence of an organization depends upon a combination of these elements appropriate to the external conditions at the moment. Its survival depends upon the maintenance of an equilibrium of the system. This equilibrium is primarily internal, a matter of proportions between the elements, but it is ultimately and basically an equilibrium between the system and the total situation external to it. This external equilibrium has two terms in it: first, the effectiveness of the organization, which comprises the relevance of its purpose to the environmental situation; and, second, its efficiency, which comprises the interchange between the organization and individuals. Thus the elements stated will each vary with external factors, and they are at the same time interdependent; when one is varied compensating variations must occur in the other if the system of which they are components is to remain in equilibrium, that is, is to persist or survive [p. 83].

Willingness to cooperate, positive or negative, is the expression of the net satisfactions or dissatisfactions experienced or anticipated by each individual in comparison with those experienced or anticipated through alternative opportunities. These alternative opportunities may be either personal and individualistic or those afforded by other organizations. That is, willingness to cooperate is the net effect, first, of the inducements to do so in conjunction with the sacrifices involved, and then in comparison with the practically available net satisfactions afforded by alternatives. The questions to be determined, if they were matters of logical reasoning, would be, first, whether the opportunity to cooperate grants any advantage to the individual as compared with independent action; and then, if so, whether that advantage is more or less than the advantage obtainable from some other cooperative opportunity [p. 85]. . . .

Willingness to cooperate, except as a vague feeling or desire for association with others, cannot develop without an objective of cooperation. Unless there is such an objective it cannot be known or anticipated what specific efforts will be required of individuals, nor in many cases what satisfactions to them can be in prospect. Such an objective we denominate the "purpose" of an organization. The necessity of having a purpose is axiomatic, implicit in the words "system," "coordination," "cooperation."

It is something that is clearly evident in many observed systems of cooperation, although it is often not formulated in words, and sometimes cannot be so formulated. In such cases what is observed is the direction or effect of the activities, from which purpose may be inferred.

A purpose does not incite cooperative activity unless it is accepted by those whose efforts will constitute the organization. Hence there is initially something like simultaneity in the acceptance of a purpose and willingness to cooperate [p. 86]. . . .

In other words we have clearly to distinguish between organization purpose and individual motive. It is frequently assumed in reasoning about organizations that common purpose and individual motive are or should be identical. With the exception noted below, this is never the case; and under modern conditions it rarely ever appears to be the case. Individual motive is necessarily an internal, personal, subjective thing; common purpose is necessarily an external, impersonal, objective thing even though the individual interpretation of it is subjective. The one exception to this general rule, an important one, is that the accomplishment of an organization purpose becomes itself a source of personal satisfaction and a motive for many individuals in many organizations. It is rare, however, if ever, and then I think only in connection with family, patriotic, and religious organizations under special conditions, that organization purpose becomes or can become the *only* or even the major individual motive [pp. 88–89]. . . .

The possibility of accomplishing a common purpose and the existence of persons whose desires might constitute motives for contributing toward such a common purpose are the opposite poles of the system of cooperative effort. The process by which these potentialities become dynamic is that of communication. Obviously a common purpose must be commonly known, and to be known must be in some way communicated. With some exceptions, verbal communication between men is the method by which this is accomplished. Similarly, though under crude and obvious conditions not to the same extent, inducements to persons depend upon communication to them [p. 89]. . . .

The size of a unit organization being usually restricted very narrowly by the necessities of communication, it follows that growth of organization beyond the limits so imposed can only be accomplished by the creation of new unit organizations, or by grouping together two or more unit organizations already existing. When an organization grows by the addition of the services of more persons it is compelled, if it reaches the limit of size, to establish a second unit; and henceforward it is a complex of two unit organizations. All organizations except unit organizations are a group of two or more unit organizations. Hence a large organization of complex character consists not of the services of individuals directly but of those of subsidiary unit organizations. Nowhere in the world, I think, can there be found a large organization that is not composed of small units. We think of them as having descended from the mass, whereas the mass can only be created from the units.

Usually when two and always when several unit organizations are combined in one complex organization, the necessities of communication impose a superleader, who becomes, usually with assistants, an "overhead" unit of organization. Similarly, groups of groups are combined into larger wholes. The most obvious case of complex structures of this type is an army. The fact that these large organizations are built up of small unit organizations is neglected in the spectacular size that ensues, and we often pass from the whole or major divisions to "men." The resulting dismissal from the mind of the inescapable practice of unit organization often leads to utterly unrealistic attitudes regarding organization problems [pp. 110–111].

In summary, we may say that historically and functionally all complex organizations are built up from units of organization, and consist of many units of "working" or "basic" organizations, overlaid with units of executive organizations; and that the essential structural characteristics of complex organizations are determined by the effect of the necessity for communication upon the size of a unit organization [p. 113].

Informal Organizations and
Their Relation to Formal Organizations

The purpose [here] has been to show (1) that those interactions between persons which are based on personal rather than on joint or common purposes, because of their repetitive character become systematic and organized through their effect upon habits of action and thought and through their promotion of uniform states of mind; (2) that although the number of persons with whom any individual may have interactive experience is limited, nevertheless the endless-chain relationship between persons in a society results in the development, in many respects, over wide areas and among many persons, of uniform states of mind which crystallize into what we call mores, customs, institutions; (3) that informal organization gives rise to formal organizations and that formal organizations are necessary to any large informal or societal organization; (4) that formal organizations also make explicit many of the attitudes, states of mind, and institutions which develop directly through informal organizations, with tendencies to divergence, resulting in interdependence and mutual correction of these results in a general and only approximate way; (5) that formal organizations, once established, in their turn also create informal organizations; and (6) that informal organizations are necessary to the operation of formal organizations as a means of communication, of cohesion, and of protecting the integrity of the individual [pp. 122–123]. . . .

[Earlier] it was shown that the primary aspect of cooperative systems was the effect of coordination of the activities of two or more persons on the overcoming of the limitations involved in the relations between the biological capacities of individuals and the natural environment. The coordination may proceed on one of two principles: on the principle of simultaneity of effort, or on that of efforts in series [p. 132]. . . .

Thus, in an important aspect, "organization" and "specialization" are synonyms. The ends of cooperation cannot be accomplished without specialization. The coordination implied is a functional aspect of organization. This function is to correlate the efforts of individuals in such a way with the conditions of the cooperative situation as a whole that purpose may be accomplished.

The way in which this correlation is accomplished is to analyze purpose into parts or detailed purposes or ends, the accomplishment of which in proper order will permit the attainment of the final objective; and to analyze the situation as a whole into parts which may be specifically coordinated by organization activity with detailed ends. These when accomplished become means toward the final attainment. The nature of this process and the function of specialization are of critical importance in the understanding of executive work.

A final observation may now be made. Since every unit of organization in a complex organization is a specialization, the general purpose of the complex must be broken into specific purposes for each unit of organization. Since purpose is the unifying element of formal organization, it is this detailed purpose at the unit level that is effective in maintaining the unit. It is this purpose which must be accepted first of all in each unit in order that there may be units of which a complex may be composed. If this local or detailed purpose is not understood or accepted, disintegration of the unit organization follows. This is not more than an induction from my personal experience and observation, as is what now follows, and it is obvious in any event that much qualification for time elements and degrees of disintegration would be required for a complete statement.

Understanding or acceptance of the *general* purpose of the complex is not, however, essential. It may be, and usually but not always is, desirable as explaining or making acceptable a detailed purpose; and if this is possible it no doubt in most cases strengthens the unit organization. But in general complex organizations are characterized by obvious lack of complete understanding and acceptance of *general* purposes or aims. Thus it is not essential and usually impossible that the company should know the specific objectives of the army as a whole; but it is essential that it know and accept an objective of its own, or it cannot function. If it feels that the whole depends upon the achievement of this objective, which it is more likely to do if it understands what the whole objective is, the intensity of its action will ordinarily be increased. It is belief in the cause rather than intellectual understanding of the objective which is of chief importance. "Understanding" by itself is rather a paralyzing and divisive element [pp. 136–138]. . . .

The individual is always the basic strategic factor in organization. Regardless of his history or his obligations he must be induced to cooperate, or there can be no cooperation [p. 139]. . . .

The net satisfactions which induce a man to contribute his efforts to an organization result from the positive advantages as against the disadvantages which are entailed. It follows that a new advantage may be increased or a negative advantage made positive either by increasing the number or the strength of the positive inducements or by reducing the number or the strength of the disadvantages [p. 140]. . . .

It will be evident, perhaps, without more elaborate illustration, that in every type of organization, for whatever purpose, several incentives are necessary, and some degree of persuasion likewise, in order to secure and maintain the contributions to organization that are required. It will also be clear that, excepting in rare instances, the difficulties of securing the means of offering incentives, of avoiding conflict of incentives, and of making effective persuasive efforts, are inherently great; and that the determination of the precise combination of incentives and of persuasion that will be both effective and feasible is a matter of great delicacy. Indeed, it is so delicate and complex that rarely, if ever, is the scheme of incentives determinable in

advance of application. It can only evolve; and the questions relating to it become chiefly those of strategic factors from time to time in the course of the life of the organization. It is also true, of course, that the scheme of incentives is probably the most unstable of the elements of the cooperative system [p. 158]. . . .

Authority is the character of a communication (order) in a formal organization by virtue of which it is accepted by a contributor to or "member" of the organization as governing the action he contributes; that is, as governing or determining what he does or is not to do so far as the organization is concerned. According to this definition, authority involves two aspects: first, the subjective, the personal, the *accepting* of a communication as authoritative. . . . and, second, the objective aspect—the character in the communication by virtue of which it is accepted [p. 163]. . . .

The necessity of the assent of the individual to establish authority *for him* is inescapable. A person can and will accept a communication as authoritative only when four conditions simultaneously obtain: (a) he can and does understand the communication; (b) *at the time of his decision* he believes that it is not inconsistent with the purpose of the organization; (c) *at the time of his decision,* he believes it to be compatible with his personal interest as a whole; and (d) he is able mentally and physically to comply with it [p. 165]. . . .

Naturally the reader will ask: How is it possible to secure such important and enduring cooperation as we observe if in principle and in fact the determination of authority lies with the subordinate individual? It is possible because the decisions of individuals occur under the following conditions [p. 167]. . . .

(a) There is no principle of executive conduct better established in good organizations than that orders will not be issued that cannot or will not be obeyed [p. 167]. . . .

(b) The phrase "zone of indifference" may be explained as follows: If all the orders for actions reasonably practicable be arranged in the order of their acceptability to the person affected, it may be conceived that there are a number which are clearly unacceptable, that is, which certainly will not be obeyed; there is another group somewhat more or less on the neutral line, that is, either barely acceptable or barely unacceptable; and a third group unquestionably acceptable. This last group lies within the "zone of indifference." The person affected will accept orders lying within this zone and is relatively indifferent as to what the order is so far as the question of authority is concerned. Such an order lies within the range that in a general way was anticipated at time of undertaking the connection with the organization [pp. 168–169]. . . .

The zone of indifference will be wider or narrower depending upon the degree to which the inducements exceed the burdens and sacrifices which determine the individual's adhesion to the organization. It follows that the range of orders that will be accepted will be very limited among those who are barely induced to contribute to the system [p. 169]. . . .

Authority has been defined in part as a "character of a communication in a formal organization." A "superior" is not in our view an authority nor does he have

authority strictly speaking; nor is a communication authoritative except when it is an effort or action or organization. This is what we mean when we say that individuals are able to exercise authority only when they are acting "officially," a principle well established in law, and generally in secular and religious practice. Hence the importance ascribed to time, place, dress, ceremony, and authentication of a communication to establish its official character. These practices confirm the statement that authority relates to a communication "in a formal organization." There often occur occasions of compulsive power of individuals and of hostile groups; but authority is always concerned with something *within* a definitely organized system. Current usage conforms to the definition in this respect. The word "authority" is seldom employed except where formal organization connection is stated or implied (unless, of course, the reference is obviously figurative) [pp. 172–173]. . . .

Thus men impute authority to communications from superior positions, provided they are reasonably consistent with advantages of scope and perspective that are credited to those positions. This authority is to a considerable extent independent of the personal ability of the incumbent of the position. It is often recognized that though the incumbent may be of limited personal ability his advice may be superior solely by reason of the advantage of position. This is the *authority of position.*

But it is obvious that some men have superior ability. Their knowledge and understanding regardless of position command respect. Men impute authority to what they say in an organization for this reason only. This is the *authority of leadership* [p. 173]. . . .

The Functions of the Executive

. . . Functions of executives relate to all the work essential to the vitality and endurance of an organization, so far, at least, as it must be accomplished though formal coordination [p. 255]. . . .

Executive work is not that of the organization, but the specialized work of *maintaining* the organization in operation [p. 215]. . . .The problem of the establishment and maintenance of the system of communication, that is, the primary task of the executive organization, is perpetually that of obtaining the coalescence of the two phases, executive personnel and executive positions [p. 218]. . . .

The second function of the executive organization is to promote the securing of the personal services that constitute the material of organizations.

The work divides into two main divisions: (1) the bringing of persons into cooperative relationship with the organization; (2) the eliciting of the services after such persons have been brought into the relationship [p. 227]. . . .

The third executive function is to formulate and define the purposes, objectives, ends, of the organization. It has already been made clear that, strictly speaking, purpose is defined more nearly by the aggregate of action taken than by any formulation in words; but that the aggregate of action is a residuum of the decisions relative to purpose and the environment, resulting in closer and closer approximations to the concrete acts. It has also been emphasized that purpose is something that must be accepted by all the contributors to the system of efforts. Again, it has been stated that purpose must be broken into fragments, specific objectives, not only ordered in time so that detailed purpose and detailed action follow in the series of progressive cooperation, but also ordered contemporaneously into the specializations, geographical, social, and functional, that each unit organization implies. It is more apparent here than with other executive functions that it is an entire executive organization that formulates, redefines, breaks into details, and decides on the innumerable simultaneous and progressive actions that are the stream of syntheses constituting purpose or action. No single executive can under any conditions accomplish this function alone, but only that part of it which relates to his position in the executive organization [p. 231].

PART IV

Integrative Approaches to Organization

While it is fair to characterize almost any organizational model, as is shown in Figure 1.1, as having a dominant theoretical perspective (rational, natural, open, or closed systems), the fact is that virtually none of them is "pure." For example, while rational models do emphasize how a firm can maximize profitability, there are some at least implicit natural model ideas in them. That is, while natural models recognize that individuals in organizations do not operate with the strictures of rules and policies and that these are modified by the member, the rational models recognize this by seeking to control and minimize such deviations. In addition, a close reading of the original theoretical approaches set out in this book will reveal that there is indeed often substantial theoretical overlap in many instances. All too often, purported differences between theoretical approaches are straw men created by a writer to justify why his or her approach is better than the alternatives. Nowhere is this more evident than in the classic by March and Simon, *Organizations* (1958), as Kilduff pointed out in *Deconstructing Organizations* (1993).

Such issues notwithstanding, however, there are some who have attempted to integrate what appear to be competing views (Scott, 2003), and two of these integrative approaches are included in this book. One is by Etzioni (1964), who develops a typology of organizations and examines how individual involvement with an organization and the type of power predominant in the various forms interact to explain compliance. This is a "structuralist" perspective that seeks a synthesis between the rational schools and the natural schools (Scott, 2003). It is *rational* in that it addresses how authority and power are structured in terms of the formal hierarchy. It is *natural* in the way that he focuses on the idea that the type of power that will result in compliance is contingent on the nature of the organization and why people are there. One of the key points by Etzioni is that

Organizations are under pressure to be effective. Hence to the degree that the environment allows, organizations tend to shift their compliance structures from incongruent to congruent types and organizations which have congruent compliance of structures tend to resist factors pushing them toward incongruent structures. (p. 13)

The second is James Thompson's *Organizations in Action* (1967). He discusses the inherent conflict between the "closed system" and "open system" models: Closed system models cannot accommodate environmental influences, and open system models overstate adaptability to the neglect of more controllable factors. His synthesis considers complex organizations as open systems that may be faced with uncertainty but at the same time are subject to criteria of rationality. He says, for instance, that

if the closed-system aspects of organizations are seen most clearly at the technical level, and the open-system qualities appear most vividly at the institutional level, it would suggest that a significant function of the managerial level is to mediate between the two extremes and the emphasis they exhibit. (p. 12)

CHAPTER 5

Organizations
Power and Compliance

Amatai Etzioni's A Comparative
Analysis of Complex Organizations[1]

Robert J. House[2]

The term "organization" as used here refers to a social unit devoted primarily to the attainment of specific goals. Organizations as discussed here are complex in that they involve many levels, specialization of efforts, departmentalization of groups within the organization, the need for both formal and informal communication and coordination and intricate relationships of authority and responsibility. This is a study of the systematic differences among various social units classed as organizations. The theory is diagrammed in Figure 5.1.

In this theory, organizations are classified on the basis of their "compliance structure." Compliance is defined as a relationship consisting of the power employed by superiors to control subordinates and the orientation of the subordinates to this power. Thus, this theory combines a structural and a motivational aspect: structural, since it concerns the kind and distribution of power in organizations; motivational, since it concerns the different commitments of the members to the organization. In this theory, Etzioni seeks to analyze organizations in terms of both social systems and personality systems.

The basic assumption underlying the theory is that there are three major sources of control, the allocation and manipulation of which account to a great extent for the foundation of social order within organizations. These control sources are: (1) coercion (threat and punishment), (2) economic assets (remuneration), and

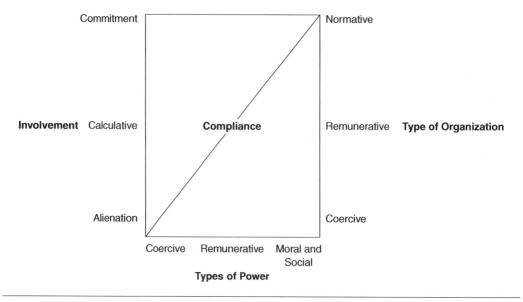

Figure 5.1 The Relationship Between Power, Involvement, and Type of Organization

(3) social and moral values (recognition, acceptance and moral involvement). Accordingly, three types of compliance serve as the basis for comparison between organizations. Compliance—the organizational equivalent of social order—is the core variable, or hub, of this theory.

Power and Involvement: The Comparative Dimensions

Using compliance as a comparative basis of analysis, organizations are analyzed in terms of two basic dimensions: *power*, which is applied by the organization to its members; and *involvement* in the organization developed by its members

Power

Power is referred to as a member's ability to induce or influence another member to carry out his directives by any other values which he supports. Power differs according to the means employed to make the subjects comply.

Thus, remunerative power is based on control over material resources and rewards through allocation of salaries and wages, commissions and contributions, "fringe benefits," services, and commodities.

Moral and social power[3] rest on the allocation and manipulation of symbolic rewards and deprivations through employment of leaders, manipulation of mass media, allocation of esteem and prestige symbols, administration of ritual, and influence over the distribution of social acceptance and positive responses by others (e.g., recognition or approval). Thus, moral or social power rests upon the manipulation of those rewards which carry high symbolic value to the respondent.

Coercive power rests on the application, or threat, of physical sanctions such as infliction of pain, deformity, or death; generation of frustration through restriction of movements; or controlling the satisfaction of needs such as those of food, sex, comfort, and the like through force.

Etzioni marshals evidence which strongly supports the proposition that most organizations tend to emphasize only one means of power, relying less on, but not completely avoiding, the other two. Most organizations, then, have both a primary and secondary compliance structure.

Involvement

The second dimension of the theory is that of involvement. Involvement is characterized in terms of intensity and direction. The intensity of involvement ranges from high to low. The direction is either positive or negative. When involvement is high, it is called commitment; when it is low, alienation. Involvement thus is a term which applies to a continuum of personal and voluntary orientation toward an organization.

Classification of Organizations

Etzioni classified organizations according to their compliance structure as coercive, remunerative, or normative.[4]

Coercive Organizations

Coercive organizations are organizations in which coercion is the major means of control over the members, and high alienation characterizes the orientation of the members. Examples of coercive organizations would be prisoner-of-war camps, concentration camps, the large majority of prisons, traditional "correctional institutions," custodial mental hospitals, forced labor camps, and relocation camps.

Remunerative Organizations

Remunerative organizations are those in which material remuneration is a major means of control over the members. This involves a determination by the member of the amount of involvement he or she feels will be most profitable. Thus, "calculative involvement" characterizes the orientation of the members to the remunerative organization. Those divisions of industrial organizations employing predominantly blue-collar workers or white-collar, nonprofessional workers (clerks and stenographic workers) and semiprofessional workers such as laboratory technicians and most college graduates would be placed in this category. This is true because wages, salaries, commissions, fringe benefits, working conditions, and similar rewards constitute the predominant source of control for such employees. . . .

White-collar employees are predominately controlled by remunerative means, but less so than blue-collar employees. Secondary, normative control, such as the manipulation of status symbols and social recognition, seems to play a more important role among white-collar employees than among blue-collar employees.

Since white-collar employees have a greater tendency toward identification with the organizational objectives, and since management usually finds it difficult to manipulate esteem and prestige symbols of blue-collar workers, the use of social and moral values for purposes of influencing most industrial employees is limited. At the same time, the manipulation of esteem and prestige symbols, which as a rule has a limited effect on blue-collar workers, seems to be more effective among white-collar employees. This point is illustrated in a study of saleswomen which emphasized the role of nonremunerative "symbolic" controls. Saleswomen who made mistakes writing out sales slips had the slips returned to them, bound with a large red rubber band, to be opened and corrected in the presence of the section manager and other saleswomen. These red bands "do not result in fines or punishments of any sort, and yet the clerks feel that to get one is a disgrace."[5] Similarly, there were "all sorts of honors bestowed upon the capable and efficient. These have small monetary value, but money is secondary to honor. To be ace—the best saleswoman in your department—is compensation enough in itself."[6]

One can imagine what the effects of similar manipulation would be if attempted with the blue-collar nonskilled worker. It is not unlikely that the person who gets the most red rubber bands would be the "ace of the day."

Normative Organizations

Normative organizations are those in which moral involvement and social acceptance are the major sources of control. The orientation of members of these organizations is characterized by high commitment to the organization. There are several frequently found types of normative organization. These are religious organizations, employing primarily professional employees such as research laboratories, law firms, and medical associations. In these kinds of organizations, social power is exercised mainly through informal sanctions (e.g., social isolation or approval), through the manipulation of prestige symbols (titles, status trappings), through the personal influence of the leader or influential members of the organization, or through the manipulation of peer groups' climate of opinion.

An organization made up of professional employees utilizes mainly moral and social controls, though calculative involvement occurs here to a greater extent than in any other kind of normative organization. In this sense, professional organizations resemble white-collar industries as borderline cases, though it seems they fall on the other side of the border, whereas in professional organizations moral and social power predominates, with remunerative compliance a close second. In white-collar industries the reverse seems to be true.

Today, with increased stress placed on creative scientific work, industries find normative, or moral, social control affecting larger segments of their member population. Typically, industrial firms consist of a large portion of production staff who are motivated primarily by remunerative means and a small but critical, and probably growing, portion of employees who are contributing toward the creative development of the product. The same is true of newspapers which have a highly remunerative section in which the newspaper is actually produced and a highly committed editorial wing in which it is written and edited. The editorial group may be more affected by normative power than the other sectors. Other communications industries, such as radio and television networks and advertising agencies, also have these characteristics.

The major means of control in professional organizations are based on prolonged and careful selection, education in professional value systems at universities and professional schools, or education on the job which the professional holds in the early part of his career. Examples of such jobs are the law student, the intern, the novice, and the seminarian. Frequently, incumbents of these positions continue their professional education as part of the job, or on a part-time basis. Social powers, formalized in the professional code of ethics and the professional association and supported by the social bonds of the professional community and professional elites, carry great weight.

High intrinsic satisfaction from work, positively associated with voluntary involvement, characterizes the work of professionals. This commitment is sometimes disassociated from the organization and vested in the work itself, for which the profession—not the organization—serves as the reference group and the object of involvement. Thus, research scientists may be more easily persuaded by senior members of their discipline than by the managers of the firm. As one would expect from the comparatively extensive use of remunerative rewards, despite the importance of intrinsic satisfaction and other symbolic gratifications, commitment to professional organizations is not as high as it is in other normative organizations with strongly ideological overtones, such as some political parties or church organizations.

Leadership, Compliance, and Organizational Specialization

Etzioni's theory has significant implications for management selection, the study of leadership, and organization. Organizations are often compared to task-performing, goal-oriented instruments. However, organizations which are seemingly committed to one set of goals must often pursue quite different subgoals in order to achieve those goals. These different goals and tasks frequently differ in their compliance requirements. Rarely are there two goals which can be served with optimal effectiveness by compliance structures which are precisely the same in both the predominant element and the weight given it.

It is because of the relationship between goals and compliance that multigoal or multitask "organizations" face a dilemma. Consistent emphasis on one pattern of compliance, perhaps appropriate for one sector of the organization, will cause a loss of effectiveness in the other because the pattern is congruent with only one task. If equal stress is given to two patterns or more, effectiveness may be reduced through neutralization.

However, segregation of tasks and/or personnel allows organizations to combine various compliance structures without losing effectiveness. Segregation may take the form of departmentalization, thereby allowing different subunits of the organization to operate at the same time with relatively independent compliance structures. Or segregation may take place on the basis of time requirements. At any given point in time, the unit is employing only one compliance structure, but at later points in time it may switch to another. An example of this form of compliance is found in the military. During combat more reliance is placed upon moral-social pressures than during peacetime activities.

Etzioni argues that successful leadership within an organization depends upon the leader's ability to gain compliance. Ability to gain compliance depends upon the control relationship between two levels; that is, the power applied and the kinds of involvement of the members, rather than on the substance of the work carried out. Therefore it is possible that the compliance requirements of a situation may be more important than the technological considerations of the task. This suggests that the character of compliance should be considered, as well as, or even prior to, the division of labor on the basis of task specialization. Etzioni does not deny the advantage of independent task specialization—he feels that such specialization is important, but that it should take place within major constraints imposed by the demands of the compliance structure.

There have been two opposing viewpoints concerning effective control of organizational performance. One point of view holds that each control relationship is a distinctive specialty to be defined in terms of performances which are controlled. The nature of the control relationship is dictated by the executive's intimate knowledge of the tasks and performances he supervises. A different position is taken by those who suggest that the control function is universal and abstract. From this point of view, control always means the ability to obtain performances through other people. The main skill required is the ability to direct the work of others and get work done by getting other people to do it. Specialized knowledge comes from experts or staff positions, not from the executive. Thus, one position maintains that control is a highly specialized function, the other that it is highly general.

Etzioni postulates that "the control function is less specialized than the performance function; it is not universal in the sense that a person who is an effective control agent in one structure will be equally effective in others. . . . Control differentiation is *not* based directly on the kind of performances which are supervised, but on the kind of compliance effective performance requires." Styles of leadership (here, Etzioni refers to modes of control) should be differentiated according to the kind of discipline the leader must attain, and not according to the nature of work supervised, though the two are, of course, related to some degree. Stated another way, Etzioni suggests that "the effectiveness of the mobile executive is limited to compliance areas rather than administrative or technical boundaries." Each type of compliance requires a distinctive set of personality characteristics, aptitudes, and inclinations. An individual may not have the characteristics required for more than one type of compliance. Thus, one would not expect effective combat leaders also to be effective "desk executives." Similarly, one would not expect a shop steward to

based on style.

be equally effective during periods of industrial harmony and in periods of labor-management conflict.

Notes

1. For a more thorough discussion of this theory, see Etzioni (1961).

2. The writer has taken the liberty of describing this theory in terms other than those used by Etzioni.

3. Etzioni refers to this kind of power as "normative power."

4. In the original work, organizations are classified as "coercive," "utilitarian," and "normative." Utilitarian organizations are called "remunerative" organizations here.

5. Donovan, F. R. (1929). *The saleslady* (p. 64). Chicago: University of Chicago Press.

6. Donovan, p. 192.

CHAPTER 6

James D. Thompson's *Organizations in Action*

Donna Goehle

J ames D. Thompson, in prefacing his *Organizations in Action* (1967), states that a "central purpose of the book is to identify a framework which might link at important points several of the now independent approaches to understanding organizations." In developing primarily a theoretical inventory of concepts and propositions about the ways in which those concepts might be related in explaining complex organizations, Thompson does not attempt to test his formulations empirically; rather, he suggests that the framework he advances may be useful for others in generating those hypotheses. From the outset, Thompson makes it clear that he is interested in focusing on the behavior of organizations and only tangentially in considering individual behavior within organizations.

Thompson has integrated various approaches to the study of organizations from several fields and disciplines which deal with observing and understanding complex organizations. According to Thompson, these interdisciplinary approaches have yielded useful concepts and propositions regarding organizations, though their contributions to the general field or organizational study have been limited by fragmentation. Therefore, rather than focusing entirely on one approach discarding critical elements of several different ones, Thompson suggests ways in which the approaches and concepts can be reconciled and used in building a more comprehensive theoretical framework which more accurately assists in explaining the complex phenomena involved in organizational analysis.

---

*Abstracted from *Organizations in Action*, by J. Thompson, 1967, New York: McGraw-Hill.

Strategies for Studying Organizations

Thompson begins his book by reviewing the complexities of organizations and the various conceptual approaches which have been developed in attempting to explain and understand the phenomena associated with complex organizations. He discusses the inherent conflict between the "closed-system" and "open-system" models and their apparent limitations in application. Finding both of these models lacking in comprehensiveness—the closed system in that it does not accommodate environmental influences and the open system in that it perhaps overemphasizes adaptability to the neglect of more controllable elements—Thompson indicates that the Simon-March-Cyert stream of study provides a way of overcoming the conflict between the two approaches. However, he also feels that even their approach is lacking in that it tends to omit some of the useful information from studies utilizing the older approaches.

Consequently, Thompson attempts a synthesis of the closed and open systems approach in his treatment of organizational behavior. Thompson says, "For purposes of this volume then, we will conceive of complex organizations as open systems, hence indeterminate and faced with uncertainty, but at the same time subject to criteria of rationality, and hence needing determinateness and certainty." The remainder of the first section of his book is devoted to explaining the nature of the conflict between these two approaches and the necessity of viewing organizations in relation to concepts advanced in both the open and closed systems approaches. He recognizes that much of the literature illustrates the adaptiveness of organizations to their environment, and also recognizes the weakness of such approaches in application to organizational design and administrative practice. Therefore, he seeks some means of building upon these concepts while holding rationality as a criterion upon which the theory must also be judged.

He does not suggest that the two approaches are equally incompatible at all ranges of organizational phenomena, but that the problems associated with each tend to fall into one of Parsons's three categories of responsibility and control—"technical, managerial, and institutional." For each of these levels, Thompson indicates that a different approach may be most suitable. For instance, "if the closed-system aspects of organizations are seen most clearly at the technical level, and the open-system qualities appear most vividly at the institutional level, it would suggest that a significant function of the managerial level is to mediate between the two extremes and the emphasis they exhibit." Since organizations are usually forced to interact with their environment in both resource-acquisition and output disposal, Thompson argues that the organization will attempt to isolate its "technical core" as much as possible from the uncertainties generated by this interaction with the environment. Because uncertainties may arise from either the technology or the environment, and since there are substantial numbers of variations observable in both categories, Thompson argues that organizations will also differ in their methods of coping with these different combinations. Since the three levels (technical, managerial, and institutional) are interdependent, organizational differences in coping with uncertainty of various types will also create differences in these levels across organizations as efforts are made to reduce uncertainty.

Rationality in Organizations

Thompson develops a framework from which the relationship between "technical rationality" and "organizational rationality" can be understood, compared, and related to the actions of complex organizations.

According to him, "instrumental action is rooted on one hand in desired outcomes and on the other hand in beliefs about cause-effect relationships. Given a desire, the state of man's knowledge at any point in time dictates the kinds of variables required and the manner of their manipulation to bring that desire to fruition." In Thompson's view, technical rationality represents "the extent to which these activities thus dictated by man's beliefs are judged to produce the desired outcomes." The measures of technical rationality can be evaluated in terms of whether or not the desired outcome is achieved (instrumental) and whether the results were achieved with the least expenditure of resources (economic). Both of these criteria are essential to a discussion of the ways in which technology may be employed by complex organizations, and consequently, its potential influence on the organization itself.

Since there are numerous technologies available in society which may be employed by organizations, three general categories of technology are proposed which are sufficiently distinct for purposes of illustrating Thompson's point. They are: "*long-linked* (involving serial interdependence); *mediating* (requiring operating in standardized ways and extensively with multiple clients or customers widely distributed in time and space); and *intensive* (a custom technology which depends on the availability of potentially necessary resources and their suitable application in an individual case or project)."

According to Thompson, since technical rationality is an abstraction concerning beliefs about cause and effect relationships, "it is only instrumentally perfect when it becomes a closed system of logic." Since organizations are forced to implement these technologies in action, the logic of the closed system does not accurately reflect the requirements nor the alternatives characterizing particular situations. Therefore, although every organization can be described as having a "core technology," the "technical core is always an incomplete representation of what the organization must do to accomplish desired results." And, according to Thompson:

> Technical rationality is a necessary component but never alone sufficient to provide *organizational rationality* which involves acquiring the inputs which are taken for granted by the technology, and dispensing outputs which again are outside the scope of the core technology.

At a minimum, organizational rationality involves three major component activities: (1) input activities, (2) technological activities, and (3) output activities. Since they are interdependent, organizational rationality requires that they be appropriately geared to one another. The inputs acquired must be within the scope of the technology, and it must be within the capacity of the organization to dispose of the technological production. (p. 19)

Given this interdependence, it is obvious that the input and output activities require an open-system type of logic and do impinge on the closed-system logic of the technology. Because of this interdependence, it is impossible to completely "seal off" the technological core in the sense of a closed system. Therefore, organizations will seek to minimize the influences of the environment through such techniques as buffering, leveling, forecasting, and rationing. The elements within the environment which Thompson feels are an influence on organizational action can be classified as "constraints" and "contingencies." Constraints are those fixed conditions which the organization cannot control. Contingencies are those factors which may or may not vary but are not subject to the arbitrary control of the organization. Organizational rationality is, therefore, some combination of constraints, contingencies, and the controllable variables cited previously.

Because it is assumed that organizations will seek some types of control over environmental interdependence and will engage in various types of action to gain that control where possible, Thompson suggests that the direction of those actions as well as the nature of them must also be examined. In order to accomplish that task, he introduces the concept of organizational "domain."

Domains of Organized Action

Organizations must establish some type of domain in terms of the "range of products, the populations served, and the services offered." Thompson then goes on to consider the relationship between domain, dependence, and environment. In Thompson's words, "The results of organizational action rest not on a single technology, but upon a technological matrix. A complicated technology incorporates the products or results of still other technologies. Although a particular organization may operate several core technologies, its domain always falls short of the total matrix."

With such a concept, Thompson illustrates the interlocking relationships among modern organizations in general and commercial enterprises in particular. Given these overlaps within the system, "the organization's domain identifies the points at which the organization is dependent on inputs from the environment." The nature of the dependencies, for a particular organization, will be primarily determined by the composition of the environment and the location of various organization-serving capacities within it. Thus, the organizational interfaces with the environment—such as sources of raw materials and markets for products—can be viewed as being dispersed, concentrated, or somewhere between the two extremes. According to Thompson, each organization will have a unique set of input and output relationships depending on the environment which it encounters and operates within.

Since environment can be taken to mean almost everything beyond the internal organization, he suggests that William R. Dill's concept of "task environment," which defines task environment as "the parts of the environment which are relevant or potentially relevant to goal setting and goal attainment," is more useful conceptually. Among the elements of task environment are the following: customers, suppliers, competitors, and regulatory groups. In the same way that no two organizational domains are exactly alike, neither are two task environments. In Thompson's view, "which individuals, which other organizations, and which aggregates constitute the task environment for a particular organization is determined by the requirements of the technology, the boundaries of the domain, and the composition of the larger environment."

In examining the relationship between task environment and domain, he argues that domain-consensus is reached through mutual expectations regarding the roles of various organizations. This consensus "defines a set of expectations both for members of the organization and for others with whom they interact about what the organization will and will not do." Thus, each organization must exchange with several elements of its task environment, each of which is also involved in a network of interdependencies characterizing its own domain and task environment. In this process of multiorganizational interaction, one or more elements in the task environment of one organization may choose to discontinue its support of that organization. Thus, according to Thompson, task environments also impose contingencies for organizations. In addition, they may also impose constraints, such as those encountered by a local high school which can only draw on the surrounding community for certain inputs. Since both constraints and contingencies can interfere with the attainment of rationality, Thompson argues that "organizations that are subject to the norms of rationality will attempt to manage dependency."

In order to manage that dependency, organizations must have some kind of power. To Thompson, power is the obverse of dependence. In his view, "an organization has power relative to an element of its task environment to the extent that the organization has capacity to satisfy the needs of that element and to the extent that the organization monopolizes that capacity." An organization's "net power" results from the interaction of the organization with the various elements comprising the pluralistic task environment. In this view, organizations with relatively little control over inputs will seek to gain power on the output side of the equation. Some organizations will also be characterized as being powerful or weak in their ability to control *both* inputs and outputs; however, those organizations gaining control over both inputs and outputs may find that countervailing power may arise within the task environment to reduce the discretion with which that power might be applied (i.e., regulatory agencies). Thompson also argues that power should not be treated as a zero-sum game in that increased interdependence among equally powerful elements may result in increased power for both parties.

Organizations want to manage the dependency of their task environment, and there are several strategies they can follow to avoid becoming subservient to any of the elements in that environment. The organization may attempt to maintain alternatives (as in the case of suppliers), acquire "prestige" (one of the "cheapest" means of gaining power since it does not increase dependency), enlarge the task environment, and engage in cooperative strategies for managing interdependencies (such as contracting, coopting, and coalescing). In attempting to manage interorganizational relations and maintain a viable domain, organizations are seeking an "optimal point between the realities of interdependence and the norms of rationality." Since the maneuvering necessary to reach that optimum point can be both costly and disruptive, organizations "subject to norms of rationality [would] seek to design themselves so as to minimize the necessity of maneuvering and compromise."

Organizational Design

In addition to dealing with contingencies through developing strategies for inter-action with the elements of the task environment, organizations may also be able to remove or reduce those contingencies through organizational design. Since the domain of an organization is influenced by technology, the population being served, and the services being rendered, a substantial change in organizational design would involve a modification of the "mix" of these elements. Some of the ways in which this modification might be achieved include vertical integration (especially with long-linked technologies), increases in the size of the populations being served (as in mediating technologies), and incorporating the object or the client into the orga-nization (as in the case of intensive technologies). Not all of these alternatives are viable for an organization at any one time since organizations may be constrained by capital requirements, the ability of the market to absorb additional production output, and/or legal restrictions, to mention only a few.

Nevertheless, if we assume there are pressures being exerted on the organization which encourage it to grow, the direction of growth will "not be random but will be guided by the nature of the technology and the task environment." Consequently, if organizations vary in design, they must also vary in structure.

Technology and Structure

In introducing the topic of organizational structure, Thompson states:

> The major components of a complex organization are determined by the design of that organization. Invariably these major components are further segmented, or departmentalized, and connections are established within and between departments. It is this internal differentiation and patterning of rela-tionships that we will refer to as structure. (p. 51)

He focuses particularly on those components of the organization which appear to be most protected from environmental influences—the technical core. Since "struc-ture is a fundamental vehicle by which organizations achieve bounded rationality," some coordination of effort, along with protection of the technical core, is achieved.

By delimiting responsibilities, control over resources, and other matters, organi-zations provide their participating members with boundaries within which effi-ciency may be a reasonable expectation. But if structure affords numerous spheres of bounded rationality, it must also facilitate the coordinated action of those *inde-pendent* elements (p. 54).

Thus, according to Thompson, before organizational structure can be under-stood, the meaning of, and different types of, interdependence and coordination must be considered. Three types of internal interdependence described by Thompson include "pooled interdependence," "sequential interdependence," and "reciprocal interdependence." **Pooled task interdependence** occurs when individuals or units can work in a relatively autonomous fashion. What they do is not entirely dependent on the others, but organization success or failure depends on the unique contribution of each to the total organization. Some professionals often have this form of interdependent relationship. Law firms and medical clinics, for example, are set up so that each lawyer or physician works with a high degree of autonomy. The work on a typical assembly line is an example of **sequential task interdependence**. This is when there are several tasks to be performed and they must be done in sequence. The work flows in a linear fashion through the production unit. **Reciprocal task interdependence** is when the tasks of two or more people are mutually dependent. Reciprocal task interdependence would exist, for example, in work in which a product must go progressively back and forth between the two workers, and each depends on the other to get the job done properly.

These three types, in the order introduced, contain increasing degrees of contingency and interdependence and are, therefore, more difficult and costly to coordinate. The three methods of coordination, each most appropriate for dealing with the different types of interdependence, are "standardization," "coordination by plan," and "coordination by mutual adjustment." Since coordination is necessary, but may also be costly, organizations will seek to minimize coordination costs. "It is the task of structure to facilitate the appropriate coordinating processes."

Operating under norms of rationality and in attempting to minimize coordination costs, organizations will localize and make "conditionally autonomous, first reciprocally then sequentially interdependent ones, and finally grouping positions homogeneously to facilitate standardization." Hierarchy is introduced because of the fact that first groupings do not totally take care of interdependence. Therefore, the organization must find some means of linking the groups involved into higher-order groups, or, in effect, establishing a hierarchy. Any interdependence not included by these arrangements will then require the establishment of committees or task forces to overcome the problems of coordination.

Organization and Structure

Since complex organizations must interface with their environment, yet cannot fully control the influences arising from those interdependencies, the structure of the boundary-spanning units within an organization must allow for the necessary adjustments to continue to be made. Here Thompson deals with the way in which environment also influences organizational structure (especially in the structure of the boundary-spanning units) as well as the way in which both technology and environment together influence the overall structure of the organization.

Although Thompson recognizes that the elements of the task environment vary for different organizations and, therefore, introduce certain constraints which are unique to that organization, he argues that generally the nature of those constraints can be classified within two major categories: "geographic space" (such as the costs involved in transportation) and in the "social composition" of their task environment. The social composition of the task environment can be viewed as being homogeneous or heterogeneous and stable or shifting. According to Thompson, "all organizations face task environments which are simultaneously located somewhere on the homogeneous-heterogeneous continuum and the stable-shifting continuum."

In summarizing the impact of the task environment on the structure of boundary-spanning units, Thompson states:

> The more heterogeneous the task environment, the greater the constraints presented to the organization. The more dynamic the task environment, the greater the contingencies presented to the organization. Under either condition, the organization seeking to be rational must put boundaries around the amount and scope of adaption necessary, and it does this by establishing structural units specialized to face a limited range of contingencies within a limited set of constraints. The more constraints and contingencies the organization faces, the more its boundary-spanning component will be segmented. (p. 73)

Having considered the influences on the structure of the units comprising the "technical core" and the "boundary-spanning" units, the concern then becomes the means by which these elements are combined to result in the overall organizational structure. Those organizations characterized as having "technical cores and boundary-spanning activities which can be isolated from each other will be centralized with an overarching layer of functional divisions." Where those activities are reciprocally interdependent rather than isolated, an organization will tend toward arranging these units in self-sufficient clusters, each having its own domain; "this is the major form of decentralization."

Thus, in Thompson's view, the organization faces internal requirements for coordinating the technical core and externally generated requirements for adjustment of the boundary-spanning units to the contingencies and constraints of the environment. Therefore, the major purpose of structure is to allow for the satisfaction of both internal and external organizational requirements. Because he assumes bounded rationality is necessary, Thompson argues that organizations facing heterogeneous task environments will not only attempt to identify homogeneous elements in that environment but also will establish structural units capable of dealing with each type. In this way, Thompson attempts to tie together the structural implications of the apparently incompatible closed-system and open-system requirements.

The Variable Human

Thompson then turns to a discussion of the characteristics of individuals and how they relate to organizations. He considers such things as the extent to which organizations can increase predictability of the behavior of their members and/or others in the task environment. He also discusses, in considerable detail, the exercise of discretion on the part of organizational members. A central argument is that "the ability or opportunity to exercise discretion is not uniformly distributed throughout the organization—that technology, task environment, design, and structure result in patterns of discretion." Thompson is interested in identifying the participants who exercise discretion, the relationships among those individuals, what "discretion" implies, and how it might be expressed or exercised.

Since Thompson has indicated from the outset that his focus is primarily on the behavior of organizations in a general sense, rather than on the behavior of specific individuals within those organizations, he builds extensively on the preceding organizational concepts and relationships which have already been discussed.

In viewing organization members, Thompson sees them as having certain aspirations and beliefs about cause and effect relationships and postulates that they (the individuals) bring these with them to an organizational setting which provides compatible opportunities and constraints. Culture, in his view, tends to be a "homogenizing" force which limits the range of diversity of these beliefs and aspirations and allows for the "channeling" of these individuals into relevant sectors of the labor market. He argues that the composition of the inducements/contribution contract is influenced by these factors and that the inducements/contribution contract itself further limits the range of behavior an individual will exhibit in an organizational setting. All of these factors, when taken together, tend to reduce the potential for heterogeneity of expression among organizational members.

Given these observations, the individual's range of discretion can be viewed in the context of "spheres of action." These action spheres also, "differ according to the technologies in which these jobs are imbedded." By locating jobs within technological contexts, individuals are therefore presented with patterned spheres of action. Since a job is "both a unit in the organization and a unit in the career of the individual, the joining of the two is a result of bargained agreement or inducements/contribution contract." Given the duality of the expectations, "it is then only reasonable to expect the resulting behavior to be patterned."

Proceeding from these initial assumptions regarding the nature of the individual behavior in an organizational setting, Thompson further illustrates the ways in which these patterns of behavior are influenced by technological factors, environmental constraints and contingencies, and the individual's position within the subunits of the organizational structure. He builds on the concepts of interdependence and power to describe the range of discretion and/or authority for an individual. In this manner, Thompson integrates a logical framework of individual behavior within the overall framework already established for the organization.

The administrative process is considered in terms of two types of administrative action necessary for the organization to survive. They are "adaptive" and "directive." Adaptive actions are necessitated primarily by environmental influences, and directive actions arise out of the basic internal requirements of the organization. Recognizing that both types of action are necessary, they must be coordinated in such a way as to allow the organization to manipulate "strategic variables" in order to survive. This manipulation of strategic variables should, therefore, result in a "viable co-alignment" with other elements in the environment. Given the fluidity of the task environment, it is apparent that the types of co-alignment are continually changing; therefore, a major task of administration, in Thompson's view, is to reduce the uncertainty involved in the process through achieving co-alignment "not merely of people (in coalitions) but of institutionalized action—of technology and task environment into a viable domain, and of organizational structure appropriate to it." As a result, "the administrative process must reduce uncertainty but at the same time search for flexibility."

Conclusions

Thompson concludes that the fundamental problem faced by complex organizations is coping with uncertainty. Coping with uncertainty is therefore the essence of the administrative process. The sources of uncertainty for an organization arise from three areas, two are external to the organization and one is internal. "External uncertainties stem from (1) *generalized uncertainty or lack* of cause/effect understanding of the culture at large, and (2) *contingency*, in which the outcomes of organizational action are in part determined by the actions of elements of the environment." The third source of uncertainty is internal; the *interdependence of components*. The way in which these uncertainties are resolved is:

> A solution of the first type [generalized uncertainty] provides a pattern against which organizational action can be ordered. Solution of the second type [contingency] affords organizational freedom to so order the action against the pattern. Solution of the third [interdependence of components] results in the actual ordering of action to fit the pattern. (p. 160)

This is the way Thompson summarizes the general nature of his view of organizations as having certain aspects of closed systems and of open systems within a context of internal and external uncertainty. Given the assumed necessity of rationality, both must be taken individually and together in explaining the behavior of complex organizations in a contemporary setting.

PART V

Open System Rational Models

The late 1950s and early 1960s was a period of ferment in the field of organizational studies that questioned the closed system models of organization that dominated thinking for the first half of the 20th century. It was a result of the belief that the ideas of administrative theory, which, critics argued, advocated highly controlled and bureaucratic structures, represented a very limited and restrictive form of organization that would work under some, but not all, circumstances. Others argued that rigid job specifications, rules, and policies implied in these models stifled the creativity, growth, development, and general effectiveness of individuals in the organization. The thrust of this argument is that the bureaucratic form of organization is incongruent with the basic needs of the healthy individual. For example, Douglas McGregor, in *The Human Side of Enterprise* (1960) said that most managers made a set of incorrect assumptions about those who worked for them, a theory he called Theory X. Theory X assumed that man was lazy, personal goals ran counter to the organization's, and that, because of this, man had to be controlled externally, a dominant theme of closed rational systems. Chris Argyris (1957, 1964) also believed that many constraints placed by organizations on human beings were self-defeating to organizational goals of effectiveness and efficiency.

Bounded Rationality. James March and Herbert Simon played a major role in this movement. In 1958, using concepts from Barnard, their seminal book, *Organizations* was published, a book that they argued was stimulated by feelings that the existing research and theory about organization and management were inadequate. They contended that principles, such as those of Fayol and other administrative theorists, were not only logically inconsistent, but they were oversimplified. They extended the Barnard view of the organization as a social system. Following Barnard, they presented a more elaborate motivational theory for organizational members than the classical writers. They emphasized individual decision making as a basis for understanding behavior in organizations. One of the salient points they developed was that of "bounded rationality." To make the optimal decisions suggested by the administrative theorists, they said, the manager would have to select the best of *all* possible alternatives. But the executive, as an "administrative man," is limited by his own perceptions and limited knowledge in making organizational decisions and cannot, therefore, make optimal decisions.

The Contingency Theories. Another set of important ideas was developed in contingency theories. Contingency theorists argued that there is no one best way to manage, as implied by scientific management and administrative theories. They were correct: There is no one best way to manage—that the best way to manage all depended. But, on what did it depend?

Some of the answers began to emerge in a very seminal way from Selznick's study of the Tennessee Valley Authority, *TVA and the Grass Roots* (1949). Selznick's work, described more extensively in this section, showed how organizations and interest groups in the outside environment of the TVA affected managerial decisions. He described clearly what the formal structure depended on, as well as how and through what kind of strategy the adjustment took place.

In 1961, Burns and Stalker published a study of British industry. They found differences in the structures of the firms they studied and traced these differences to the nature of the technology used and the markets served. When the technological and market environments were uncertain, a loose organization was found. When the environment was more predictable, a more traditional bureaucracy seemed to be most effective. Burns and Stalker not only saw the environment effect as important, but they specified more precisely than had been done before what the internal structure should look like, given a certain kind of environment.

Another important English study, by Woodward (1965), following the Burns and Stalker model, showed that the type of organizational structure used was related to a firm's economic performance when type of technology was taken into account.

Lawrence and Lorsch (1967) studied a highly effective and a less effective organization in three different industries: plastics, food, and container. These industries were chosen because they operated in environments that differed with respect to rate of technological change for the products they produced and the production methods used. The industries also differed with respect to the type of competitive situation they were in. These factors led to differences in the amount of environmental uncertainty. Lawrence and Lorsch found that in the plastics and food industries, companies were faced with much change and uncertainty, while the container industry was much more stable and predictable. They concluded that the closer the organizational structure matched the requirements imposed on it by the environment, the more successful was the firm. The effective organization had, for example, a high degree of coordinated effort when the environment required it. And a high degree of task specialization was present in high-performance firms when the environment demanded this. In general, they concluded that organizations in a stable environment are more effective if they have more detailed procedures and more centralization of the decision-making process, while organizations in an unstable environment have decentralization, participation, and less emphasis on rules and standard procedures.

Charles Perrow (1970), a sociologist, examined the research extant and other case studies of many large U.S. companies and concluded that it is very important that a proper fit exist between an organization and its environment and that one organization's structure and style of management may be effective in one type of environment and quite ineffective in another.

Henry Mintzberg, in *The Structuring of Organizations* (1979), outlines a typology of five "pure types" of organization. Each of these has a configuration of structural elements that differs from others. These different structures emerge in response to the environment and as a result of managerial decisions about the design of the organization. He argues that an organization is driven toward a particular natural cluster, or configuration, based on the strength (power) of the various parts of the organization, the ways in which the parts of the organization coordinate their work, the structural design parameters, and contingency factors such as age, size, and environment.

The Economists and Organization. The concepts used most frequently in organization theory are taken primarily from sociology and psychology. Little had been drawn from the field of economics until the 1970s, when the field of economics developed a focus on organizations much different from that of classical and neoclassical economics. In those traditional approaches, the organization and the entrepreneur–owner were one and the same. Building on the theory of managerial capitalism (Berle & Means, 1932), which described effects on the firm when there was the separation of ownership from the management of the firm, agency theorists addressed the question of how owners could control managers, who actually directed the firm. Agency theory applies classical economic thinking to problems of organizational control and design. Agency theory views a firm as a legal entity that serves as a nexus for a complex set of formal and informal contracts among different individuals (Spence & Zeckhauser, 1971; Ross, 1973). The agency relationship is defined as "a contract under which one or more persons (the principal(s)) engage another person (the agent) to perform some service on their behalf which involves delegating some decision making authority to the agent" (Jensen & Meckling, 1976, p. 308). In the agency literature that focuses on the internal management of the firm, the typical view is that shareholders or the board of directors are principals, and top managers, more specifically the CEOs, are agents.

Both owners and managers are rational actors with divergent interests, and the owners, through the board of directors, seek to ensure that managers put forth the requisite effort and do not misrepresent the condition of the firm. This is done by aligning managerial incentives with owners' interests and the creation of monitoring procedures, supervision, added hierarchical levels to the organization, information systems, budgeting systems, reporting procedures, and boards of directors (Eisenhardt, 1989; McGuire, 1964). All of these are costly to owners, who seek to minimize these control costs through the design of an effective organization structure.

The transaction cost approach by Oliver Williamson (1976b), an economist, tempers standard economic assumptions about rationality by using March and Simon's concept of bounded rationality. He uses transaction costs, environmental certainty, and opportunism to explain how hierarchies (organizations) emerge to manage conditions where markets are not efficient regulating mechanisms. The appropriate form of organization depends on uncertainty, the frequency of transactions, and the extent to which transaction-specific investments are necessary. These determine what Williamson calls transaction governance modes: markets, internal organization, and a form of market contracting.

CHAPTER 7

James March and Herbert Simon, *Organizations*

Henry L. Tosi

M arch and Simon's work *Organizations* (1958) is described by them as one in which they

> surveyed the literature on organization theory, starting with those theories that viewed the employee as an instrument and physiological automaton, proceeding through theories that were centrally concerned with the motivational and affective aspects of human behavior, and concluding with theories that placed particular emphasis on cognitive processes. (p. 5)

They assert that the literature about organizations to the time that they wrote was the result of the experience of executives, the scientific management movement, sociologists, social psychologists, political scientists, and economists, little of which had been well substantiated empirically.

Much organization theory was developed by the "classical" school and had been directed largely into two areas. The first is "scientific management." Theorists such as Taylor and Gilbreth brought a great deal of precision into the analysis, management, and reorganization of routine tasks. They attempted to develop a prescribed set of operating procedures to be used in analyzing and setting forth guidelines for effectiveness in organization. The second category is called the "administrative management school." These writers were generally concerned with the most effective way to organize tasks in order to achieve organizational goals, dealing with problems such as how to group tasks into jobs, jobs into larger administrative units, these administrative units into larger units, and so on to minimize the cost of performing these activities. In general, these theorists attempt to develop principles of organization to be applied across organization types.

These theories were untested. The motivational assumptions they make about individuals and work tend to be inaccurate. There is little appreciation of intraorganizational conflict. By and large they may be criticized for their lack of consideration of the human factor. They give little attention to the role of cognition in task identification, nor does the concept of program elaboration receive much attention. It is with these limitations regarding classical organization theory that March and Simon begin their work.

Some Assumptions

An organization is a system of interrelated social behaviors of a number of participants. While the definitions generally used by the classical school fall within this construct, March and Simon derive their conclusions from the model of influence processes in organizations.

Behavior results from a stimulus. Stimuli are perceived by the individual. They act upon memory. Memory is composed of values, perceptions, beliefs, experiences, programs, alternatives, and other knowledge stored in the psychological bank of the individual. As a result of perceiving external changes in the environment, or stimuli, the individual evokes, or calls forth, certain of these stored values, experiences, and perceptions which he or she believes particularly pertinent to the situation. The "evoked set" is that part of the memory which influences the behavior of the individual: It contains some behavior programs which the individual will enact.

Behavior can be changed, or influenced, in at least two ways. First, behavior may be changed by learning, or changing the memory of the individual. Then, in reacting to stimuli, the individual may evoke part of the new memory content. This, then, should impact his or her behavior. Second, change in the stimuli may change behavior. Different stimuli may evoke different sets, which include different behavior programs, resulting in different behaviors.

There are several possible outcomes that may occur. First, the stimuli may act upon the memory and may obtain the desired behavior. Another possibility is that the stimuli is misunderstood by the individual and may evoke a different set than originally intended. The resulting behavior may be undesired. For example, a person may perceive an unintended stimulus; that is, changes in the environment which were not planned by one who might have some control over it. These perceived stimuli may then evoke a certain set and perhaps trigger responses other than those intended.

In earlier theories, most of these possibilities were overlooked or not dealt with. The classical theorists and the administrative theorists did not consider in detail the fact that stimuli may generate unanticipated consequences because they may evoke a larger, or a different, memory set than expected. They believed that the environment contained well-defined stimuli which evoked a predictable memory set. This included a program for generating the appropriate, desirable response. For instance, use of the concept of economic rationality may result in offering increases in economic well-being to the organization member as a stimulus. This presumably would evoke a set which contained values oriented toward improving one's economic status, a belief that such improvement is desirable, and a behavior program which includes the "appropriate" response of engaging in the activity desired by the management.

Organization Equilibrium: The Decision to Participate

The individual is essentially faced with two different decisions about organizations, each reflecting different considerations. The first is the decision to participate and the second is the decision to produce. The *decision to participate* is based on the concept of organization equilibrium, which refers to the balance of payments to members for their continued participation and contribution to the organization. The underlying concepts of organization equilibrium state that:

1. The organization is a system of interrelated social behavior of participants.

2. Each participant and group receives inducements from the organization for their contribution.

3. The individual continues to participate so long as the inducements he or she receives are greater than his or her contribution. This evaluation is measured by the individual in terms of his or her own values, which may reflect or include those other than economic.

4. The contributions of various groups are sources from which the organization creates inducements to pay the others.

5. Equilibrium (or solvency) occurs when the organization can continue to provide inducement to members to obtain their contributions.

The general scope of the concept of organization equilibrium considers managers, employees, customers, suppliers, investors, the communities, and lenders. These are individuals and subgroups which make some sort of contribution to the existence of the organization. In short, anyone providing input needed by the organization for its continued existence and survival must be viewed as an integral part of the system. Should one group leave, or change basically in nature, then the organization's equilibrium is disturbed, and a new level must be sought and achieved. This may require a redistribution of inducements to others in order to obtain their participation.

The basic notion of organization equilibrium is: Increases in the balance of inducement utilities over contribution utilities decrease the propensity of the individual to move; decreases in the balance of inducement utilities over contribution utilities increase the propensity to move. Inducement utilities received by an individual or group represent more than economic consideration such as wages. Satisfaction with the organization, identification with group members, and other noneconomic values all contribute to the inducement-contribution balance.

This balance is affected by two major considerations: (1) the perceived desirability of leaving the job, and (2) the perceived ease of movement from the organization. The perceived desirability of leaving is a function of the individual's job satisfaction and the possibility of intraorganizational transfer. When individual job satisfaction is high, it may be less desirable for one to move. Several factors may affect job satisfaction (such as compatibility of work requirements with other roles, conformity of the work roles with the individual's self-characterization, and the predictability of instrumental relationships on the job), and when the person is not satisfied with his or her job, he or she may consider the possibility of an intraorganizational transfer. If this is possible, then there is less likelihood of leaving the organization. Intraorganizational transfer possibilities may be related to the organizational size; that is, in large organizations there is a greater possibility of internal transfer than in small.

The second factor that affects the inducement-contribution balance is the person's perceived ease of movement, or the number of job alternatives available. The more job offers he or she believes to have, the greater the perceived ease of movement. Personal characteristics, such as sex, age, and social status, may affect the degree to which external alternatives are perceived to be available. Skill and organizational tenure may reduce the external alternatives perceived to be available.

Thus, the likelihood of the individual leaving is a function of the desire to leave and the perceived ease of movement. If there is no desire to leave, then perceived ease of movement is not important. When one is highly dissatisfied with the organization and does wish to leave, but has few perceived external alternatives available, then it is not likely that he or she will leave and, thus, decide to remain in the organization—or participate.

The Decision to Produce

The *decision to produce* is based on a set of factors different from those that affect the decision to participate. It is a function of the character of, and the perceived consequences of, the evoked set of alternatives that emerges from the cues perceived within the environment, both internal and external to the organization that are then weighed against the individual's goals and values.

One factor which affects the motivation to produce may be the perceived external alternatives, discussed above. It may be more desirable to leave the organization than to comply with the performance requirements or group norms. A second factor, the work group and its norms, also affects the individual's evaluation of alternatives. One evaluates alternatives in terms of group norms, or those behaviors which the group may define acceptable. Thus, behavior of those in close social and physical proximity affects alternatives one may consider.

By and large, these alternatives represent possible actions. We simultaneously consider behavior possibilities and assess the perceived consequences of the evoked set. Conformity to organizational requirements will be less important when the individual perceives other alternatives to participation, which may be largely determined by his or her perception of the job market or general labor market conditions.

It is also a function of the perceived ease of movement to other organizations. When the individual feels that it would be difficult to move, that few jobs are available, he or she may view organizational conformity as important, and thus conform.

The degree to which the desired alternatives violate organizational requirements is another important individual consideration in the evaluation of alternatives. Effective compliance with organizational requirements is intended to result in the attainment and acquisition of organizational rewards. The reward system in an organization will have an effect on activity of members. Obtaining organizationally based values is largely a function of an individual's ability to meet the performance requirements of the organization.

However, it is often difficult to determine organizational performance criteria. These criteria may be a function of work group size; that is, the larger the work group, the more difficult it is to develop performance criteria and apply incentive systems. Second, the degree to which activities have been routinized and measured are important dimensions in criteria development. Organizational level is relevant here. Activities at the lowest level of the organization are more routine and programmed than higher-level activities. Performance criteria are generally more difficult to determine for higher-level officials, making it extremely difficult to tie organizational rewards to current performance at high levels. For example, the success of an organization today may be a result of decisions made three, five, or ten years ago by some other chief executive, yet it is the incumbent chief executive who receives praise or criticism.

Identification with internal or external groups affects one's evaluations of the consequences. Group pressures will largely be a function of the degree to which the individual identifies with the group. The stronger the group identification, the greater the potential group pressures.

Group pressures are significant for other reasons. Group consensus and the extent to which the group controls the environment represent pressures that may have an impact on the individual even though he or she may not identify with the group. If the group is able to influence organizational activity, or control the reward-sanction system, the individual may be forced to respond to group pressures even though he or she does not identify with the group.

When an individual perceives a stimulus to engage in behavior, a set is evoked which includes alternative actions. Each of these alternatives is evaluated in terms of its perceived consequences. They are compared to some values, or standards, which are a function of the individual's goals. These do not develop in a sterile environment. Humans, in general, evaluate their own positions in relation to the values of others and may accept other's goals as their own. Individual goals emerge from the process of identification with others. Here the concern is with the degree to which groups of one sort or the other affect and condition the goals of the individual.

An individual may identify with any or all, at different points in time, of the following types of groups:

Professional associations, family, or other types of extraorganizational groups.

Friendship groups and other social-emotional subgroups within the organization environment.

The organization itself.

Task groups in the organization involved in the performance of specific organizational assignment, similar perhaps to departments.

Obviously, the stronger the group identification, the more likely it is that individual's goals will conform to those prescribed by group norms. Group identification will be greater as a function of the following:

1. The greater the perceived prestige of the group. Prestige may be a function of success, status, or the individual's perception.

2. The greater the extent to which perceived goals are shared by members.

3. The more the perceived goals are shared by group members, the greater interaction of members.

4. The more frequent the interaction among members, the greater the propensity to identify with the group.

5. The greater the number of needs satisfied in the group, the greater the propensity of any individual to identify with the group.

6. The amount of competition between the individual and the group is negatively related to the degree of individual identification with the group.

Group Conflict

Simply because one elects to remain in an organization and operate at a given activity level, internal conflict and bargaining among members and member units are not precluded. The inducements/contributions balance permits some degree of latitude within which organization conflict and bargaining can occur because it is flexible and the level of productive activity is elastic. The decision to produce and to participate may be within the range of "semiconscious" motivational factors but conflict is more a "conscious and deliberate power phenomenon."

Conflict among organizational units arises from the following factors: the existence of a "felt need for joint decision making," differences in goals, and differences in perceptions of reality. Individuals may feel that certain decision-making situations call for representatives from several units. There may be a high degree of instrumental interdependence among units. Unit A may perform an operation on a product which may limit or condition the degree of success of Unit B. For instance, if Unit A is a metal-finishing department and Unit B is a paint shop, then the metal finish may significantly affect the quality of the paint job. Mutual dependence upon limited resources may increase the need for joint decision-making. Where several units rely on a limited budget for support, it is likely that members desire to jointly determine budget allocations.

Differences in perceived goals may be a condition that precedes conflict. Different organizational units may perceive different ends as justified. Organizational units may view their function as being more significant than other units, justifiably believing they should have a larger share of resources. Differences in goals may be a function of the size of the unit, particularly when it is reflected in the existence of a greater number of departments, which results in a larger number of differentiated goals.

Individual perceptions of reality may foster intergroup conflict. There may be substantial difference between the goals of individual members. The departmental affiliation of a member may affect perception of problems. The kind of information and the communication channels through which it flows affect the perceptions of the reality of the problem. As the number of communications channels increases, the possibility for increased differentiation of perception within the organization occurs. When the same information passes through many different channels, each may distort, filter, and edit it to suit its own needs.

When intergroup conflict exists, it must be resolved to obtain equilibrium. Conflict may be resolved by analytic or bargaining processes. Analytic processes are methods where public and private agreement among the conflicting groups is sought. Problem-solving and resolution of conflict by higher-level officials are *analytic* processes. These tend to be used when the conflict situation is more a function of individuals than intergroup differences. The general characteristic of these processes is increased information of alternatives and evaluation of the consequences of them.

Bargaining processes are attempts to resolve conflicts through the use of politics or gamesmanship. These methods are predominant when the differences are between groups rather than individuals. Bargaining processes, however, require the use of power and status, and this may have a negative impact on members. Power and status differences may be strengthened or weakened in the process. In either event, one group may suffer. Hence, there will be a tendency to treat conflict as "individual" and resolve it using an analytical method.

The Cognitive Limits of Rationality

The classical concept of the "rational" decision-making situation is limited in practice. Rational, or optimum, decisions require that all alternatives to a problem are perceived by the problem-solver. Criteria must be available which permit these to be evaluated and compared. The alternative finally selected should be that preferred above all others.

This is hardly the case in organizational life, where it is unlikely that all alternatives are known. It is even less likely that criteria exist for adequate comparison of all alternatives. Thus, decision making can only be rational within certain limits. The known alternatives, then, represent the boundaries, or parameters, of decision rationality.

Rather than "optimizing" as an organizational decision-making methodology, decision makers "satisfice." Most human decision making, whether individual or organizational, is concerned with the discovery and selection of satisfactory alternatives. Only in exceptional cases is it concerned with the discovery and selection of optimal alternatives.

An alternative is considered satisfactory if

1. a set of criteria exists that describe minimally satisfactory alternatives, and

2. the alternative in question meets or exceeds all these criteria.

Types of decision making may vary, ranging from a case in which an individual searches for various alternative behavior to one where environmental stimuli evoke a highly complex and organized set of responses. These highly complex sets of responses are called "programs." The existence of programs accounts, in large part, for the predictability of individual performance and behavior. Programs may be viewed as a part of the organizational control system. Individuals in the organization accept programs based on the factors discussed previously under the "decision to produce."

Programs exist as a function of the ability to group activities and a need for coordination. When it is relatively easy to observe and relate job output and activities, then it is possible to develop programs. As the difficulty of observing this relationship increases, the difficulty of devising organizational programs increases. Programs may also exist, or be developed, when there is a need for coordination of either activity or output. Where there is a need for a high level of coordination, then some method will be developed to ensure that it occurs.

Programs are not meant to be extremely rigid behavioral specifications in all cases, but they may be. For instance, a program which prescribes behavior for an emergency breakdown of a production line may be highly specific. On the other hand, a program dealing with price determination of special job-lot-produced equipment may be relatively flexible. Individual discretion in the use of programs is determined by whether it specifies outcome, or ends, to a greater degree than it specifies the means of achieving these ends. Programs which describe how to do something allow less discretion than programs which simply state the results desired. The hierarchical structure of programs within the organization is related to the concept of organizational levels. Higher-level officials in an organization modify programs implemented by lower-level personnel.

The organization's structure may be viewed as a function of the problem-solving process. The existence of structure, or programs, provides boundaries or parameters of rationalities for the decision-making process. Its existence provides some degree of stability and permanency to behavior within an organization, and this is a necessary characteristic of an organization's behavior.

Rational behavior rests upon the concept of "goal." The individual defines his or her behavior in terms of goal attainment. Selection of alternatives which enhance the probability of obtaining goals may be viewed as rational behavior. Thus, the goals of the individual condition whether his or her behavior is "rational" or "irrational." The behavior of one unit may be viewed by another as being nonrational behavior because of discrepant goal perception. This may be due to factoring organizational goals into subgoals for lower-level units.

Goal factoring may be viewed as a type of means-end analysis: if the overall organizational goal is viewed as the end, then those units at the highest level engage in the means of achieving that end. When one of these units is subdivided into small organization components, the means of the larger unit become the objective (or the end) of the smaller unit. This continues until the overall organizational goal has been factored into small behavior components. The factoring of overall organizational goals may result in units directing attention to their own goals. The degree of goal differentiation is important, since members of units often see goals in some particular frame of reference. Thus the number of departmental units, and the one with which an individual is affiliated, affects his or her goal perception.

As the goal becomes factored at lower and lower organizational levels, specialization of function and labor occur. Specialization of labor allows the organization to take advantage of repetitive programs. The type of specialization of labor, or the manner in which the goals have been factored, will affect the interdependence relationships among various departments. For instance, the greater the process specialization, the greater the interdependencies among departments.

The interdependencies and complexities that can occur within an organization are limited by the effectiveness of the communication processes and channels. The communication channels, or systems, in an organization are both planned and spontaneous. Certain methods for transmission of specific types of information must be provided to satisfy formal organization requirements. Additionally, there may be a need for information that is not specifically formally sanctioned. Where this information gap exists, a channel will develop to provide it. The greater the efficiency in communications, the greater the tolerance among members for departmental interdependence.

The Innovation and Elaboration of Programs

When the structure of active programs does not contain any which are adequate to meet organizational criteria, then new ones will be initiated to solve the problem. Programmed activity involves routine problem-solving. The details of behavior are relatively well-defined. Changing old programs, or devising new ones, requires a process of innovation and initiation. New program possibilities must be generated and their consequences examined. This innovating process is closely related to "problem-solving processes." In searching for programs, variables within the control of the individual or the organization will be first considered. If a satisfactory program is not developed, then an attempt will be made to change variables not within the discretion of the problem solvers. If this fails, then the criteria may be relaxed.

The criteria for satisfactory performance are closely related to the psychological concept of "level of aspiration." Aspiration levels change, but in general the adjustment process is a relatively slow, though constant one pressing upward. The aspiration level may be based on past organizational performance, but also on other bases of comparison. Firms compare themselves to other firms. When there is an awareness that better results can be obtained with other programs, there will be a revision in the standards of satisfaction.

The rate of innovation is likely to increase when changes in the internal or external environment make existing programs unsatisfactory. These environmental changes may result from deliberate design, or by accident. A "natural" process of innovation, that is, a response to environmental stimuli, may be supplemented by organizational mechanisms to facilitate innovation. Whether or not members engage in research for new programs is a function of time pressures or deadlines and the degree to which clear goals can be associated with the activities.

The discovery, development, and implementation of a new program in the organization may result in the creation of a new unit to develop, elaborate, and implement it. The development phase of new programs may be a period of high activity and excitement, while the implementation phase tends to spur less interest since the program is becoming more routine. New programs may be invented, or borrowed. If a program exists outside the boundaries of the innovating organization, then it is likely that the organization will "borrow" it. When such is not the case, organization members will first call on their "stored" program solutions. As more people in the organization become aware of the problem, the number of available solutions will increase. The development and elaboration of these new programs is through the process of means-end analysis. The solution to the general problem is by a set of generally specified means. Each of these means becomes a subgoal, and a set of means must be discovered for achieving it. This process continues until the level of detail is such that programs exist to achieve the subgoal, for which criteria must be developed. Sensitivity to innovations is a function of the relevance of the innovation to needs of the specific unit involved. When the goal of the innovation does not "fit" with that of the reviewing organization level, it is less apt to receive high priority, or it may be referred to the appropriate level. The location of innovation is important to the power and influence structure of an organization. Organizational activity is affected by the processes that originate and evaluate proposals. The right to initiate is a source of power. It is one control over organizational activities.

CHAPTER 8

Burns and Stalker, *The Management of Innovation**

... The utility of the notions of "mechanistic" and "organic" management systems resides largely in their being related as dependent variables to the rate of "environmental" change. "Environmental," in this connection, refers to the technological basis of production and to the market situation. . . . The increasing rate of technological change characteristic of the last generation could plausibly be regarded as a function of fundamental changes in the relationship of production to consumption.

If the form of management is properly to be seen as dependent on the situation the concern is trying to meet, it follows that there is no single set of principles for "good organization," an ideal type of management system which can serve as a model to which administrative practice should, or could in time, approximate. It follows also that there is an overriding management task in first interpreting correctly the market and technological situation, in terms of its instability or of the rate at which conditions are changing, and then designing the management system appropriate to the conditions, and making it work. "Direction," as I have labelled this activity, is the distinctive task of managers-in-chief. . . .

For the individual, much of the importance of the difference between mechanistic and organic systems lies in the extent of his commitment to the working organization. Mechanistic systems (namely "bureaucracies") define his functions, together with the methods, responsibilities, and powers appropriate to them; in other words, however, this means that boundaries are set. That is to say, in being told what he has to attend to, and how, he is also told what he does not have to bother with, what is not his affair, what is not expected of him, what he can post

---

*Excerpted with permission of the publisher from *The Management of Innovation*, by T. Burns and G. M. Stalker, 1961, London: Tavistock.

elsewhere as the responsibility of others. In organic systems, the boundaries of feasible demands on the individual disappear. The greatest stress is placed on his regarding himself as fully implicated in the discharge of any task appearing over his horizon, as involved not merely in the exercise of a special competence but in commitment to the success of the concern's undertakings approximating somewhat to that of the doctor or scientist in the discharge of his professional functions. . . .

Mechanistic and Organic Systems

We are now at the point at which we may set down the outline of the two management systems which represent for us . . . the two polar extremities of the forms which such systems can take when they are adapted to a specific rate of technical and commercial change. The case we have tried to establish from the literature, as from our research experience . . . , is that the different forms assumed by a working organization do exist objectively and are not merely interpretations offered by observers of different schools.

Both types represent a "rational" form of organization, in that they may both, in our experience, be explicitly and deliberately created and maintained to exploit the human resources of a concern in the most efficient manner feasible in the circumstances of the concern. Not surprisingly, however, each exhibits characteristics which have been hitherto associated with different kinds of interpretation. For it is our contention that empirical findings have usually been classified according to sociological ideology rather than according to the functional specificity of the working organization to its task and the conditions confronting it.

We have tried to argue that these are two formally contrasted forms of management system. These we shall call the mechanistic and organic form.

A *mechanistic* management system is appropriate to stable conditions. It is characterized by:

1. The specialized differentiation of functional tasks into which the problems and tasks facing the concern as a whole are broken down.

2. The abstract nature of each individual task, which is pursued with techniques and purposes more or less distinct from those of the concern as a whole (i.e., the functionaries tend to pursue the technical improvement of means, rather than the accomplishment of the ends of the concern).

3. The reconciliation, for each level in the hierarchy, of these distinct performances by the immediate superiors, who are also, in turn, responsible for seeing that each is relevant in his own special part of the task.

4. The precise definition of rights and obligations and technical methods attached to each functional role.

5. The translation of rights and obligations and methods into the responsibilities of a functional position.

6. Hierarchic structure of control, authority, and communication.

7. A reinforcement of the hierarchic structure by the location of knowledge of actualities exclusively at the top of the hierarchy, where the final reconciliation of distinct tasks and assessment of relevance is made.

8. A tendency for interaction between members of the concern to be vertical (i.e., between superior and subordinate).

9. A tendency for operations and working behavior to be governed by the instructions and decisions issued by superiors.

10. Insistence on loyalty to the concern and obedience to superiors as a condition of membership.

11. A greater importance and prestige attaching to internal (local) than to general (cosmopolitan) knowledge, experience, and skill.

The *organic* form is appropriate to changing conditions, which give rise constantly to fresh problems and unforeseen requirements for action which cannot be broken down or distributed automatically arising from the functional roles defined within a hierarchic structure. It is characterized by:

1. The contributive nature of special knowledge and experience to the common task of the concern.

2. The "realistic" nature of the individual task, which is seen as set by the total situation of the concern.

3. The adjustment and continual re-definition of individual tasks through interaction with others.

4. The shedding of "responsibility" as a limited field of rights, obligations, and methods. (Problems may not be posted upwards, downwards, or sideways as being someone else's responsibility.)

5. The spread of commitment to concern beyond any technical definition.

6. A network structure of control, authority, and communication. The sanctions which apply to the individual's conduct in his working role derive more from presumed community of interest with the rest of the working organization in the survival and growth of the firm, and less from a contractual relationship between himself and a nonpersonal corporation, represented for him by an immediate superior.

7. Omniscience no longer imputed to the head of the concern; knowledge about the technical or commercial nature of the here and now task may be located anywhere in the network; this location becoming the ad hoc center of control authority and communication.

8. A lateral rather than a vertical direction of communication through the organization, communication between people of different rank, also, resembling consultation rather than command.

9. A content of communication which consists of information and advice rather than instructions and decisions.

10. Commitment to the concern's tasks and to the "technological ethos" of material progress and expansion is more highly valued than loyalty and obedience.

11. Importance and prestige attach to affiliations and expertise valid in the industrial and technical and commercial milieux external to the firm.

One important corollary to be attached to this account is that while organic systems are not hierarchic in the same sense as are mechanistic, they remain stratified. Positions are differentiated according to seniority (i.e., greater expertise). The lead in joint decisions is frequently taken by seniors, but it is an essential presumption of the organic system that the lead (i.e., "authority,") is taken by whoever shows himself most informed and capable (i.e., the "best authority"). The location of authority is settled by consensus.

A second observation is that the area of commitment to the concern—the extent to which the individual yields himself as a resource to be used by the working organization—is far more extensive in organic than in mechanistic systems. Commitment, in fact, is expected to approach that of the professional scientist to his work, and frequently does. One further consequence of this is that it becomes far less feasible to distinguish "informal" from "formal" organization.

Thirdly, the emptying out of significance from the hierarchic command system, by which cooperation is ensured and which serves to monitor the working organization under a mechanistic system, is encountered by the development of shared beliefs about the values and goals of the concern. The growth and accretion of institutionalized values, beliefs, and conduct, in the forms of commitments, ideology, and manners, around an image of the concern in its industrial and commercial setting make good the loss of formal structure.

Finally, the two forms of system represent a polarity, not a dichotomy; there are . . . intermediate stages between the extremities empirically known to us. Also, the relation of one form to the other is elastic, so that a concern oscillating between relative stability and relative change may also oscillate between the two forms. A concern may (and frequently does) operate with a management system which includes both types.

The organic form, by departing from the familiar clarity and fixity of the hierarchic structure, is often experienced by the individual manager as an uneasy, embarrassed, or chronically anxious quest for knowledge about what he should be doing, or what is expected of him, and similar apprehensiveness about what others are doing. Indeed . . . , this kind of response is necessary if the organic form of organization is to work effectively. Understandably, such anxiety finds expression in resentment when the apparent confusion besetting him is not explained. In these situations, all managers some of the time, and many managers all the time, yearn for more definition and structure.

On the other hand, some managers recognize a rationale of nondefinition, a reasoned basis for the practice of those successful firms in which designation of status, function, and line of responsibility and authority has been vague or even avoided.

The desire for more definition is often in effect a wish to have the limits of one's task more neatly defined—to know what and when one doesn't have to bother about as much as to know what one does have to. It follows that the more definition is given, the more omniscient the management must be, so that no functions are left wholly or partly undischarged, no person is overburdened with undelegated responsibility, or left without the authority to do his job properly. To do this, to have all the separate functions attached to individual roles fitting together and comprehensively, to have communication between persons constantly maintained on a level adequate to the needs of each functional role, requires rules or traditions of behavior proved over a long time and an equally fixed, stable task. The omniscience which may then be credited to the head of the concern is expressed throughout its body through the lines of command, extending in a clear, explicitly titled hierarchy of officers and subordinates.

The whole mechanistic form is instinct with this twofold principle of definition and dependence which acts as the frame within which action is conceived and carried out. It works, unconsciously, almost in the smallest minutiae of daily activity. "How late is late?" The answer to this question is not to be found in the rule book, but in the superior. Late is when the boss thinks it is late. Is he the kind of man who thinks 8:00 is the time . . . ? Does he think that 8:15 is all right occasionally if it is not a regular thing? Does he think that everyone should be allowed a 5-minutes grace after 8:00 but after that they are late?

Settling questions about how a person's job is to be done in this way is nevertheless simple, direct, and economical of effort. . . .

One other feature of mechanistic organization needs emphasis. It is a necessary condition of its operation that the individual "works on his own," functionally isolated; he "knows his job," he is "responsible for seeing it's done." He works at a job which is in a sense artificially abstracted from the realities of the situation the concern is dealing with, the accountant "dealing with the costs side," the works manager "pushing production," and so on. As this works out in practice, the rest of the organization becomes part of the problem situation the individual has to deal with in order to perform successfully (i.e., difficulties and problems arising from work or information which has been handed over the "responsibility barrier" between two jobs or departments are regarded as "really" the responsibility of the person from whom they were received). As a design engineer put it, "When you get designers handing over designs completely to production, it's their responsibility now. And you get tennis games played with the responsibility for anything that goes wrong. What happens is that you're constantly getting unsuspected faults arising from characteristics which you didn't think important in the design. If you get to hear of these through a sales person, or a production person or somebody to whom the design was handed over to in the dim past, then, instead of being a design problem, it's an annoyance caused by that particular person, who can't do his own job—because you'd thought you were finished with that one, and you're on to something else now."

When the assumptions of the form of organization make for preoccupation with specialized tasks, the chances of career success, or of greater influence, depend rather on the relative importance which may be attached to each special function by the superior whose task it is to reconcile and control a number of them. And, indeed, to press the claims of one's job or department for a bigger share of the firm's resources is in many cases regarded as a mark of initiative, of effectiveness, and even of "loyalty to the firm's interests." The state of affairs thus engendered squares with the role of the superior, the man who can see the wood instead of just the trees, and gives it the reinforcement of the aloof detachment belonging to a court of appeal. The ordinary relationship prevailing between individual managers "in charge of" different functions is one of rivalry, a rivalry which may be rendered innocuous to the persons involved by personal friendship or the norms of sociability, but which turns discussion about the situations which constitute the real problems of the concern—how to make products more cheaply, how to sell more, how to allocate resources, whether to curtail activity in one sector, whether to risk expansion in another, and so on—into an arena of conflicting interests.

The distinctive feature of the second, organic system is the pervasiveness of the working organization as an institution. In concrete terms, this makes itself felt in preparedness to combine with others in serving the general aims of the concern. Proportionately to the rate and extent of change, the less can the omniscience appropriate to command organizations be ascribed to the head of the organization; for executives, and even operatives, in a changing firm it is always theirs to reason why. Furthermore, the less definition can be given to status, roles, and modes of communication, the more do the activities of each member of the organization become determined by the real tasks of the firm as he sees them than by instruction and routine. The individual's job ceases to be self-contained; the only way in which "his" job can be done is by his participating continually with others in the solution of problems which are real to the firm, and put in a language of requirements and activities meaningful to them all. Such methods of working put much heavier demands on the individual. . . .

We have endeavored to stress the appropriateness of each system to its own specific set of conditions. Equally, we desire to avoid the suggestion that either system is superior under all circumstances to the other. In particular, nothing in our experience justifies the assumption that mechanistic systems should be superseded by organic in conditions of stability. The beginning of administrative wisdom is the awareness that there is no optimum type of management system.

CHAPTER 9

Woodward's *Industrial Organization**

Donna Goehle

The First Survey and Initial Conclusions

In the first study of 100 industrial firms conducted between September 1954 and September 1955, Woodward and her colleagues attempted to obtain information regarding the formal organization and operating procedures. It was felt that the large number of firms involved in the first phase of the study would preclude attempts to find out very much about the informal social relationships within the firm; therefore, the information sought by the researchers was limited to the following categories:

1. History, background, and objectives.

2. Description of the manufacturing processes and methods.

3. Forms and routines through which the firm was organized and operated.

4. Facts and figures that could be used to make an assessment of the firm's commercial success.

In evaluating the information regarding history, background, and objectives, it became evident that although all firms were engaged in manufacturing, there were substantial differences among them. "The nature of their markets, the type of customers they served, the methods they employed, and the targets they set for themselves differed considerably." The differences in manufacturing processes were also

---

*From *Industrial Organization: Theory and Practice*, by J. Woodward, 1965, London: Oxford University Press.

noticeable and were grouped according to the following "technical variables": "the density of production, the flexibility of production, facilities, the diversity of products, the time span of operations, and the way in which production programs were initiated and controlled." (This classification of technical variables related to production types becomes a critical element throughout the entire period of the study.)

Third, the researchers obtained organization charts where they were available, and tried to construct them through interviewing when they were not. Information in this category focused on determining the pattern of prescribed relationships as well as duties and responsibilities of each office studied. In addition, they studied "the history and responsibilities of the principal staff and specialist departments, including sales, research, development, personnel, inspection, maintenance, and purchasing; they examined the documentation associated with planning and control procedures and the methods used in costing and budgetary control." Considerable attention was also given to analyzing the labor structure for each firm.

Since the researchers were not only interested in determining how the various firms were organized and operated, but also in discovering whether particular forms of organization were associated with managerial efficiency and success, they also attempted to assemble information regarding the ways in which a firm's success might be evaluated internally and externally. Some of the factors used in assessing the "success" of the enterprise included such things as market position and market share, annual reports and financial statements for a five-year period, fluctuations in the market price of the firm's stock, reputation among competitors and labor unions, and internally generated information thought to be significant in explaining the relationship between internal operations and enterprise success.

In developing a measure of commercial success which could be used in testing the relationship between organizational form and that success, the methods used by the researchers seem to be imprecise and are not treated as rigorously as some of the other variables utilized. Internal efficiency, although mentioned, does not appear to be fully developed in either of the studies; however, some oblique references to the efficiency of certain production technologies do appear in the analysis of both studies. Aside from grouping the firms on the basis of the general categories of "average," "above average," and "below average," the researchers did not concentrate their analysis on linking more specific measures of commercial success to particular organizational forms.

In their analysis of organization, Woodward and her colleagues focused primarily on the types of organization traditionally associated with the "classical" school of organizational thought: line organization, functional organization, and line-staff organization. They divided the firms into these categories and found the following distribution of types among the firms surveyed: 35 predominately line organizations; 2 functional organizations; 59 line-staff organizations; and 4 unclassifiable organizations.

A considerable degree of variation, especially in the manner in which specialist departments evolved, existed among the firms surveyed; however, there seemed to be no consistent pattern of evolution which held true across the sample. In addition, firms rated at both ends of the success continuum illustrated diverse organizational forms. According to the study, there did not appear to be a direct interrelationship between organizational structure and commercial success. When other variables were examined, such as the length of the command hierarchy, the sizes of the span of control at various levels, the size of the firm based on total employees, the industry type, and managerial qualifications, no link between one or more variables and commercial success could be established.

Woodward and her associates also utilized Burns's approach to classifying industrial organizations as "mechanistic" and "organic" systems. Applying this classification to the firms being studied they found that "Organic systems, both those consciously planned on organic lines and those planned on mechanistic lines but operated on organic principles, outnumbered mechanistic systems by approximately two to one." The results of the analysis of the participating firms, based on the criteria Burns's work suggested, seem to substantiate his earlier findings. Woodward reports the results in the following manner:

> As a result of his researches he came to the conclusion that mechanistic systems are appropriate to stable conditions and organic systems to conditions of change. It will be recalled that South Essex is an area in which the newer and developing industries predominate, and it might therefore be expected that organic systems would predominate. (p. 24)

Having reached these general conclusions in their initial analysis of the data, the researchers turned to a more detailed examination of the technical variables. Although some social scientists, including Weber and Veblen, have suggested a link between technological circumstances and the structure and behavior of social systems, there had been relatively little empirical work undertaken which would delineate this suggested relationship. In the absence of such a framework, Woodward's researchers initially grouped the firms on the basis of similarities in manufacturing processes and methods. Once the initial classification was complete, they were able to determine that "firms with similar goals and associated manufacturing policies had similar manufacturing processes—the range of tools, instruments, machines and technical formulas was limited and controlled by the manufacturing policy." The first breakdown of firms studied included those enterprises "where production was one of a kind to meet customers' individual requirements, and those where production was standardized."

This initial breakdown quickly developed into many more categories based on the size of the unit being produced, the technical complexity of the product being produced, and the diversity of products being manufactured, to mention only a few. It became obvious to the researchers that each of the manufacturing processes was unique in some way; therefore, some method of systematizing the firms according to technical variables had to be developed. "It was felt that the system of division normally used by production engineers into the three categories of jobbing, batch, and mass production were inadequate. . . ." Consequently, a more expanded grouping of eleven categories, based on these basic production types, was devised. Table 9.1 represents the distribution of firms by production system.

Table 9.1   Production Systems of Firms in the Study

	Unit & Small Batch	Large Batch & Mass	Process Industries
1. Equipment	General Purpose	Special Purpose	Special Purpose
2. Layout	Colonies	Line	Flow
3. Flexibility	High	Low	Low
4. Skill & Training	High	Low	High
5. Design/Mkt./Mfg. Sequence	Mkt./Des./Mfg.	Des./Mfg./Mkt.	Des./Mkt./Mfg.
6. Labor/Capital Intensive	Labor	Capital/Labor	Capital
7. Control	Decentralized	Centralized	Centralized
8. In-Process Inventory	High	Low	Low
9. Finished Inventory	Low	High or Low	Low or High
10. Adaptability to Econ. Change	High	Low	Low
11. Input/Output Dependence	Low	Low	Low
12. Make/Buy	Make (buy)	Buy (make)	Buy
13. Optimal "Style"	Organic	Mechanistic	Organic
14. Staff Role	Supportive	Dominant	Supportive
15. Typical Scale	Small	Large	Large
16. Technology	Variable	High	High
17. Quality Control	Random	In-Line	Continuous

In relating the production categories to the ways in which the various firms were organized and operated, the first significant pattern emerged. It was determined that "firms with similar production systems appeared to have similar organizational structures." According to Woodward, the differences between some of the firms placed in the same category were not as significant as the differences observed between the various categories. Furthermore, "the figures relating to the various organizational characteristics tended to cluster around the medians, the medians varying from one category to another." Based on these observations, the

> . . . main conclusion reached through this research project was that the existence of the link between technology and social structure first postulated by Thorstein Veblen (1919) can be demonstrated empirically. (p. 50)

Although Woodward is careful to note that the research did not prove technology was the only important variable in determining the organizational structure, it was one which could be isolated for further study without much difficulty. In addition, "the only variable found to be demonstrably related to variations in organization was the system of production in operation." In examining this relationship, the following characteristics were also considered: "the length of the line of command;

the span of control of the chief executive; the percentage of total turnover allocated to the payment of wages and salaries; and the ratio of managers to total personnel, of clerical and administrative staff to manual workers, of direct to indirect labor, and of graduate to non-graduate supervision in the production departments."

Throughout this phase of the report, Woodward distinguishes the predominant characteristics of firms operating at both ends of the production continuum as well as in the middle ranges and relates them in a systematic fashion to the variables. She then develops a discussion of the relationship between technology, organization, and success. Since one of the objectives in conducting the study was to determine whether or not management principles were being applied in practice and whether they were influential in ensuring business success, the researchers wanted to determine what type of organizational system might prove to be most appropriate for a particular production system. On the basis of analyzing the preceding organizational characteristics (i.e., the number of levels in the chain of command, labor costs, and various labor ratios—with measures of organizational success), Woodward concludes that:

> The fact that organizational characteristics, technology and success were linked together in this way suggested that not only was the system of production an important variable in the determination of organizational structure, but also that one particular form of organization was most appropriate to each system of production. In unit production, for example, not only did short and relatively broadly based pyramids predominate, but they also appeared to ensure success. Process production, on the other hand, would seem to require the taller and more narrowly based pyramid. (p. 71)

Woodward also found that "successful firms inside the large-batch production range tended to have mechanistic management systems. On the other hand, successful firms outside this range tended to have organic systems."

In explaining the observations of the Woodward team and their relationship to the concepts associated with classical management theory, she says:

> In general, the administrative expedients associated with success in large-batch firms were in line with the principles and ideas on which the teaching of management subjects is based. In all successful large-batch production firms there was not only a clear definition of duties and responsibilities of the kind already referred to, but also an adherence to the principles of unity of command; a separation (at least on paper) of advisory from executive responsibilities, and a chief executive who controlled no more than the recommended five or six direct subordinates.

> The tendency to regard large-batch production as the typical system of modern industry may be the explanation of this link between success and conformity with management theory. The people responsible for developing management theory no doubt had large-batch production in mind as they speculated about management. In general, the experience on which their generalizations were based had been obtained in large-batch production industry. (pp. 71–72)

In summarizing the results of the survey, Woodward states that "While at first sight there seemed to be no link between organization and success, and no one best way of organizing a factory, it subsequently became apparent that there was a particular form of organization most appropriate to each technical situation." According to the survey, "within a limited range of technology this was also the form of organization most closely in line with the principles and ideas of management theory.... Outside this limited range, however, the rules appear to be different, the most suitable form of organization being out of line with these ideas." It should be noted that Woodward carefully states that the researchers found a link between organization, technology, and success, but that a *precisely defined causal* relationship was not found.

The researchers were also interested in evaluating the relationship between technology, social structure, and administrative practices in general. Viewing the firm as a social system within a larger social system, Woodward defines social structure as the "framework on which the system operates." According to Woodward, the variables in the system include: "occupational structure, the enterprise consisting of members of different occupational groups in the community, formal organization (i.e., the stable and explicit pattern of prescribed relationships designed to enable those employed to work together in the achievement of objectives), and informal organization (i.e., the pattern of relationships which actually emerges from day-to-day operations"). Since the researchers were interested in determining to what degree management theory, as it was being taught, was being applied in designing and administering organizations, it was natural that the analysis would probably move in the direction of further defining the link between technology and organization.

From the information obtained in the survey, Woodward and her colleagues determined that formal organization was considerably affected by technical factors. Although they found that there was less conscious planning of formal organization in the firms they studied than one would expect, given the findings of several other social scientists in the industrial field, they did discover some interesting relationships between formal planning of organizational structure, formalization of the informal structure, and the type of production being employed in the enterprise. In the successful firms of the first group (utilizing formal organizational planning), "unit and small-batch production and continuous-flow production predominated, while the majority of successful firms in the second category were in the large-batch production category." This finding would tend to suggest that "conscious planning produces better results in some kinds of industry than in others."

Since other social scientists have frequently assumed that "formal organization is the part of social structure least affected by technology," the conclusions drawn by Woodward seem especially interesting: "the survey findings suggested that the link between technology and organization persists in spite of, rather than because of, the conscious behavior or deliberate policy, and in defiance of the tendency in management education to emphasize the independence of the administrative process from technical considerations." Through her analysis of these findings, she suggests that technical environments can and do affect the structure of both the formal and the informal organization of the enterprise. Furthermore, she contends that "technology, because it influences the roles defined by formal organization, must therefore influence industrial behavior, for how a person reacts depends as much on the demands of his role and the circumstances in which he finds himself, as well as on his personality." Woodward goes on to state that "there can be occasions when the behavior forced on him by his role will conflict with his personality." To her way of thinking, the individual will resolve the conflict in one of two ways—modifying his personality to conform to the role considerations or leaving the organization. In light of the hypothesized relationship between technical variables and organizational roles and the concomitant possibilities for conflict for the individual, Woodward concludes that perhaps top managers are brought to the upper levels of the organization through having those "personalities which best fit the technical background in which they have to operate."

Although explicit causal relationships were not defined, Woodward and her associates suggest that a number of other initial observations could be made from analyzing the results of this first survey. It was determined, for instance, that certain technical environments seem to impose greater strains than others might on members of all levels of the hierarchy. In addition, intermanagerial and employee-employer relationships appeared to "be better at the extremes of the scale than they were in the middle; pressure was greatest in the middle and it seemed more important to build mechanisms into the organizational structure which would resolve the conflicts likely to occur." Woodward then summarizes the findings and their implications for formulating the next stage of the study.

> Thus it seems that an analysis of situational demands could lead not only to the development of better techniques for appraising organizational structure and for conscious planning, but also to an increased understanding of the personal qualities and skills required in different industrial situations, and to improved methods of training directed towards giving those concerned a better understanding of the strains and stresses associated with the roles they are likely to occupy. (p. 80)

The Case Studies

In order to investigate some of their initial observations, the group undertook a more detailed case study of 20 selected firms in which manufacturing methods were either changing or mixed. It was felt that if technology and organization were linked in the manner suggested by the earlier findings, more difficult organizational challenges and problems would arise in firms with these characteristics. Therefore, they wanted to examine firms which were characterized as undergoing a change in production systems (caused by technological developments) and which might require that the formal organization be modified to a new set of situational demands.

Firms utilizing mixed production systems were also chosen for additional study because of the possibilities they presented for studying potentially incompatible situational demands arising from the technology. If those organizations were found to have conflicting situational demands, study of the organizational structure might reveal the way in which these demands might be reconciled. Thus, this phase of the study was intended to evaluate in more detail the relationship between the technology of production and the associated organizational pattern. Consequently, the three main aspects of organization selected for examination in this phase of the study were: "the type of organization with particular reference to the breakdown between line and staff roles; the relationships between the three main functions of manufacturing research and development, production, and marketing; and the organization of production, including the way in which results were predicted and controlled."

The researchers began by examining the relationship between situational demands arising from the technology and the organizational structure. In general, the "follow-up studies confirmed that in many firms the conscious process of organization-building proceeds independently of technical change and development, and that the link between technology and organization was not the product of conscious behavior or deliberate policy." In fact, many of those interviewed seemed to feel that there was no one best way for organizing a firm and that there were a number of alternatives which could potentially be as effective as the one they happened to be using. It appeared in some firms, that there were changes in organization which followed a change in technology and resulted from the apparent inability of the preceding organization to cope with that change.

Although the observations made in the second phase of the research seemed to support the conclusions of the initial study, a number of interesting points emerged in the more detailed phase of analysis. "The research workers realized as they studied firms more deeply that not only the type of organization but also the functions of the organization were linked with technology." Although the organization is often thought of as having a dual function in serving both technical and social ends, Woodward and her colleagues found rather substantial differences between the functions of organization required for one type of firm (or production process) and those of a firm utilizing a less advanced system of production. They discovered that "in the process industry, the design or mechanism for coordinating work is intrinsic in the plant itself," and in some of the mass-production firms they studied, "the control system fulfilled a similar function." Consequently, "in both these systems, production emerged almost automatically once the production process had been set in motion." Summarizing the relationship between organization structure, functions, and technology among observed firms, Woodward states:

> This means that in the technically advanced firm organization serves primarily social ends, its function being to define roles and relationships within a social system. This means that the organization planner can concentrate on establishing the network of relationships which is best for people. Moreover, because coordination is independent of organization, the form of organization is not likely to have a critical effect on business success.

> In the less advanced systems of production, where organization serves both technical and social ends, there is likely to be a much closer link between business success and the form of organization, and the two functions can come into conflict. The network of relationships best for production is not necessarily best for people. (p. 123)

Based on these observations, Woodward suggests that the initial step in designing an organizational structure compatible with the situational demands imposed by the technology is to determine the purposes of the organization. Unfortunately, according to Woodward's view, classical management thought is inadequate in relating organizational structure to business success in this manner, particularly when considered in light of the situational demands imposed by a particular technology.

After having made the distinction between task and element functions and their relationship to organizational structure, Woodward turned her analysis toward examining the relationship between the task functions and the personnel charged with carrying them out. This phase of the analysis focused on the relationship between task functions and the three major manufacturing tasks mentioned earlier: manufacturing, marketing, and development. In evaluating the task functions associated with each of these functions, Woodward and her colleagues discovered that in the technically advanced systems, the functions could be separated quite easily; however, in the unit and small-batch process firms, the separation between these three functions was much more difficult to achieve.

In addition, they determined that "the relative importance of the various functions was also related to the system of production," and that within each production organization, one task element seemed to be central and critical to both success and survival. Although they recognized that this difference in emphasis between firms could certainly be due to more than a dependency on a certain type of technology, they concluded that "in the long run, technology remained the dominant factor in the determination of the critical factor."

Through their analysis of the status system, they observed that the successful firms accorded adequate recognition to the importance of the critical function. They also discovered that the department in which the chief executive had previously worked was also the department with the highest status. Taking this link between the status system and technology as well as the background of the chief executive, they concluded that "there was a tendency for firms whose chief executive had been closely associated with the critical function earlier in his career to be the more successful ones."

The general outcome of this phase of the study can be summarized as follows:

As we have seen, in unit production and large-batch and mass production, organization has to serve both technical and social ends; the coordination of basic activities depends upon organization, the difference between these two types of production being that whereas in unit production there is no conflict between technical and social ends, in large-batch and mass production such conflict can and does arise.

Process production is different again. This is the type of industry where organization does not have to provide a mechanism for the coordination of work; its main purpose is therefore social.

The fact that organization does not provide the mechanism for the coordination of work may be the fundamental reason why relationships between development, production, and marketing were more harmonious in process firms than in large-batch and mass-production firms even though roles were in general less clearly defined. (p. 127)

When the researchers turned their attention from the overall organizational structure to the more detailed elements of planning and controlling production, they found that the link between technology and organization was not always as apparent. When production organization was considered, it did not appear to be as closely related to technology as some of the other aspects of organization. In evaluating this situation further, Woodward and her colleagues observed that "there was greater variation in the way production operations were planned and controlled in the firms in the middle ranges of the scale. . . ." As far as the organization of production was concerned, situational demands impose themselves more rigidly and obviously at the extremes than in the middle ranges of the scale.

It appeared that at either end of the continuum, the possible ranges in organizational choice were much more confined by the type of production technology than in the middle ranges; consequently, those in the middle ground had much more latitude in determining organizational issues related to production. In fact, it was determined that within this middle range, even an unsuitable organization had relatively little immediate impact on the success of the enterprise. Therefore, Woodward concludes that, in the case of firms in the middle ranges of the production spectrum, technology was an important variable; however, other variables were equally important.

It was in her analysis of the production organization that Woodward seemed to find classical management theory most noticeably inadequate for analyzing and understanding the behavior and the relationships associated with complicated production processes. Although the conventional line-staff classifications were evidently useful to the researchers in identifying and categorizing some of the problem areas in organization, they were unable to utilize these concepts in fully explaining the nature of their findings. This seemed to be particularly evident in those situations where they were attempting to evaluate the relationship between control systems and the human relations problems they observed in several situations.

The Follow-up Investigations

Throughout their extensive study of manufacturing organizations in the South Essex area, Woodward and her associates had demonstrated and evaluated the existence of a link between technology and organizational characteristics. They were not interested in deepening their understanding of the apparent interaction between technical and behavioral factors. To this end, additional and more intensive studies of three firms were begun. The researchers now wanted to refine the instrument used in classifying technology and detail the appropriate technical characteristics for the various production processes considered earlier. In addition, they wanted to further examine the relationship between technology and organization in those enterprises undergoing technical changes. One other objective of the study was to further examine the effects of formalization on control procedures.

The analysis of the control system was, to some degree, to serve as a basis for further studies in the area, and some comments on the background of this aspect of the project seem appropriate.

Briefly, this project is based on the assumption that when the management of a firm makes a decision to manufacture a product or series of products a control system is automatically brought into existence. Objectives have to be determined in relation to the product and a sequence of activities planned in order to achieve these objectives. Plans then have to be executed and information generated to enable the results to be assessed. If activities are to be repeated, corrective action may have to be taken or the objectives modified in the light of the result obtained. For those concerned with the product at all levels of the hierarchy, the control system is the framework in which they operate, determining the amount of discretion they have in the organization of their own activities. It is hoped that some way of describing control systems in terms of such parameters as degrees of formalization, complexity, and fragmentation will be found, and the behavior associated with them.

The researchers discovered that substantially less organizational disturbance and modification had resulted in the one firm which experienced a change in moving from process production to automated, continuous-flow production than occurred in the two plants characterized as having substantially different production technologies. This would seem to support their initial hypothesis that: "Technical changes involving a change in the nature of the production system have the greatest effect on organization and behavior."

In continuous-process production plants, the commercial success of the enterprise was more closely linked to the assurances of a long-range market potential for its products; therefore, the "number of imponderables was relatively few and the consequences of taking a particular course of action could be predicted with a certain degree of certainty." Although Woodward does not elaborate on the topic of uncertainty in markets as it might affect intra-firm organizational issues, she seems to suggest that the problems faced by some of the other firms—having different production technologies—may be related to the uncertainties in marketing of products and the interrelationship of those uncertainties with production scheduling, control, and plant organization and administration.

The role of the chief executive also differed in the three types of companies. Again, because of the rigid framework of control provided by the production process itself in process industries, relationships were characterized as being less stressful than those in the other two firms. In addition, although the members of the organization were working under a relatively rigid framework of control—based on the process technology—there appeared to be fewer complaints in this organization regarding limitations on individual action and authority. Interestingly, chief executives in the process production industry were observed as spending less time on purely technical matters than their counterparts in other firms. Since technical decisions in crisis situations were delegated to those which technical expertise and long-range planning decisions were too important to be left to one person, the observers felt that the chief executive in this industry was more involved in the social organization of the firm than his counterparts in other types of production plants.

In evaluating the other two plants which were moving into the batch-production type of technology from opposite ends of the continuum, results concerning the effect of change on these two organizations indicated that the most "recalcitrant problems of organization and behavior are likely to be found in the batch-production area of technology." Since it was anticipated that the problems in adjusting to change in each of these organizations would probably take a greater period of time than in the process industry and might prove to be more costly, the researchers were interested in examining further the relationship between the degree of adjustment required and the duration of the period of tension accompanying these changes. Since the researchers sought to study a "before and after" situation, and already had considerable data on these firms, these studies allowed the researchers to control the experiment somewhat by holding the factors other than technology constant.

The researchers concluded that their initial predictions of the effect of technological change on organization and behavior were substantiated. In brief, they determined that the batch-production technology brought with it some of the most difficult problems in both behavior and organization. "Moreover, the differences in the ease with which firms adapted to technical change could be explained in terms of the senior managers' ability to anticipate these problems, and the initiative shown in simultaneous planning of organizational and technical change." According to Woodward, the results of this phase of the study:

> Provided a further demonstration of the main thesis put forward. . . . , i.e., that meaningful explanations of behavior can be derived from an analysis of the work situation. It seemed that in identifying technology as one of the primary variables on which behavior depended, a step forward had been made in the determination of the conditions under which behavior becomes standardized and predictable. (p. 208)

In evaluating the effects of technical change on organization and behavior, the researchers also examined the relationship between informal and formal organization within the firms being studied and found that the organizational objectives were frequently achieved by the informal organization. Furthermore, they found that "a disfunctional organization could be compensated by contributive informal relationships," and that this observation was particularly notable when viewed in relation to technical change.

When technical change was introduced, the researchers found that organizations varied in the way in which the formal and informal organizations responded to the new requirements. In some firms, where technical change and organizational change were simultaneously planned and initiated, adjustment of the informal to the formal organization seemed much more rapid. Conversely, where organizational change and technical change were not simultaneously introduced and/or planned for, the informal organization was the primary means by which the organizational goal was effected. It was only later that the adjustment was made in the formal organization. The possible advantages in control gained through proper attention to planning both organizational and technical change seem evident and appear to be supported by Woodward's analysis.

Conclusions

Table 9.1 presents a summary of her findings. The conclusions she reached tend to support the view that the "rules of classical management theory do not always work in practice." However, classical theory was not dismissed as useless in the analysis of organizations. She concluded that the existing classical theory is not able to incorporate the formal and informal aspects of organizational behavior. She also found the human relations school to be inadequate in explaining the complexities of organization and behavior. Consequently, "far from casting away management principles altogether, one of the more significant factors in the research findings was the confirmation that these principles were positively linked to business success in one particular area of technology." But there is still the absence of clear cut guides for application in differing settings which would enhance both stability in application and improved predictability.

CHAPTER 10

Organization Analysis*

A Sociological Point of View

Charles Perrow

The Mixed Model

Let us assume, for a moment, that we are talking about organizations where all three of the following functions are important: research, production, and marketing. Though industrial terminology is being used here, it should be recognized that all organizations have, to at least some limited extent, all these functions. A correctional institution, an employment agency, the social security administration, or various military units all not only produce products but must also market them in some form or other. The manner in which they produce and market these products is based upon an appropriate technology. To find, change, develop, and improve the technology constitutes a research function, as does the determination of what the new products will be. Of course, for some organizations, marketing is a minor problem, while for others it is a major one, and the same is true of research and even of production. Assuming all three are important, however, how should they be organized?

The organizational form will depend upon the state of the art in each function and the changes required by the environment. Preferably production and marketing would be routinized: Even fairly routine research functions would be preferred. If all three are routine (or nonroutine), the organization has little difficulty in determining the best method of organizing the whole. All can be structured alike and integration problems are minimized.

However, it is far more common to find varying degrees of routinization among the three functions. Typically, production is fairly routine and exists in a stable environment; research is nonroutine, and marketing is in-between. This situation presents problems of coordination beyond those normally encountered when there are different units, since the three units will think differently and will be accustomed to different ways of getting things done. Production, for example, may think only in terms of the very short run. This is the basis upon which this function is judged; the unit is not responsible for, nor in a position to anticipate, new products or techniques. Marketing, however, must take a somewhat longer perspective. (If the marketing function is not developed, and only a sales division exists, its perspective may be as short-range as production.) Development, and especially research, however, should have a relatively long perspective compared to production and marketing. Time perspectives establish priorities, and thus the units may clash. They will disagree about such matters as the allocation of resources or the urgency of solving a particular problem. Not only perspectives are involved, but also active and precise goals which can affect actual structures. With its short-range perspective and precise goals which can be measured, production is likely to have highly specialized subunits, clear lines of authority, precise rules and procedures. Research, at the other extreme, may depend more upon lateral and diagonal communication among its members, resulting in a good deal of informal contact; there may be few intermediate measures of productivity and few binding rules or procedures. It may be difficult for members of these two departments to work together, or even to communicate information easily, because of their different "styles."

Technology Models

So far we have been content with a simple polar contrast between bureaucratized organizations or units and nonbureaucratized units. The key to the distinction has been the kind of work performed in the organization or unit of the organization: its degree of routine or lack of routine. But if we analyze the term "routine" more closely, it appears that we mean that two conditions are present—there are well-established techniques which are sure to work, and these are applied to essentially similar raw materials. That is, there is little uncertainty about methods and little variety or change in the tasks that must be performed.

Similarly, nonroutineness means that there are a few well-established techniques; there is little certainty about methods, or whether or not they will work. But it also means that there may be a variety of different tasks to perform, in the sense that raw materials are not standardized, or orders from customers ask for many different or custom-made products.

The operations of some firms may have little variety, yet quite a bit of uncertainty; others may have little uncertainty, but a great deal of variety. These two types are neither highly routine nor highly nonroutine. They are in the middle somehow, but they are not in the same middle; they themselves differ from one another. So it is possible to be nonroutine in one sense and not another, or routine in one sense but not in another. . . .

Variability and Search

. . . Organizations are designed to get some kind of work done. To do this work they need techniques or technologies. These techniques are applied to some kind of "raw material" which the organization transforms into a marketable product. It doesn't matter what the product is; it may be reformed delinquents, TV programs, advertising symbols, governmental decisions, or steel. But some technology is required, not only in the actual production process, but also for procuring the input of materials, capital, and labor and disposing of the output to some other organization or consumer, and for coordinating the three "functions" or "phases" of input-transformation-output.

How does one think about, or conceptualize, technology so that it may be analyzed in this way as a means of transforming raw materials (human, symbolic, or material) into desirable goods and services? In this view of technology, machines and equipment are merely tools; they are not the technology itself. Indeed, the [human resource manager] uses a technology that has little to do with tools. Nor can we use the actual techniques such as are found in production manuals, for these are too specific to the particular organization. Instead, let us consider the individual who is assigned to do a specific task.

He receives stimuli (orders, signals), to which he must respond. Even the decision to ignore the stimulus or not even to "see it" is a response. He "searches" his mind to decide what kind of response to make. So far we have two concepts with which to work: the stimulus and the response. The response is conceived of as "search behavior": If the stimulus is familiar and the individual has learned in the past what to do in the face of it, little search behavior is required. He may respond automatically or after a moment's thought. . . .

If the stimulus is unfamiliar, however, and the individual decides not to ignore it or to panic, considerable search behavior must be instituted, and the search is of a different kind. The problem presented by the stimulus is not immediately analyzable; search must take place without manuals, computers, or clerks who have the requisite information and programs. . . .

If we substitute a more general term for stimuli—raw material—we can see that the nature of the search procedure depends a good deal upon what is known about the material that one is to transform through techniques. If a good deal is known that is relevant to the transformation process, search can be quite routine and analyzable. . . .

The other dimension of technology which will be used here is the variability of the stimuli presented to an individual—the variety of problems which may lead to search behavior. Sometimes the variety is great and every task seems to be a new one demanding the institution of search behavior of some magnitude (whether analyzable or unanalyzable). Sometimes stimuli are not very varied and the individual is confronted chiefly with familiar situations and a few novel ones. Note that, in industrial firms, this is not necessarily a distinction between a great or small variety of products. Automobile firms produce an amazing variety of models and a staggering variety of parts, but these are not novel situations requiring search behavior (except in the design and engineering of model changes).

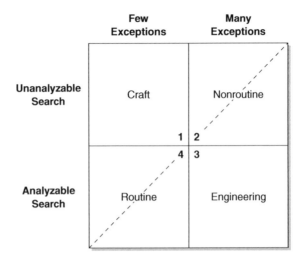

Figure 10.1 Technology Variables

Note also that the difference between analyzable or routine search is not necessarily the same as the distinction between technologically advanced and technologically backward industries. Some semiconductors, such as auto diodes, are a product of advanced technology but they can be made in a quite routine fashion. Certain kinds of ferro castings for the auto industry—a technologically "backward" process—cannot be made on a routine basis. To routinize production would require the solution of problems that have yet to be analyzed.

We now have two dimensions, the degree of variability of stimuli and the degree to which search procedures are analyzable. Let us refer to the first as simply the number of *exceptions* encountered by the individual. If we dichotomize and then cross-classify these there are four possibilities which, in Figure 10.1, we have labeled craft, nonroutine, routine, and engineering.

A factory manufacturing a standard product like heating elements for electric stoves (cell 4), and an engineering firm building made-to-order machines such as drill presses or electric motors (cell 3), may both be routine to the extent to which search behavior is analyzable. Still, they differ in the variety of occasions when search must be instituted—rarely in the factory, and quite frequently in the engineering firm. The engineering firm must continually modify designs and introduce modifications to meet the customers' needs. In a firm making fine glassware (cell 1), search may be as unanalyzable as in the factory which makes nuclear-propulsion systems (cell 2). Yet the variety of the stimuli in the glassware factory is small, while the varying requirements of the customers of the other firm present a great variety of problems or stimuli. The work of the nuclear fuel system firm would be highly nonroutine, combining unanalyzable problems with great variability of problems; the operations of a heating-element factory or a mill making reinforcing bars for concrete structure would be highly routine—a small variety of problems, while those which do occur would be subject to analyzable search procedures. The glass firm is low on variability but high on unanalyzable search procedures (therefore, referred to as a craftsman model). The engineering firm is high on variability but has analyzable search procedures—an engineering model.

Note that if one were discussing only routine and nonroutine companies or bureaucratic and nonbureaucratic structures, only cells 4 and 2 would be relevant. These are represented by a two-dimensional continuum characterized by a broken line; this is the sort of operation to which we have previously limited our discussion. However, organizations can fall into the categories represented by cells 1 and 3 though they probably would cluster rather close to the center of the figure.

The same kind of analysis can be used for people-changing organizations. . . .

Technology and Structure

What, then, does technology have to do with the *structure* of the organization? The answer has already been strongly hinted at in the discussion of nonbureaucratic and bureaucratic structures. But now it is possible to be a little more specific. We must assume here that, in the interest of efficiency, organizations wittingly or unwittingly attempt to maximize the congruence between their technology and their structure. Many which fail to make such a match should be more or less bureaucratically organized than they are. But let us assume that they have all studied the sociology of complex organizations and have adapted their structures to fit their technology. What would the four types of firms look like?

There are many, many ways to conceptualize structure. For our purposes here let me choose the following variables: the discretion of subgroups; their power; the basis of coordination within a group; and the interdependence of groups. For the moment, let us also deal only with production, although these concepts are equally applicable to marketing and perhaps even to the research aspects of organizations. If we single out middle and lower management we can make some predictions about the organization of each group and the relationship between them. Middle management here will, in general, mean the people who are concerned with the administration of production; we will call this the technical level. Lower management is concerned with the supervision of production.

Figure 10.2 suggests some of the structural characteristics of the four types of firms. In the nonroutine type of firm—characterized by unanalyzable search procedures and the need to deal with many exceptions—both discretion and power are high in both groups; in both, coordination is through feedback (mutual adjustment) rather than through advance planning (programmed), and finally, the interdependence of the groups is high. What this means is that the supervisors of production work closely with the technical people in the administration of production since the latter cannot call the shots for the former on the basis of routine information sent upstairs. Indeed, job descriptions may be such that it is difficult to distinguish the supervisory level from the technical level. Both groups are free to define situations as best they can. Therefore, both have considerable power with respect to such matters as resources and organizational strategies.

	Discretion	Power	Coordination Within Groups	Interdependence of Groups	Discretion	Power	Coordination Within Groups	Interdependence of Groups
Technical	Low	Low	Plan		High	High	Feed	
				Low				High
Supervision	High	High	Feed		High	High	Feed	
			Decentralized				Flexible, polycentralized	
				1	**2**			
				4	**3**			
Technical	Low	High	Plan		High	High	Feed	
				Low				Low
Supervision	Low	Low	Plan		Low	Low	Plan	
			Formal, centralized				Flexible, centralized	

Figure 10.2   Task Structure—Task-Related Interaction

This model resembles what others have called the organic as opposed to the mechanistic structure, or the professional or collegial as opposed to the bureaucratic structure. This type of structure is probably efficient only for highly nonroutine organizations. There are few of these, even though they are quite visible and attractive to social scientists who see in them reflections of their academic institutions and values.

Most firms fit into the quite routine cell. It is in their interest to fall in this category because it means greater control over processes and much more certainty of outlook (we are ignoring market situations). In routine firms, the discretion allowed to both supervisors of production and administrators of production is minimal—there is little ambiguity in these situations. The power of the technical middle-management level, however, is high, for it controls the supervisory level on the basis of routine reports. In both cases coordination within the levels comes through planning (giving further power to the technical level) because events can be foreseen. Interdependence between the two groups is likely to be low. This arrangement approaches the bureaucratic model. Where it is appropriate, it is undoubtedly the most efficient.

In the engineering model—characterized by analyzable problems with many exceptions—the technical-level functions more like the nonroutine firm. There is great discretion in choosing among programs and considerable power, and coordination is achieved through the feedback of information for problem solving. But on the shop floor, discretion and power are—should be—minimal. Planning is the basis of coordination here, and there is little interdependence between the two levels—designs are sent down and executed. In the craftsman model—characterized by unanalyzable problems and a few exceptions—it is the supervisory level which has discretion and high power and coordinates through feedback. The technical level is weak, responds to the supervisors of production, and needs little discretion and little power. Coordination is on the basis of planning in the technical level. Interdependence of the two levels can be low.

To become even bolder in our speculation, Figure 10.3 may be revised to include two more unusual types of industrial organizations—the research and development firm or unit, which would be very nonroutine, and the continuous processing industry, such as oil or chemicals, or, to some extent, beer and other beverages, which would be very routine. Other examples of craft and engineering firms can also be added. (See Figure 10.3.)

The elliptical character of the model suggests that it is somewhat unusual to find organizations at the extreme of the axis represented by the dotted line. Still, examples do exist on that continuum. The distinction is not simply between routine and nonroutine or between bureaucratic and nonbureaucratic, as represented by the broken line. . . .

We have gone into this particular theory in such detail in order to suggest at least one way of conceptualizing differences among organizations and to show that these differences indicate different kinds of strategies, none of which are either good or bad in themselves. As noted, most social scientists consider the nonbureaucratic, or

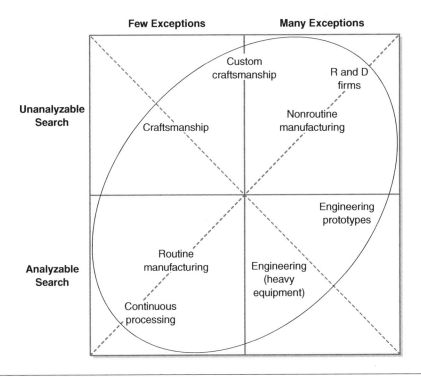

Figure 10.3   Examples of More Unusual Types of Organizations

nonroutine, organization to be good and the bureaucratic or routine organization to be bad (it impedes progress, is old-fashioned, is hard on its employees, etc.). But this judgment is debatable. One of the purposes of the R and D firm, or the non-routine organization, is to generate ways of routinizing production and building better bureaucratic controls into organizations. Furthermore, for routine work, the bureaucratic structure may be both the most efficient and the most humane. Not all people prefer the hectic, open-ended, and uncertain character of nonroutine tasks, not even top management.

In addition, this little exercise in speculation suggests a way of looking at problems in organizational structure. For example, going back to Figure 10.1, to simplify matters, if an organization in cell 1 (craft) hires an engineer at the middle-management level who is used to working in an organization in cell 3 (engineering), and if he tries through the use of discretion and personal power to coordinate the work in his unit by means of on-the-spot feedback, he is likely to be in for trouble. In this type of firm, many production problems have no analyzable solution. An engineer cannot dictate the solution of such problems nor can he exercise a high degree of discretion in helping or controlling staff members at the supervisory level. Furthermore, because problems vary very little and exceptional occasions seldom occur, he will find that he must do a great deal more advance planning within the technical group in order to support the supervisory level. He cannot expect supervisors to coordinate their own activities primarily through advance planning because of the unanalyzable nature of the problems which do occur.

Or, suppose that a successful production supervisor from a firm in cell 4 (routine) is moved to a position in a different division of the company where the work is more characteristic of cell 2 activities (nonroutine). Such a supervisor might find it quite difficult to become accustomed to exercising a high degree of discretion and power within this supervisory level. He might also be unable to adjust to coordination achieved through on-the-spot discussion when he has been used to coordination by means of fairly routine advance planning.

However, these examples relate to the problems of individuals. A more striking instance might be a case involving the recommendations of a management consultant firm which is accustomed to dealing with organizations within cell 4 (routine). Should the consultants try to apply their customary solutions to an organization in one of the other cells, they well might fail. (The Hoover Commission, charged with reorganizing much of the federal government, consistently made this error.) Similarly, a management-training program designed to increase the independence and autonomy of managers and the interdependence of groups could be quite successful in cell 2 (nonroutine), but be a waste of time in cell 4. To cite a final example: We have noted that organizations may attempt to move into cell 4 by reducing the number of exceptions that may occur, by decreasing the variability of raw materials, and by finding analyzable ways of solving their problems. However, this victory may be short-lived. If the market suddenly changes, or the technology changes, such an organization may find itself back in cells 3, 2, or 1. It would be well to be prepared to change the organizational structure when such events occur.

More important than the specific examples or recommendations, however, is the perspective illustrated here. This view holds that organizations are not all alike and that the way in which they may vary is in terms of their technology. Two aspects of technology exceptions and search are abstracted and analyzed independently and concurrently. Whether or not the scheme just presented is verified by empirical research, and whether or not it proves to have predictive value, matters less than this: Before an organization's problems can be solved, it is essential to determine the nature of the organization. Once the determination is made, some administrative and management proverbs may apply very well but others may be irrelevant or even invalid.

The Woodward Model

[As Woodward concluded] it appeared that firms with similar production systems had similar organizational structures—despite the variety of products involved. . . .

The critical function is different for each type of organization. Unit firms tend to be dominated by engineering personnel; mass-production firms by production people; process firms by marketers. Similarly, the relationships between these groups, the amounts and kinds of stresses, the difficulties of integration and cooperation vary in rather complex ways in each type. But the most important conclusion is that there is no evidence to prove that sales, production, or development is most important in all organizations. The importance of a function depends upon the specific technology employed.

With a comparative perspective like this, which shows that there is no "one best way" of doing things in all organizations, many well-accepted and even commonplace generalizations are challenged. Instead of applying to all or most cases, such generalizations hold true only for specific types, as we have just seen in terms of the importance of sales or production. . . .

Only when we begin to look at the differences between organizations and to categorize them in some meaningful way, such as by technology (though there are undoubtedly other ways), can we begin selectively to apply the multitude of insights offered by organizational analysis.

CHAPTER 11

Henry Mintzberg, *The Structuring of Organizations**

Janice H. Zahrly

Elements of the Basic Organization Structures

The variables in Mintzberg's organization structure model are the various parts of the organization, mechanisms to coordinate the diverse tasks, and design parameters. The design parameters are used by the organization to establish formal and informal relationships.

Coordinating Mechanisms

Mintzberg defines the organization structure as the sum total of the way in which it divides its labor into distinct tasks and then achieves coordination among them. Coordination is the basic element of structure, that which holds an organization together. There are five coordinating mechanisms.

Direct supervision results when one individual has the responsibility for the work of others and gives them direct orders which coordinate their work. The quarterback on a football team, for example, engages in direct supervision when he gives direct orders by calling the plays.

Standardization of work processes occurs when the content of the work, the actual process, is specified or programmed. Typically, assembly lines have most

*From *The Structuring of Organizations* (1st ed.) (pp. 20, 286, 307, 325, 355, 393, 443), by H. Mintzberg, 1979, Upper Saddle River, NJ: Pearson. Reprinted by permission of Pearson Education, Inc.

work processes specified, leaving the operator with little discretion in performance of the task.

Standardization of outputs is the coordinating mechanism whereby the results of the work (e.g., the dimensions of the product or the performance) are specified. A craftperson may be told to make picture frames of a particular size but is not given instructions about how to make them or a plant supervisor is told to reduce costs by 10 percent but it is not told how; only the desired outcomes are specified.

Standardization of skills is the coordinating mechanism when the type of training required in order to perform the work is specified. Individuals learn how to coordinate before they perform the task. The surgeon and anesthesiologist know what to expect of each other as a result of their training and socialization. They, therefore, spend little time communicating with each other about who will do what before or during an operation.

Mutual adjustment occurs when two or more people communicate informally to accomplish a task. This type of coordination occurs in very simple situations such as two people in a canoe, or in organizations such as a small shop where the owners are also operators. Mutual adjustment may also occur in the most complicated, dynamic organizations such as NASA, where highly skilled people design and build complex machines and equipment.

When the various coordinating mechanisms are placed on a task complexity continuum as in Figure 11.1, mutual adjustment is at each end of the continuum. Direct supervision is near mutual adjustment on the least complex end, followed by standardization of work, standardization of output, and standardization of skills. Skill standardization is near mutual adjustment on the most complex end of the continuum, with standardization of the work process and output near the center.

Parts of the Organization

The simplest organization has almost no division of labor and relies on mutual adjustment to coordinate the work procedures that lead to a product or service. However, as the organization grows, there are needs for formal coordinators (i.e., managers), an administrative hierarchy, analysts to plan and manage the standardization, and support staffs. There are five distinct parts of the organization, each with a particular function (see Figure 11.2).

Task Complexity

Low					High
Mutual adjustment	Direct supervision	Standardization of work processes	Standardization of output	Standardization of skills	Mutual adjustment

Coordinating Mechanisms

Figure 11.1   Task Complexity/Coordinating Mechanisms

The **operating core** of an organization is composed of operators who perform the basic work directly related to the production of goods and services. It is that part of the organization which produces essential outputs to keep the organization alive. The operating core has several functions: to secure inputs, to transform inputs to outputs, to distribute outputs, and to provide direct support for the input, output, and transformation processes. The professor is part of the operating core in a university as is the machine operator who stamps out aluminum can tops in the factory. Standardization of any type (work process, output, or skill) is the usual means of coordination in the operating core.

The **strategic apex** is at the top of the organization. It is "charged with ensuring that the organization serve its mission in an effective way, and also that it serve the needs of those people who control or otherwise have power over the organization (such as owners, government agencies, unions of the employees, pressure groups)." Functions of the strategic apex include direct supervision, management of the organization's relations with the environment, and development of organization strategy.

Strategy formulation is the most important role of this part of the organization. Strategy formulation is the determination of how the organization can and must deal with the environment. Work activities in the strategic apex are characterized by long decision cycles, little routine and standardization, and the members have much discretion. Mutual adjustment is the major coordinating mechanism at this level.

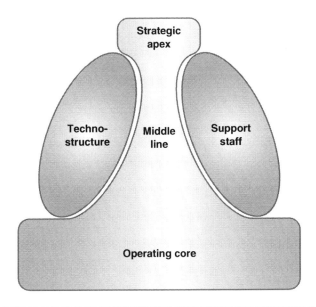

Figure 11.2   The Five Parts of the Organization

SOURCE: From *The Structuring of Organizations* (1st ed.), by H. Mintzberg, 1979, Upper Saddle River, NJ: Pearson. Reprinted by permission of Pearson Education, Inc.

The **middle line** is the formal authority chain which joins the strategic apex to the operating core. Direct supervision is the usual coordinating mechanism in this segment. The functions of this part of the organization, in addition to direct supervision, are feedback (including upward communication of information), management of boundary conditions for the environment relevant to the individual units, and other managerial duties, which are part of supervising a particular unit (e.g., figurehead, liaison role, and allocator of resources).

The middle line managers' job can vary dramatically, depending on where the manager is in the chain of authority. At lower levels of the organization and administration, tasks are detailed and elaborate, less abstract, and more focused on work flow. The work is more structured as it approaches the operating core. When these positions are near the strategic apex they are more abstract and have less structure.

As the organization becomes larger, it relies more on all types of standardization as a means of becoming more efficient. The **technostructure** is composed of control analysts who seek to increase standardization. There are three types of control analysts: The work study analyst (such as an industrial engineer) standardizes work processes; the planning and control analyst (such as the accountant) standardizes outputs; the personnel analyst (such as a recruiter or trainer) standardizes skills. The control analysts, who coordinate their work by mutual adjustment, influence the work of others by designing or changing work procedures, planning work flows, [and] training employees for certain tasks. Control analysts do not actually produce the outputs that keep the organization alive in the marketplace. They perform a support function. The technostructure is effective if it makes the work of other parts of the organization more effective.

The function of the technostructure varies according to the organization level with which it operates. For the operating core, control analysts might standardize the operating work flow or the quality control system. The intellectual work of the middle level might be standardized by training middle managers. At the strategic apex, the control analysts might develop strategic planning models or financial systems which control the individual units.

Finally, the **support staff** exists to provide support to various organization units outside the operating work flow. Examples of support staff are company cafeterias, legal services, and public relations departments. The support staff does not directly produce the product or service, but makes it easier for other units to do so. The support systems are often self-contained (i.e., a miniorganization) and are found at all levels of the organization. Although they use a variety of coordinating mechanisms most support units, because they are highly specialized and rely on professional people, coordinate by means of skill standardization.

Design Parameters

In order to establish stable patterns of behavior, organizations use formal and semiformal methods, called design parameters, to differentiate and coordinate work activities. Their particular configurations establish the structure of each organization. There are nine design parameters that are grouped into four categories. The choice and configuration of design parameters determine the structure of the organization.

The **design of positions** is the first category of decisions concerning the organization structure. Job positions are designed by *job specialization, behavior formalization, and training and indoctrination.*

Job specialization reflects the division of labor (the number of tasks assigned to a worker) and the worker's control over the assigned tasks. A job may be horizontally specialized or vertically specialized. In horizontal specialization the worker has a few narrowly defined tasks. In vertical specialization, work performance is separated from the administration, giving the worker little or no control over the task. Job enlargement increases the number of tasks performed (i.e., worker control).

Managerial jobs tend to be less specialized than most other jobs. Unskilled jobs are usually highly specialized, both vertically and horizontally. Complex jobs which are specialized horizontally but not vertically are called professional jobs.

Another way to design positions is through *behavior formalization.* Behavior is regulated by the standardization of work content. This regulation will result in formalization of the job (where behavioral specifications of the job are listed), formalization of the work flow (such as imposition of operating instructions), or formalization by rules and regulations. Bureaucratic organizations rely primarily on standardization. Organic organizations have little standardization. Behavior formalization is most common in the operating core, making it bureaucratic. The strategic apex tends to have an organic structure. As work progresses down the hierarchy, it usually becomes more formalized. Organizations use behavior formalization to reduce variability of performance. This means that it is easier to more accurately predict and to control behaviors.

A third method of designing positions is through *training and indoctrination.* Training occurs when job-related skills and knowledge are taught. Indoctrination, or socialization, is the process of acquiring organizational norms. Training is a major design parameter for the operating core, the technostructure, and for staff units. However, indoctrination is the major approach at the strategic apex and middle line portions of the organization.

Training and behavior formalization are often substitutable. Both seek to control, organize, and promote standard behavior. While the technostructure within the organization designs the work activities of the unskilled employee, outside institutions often direct the behavior of the professional. The professional learns norms as well as skills while in educational institutions, which are controlled by other professionals. By the time the professional gets to the work organization most of his behaviors are set.

The **design of the superstructure** is the second category of design parameters which fashion the structure of an organization. Included in this category are decisions about *unit grouping* and *unit size.*

Unit grouping is the basic means of clustering positions to coordinate work. It establishes a system of common supervision among positions and units, requires the sharing of common resources, creates common measures of performance, and encourages mutual adjustment. But unit grouping also creates the problem of coordination among units. When significant interdependencies among units occur, such as sequential or reciprocal interdependencies, coordination becomes costly.

Units can be grouped on the bases of knowledge, output, client, and work process, but the fundamental grouping bases are function and product. Functional grouping is concerned with the work process and scale interdependencies. This occurs when some unit autonomy is sacrificed to obtain economies of scale, such as the installation of a company data processing system that processes all records in a central location. This method of grouping lacks a built-in mechanism to coordinate the work flow. This approach tends to be bureaucratic.

Unit grouping by product is more flexible, less bureaucratic, has fewer economies of scale, and is less efficient. There is a concern for work flow coordination at the expense of process specialization. Functional grouping is more common at the lower levels of the organization, particularly in the operating core, while unit grouping by product occurs more often at higher levels. Support staff and analysts will usually be in functional units.

The second consideration when designing the superstructure (i.e., the structure of the entire organization) is the *unit size*, or the number of positions contained in a single unit. In general, the larger the unit size, the greater the use of standardization for coordination. Conversely, the greater the reliance on mutual adjustment as a coordinating mechanism, the smaller the size of the work unit. The work unit can be quite large if there are no sequential or reciprocal interdependencies. In most organizations, the operating core will have the largest units. Staff units may be large or small. Unskilled staff such as cafeteria workers will be large units and operate in a bureaucratic manner. Skilled staff will be professional and will be grouped into small units which tend to be organic.

The redesign of the superstructure can come from two directions. First, if the organization's goals and missions change, structural redesign is initiated from the top downward. Second, if the technical system of the operating core changes, the redesign proceeds from the bottom up.

The **design of lateral linkages** is the third design parameter. Organizations are able to influence their structures by designing specific coordinating procedures for lateral relationships. The design of these linkages is accomplished by *planning and control systems* and *liaison devices.*

The purpose of *planning and control systems* is to standardize outputs. Action planning specifies the desired results of specific activities, such as the particular dimensions of holes to be drilled. Action planning occurs before the activity is undertaken. Work-flow interdependencies often require action planning.

Performance control systems regulate the overall results of a given unit; for example, such a system may seek a 10 percent increase in sales for the total organization. Performance control systems are used with pooled interdependencies. They specify the desired results of many activities after the fact. That is, activities are not specified. Only final objectives are detailed.

Another way to design lateral linkages is to use *liaison devices.* Liaison positions may be created in the formal structure, such as the design engineer who moves between the development lab and the preproduction engineering group. Temporary task forces and permanent standing committees may be part of the formal structure. Integrating managers (such as brand, project, or program managers) bring together representatives from many functional areas.

The matrix organization structure is an example of the most complex liaison device. While a dual authority structure is created, the matrix organization has proven most effective in coordinating complex interdependencies and in responding rapidly to uncertainty in the environment.

Liaison devices encourage informality and more organic structures. In general, the more liaison devices, the smaller the unit. When work is horizontally specialized, complex, and highly interdependent, liaison devices are necessary. They are best suited for work at the middle levels of the organization. Liaison devices are rarely found in the operating core. The exception is found where professionals make up the operating core, as in the university. The strategic apex does not often use liaison devices.

The **design of the decision-making system**, or *vertical and horizontal decentralization,* is the last category of design parameters. A centralized system gives the decision-making power to one or a few persons near the top of the organization. Decentralization disperses authority to make decisions among many organization members at lower levels.

The organization decentralizes because the underlying factors of decisions cannot be understood by one person or even a small group. Decentralization allows a quick response to relevant environmental conditions. On the other hand, centralization places all decision-making activities (e.g., information gathering, determining alternatives, analyzing the information, etc.) into one person or unit. In general, centralization will often lead to higher efficiency but may also contribute to lower morale since organization members may feel they no longer control their work lives.

Vertical decentralization is the delegation of decision making down the chain of authority. When decision-making power shifts laterally to nonmanagers, this is called horizontal decentralization. Vertical decentralization may be selective (for specific decisions or groups of decisions) or parallel, such as a market-based organization that is divided into divisions. Each division may vertically decentralize to differing degrees. Horizontal decentralization may shift the decision-making authority to a single person in a particular organization position, to analysts (who standardize), to experts (who have the technical expertise), or to the members.

Centralization may be related to other design parameters. Behavior formalization often exists when there is centralization. Training and indoctrination lead to decentralization. Liaison devices are used in decentralized organizations; planning and control systems are preferred in centralized organizations.

Contingency Factors

Situational or contingency factors are viewed as independent variables, influenced by mediating variables such as the predictability or diversity of work. The structural variables, or design parameters, are the dependent variables in this model. Mintzberg hypothesizes that "effective structuring requires a consistency among the design parameters and contingency factors." Significant contingency factors that influence structure are age, size of the organization, the technical production system, environment, and the organization's power system.

Age and Size

The organization's age and size affect behavior formalization and the administrative structure at the middle level. The size of an organization often changes incrementally, but the transition is seldom smooth. It is often disruptive. The first stage of organization development usually is a craft or entrepreneurial organization: small, informal, and organic with owners as both operators and managers. In the next stage, ownership is separated from management, bureaucracy begins to occur, and standardization emerges. If organizations move beyond the bureaucratic stage, they become divisionalized, that is, with several functional bureaucracies. Each of these functional bureaucracies has an operating core to serve a unique market. The final developmental stage is a matrix organization with grouping by two or more bases (such as function, product, geography, client, etc.) and a return to a more organic structure.

In general, there is more formalized behavior in older organizations. Organization structures often reflect the age of the industry. Job specialization and the use of professionals in staff positions are related inversely to the age of the industry. For example, farming (an old industry) has little job specialization and few staff positions, and few professionals to fill them. On the other hand, aerospace is a young industry, NASA has high job specialization and many staff positions filled with professionals.

Larger organizations will tend to have more elaborate structures (more specializations, more differentiation, etc.), larger work units, and more formalized behavior. As organizations grow, the proportion of line managers decreases and the proportion of staff specialists increases.

The Technical System

The organization's technical system is the second contingency factor that will influence structure. It is closely associated with the operating core. The technical system is composed of the collective instruments used by operators to complete their work. Two dimensions of this system are the degree of regulation (the influence of the technical system on the operators) and the degree of sophistication (complexity).

The regulation imposed by the technical system is the extent to which the operator's work is controlled by the instruments or machinery which he or she uses. The surgeon's use of a scalpel is an example of the case where the "instrument" imposes only a minimal amount of regulation. On the other hand, the machinery in an oil refinery exerts a high degree of regulation, and extensively controls the operator's work. Technical system sophistication determines the difficulty of understanding the work process. Flying a giant modern aircraft requires more complex cognitive processes than does baking a cake.

In general, if the technical system is highly regulated, the work processes will be more formalized, and the structure of the operating core will be more bureaucratic. As the technical system becomes more sophisticated (more complex), the administrative structure becomes more elaborate, there is more selective decentralization to the staff, and more liaison devices are used. However, if the operating core is automated, there is little need for rules and procedures (formalization). The administrative structure may be organic and the operators and first line supervisors are specialists.

The Environment

A third contingency factor is the organization's external environment. This is more important at the strategic apex where strategies and policies are established. Relevant environmental dimensions are the degree of stability, degree of complexity, market diversity, and degree of hostility toward the organization.

As the environment becomes more dynamic, the structure becomes more organic. Extreme hostility in the environment drives the administration to temporarily centralize control, whereas disparities in the environment lead the organization to decentralize selectively to various differentiated work groups. If the organization's markets are diversified, there is a propensity to divisionalize, or split the organization into market-based units.

The more complex the environment, the greater the need for decentralization. The relationship between environmental complexity and stability suggests four types of structures, shown in Figure 11.3.

Power

The final contingency factor includes external control, personal power needs, and the style of power that is fashionable. The more an organization is controlled

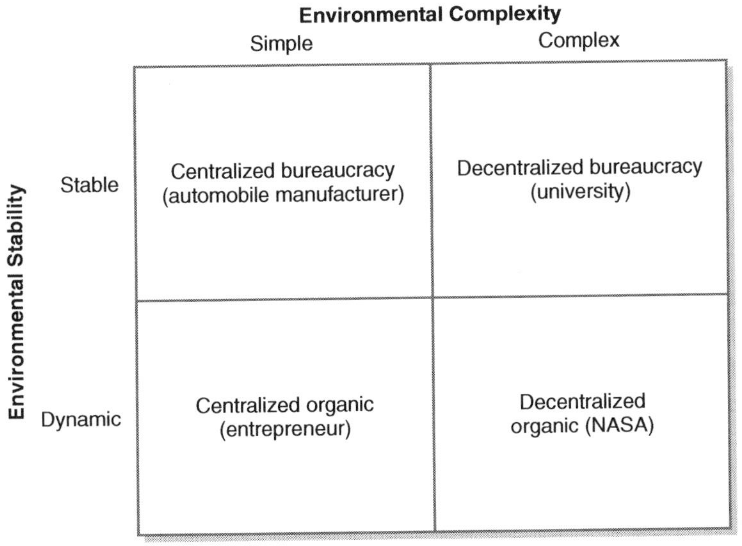

Figure 11.3   Environmental Complexity and Stability

SOURCE: *The Structuring of Organizations* (1st ed.), by H. Mintzberg, 1979, Upper Saddle River, NJ: Pearson. Reprinted by permission of Pearson Education, Inc.

externally, the more its structure will be centralized and bureaucratic. If the CEO is held accountable by external decision makers, he or she will tend to centralize in order to control more carefully. Also, because the organization must justify its actions to outsiders, there will be greater behavior formalization.

Excessive individual power needs in top executives will lead to unwarranted centralization. Moreover, the organization structure preferred by those with power is often adopted—even if it is inappropriate for the particular organizational circumstances.

Structural Configurations

Relating the organization elements (coordinating mechanisms, parts of the organization, and the design parameters) with the contingency factors, five natural clusters or configurations of organization structure emerge. That is, certain types of coordination are used more often with certain levels of decentralization, and certain parts of the organization have more strength when particular lateral linkages are used, etc. The five basic structures are (1) the simple structure, (2) machine bureaucracy, (3) professional bureaucracy, (4) divisionalized form, and (5) adhocracy.

The Simple Structure

The simple structure is illustrated in Figure 11.4. The strategic apex is the most important organizational part in the simple structure. Little or no technostructure and support staff exist. The managerial hierarchy is small. There is almost no division of labor and minimal differentiation occurs between units. Most coordination is a result of direct supervision and decision making is highly centralized. Formal planning, training, and liaison devices are unnecessary. The organization is organic with flexible work flow and decision-making processes. The entrepreneurial firm is an example of the simple structure.

Simple, dynamic environments are conducive to simple structures. Simple structures tend to be small. A simple structure often describes the formative years of many organizations. Organizations may revert to a simple structure in times of crisis. Leaders in the simple structure are often autocratic or charismatic.

There are several important facets of the simple structure. The strategic apex is usually involved in both production and strategy. While this allows rapid reaction to any change, the entrepreneur/owner/manager is the center of the firm and all relevant knowledge rests in one person. This structure has high risk in that it is dependent on one person or, at best, only a few persons. Furthermore, the decision maker (i.e., the owner) may not recognize the need for growth, for staff, for technical expertise, and so forth.

Technical systems are, in general, nonsophisticated and nonregulating. A major advantage of this structure is that it is easy to transmit a sense of mission to those in the organization. The owner and employees know the goals of the firm and work

Figure 11.4   The Simple Structure

SOURCE: From *The Structuring of Organizations* (1st ed.), by H. Mintzberg, 1979, Upper Saddle River, NJ: Pearson. Reprinted by permission of Pearson Education, Inc.

toward them. This structure also allows a great deal of flexibility that is not present in other organization structures.

The Machine Bureaucracy

The machine bureaucracy, shown in Figure 11.5, is a performance organization, not a problem-solving one. Production is the goal, not problem solving. There are always specific tasks leading to a particular performance. The operating core is characterized by standardization of work processes, formalized behavior, and narrow, specialized jobs. The administrative hierarchy (the middle line) is tall and fairly narrow. Because of the standardization of work, the technostructure is the dominant part of the organization. The support staff is also large and has much informal power. Line and staff are sharply differentiated in that there is a clear division between them.

Rules and regulations permeate the organization. Formal authority structures and formal communication systems exist and are fully utilized. There is an inflexibility and an obsession with control. In an attempt to remove uncertainty, the operating core is often sealed off from external influences. The support staff increases in an attempt to remove all uncertainty. This structure inherently promotes conflict, because of the line-staff division, the specialized narrow work which is routine, and the extreme division of labor.

Even though the technostructure is dominant, the strategic apex also maintains great power. Strategy tends to be transmitted from the top down with a heavy emphasis on action planning. Decision making is vertically centralized with selective horizontal decentralization to the technostructure. The strategic apex delegates some power to parts of the technostructure when appropriate. There is only a small administrative component because many rules and regulations control the organization.

The machine bureaucracy operates in large, mature organizations. The environment is simple and stable and the technical systems are regulating. This structure is typified by mass-production firms, often with much external control. This external control may be exercised by owners (i.e., stockholders) as in industrial firms or by a government agency as the nature of control over veterans' hospitals. While the

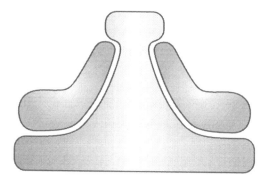

Figure 11.5   The Machine Bureaucracy

SOURCE: From *The Structuring of Organizations* (1st ed.), by H. Mintzberg, 1979, Upper Saddle River, NJ: Pearson. Reprinted by permission of Pearson Education, Inc.

machine bureaucracy is a dominant structure today, it is not a fashionable or popular design. However, it is an indispensable configuration, particularly in a society that demands mass-produced goods where full automation is not yet possible or reasonable.

The machine bureaucracy is the most effective structure for mass production because it is the most efficient system for the performance of routine tasks. Because of a propensity to treat workers as machines, coordination is difficult. Only vertical communication is allowed, which can lead to an abuse of power (e.g., the supervisor who insists on controlling all communication). This will certainly lead to centralization. It also often leads to information overload on the part of supervisors and managers. The strategic apex is overburdened with superfluous data and incomplete or old information which is often used as the basis for significant decisions.

The Professional Bureaucracy

The operating core of the professional bureaucracy (see Figure 11.6) is made up of professionals and is the most significant component in this structure. Tasks are specialized horizontally. The professionals have much control over their work and they often work closely with clients. This is very different from the machine bureaucracy where the work processes are routine and which attracts unskilled or semi-skilled workers.

Coordination is accomplished by standardization of skills. Such standardization occurs after much training and indoctrination. Professionals are extensively trained by institutions other than the employing organization. Therefore, standards are usually set by the professions, outside the organization. This is in contrast to the machine bureaucracy where the technostructure sets work standards.

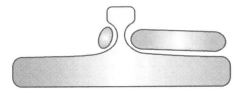

Figure 11.6   The Professional Bureaucracy

SOURCE: From *The Structuring of Organizations* (1st ed.), by H. Mintzberg, 1979, Upper Saddle River, NJ: Pearson. Reprinted by permission of Pearson Education, Inc.

The professional bureaucracy is, however, bureaucratic in nature. There are many rules and regulations, authority is based on expertise, and organizational tenure is pervasive.

The operating core is large and there is a large support staff to support that operating core. The middle line and technostructure are small, as is the strategic apex.

Horizontal and vertical decentralization characterize this structure. The tasks performed by the professional are too complex to be directly supervised or standardized. The diagnosis of the situation is a fundamental task in the professional bureaucracy and that requires the operator (i.e., the professional) to be well versed in relevant areas. Since the professional has expertise, he or she derives some power from this expertise and the professional's services are often in great demand. Because of expert power, the professional is allowed high autonomy. He or she may be subject to little outside control but is subject to the censure of colleagues should the professional behave in an inappropriate manner.

The administrative hierarchy is made up of professionals, often serving at the pleasure of the professional operators. The organization is very democratic. Information and decisions tend to flow from the bottom up. The professional administrator is both a negotiator, handling disturbances within the organization, and a boundary spanner, interacting with external people and organizations. Strategies are often formulated by individuals within the system, professional associations, or external entities with control, such as the board which controls state university systems.

The environment is the most significant contingency factor for the professional bureaucracy. A stable and complex environment leads to standardized skills. This structure has no typical age or size. The technical system (i.e., the system of instruments used to apply knowledge) is not highly regulated or complex. However, the technology (i.e., the knowledge base) is sophisticated but not regulated. Power rests with the operator.

Issues unique to the professional bureaucracy are based on the professional as an operator. No other structure claims democracy for its workers. The operators have more autonomy than in any other type of organization. Unfortunately, because there is little outside control, professionals can be quite unproductive, yet often keep their positions and salaries. The professional often ignores problems and, in so doing, ignores the needs of both clients and the organization. Conflict is rampant between the support staff and the operator/professionals. Professionals are often unable to deal with incompetent and unconscientious colleagues, leaving the client or organization to bear the brunt of the unprofessional behavior. Professional bureaucracies are inflexible structures. They are not suited to innovation and can be very inefficient by retaining old policies or procedures that are no longer useful.

The Divisionalized Form

The divisionalized form, shown in Figure 11.7, is a structure that is superimposed on several division structures, with each division being driven toward a machine bureaucracy. Market grouping is the usual basis for the divisionalization. Usually the separate divisions have duplicate operating functions. The divisions are quasi-autonomous and loosely coupled to the superstructure, which permits limited vertical decentralization to division managers. However, divisions may be quite centralized within themselves. This structure is often a result of mergers and consolidations.

Performance control systems, which focus on outputs and standards, are the predominant control devices. In turn, the primary coordinating mechanism is standardization of outputs. The middle line (i.e., the division managers) is the critical part of this organization. Division managers have great power and often have standardized skills. In essence, they are chief executive officers for their divisions.

The sharp division of labor between the strategic apex (headquarters) and the divisions occurs because the divisions control operations and determine the strategies for specific markets. However, headquarters manages the overall strategy and resources, designs the performance control system, and monitors divisional performance while remaining small relative to the divisional units. The technostructure and support staff are small while the operating core is very large, since it is composed of the actual divisions.

Market diversity leads to divisionalization, but this structural form is only possible when the organization's technical system can be segmented, with each division controlling a different segment. The divisionalized structure tends to be in older, larger organizations. The environment is similar to that of a machine

Figure 11.7   The Divisionalized Form

SOURCE: From *The Structuring of Organizations* (1st ed.), by H. Mintzberg, 1979, Upper Saddle River, NJ: Pearson. Reprinted by permission of Pearson Education, Inc.

bureaucracy—stable, simple with horizontal diversification. However, hybrid structures tend to develop when the environment is dynamic or complex. Hybrids also develop when coordinating mechanisms other than standardization of output exist. These hybrid structures take parts of the five pure structures and must be classified in terms of their unique characteristics, rather than as one of the five aggregate structural forms.

The divisionalized form is most effective in the private sector. It seems to be ill suited for the nonbusiness sector since it operates best with machine bureaucracy divisions and it needs quantifiable goals with the performance control system.

There are several unique aspects of the divisionalized form. Economic advantages of divisionalization are that it encourages efficient allocation of capital within the division, trains general managers as they move through the divisions, diversifies risk, and is strategically responsive to the market. These can be disadvantages if they are abused, however. Headquarters managers have a tendency to usurp divisional powers, to centralize, and to design stronger performance control systems. In turn, the quantitative nature of the control system can drive the firm to act in socially unresponsive or irresponsible ways. This concentration of power in headquarters can lead to anticompetitiveness and is the basis for the tendency to move toward machine bureaucracy.

The divisionalized form has the narrowest range of any of the structures in that it is only applicable in limited circumstances. It can occur in any environment but tends to move toward the simple, stable environment. The economic advantages occur only because of fundamental inefficiencies in the capital markets, the finished goods markets, and stockholder control systems. This structure is perhaps the "ideal type," one that is approached but never reached. It is positioned to adapt rapidly to environmental changes, yet has the superstructure for support.

The Adhocracy

The most complex structure, and the one most appropriate for organization innovation, is the adhocracy (see Figure 11.8). It is an organic structure with little formalization of behavior, highly trained specialists, and multidisciplinary project teams or matrix teams with functional and market grouping. The many managers (project, functional, integrating, etc.) coordinate by mutual adjustment using several liaison devices. The managers themselves occupy liaison roles much of the time. It is difficult for one person to become powerful in this dynamic organizational environment. There is selective decentralization, both horizontal and vertical.

There are two types of adhocracies, differing as a function of the ultimate consumer: the operating adhocracy and the administrative adhocracy. The operating adhocracy innovates and solves problems directly on behalf of its clients. Examples are the creative advertising agency or the design engineering firm which makes prototypes for clients. Output of an operating adhocracy is similar to output from a professional bureaucracy. In actuality, there is a professional bureaucracy that corresponds to each operating adhocracy. Both organizations produce the same product, but use different structures. For example, an experimental theater company is an adhocracy while the permanent theater company, which works to improve or perfect its standard fare, is a professional bureaucracy. Yet both provide theatrical entertainment. The area above the dotted line in Figure 11.8 is an operating adhocracy.

The administrative adhocracy differs from the operating adhocracy in that it engages in project work on its own behalf. There is a sharp distinction between the administrative and operating components, which is shown as the complete figure in Figure 11.8. The administration is organic but the operations (1) are carried out by a separate part of the organization, (2) are contracted out, or (3) are automated. Magazine production is an excellent example of the administrative adhocracy. While the creation of the copy, the marketing, and the strategy are highly dynamic, the actual printing of the magazine is routine, and usually delegated to a machine bureaucracy.

The support staff is the most significant part of the adhocracy, but it does not stand alone as a separate organization element. All parts of the organization blend together. The line-staff distinction is blurred, and the strategic apex tends to blend with the middle line and the operating core. Strategy and planning tend to be dynamic and continuous.

Environments conducive to the use of adhocracies are dynamic and complex. These allow organic, relatively decentralized operations. Frequent product changes drive the firm toward adhocracy. Many hybrid adhocracies exist, particularly with multinational interdependent organizations. The adhocracy is fashionable, perhaps because it is so suited for innovative work.

Adhocracies tend to be young and are the least stable structure of the five configurations. The operating adhocracy is particularly prone to a short life in that lack of success will cause the firm to disappear, but success breeds stability and bureaucracy.

The administrative adhocracy has a tendency to grow large while the operating adhocracy is often small or midsize. The technical systems are different—the operating adhocracy has a simple, nonregulating system while the technical system for the administrative adhocracy is sophisticated and often automated.

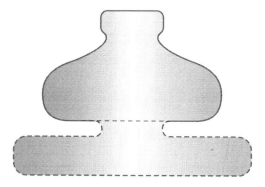

Figure 11.8   The Adhocracy

SOURCE: From *The Structuring of Organizations* (1st ed.), by H. Mintzberg, 1979, Upper Saddle River, NJ: Pearson. Reprinted by permission of Pearson Education, Inc.

Power goes to the experts but is not concentrated in one area. Adhocracy is unique in that it is the most political structure of the five forms. Task ambiguity, high expert power, and matrix formats combine to institutionalize conflict, leading to the many managers and coordination by mutual adjustment. This structure is inefficient, loses economies of scale, and sacrifices the advantages of specialization. The high cost of communication and integration make the structure prohibitive in some situations. Adhocracy is best suited for performing complex, ill-structured programs.

Concluding Overview

An organization is driven toward one of the configurations based on the contingency factors and the strength of the organizational parts. The strategic apex moves toward direct supervision and centralization. Standardized work processes are urged by the technostructure while standardized skills are promoted by operators. The middle managers want to have autonomy to manage their individual units and have standard outputs. The pull by the support staff, and by operators in the operating adhocracy, is for collaboration and mutual adjustment. Each structure is unique in that different parts of the organization are strong, different design parameters are significant, and different contingency factors are important. Table 11.1 indicates how the several factors differ among the various structures.

Hybrid structures emerge when the organization responds to more than one force at the same time. This is reflected in one of two ways. Either the structure adopted will be a mixture of two configurations or different units in the organization will have different structures. Organizations usually begin with a simple structure or an operating adhocracy and make transitions to other forms based on the design parameters and contingency factors. Structural transitions often lag behind the new conditions that evoke them. There is no one best structure. There are only structures that are internally consistent and in harmony with the contingency factors.

Table 11.1 Dimensions of the Five Configurations

	Simple Structure	Machine Bureaucracy	Professional Bureaucracy	Divisionalized Form	Adhocracy
Key coordinating mechanism	Direct Supervision	Standardization of work	Standardization of skills	Standardization of outputs	Mutual adjustment
Key part of organization	Strategic apex	Technostructure	Operating core	Middle line	Support staff (with operating core in operating adhocracy)
DESIGN PARAMETERS					
Specialization of jobs	Little specialization	*Much horizontal and vertical specialization*	*Much horizontal specialization*	Some horizontal and vertical specialization (between divisions and HQ)	*Much horizontal specialization*
Training and indoctrination	Little training and indoctrination	Little training and indoctrination	*Much training and indoctrination*	Some training and indoctrination (of division managers)	Much training
Formalization of behavior Bureaucratic/organic	Little formalization *Organic*	*Much formalization Bureaucratic*	Little formalization *Bureaucratic*	Much information (within divisions Bureaucratic)	Little formalization *Organic*
Grouping	Usually functional	*Usually functional*	Functional and market	*Market*	*Functional and market*
Unit size	Wide	Wide at bottom, narrow elsewhere	Wide at bottom, narrow elsewhere	Wide (at top)	*Narrow throughout*
Planning and control systems	Little planning and control	Action planning	Little planning and control	*Much performance control*	Limited action planning (esp. in administrative adhocracy)
Liaison devices	Few liaison devices	Few liaison devices	Liaison devices in administration	Few liaison devices	*Many liaison devices throughout*
Decentralization	*Centralization*	*Limited horizontal decentralization*	*Horizontal and vertical decentralization*	*Limited vertical decentralization*	*Selective decentralization*

Table 11.1 (Continued)

	Simple Structure	Machine Bureaucracy	Professional Bureaucracy	Divisionalized Form	Adhocracy
CONTINGENCY FACTORS					
Age and size	Typically young and small	Typically old and large	Varies	Typically old and very large	Typically young (operating adhocracy)
Technical system	Simple, not regulating	Regulating but not automated, not very complex	Not regulating or complex	Divisible, otherwise typically like machine bureaucracy	Very complex, often automated (in administrative adhocracy), not regulating or complex (in operating adhocracy)
Environment	Simple and dynamic; sometimes hostile	Simple and stable	Complex and stable	Relatively simple and stable; diversified markets (especially products and services)	Complex and dynamic; sometimes disparate (in administrative adhocracy)
Power	Chief executive control, often owner-managed, not fashionable	Technocratic and external control; not fashionable	Professional operator control; fashionable	Middle line control; fashionable (especially in industry)	Expert control; very fashionable

SOURCE: From "Configurations of Organization Structure," by H. Mintzberg, in *Making Organizations Humane and Productive*, by H. Meltzer and W. Nord, 1981, New York: Wiley. Reprinted by permission of the publisher.

CHAPTER 12

Agency Theory

An Assessment and Review*

Kathleen Eisenhardt

Agency theory has been used by scholars in accounting (e.g., Demski & Feltham, 1978), economics (e.g., Spence & Zeckhauser, 1971), finance (e.g., Fama, 1980), marketing (e.g., Basu, Lal, Srinivasan, & Staelin, 1985), political science (e.g., Mitnick, 1986), organizational behavior (e.g., Eisenhardt, 1985, 1988; Kosnik, 1987), and sociology (e.g., Eccles, 1985; White, 1985). Yet, it is still surrounded by controversy. Its proponents argue that a revolution is at hand and that "the foundation for a powerful theory of organizations is being put into place" (Jensen, 1983, p. 324). Its detractors call it trivial, dehumanizing, and even "dangerous" (Perrow, 1986, p. 235).

Which is it: grand theory or great sham? The purposes of this paper are to describe agency theory and indicate ways in which researchers can use its insights. The paper is organized around four questions that are germane to organizational research. The first asks the deceptively simple question, What is agency theory? Often, the technical style, mathematics, and tautological reasoning of the agency literature can obscure the theory. Moreover, the agency literature is split into two camps (Jensen, 1983), leading to differences in interpretation. For example, Barney and Ouchi (1986) argued that agency theory emphasizes how capital markets can affect the firm, whereas other authors made no reference to capital markets at all (Anderson, 1985; Demski & Feltham, 1978; Eccles, 1985; Eisenhardt, 1985).

---

*From "Agency Theory: An Assessment and Review," by K. Eisenhardt, 1989, *Academy of Management Review, 14*, pp. 57–74.

The second question is, What does agency theory contribute to organizational theory? Proponents such as Ross (1973, p. 134) argued that "examples of agency are universal." Yet other scholars such as Perrow (1986) claimed that agency theory addresses no clear problems, and Hirsch and Friedman (1986) called it excessively narrow, focusing only on stock price. For economists long accustomed to treating the organization as a "black box" in the theory of the firm, agency theory may be revolutionary. Yet, for organizational scholars the worth of agency theory is not so obvious.

The third question is, Is agency theory empirically valid? The power of the empirical research on agency theory to explain organizational phenomena is important to assess, particularly in light of the criticism that agency theory is "hardly subject to empirical test since it rarely tries to explain actual events" (Perrow, 1986, p. 224). Perrow (1986) also criticized the theory for being unrealistically one-sided because of its neglect of potential exploitation of workers.

The final question is, What topics and contexts are fruitful for organizational researchers who use agency theory? Identifying how useful agency theory can be to organizational scholars requires understanding the situations in which the agency perspective can provide theoretical leverage.

The principal contributions of the paper are to present testable propositions, identify contributions of the theory to organizational thinking, and evaluate the extant empirical literature. The overall conclusion is that agency theory is a useful addition to organizational theory. The agency theory ideas on risk, outcome uncertainty, incentives, and information systems are novel contributions to organizational thinking, and the empirical evidence is supportive of the theory, particularly when coupled with complementary theoretical perspectives.

Origins of Agency Theory

During the 1960s and early 1970s, economists explored risk sharing among individuals or groups (e.g., Arrow, 1971; Wilson, 1968). This literature described the risk-sharing problem as one that arises when cooperating parties have different attitudes toward risk. Agency theory broadened this risk-sharing literature to include the so-called agency problem that occurs when cooperating parties have different goals and division of labor (Jensen & Meckling, 1976; Ross, 1973). Specifically, agency theory is directed at the ubiquitous agency relationship, in which one party (the principal) delegates work to another (the agent), who performs that work. Agency theory attempts to describe this relationship using the metaphor of a contract (Jensen & Meckling, 1976).

Agency theory is concerned with resolving two problems that can occur in agency relationships. The first is the *agency problem* that arises when (a) the desires or goals of the principal and agent conflict and (b) it is difficult or expensive for the principal to verify what the agent is actually doing. The problem here is that the principal cannot verify that the agent has behaved appropriately. The second is the *problem of risk sharing* that arises when the principal and agent have different

Table 12.1   Agency Theory Overview

Key idea	Principal-agent relationships should reflect efficient organization of information and risk-bearing costs
Unit of analysis	Contract between principal and agent
Human assumptions	Self-interest
	Bounded rationality
	Risk aversion
Organizational assumptions	Partial goal conflict among participants
	Efficiency as the effectiveness criterion
	Information asymmetry between principal and agent
Information assumption	Information as a purchasable commodity
Contracting problems	Agency (moral hazard and adverse selection)
	Risk sharing
Problem domain	Relationships in which the principal and agent have partly differing goals and risk preferences (e.g., compensation, regulation, leadership, impression management, whistle-blowing, vertical integration, transfer pricing)

attitudes toward risk. The problem here is that the principal and the agent may prefer different actions because of the different risk preferences.

Because the unit of analysis is the contract governing the relationship between the principal and the agent, the focus of the theory is on determining the most efficient contract governing the principal-agent relationship given assumptions about people (e.g., self-interest, bounded rationality, risk aversion), organizations (e.g., goal conflict among members), and information (e.g., information is a commodity which can be purchased). Specifically, the question becomes, Is a behavior-oriented contract (e.g., salaries, hierarchical governance) more efficient than an outcome-oriented contract (e.g., commissions, stock options, transfer of property rights, market governance)? An overview of agency theory is given in Table 12.1.

The agency structure is applicable in a variety of settings, ranging from macrolevel issues such as regulatory policy to microlevel dyad phenomena such as blame, impression management, lying, and other expressions of self-interest. Most frequently, agency theory has been applied to organizational phenomena such as compensation (e.g., Conlon & Parks, 1988; Eisenhardt, 1985), acquisition and diversification strategies (e.g., Amihud & Lev, 1981), board relationships (e.g., Fama & Jensen, 1983; Kosnik, 1987), ownership and financing structures (e.g., Argawal & Mandelker, 1987; Jensen & Meckling, 1976), vertical integration (Anderson, 1985; Eccles, 1985), and innovation (Bolton, 1988; Zenger, 1988). Overall, the domain of agency theory is relationships that mirror the basic agency structure of a principal and an agent who are engaged in cooperative behavior, but have differing goals and differing attitudes toward risk.

Agency Theory

From its roots in information economics, agency theory has developed along two lines: positivist and principal-agent (Jensen, 1983). The two streams share a common unit of analysis: the contract between the principal and the agent. They also share common assumptions about people, organizations, and information. However, they differ in their mathematical rigor, dependent variable, and style.

Positivist Agency Theory

Positivist researchers have focused on identifying situations in which the principal and agent are likely to have conflicting goals and then describing the governance mechanisms that limit the agent's self-serving behavior. Positivist research is less mathematical than principal-agent research. Also, positivist researchers have focused almost exclusively on the special case of the principal-agent relationship between owners and managers of large, public corporations (Berle & Means, 1932).

Three articles have been particularly influential. Jensen and Meckling (1976) explored the ownership structure of the corporation, including how equity ownership by managers aligns managers' interests with those of owners. Fama (1980) discussed the role of efficient capital and labor markets as information mechanisms that are used to control the self-serving behavior of top executives. Fama and Jensen (1983) described the role of the board of directors as an information system that the stockholders within large corporations could use to monitor the opportunism of top executives. Jensen and his colleagues (Jensen, 1984; Jensen & Roeback, 1983) extended these ideas to controversial practices, such as golden parachutes and corporate raiding.

From a theoretical perspective, the positivist stream has been most concerned with describing the governance mechanisms that solve the agency problem. Jensen (1983, p. 326) described this interest as "why certain contractual relations arise." Two propositions capture the governance mechanisms which are identified in the positivist stream. One proposition is that outcome-based contracts are effective in curbing agent opportunism. The argument is that such contracts coalign the preferences of agents with those of the principal because the rewards for both depend on the same actions, and, therefore, the conflicts of self-interest between principal and agent are reduced. For example, Jensen and Meckling (1976) described how increasing the firm ownership of the managers decreases managerial opportunism. In formal terms,

> *Proposition 1: When the contract between the principal and agent is outcome based, the agent is more likely to behave in the interests of the principal.*

The second proposition is that information systems also curb agent opportunism. The argument here is that, since information systems inform the principal about what the agent is actually doing, they are likely to curb agent opportunism because the agent will realize that he or she cannot deceive the principal. For example, Fama (1980) described the information effects of efficient capital and labor markets on managerial opportunism, and Fama and Jensen (1983) described the information role that boards of directors play in controlling managerial behavior. In formal terms,

> *Proposition 2: When the principal has information to verify agent behavior, the agent is more likely to behave in the interests of the principal.*

At its best, positivist agency theory can be regarded as enriching economics by offering a more complex view of organizations (Jensen, 1983). However, it has been criticized by organizational theorists as minimalist (Hirsch, Michaels, & Friedman, 1987; Perrow, 1986) and by microeconomists as tautological and lacking rigor (Jensen, 1983). Nonetheless, positivist agency theory has ignited considerable research (Barney & Ouchi, 1986) and popular interest ("Meet Mike," 1988).

Principal-Agent Research

Principal-agent researchers are concerned with a general theory of the principal-agent relationship, a theory that can be applied to employer-employee, lawyer-client, buyer-supplier, and other agency relationships (Harris & Raviv, 1978). Characteristic of formal theory, the principal-agent paradigm involves careful specification of assumptions, which are followed by logical deduction and mathematical proof.

In comparison with the positivist stream, principal-agent theory is abstract and mathematical and, therefore, less accessible to organizational scholars. Indeed, the most vocal critics of the theory (Perrow, 1986; Hirsch et al., 1987) have focused their attacks primarily on the more widely known positivist stream. Also, the principal-agent stream has a broader focus and greater interest in general, theoretical implications. In contrast, the positivist writers have focused almost exclusively on the special case of the owner/CEO relationship in the large corporation. Finally, principal-agent research includes many more testable implications.

For organizational scholars, these differences provide background for understanding criticism of the theory. However, they are not crucial. Rather, the important point is that the two streams are complementary: Positivist theory identifies various contract alternatives, and principal-agent theory indicates which contract is the most efficient under varying levels of outcome uncertainty, risk aversion, information, and other variables described below.

The focus of the principal-agent literature is on determining the optimal contract, behavior versus outcome, between the principal and the agent. The simple model assumes goal conflict between principal and agent, an easily measured outcome, and an agent who is more risk averse than the principal. (Note: The argument behind a more risk averse agent is that agents, who are unable to diversify their employment, should be risk averse, and principals, who are capable of diversifying their investments, should be risk neutral.) The approach of the simple model can be described in terms of cases (e.g., Demski & Feltham, 1978). The first case, a simple case of complete information, is when the principal knows what the agent has done. Given that the principal is buying the agent's behavior, then a contract that is based on behavior is most efficient. An outcome-based contract would needlessly transfer risk to the agent, who is assumed to be more risk averse than the principal.

The second case is when the principal does not know exactly what the agent has done. Given the self-interest of the agent, the agent may or may not have behaved as agreed. The agency problem arises because (a) the principal and the agent have different goals and (b) the principal cannot determine if the agent has behaved appropriately. In the formal literature, two aspects of the agency problem are cited. *Moral hazard* refers to lack of effort on the part of the agent. The argument here is that the agent may simply not put forth the agreed-upon effort. That is, the agent is shirking. For example, moral hazard occurs when a research scientist works on a personal research project on company time, but the research is so complex that corporate management cannot detect what the scientist is actually doing. *Adverse selection* refers to the misrepresentation of ability by the agent. The argument here is that the agent may claim to have certain skills or abilities when he or she is hired. Adverse selection arises because the principal cannot completely verify these skills or abilities either at the time of hiring or while the agent is working. For example, adverse selection occurs when a research scientist claims to have experience in a scientific specialty and the employer cannot judge whether this is the case.

In the case of unobservable behavior (due to moral hazard or adverse selection), the principal has two options. One is to discover the agent's behavior by investing in information systems such as budgeting systems, reporting procedures, boards of directors, and additional layers of management. Such investments reveal the agent's behavior to the principal, and the situation reverts to the complete information case. In formal terms,

> *Proposition 3: Information systems are positively related to behavior-based contracts and negatively related to outcome-based contracts.*

The other option is to contract on the outcomes of the agent's behavior. Such an outcome-based contract motivates behavior by coalignment of the agent's preferences with those of the principal, but at the price of transferring risk to the agent. The issue of risk arises because outcomes are only partly a function of behaviors. Government policies, economic climate, competitor actions, technological change, and so on, may cause uncontrollable variations in outcomes. The resulting outcome uncertainty introduces not only the inability to preplan, but also risk that must be borne by someone. When outcome uncertainty is low, the costs of shifting risk to the agent are low and outcome-based contracts are attractive. However, as uncertainty increases, it becomes increasingly expensive to shift risk despite the motivational benefits of outcome-based contracts. In formal terms,

> *Proposition 4: Outcome uncertainty is positively related to behavior-based contracts and negatively related to outcome-based contracts*

This simple agency model has been described in varying ways by many authors (e.g., Demski & Feltham, 1978; Harris & Raviv, 1979; Holmstrom, 1979; Shavell, 1979). However, the heart of principal-agent theory is the trade-off between (a) the cost of measuring behavior and (b) the cost of measuring outcomes and transferring risk to the agent.

A number of extensions to this simple model are possible. One is to relax the assumption of a risk-averse agent (e.g., Harris & Raviv, 1979). Research (MacCrimmon & Wehrung, 1986) indicates that individuals vary widely in their risk attitudes. As the agent becomes increasingly less risk averse (e.g., a wealthy agent), it becomes more attractive to pass risk to the agent using an outcome-based contract. Conversely, as the agent becomes more risk averse, it is increasingly expensive to pass risk to the agent. In formal terms,

> *Proposition 5: The risk aversion of the agent is positively related to behavior-based contracts and negatively related to outcome-based contracts.*

Similarly, as the principal becomes more risk averse, it is increasingly attractive to pass risk to the agent. In formal terms,

> *Proposition 6: The risk aversion of the principal is negatively related to behavior-based contracts and positively related to outcome-based contracts.*

Another extension is to relax the assumption of goal conflict between the principal and agent (e.g., Demski, 1980). This might occur either in a highly socialized or clan-oriented firm (Ouchi, 1979) or in situations in which self-interest gives way to selfless behavior (Perrow, 1986). If there is no goal conflict, the agent will behave as the principal would like, regardless of whether his or her behavior is monitored. As goal conflict decreases, there is a decreasing motivational imperative for outcome-based contracting, and the issue reduces to risk-sharing considerations. Under the assumption of a risk-averse agent, behavior-based contracts become more attractive. In formal terms,

> *Proposition 7: The goal conflict between principal and agent is negatively related to behavior-based contracts and positively related to outcome-based contracts.*

Another set of extensions relates to the task performed by the agent. For example, the programmability of the task is likely to influence the ease of measuring behavior (Eisenhardt, 1985, 1988). *Programmability* is defined as the degree to which appropriate behavior by the agent can be specified in advance. For example, the job of a retail sales cashier is much more programmed than that of a high-technology entrepreneur. The argument is that the behavior of agents engaged in more programmed jobs is easier to observe and evaluate. Therefore, the more programmed the task, the more attractive are behavior-based contracts because information about the agent's behavior is more readily determined. Very programmed tasks readily reveal agent behavior, and the situation reverts to the complete information case. Thus, retail sales clerks are more likely to be paid via behavior-based contracting (e.g., hourly wages), whereas entrepreneurs are more likely to be compensated with outcome-based contracts (e.g., stock ownership). In formal terms,

Proposition 8: Task programmability is positively related to behavior-based contracts and negatively related to outcome-based contracts.

Another task characteristic is the measurability of the outcome (Anderson, 1985; Eisenhardt, 1985). The simple model assumes that outcomes are easily measured. However, some tasks require a long time to complete, involve joint or team effort, or produce soft outcomes. In these circumstances, outcomes are either difficult to measure or difficult to measure within a practical amount of time. When outcomes are measured with difficulty, outcome-based contracts are less attractive. In contrast, when outcomes are readily measured, outcome-based contracts are more attractive. In formal terms,

Proposition 9: Outcome measurability is negatively related to behavior-based contracts and positively related to outcome-based contracts.

Finally, it seems reasonable that when principals and agents engage in a long-term relationship, it is likely that the principal will learn about the agent (e.g., Lambert, 1983) and so will be able to assess behavior more readily. Conversely, in short-term agency relationships, the information asymmetry between principal and agent is likely to be greater, thus making outcome-based contracts more attractive. In formal terms,

Proposition 10: The length of the agency relationship is positively related to behavior-based contracts and negatively related to outcome-based contracts.

Agency Theory and the Organizational Literature

Despite Perrow's (1986) assertion that agency theory is very different from organization theory, agency theory has several links to mainstream organization perspectives (see Table 12.2). At its roots, agency theory is consistent with the classic works of Barnard (1938) on the nature of cooperative behavior and March and Simon (1958) on the inducements and contributions of the employment relationship. As in this earlier work, the heart of agency theory is the goal conflict inherent when individuals with differing preferences engage in cooperative effort, and the essential metaphor is that of the contract.

Agency theory is also similar to political models of organizations. Both agency and political perspectives assume the pursuit of self-interest at the individual level and goal conflict at the organizational level (e.g., March, 1962; Pfeffer, 1981). Also, in both perspectives, information asymmetry is linked to the power of lower order

Table 12.2   Comparison of Agency Theory Assumptions and Organizational
Perspective

| | Perspective | | | | |
| | Political | Contingency | Organization Control | Transaction Cost | Agency |
Assumption					
Self-interest	X			X	X
Goal conflict	X			X	X
Bounded rationality		X	X	X	X
Information asymmetry		X		X	X
Preeminence of efficiency		X	X	X	X
Risk aversion					X
Information as a commodity					X

participants (e.g., Pettigrew, 1973). The difference is that in political models goal conflicts are resolved through bargaining, negotiation, and coalitions—the power mechanism of political science. In agency theory they are resolved through the coalignment of incentives—the price mechanism of economics.

Agency theory also is similar to the information processing approaches to contingency theory (Chandler, 1962; Galbraith, 1973; Lawrence & Lorsch, 1967). Both perspectives are information theories. They assume that individuals are boundedly rational and that information is distributed asymmetrically throughout the organization. They also are efficiency theories; that is, they use efficient processing of information as a criterion for choosing among various organizing forms (Galbraith, 1973). The difference between the two is their focus: In contingency theory researchers are concerned with the optimal structuring of reporting relationships and decision-making responsibilities (e.g., Galbraith, 1973; Lawrence & Lorsch, 1967), whereas in agency theory they are concerned with the optimal structuring of control relationships resulting from these reporting and decision-making patterns. For example, using contingency theory we would be concerned with whether a firm is organized in a divisional or matrix structure. Using agency theory, we would be concerned with whether managers within the chosen structure are compensated by performance incentives.

The most obvious tie is with the organizational control literature (e.g., Dornbusch & Scott, 1974). For example, Thompson's (1967) and later Ouchi's (1979) linking of known means/ends relationships and crystallized goals to behavior versus outcome control is very similar to agency theory's linking task programmability and measurability of outcomes to contract form (Eisenhardt, 1985). That is, known means/ends relationships (task programmability) lead to behavior control, and crystallized goals (measurable outcomes) lead to outcome control. Similarly, Ouchi's (1979) extension of Thompson's (1967) framework to include clan control is similar to assuming low goal conflict (Proposition 7) in agency theory. Clan control implies goal congruence between people and, therefore, the reduced need to monitor behavior or outcomes. Motivation issues disappear. The major differences between agency theory and the organizational control literature are the risk implications of principal and agent risk aversion and outcome uncertainty (Propositions 4, 5, 6).

Not surprisingly, agency theory has similarities with the transaction cost perspective (Williamson, 1975). As noted by Barney and Ouchi (1986), the theories share assumptions of self-interest and bounded rationality. They also have similar dependent variables; that is, hierarchies roughly correspond to behavior-based contracts, and markets correspond to outcome-based contracts. However, the two theories arise from different traditions in economics (Spence, 1975): In transaction cost theorizing we are concerned with organizational boundaries, whereas in agency theorizing the contract between cooperating parties, regardless of boundary, is highlighted. However, the most important difference is that each theory includes unique independent variables. In transaction cost theory these are asset specificity and small numbers bargaining. In agency theory there are the risk attitudes of the principal and agent, outcome uncertainty, and information systems. Thus, the two theories share a parentage in economics, but each has its own focus and several unique independent variables.

Contributions of Agency Theory

Agency theory reestablishes the importance of incentives and self-interest in organizational thinking (Perrow, 1986). Agency theory reminds us that much of organizational life, whether we like it or not, is based on self-interest. Agency theory also emphasizes the importance of a common problem structure across research topics. As Barney and Ouchi (1986) described it, organization research has become increasingly topic, rather than theory, centered. Agency theory reminds us that common problem structures do exist across research domains. Therefore, results from one research area (e.g., vertical integration) may be germane to others with a common problem structure (e.g., compensation).

Agency theory also makes two specific contributions to organizational thinking. The first is the treatment of information. In agency theory, information is regarded as a commodity. It has a cost, and it can be purchased. This gives an important role to formal information systems, such as budgeting, MBO, and boards of directors, and informal ones, such as managerial supervision, which is unique in organizational research. The implication is that organizations can invest in information systems in order to control agent opportunism.

An illustration of this is executive compensation. A number of authors in this literature have expressed surprise at the lack of performance-based executive compensation (e.g., Pearce, Stevenson, & Perry, 1985; Ungson & Steers, 1984). However, from an agency perspective, it is not surprising since such compensation should be contingent upon a variety of factors including information systems. Specifically, richer information systems control managerial opportunism and, therefore, lead to less performance-contingent pay.

One particularly relevant information system for monitoring executive behaviors is the board of directors. From an agency perspective, boards can be used as monitoring devices for shareholder interests (Fama & Jensen, 1983). When boards provide richer information, compensation is less likely to be based on firm performance. Rather, because the behaviors of top executives are better known, compensation based on knowledge of executive behaviors is more likely. Executives would then be rewarded for taking well-conceived actions (e.g., high risk/high potential R&D) whose outcomes may be unsuccessful. Also, when boards provide richer information, top executives are more likely to engage in behaviors that are consistent with stockholders' interests. For example, from an agency viewpoint, behaviors such as using greenmail and golden parachutes, which tend to benefit the manager more than the stockholders, are less likely when boards are better monitors of stockholders' interests. Operationally, the richness of board information can be measured in terms of characteristics such as frequency of board meetings, number of board subcommittees, number of board members with long tenure, number of board members with managerial and industry experience, and number of board members representing specific ownership groups.

A second contribution of agency theory is its risk implications. Organizations are assumed to have uncertain futures. The future may bring prosperity, bankruptcy, or some intermediate outcome, and that future is only partly controlled by organization members. Environmental effects such as government regulation, emergence of new competitors, and technical innovation can affect outcomes. Agency theory extends organizational thinking by pushing the ramifications of outcome uncertainty to their implications for creating risk. Uncertainty is viewed in terms of risk/reward trade-offs, not just in terms of inability to preplan. The implication is that outcome uncertainty coupled with differences in willingness to accept risk should influence contracts between principal and agent.

Vertical integration provides an illustration. For example, Walker and Weber (1984) found that technological and demand uncertainty did not affect the "make or buy" decision for components in a large automobile manufacturer (principal in this case). The authors were unable to explain their results using a transaction cost framework. However, their results are consistent with agency thinking if the managers of the automobile firm are risk neutral (a reasonable assumption given the size of the automobile firm relative to the importance of any single component). According to agency theory, we would predict that such a risk-neutral principal is relatively uninfluenced by outcome uncertainty, which was Walker and Weber's result.

Conversely, according to agency theory, the reverse prediction is true for a new venture. In this case, the firm is small and new, and it has limited resources available to it for weathering uncertainty: The likelihood of failure looms large. In this case, the managers of the venture may be risk-averse principals. If so, according to agency theory we would predict that such managers will be very sensitive to outcome uncertainty. In particular, the managers would be more likely to choose the "buy" option, thereby transferring risk to the supplying firm. Overall, agency theory predicts that risk-neutral managers are likely to choose the "make" option (behavior-based contract), whereas risk-averse executives are likely to choose "buy" (outcome-based contract).

Results of [Research in] the Positivist Stream

In the positivist stream, the common approach is to identify a policy or behavior in which stockholder and management interests diverge and then to demonstrate that information systems or outcome-based incentives solve the agency problem. That is, these mechanisms coalign managerial behaviors with owner preferences. Consistent with the positivist tradition, most of these studies concern the separation of ownership from management in large corporations, and they use secondary source data that are available for large firms.

One of the earliest studies of this type was conducted by Amihud and Lev (1981). These researchers explored why firms engage in conglomerate mergers. In general, conglomerate mergers are not in the interests of the stockholders because, typically, stockholders can diversify directly through their stock portfolio. In contrast, conglomerate mergers may be attractive to managers who have fewer avenues available to diversify their own risk. Hence, conglomerate mergers are an arena in which owner and manager interests diverge. Specifically, these authors linked merger and diversification behaviors to whether the firm was owner controlled (i.e., had a major stockholder) or manager controlled (i.e., had no major stockholder). Consistent with agency theory arguments (Jensen & Meckling, 1976), manager-controlled firms engaged in significantly more conglomerate (but not more related) acquisitions and were more diversified.

Along the same lines, Walking and Long (1984) studied managers' resistance to takeover bids. Their sample included 105 large U.S. corporations that were targets of takeover attempts between 1972 and 1977. In general, resistance to takeover bids is not in the stockholders' interests, but it may be in the interests of managers because they can lose their jobs during a takeover. Consistent with agency theory (Jensen & Meckling, 1976), the authors found that managers who have substantial equity positions within their firms (outcome-based contracts) were less likely to resist takeover bids.

The effects of market discipline on agency relationships were examined in Wolfson's (1985) study of the relationship between the limited (principals) and general (agent) partners in oil and gas tax shelter programs. In this study, both tax and agency effects were combined in order to assess why the limited partnership governance form survived in this setting despite extensive information advantages and divergent incentives for the limited partner. Consistent with agency arguments (Fama, 1980), Wolfson found that long-run reputation effects of the market coaligned the short-run behaviors of the general partner with the limited partners' welfare.

Kosnik (1987) examined another information mechanism for managerial opportunism, the board of directors. Kosnik studied 110 large U.S. corporations that were greenmail targets between 1979 and 1983. Using both hegemony and agency theories, she related board characteristics to whether greenmail was actually paid (paying greenmail is considered not in the stockholders' interests). As predicted by agency theory (Fama & Jensen, 1983), boards of companies that resisted greenmail had a higher proportion of outside directors and a higher proportion of outside director executives.

In a similar vein, Argawal and Mandelker (1987) examined whether executive holdings of firm securities reduced agency problems between stockholders and management. Specifically, they studied the relationship between stock and stock option holdings of executives and whether acquisition and financing decisions were made consistent with the interests of stockholders. In general, managers prefer lower risk acquisitions and lower debt financing (see Argawal & Mandelker, 1987, for a review). Their sample included 209 firms that participated in acquisitions and divestitures between 1974 and 1982. Consistent with agency ideas (e.g., Jensen & Meckling, 1976), executive security holdings (outcome-based contract) were related to acquisition and financing decisions that were more consistent with stockholder interest. That is, executive stock holdings appeared to coalign managerial preferences with those of stockholders.

Singh and Harianto (1989) studied golden parachutes in a matched sample of 84 Fortune 500 firms. Their study included variables from both agency and managerialist perspectives. Consistent with agency theory (Jensen & Meckling, 1976; Fama & Jensen, 1983), the authors found that golden parachutes are used to coalign executive interests with those of stockholders in takeover situations, and they are seen as an alternative outcome-based contract to executive stock ownership. Specifically, the authors found that golden parachutes were positively associated with a higher probability of a takeover attempt and negatively associated with executive stock holdings.

Finally, Barney (1988) explored whether employee stock ownership reduces a firm's cost of equity capital. Consistent with agency theory (Jensen & Meckling, 1976), Barney argued that employee stock ownership (outcome-based contract) would coalign the interests of employees with stockholders. Using efficient capital market assumptions, he further argued that this coalignment would be reflected in the market through a lower cost of equity. Although Barney did not directly test the agency argument, the results are consistent with an agency view.

In summary, there is support for the existence of agency problems between shareholders and top executives across situations in which their interests diverge—that is, takeover attempts, debt versus equity financing, acquisitions, and divestitures, and for the mitigation of agency problems (a) through outcome-based contracts such as golden parachutes (Singh & Harianto, 1989) and executive stock holdings (Argawal & Mandelker, 1987; Walking & Long, 1984) and (b) through information systems such as boards (Kosnik, 1987) and efficient markets (Barney, 1988; Wolfson, 1985). Overall, these studies support the positivist propositions described earlier. Similarly, laboratory studies by DeJong and colleagues (1985), which are not reviewed here, are also supportive.

Results of [Research on] the Principal-Agent Stream

The principal-agent stream is more directly focused on the contract between the principal and the agent. Whereas the positivist stream lays the foundation (that is, that agency problems exist and that various contract alternatives are available), the principal-agent stream indicates the most efficient contract alternative in a given situation. The common approach in these studies is to use a subset of agency variables such as task programmability, information systems, and outcome uncertainty to predict whether the contract is behavior- or outcome-based. The underlying assumption is that principals and agents will choose the most efficient contract, although efficiency is not directly tested.

In one study, Anderson (1985) probed vertical integration using a transaction cost perspective with agency variables. Specifically, she examined the choice between a manufacturer's representative (outcome-based) and a corporate sales force (behavior-based) among a sample of electronics firms. The most powerful explanatory variable was from agency theory: the difficulty of measuring outcomes (measured by amount of nonselling tasks and joint team sales). Consistent with agency predictions, this variable was positively related to using a corporate sales force (behavior-based contract).

In other studies, Eisenhardt (1985, 1988) examined the choice between commission (outcome-based) and salary (behavior-based) compensation of salespeople in retailing. The original study (1985) included only agency variables, while a later study (1988) added additional agency variables and institutional theory predictions. The results supported agency theory predictions that task programmability, information systems (measured by the span of control), and outcome uncertainty variables (measured by number of competitors and failure rates) significantly predict the salary versus commission choice. Institutional variables were significant as well.

Conlon and Parks (1988) replicated and extended Eisenhardt's work in a laboratory setting. They used a multiperiod design to test both agency and institutional predictions. Consistent with agency theory (Harris & Raviv, 1978), they found that information systems (manipulated by whether or not the principal could monitor the agent's behavior) were negatively related to performance-contingent (outcome-based) pay. They also found support for the institutional predictions.

Finally, Eccles (1985) used agency theory to develop a framework for understanding transfer pricing. Using interviews with 150 executives in 13 large corporations, he developed a framework based on notions of agency and fairness to prescribe the conditions under which various sourcing and transfer pricing alternatives are both efficient and equitable. Prominent in his framework is the link between decentralization (arguably a measure of task programmability) and the choice between cost (behavior-based contract) and market (outcome-based contract) transfer pricing mechanisms.

In summary, there is support for the principal-agent hypotheses linking contract form with (a) information systems (Conlon & Parks, 1988; Eccles, 1985; Eisenhardt, 1985), (b) outcome uncertainty (Eisenhardt, 1985), (c) outcome measurability (Anderson, 1985; Eisenhardt, 1985), (d) time (Conlon & Parks, 1988), and (e) task programmability (Eccles, 1985; Eisenhardt, 1985). Moreover, this support rests on research using a variety of methods including questionnaires, secondary sources, laboratory experiments, and interviews.

Conclusion

This paper began with two extreme positions on agency theory—one arguing that agency theory is revolutionary and a powerful foundation (Jensen, 1983) and the other arguing that the theory addresses no clear problem, is narrow, lacks testable implications, and is dangerous (Perrow, 1986). A more valid perspective lies in the middle. Agency theory provides a unique, realistic, and empirically testable perspective on problems of cooperative effort. The intent of this paper is to clarify some of the confusion surrounding agency theory and to lead organizational scholars to use agency theory in their study of the broad range of principal-agent issues facing firms.

CHAPTER 13

Theory of
Managerial Capitalism

Henry L. Tosi

L ike agency theory, managerial capitalism also posits that managers will maximize their self-interest at the expense of owners: There is no "justification for assuming that those in control of a modern corporation will also choose to operate it in the interest of the owners" (Berle & Means, 1932, p. 121). The core of the managerialism argument is that managers have discretion and control of the firm because of the dispersion of stock ownership. Many of the possible constraints on managers are eliminated when ownership is so widely dispersed that the gain to any individual stockholder (through an increase in share value) is greatly offset by the cost of that action (Hindley, 1970). This allows managers the freedom to pursue their own interests of increased personal financial gain, increased power, working conditions above those required by competitive conditions, and job security or labor–leisure tradeoff, goals that diverge from the profitability goals of owners (Berle & Means, 1932; McEachern, 1975).

Executives in charge of the firm will prefer organizational growth as a primary firm goal, although they recognize the need to maintain a satisfactory level of profits to obtain capital to further increase sales and protect against unwanted acquisitions (Marris, 1964; Baumol, 1967). Growth serves several functions for managers who control the firm. First, salaries are far more closely correlated with firm size than firm profits, thereby reducing income risk (Baumol). Second, firm growth leads to increased power, salary, and status for managers (Marris). Lastly, growth helps ensure survival because larger firms are more insulated against environmental threats, thus providing increased job security for managers (Galbraith, 1967).

The Ownership Structure

Discretion, or the control of a firm, "lies in the hand of the individual or group who have the actual power to select the board of directors (or its majority), either by mobilizing the legal right to choose them—'controlling' a majority of the votes directly or through some legal device—or by exerting pressure which influences their choice" (Berle & Means, 1932, p. 69). The degree of managerial discretion is defined in terms of the ownership structure, which refers to the distribution of equity holdings. The most common approach is to differentiate between manager-controlled, owner-managed, and owner-controlled firms using an equity concentration measure, or the minimum percentage of stock held by the largest single non-management shareholder (Hunt, 1986). A firm is classified as *owner controlled* when there is a single non-management equity holder with at least a 5% stock holding. Firms are then called *manager controlled*, unless a member of management holds more than 5% of the outstanding equity. Then firms are called *owner managed*.

Support for Managerialism

There are numerous studies from accounting (e.g., Hunt, 1985), economics (e.g., McEachern, 1975), management, and sociology (e.g., Allen, 1981) that have shown self-serving managerial behaviors in management-controlled firms. For example, Grabowski and Mueller (1972) pitted a managerialism model against a pure stockholder welfare maximization model in dividend and investment decisions. They concluded that the managerial model was conceptually and statistically superior. In a study of merger decisions, Lewellen, Loderer, and Rosenfeld (1985) found that senior managers with large personal stockholdings in their firms were less likely to engage in acquisitions that reduce shareholder wealth than were managers with small stockholdings.

Other research shows how different, specific classes of top management decisions may transfer greater risks and higher agency costs to owners when managers control the firm:

1. Managers may choose accounting methods that state results in ways more favorable to them than to stockholders (Biddle, 1980; Biddle & Lindahl, 1982; Bowen, Noreen, & Lacey, 1981; Dyl, 1989; Groff & Wright, 1989; Hagerman & Zmijewski, 1979; Holthausen & Leftwich, 1983; Morse & Richardson, 1983; Sunder, 1973, 1975).

2. Managers may make investment decisions that are less optimal for owners but that minimize managerial downside risk (Coffee, 1988; Hill & Hansen, 1989; Hill, Hitt, & Hoskinsson, 1988; Morck, Schleifer, & Vishny, 1989; Walsh & Seward, 1990).

3. Managers may undertake acquisitions and mergers that transfer higher agency costs to owners (Amihud & Lev, 1981; Halpern, 1973, 1983; Herman & Lowenstein, 1988; Jarrell, Brickley, & Netter, 1988; Kroll, Simmons, & Wright, 1990; Magenheim & Mueller, 1988; Ramanujan & Varadarajan, 1989; Ravenscraft & Scherer, 1987; Roll, 1987).

4. Managers may use internal political strategies to block organizational control mechanisms intended to provide checks on managerial discretion (Alderfer, 1986; Coughlan & Schmidt, 1985; Fierman, 1990; Meyer & Rowan, 1977; Salancik & Pfeffer, 1980; Schleifer & Vishny, 1988; Williams, 1985).

5. Managers may use organization resources to insulate themselves from the disciplining effects of external markets (Angelo & Rice, 1983; Bradley & Wakeman, 1983; Dann & DeAngelo, 1983; Malatesta & Walking, 1988; Ryngaert, 1988).

CHAPTER 14

The Markets and Hierarchies Program of Research

Origins, Implications, Prospects[1]

Oliver Williamson

William Ouchi

[The field of organizational theory] is interdisciplinary to an unusual degree, and is incompletely informed by exclusive reliance on any single social science. We contend that organization theory is seriously underdeveloped with respect to its economic content, and argue that it needs greater appeal to economics, although economics of a nontraditional kind. Specifically, we suggest that organization theory in general and organizational design and assessment in particular need to be more sensitive to transaction costs and to the importance of economizing on those.

But economics and organization theory have a reciprocal relation (Ouchi and van de Ven, 1980). Economics stands to benefit by drawing upon organization theory. This applies both to the refurbishing of its behavioral assumptions, which tend to be stark and sometimes implausible, and to the level of analysis, which in economics tends to be rather aggregative. The Markets and Hierarchies (M&H) program of research is based precisely on such a strategy. Thus it draws on organization theory to enrich its behavioral assumptions, and it regards the transaction, rather than the firm or market, as the basic unit of analysis.[2] Joining these behavioral assumptions and microanalytic focus with the economizing concepts and systems orientation characteristic of economics yields new and deeper insights into economic and social organization. [Here we review] the origins and applications of the Markets and Hierarchies approach with special emphasis on its organization theory aspects [and develop its] ramifications for organizational design, and address research agenda issues of special interest to organization theory specialists.

Origins

It is rarely possible to do justice to earlier work on which subsequent research relies; nevertheless, the following brief statement indicates the origins and background of our research.

Where to begin is somewhat arbitrary, but one decisive contribution to the evolution of the M&H approach was the interdisciplinary program of research and teaching at Carnegie Tech (now Carnegie-Mellon) in the early 1960s. The central figures at Carnegie were Richard Cyert, James March, and Herbert Simon. Williamson was a student in the economics program at Carnegie during this period and was greatly influenced by the prevailing interdisciplinary research atmosphere. The strategy of using organization theory to inform economics in the study of firm and market structures is evident in his work on managerial discretion and in other early papers (see Williamson, 1964, 1965, 1967).

It was not until later that the possibility of accomplishing a genuine synthesis between economics[3] and organization theory became evident. Two papers were of special significance. The first of these was "The Vertical Integration of Production: Market Failure Considerations" (Williamson, 1971), which was an effort to assess the question of make-or-buy in a fully symmetrical way. Ronald Coase, in a remarkably insightful paper, had posed this issue in 1937 and recognized that transaction costs were central to its resolution. Coase observed that vertical integration permitted the firm to economize on the "cost of negotiating and concluding" many separate intermediate product market contracts by substituting a flexible employment agreement (Coase, 1952, p. 336). But because the factors that were responsible for differential transaction costs in the intermediate product market were not identified, the argument lacked testable implications. Why not use a flexible employment agreement to organize all transaction costs rather than just some? Until such a time as the transaction cost argument was able to explain the organization of transactions in a discriminating way, it remained rather tautological (Alchian and Demsetz, 1972). Coase's observation, some 35 years later, that his 1937 article was "much cited and little used" (Coase, 1972) is presumably explained by the failure to make the issues operational over that interval.

If, as Coase asserted, differential transaction costs were responsible for decisions to organize some activities one way and some another, a level of analysis that was sensitive to transaction cost differences was evidently needed. Williamson accomplished this by (1) making the transaction the basic unit of analysis, (2) expressly identifying alternative market and internal modes of "contracting," (3) identifying the critical dimensions with respect to which transactions differed, (4) tracing out the transaction cost ramifications, and (5) matching modes to transactions in a discriminating way. Once the vertical integration problem had been made operational in this way, a variety of related applications followed. In this sense, the puzzle of vertical integration was a paradigm problem that, once solved, provided a research strategy that could be repeated. Any problem that could be posed, directly or indirectly, as a contracting problem could be assessed in terms of the identical conceptual apparatus.

These paradigm features were not entirely evident, however, until the paper "Markets and Hierarchies: Some Elementary Considerations" took shape (Williamson, 1973). This paper had its origins in a class discussion of market failures, with special emphasis on Arrow's classic statement of the problem (Arrow, 1969). For each type of market failure that was identified (public goods problem, appropriability problem, information asymmetry, small numbers exchange, etc.), the object was to move the explanation for the condition back to a statement of primitives. The same basic human and environmental conditions that arose in assessing vertical integration kept reappearing. *Bounded rationality and opportunism* were the recurring human factors. The environmental factors were *uncertainty-complexity* and *small numbers exchange*. The patterned way in which these human and environmental factors were paired is shown in Figure 14.1.

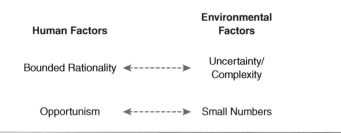

Figure 14.1   The Organizational Failures Framework

Conceptual Framework

The rudiments of the conceptual framework upon which the Markets and Hierarchies program of research relies have now been identified. What follows is an elaboration on these.

Behavioral Assumptions

Bounded rationality and opportunism are the key behavioral assumptions. These assumptions about the characteristics of human actors are joined with the assertion that viable modes of organization (market, quasi market, or internal) are ones that serve to *economize* on transaction costs. While organization theory specialists related easily to the concept of bounded rationality, many economists resist it. By contrast, economizing is a much more congenial notion to economists than it is to organization theorists. Opportunism is a concept of which both are wary.

Arrow has characterized an economist as one who "by training thinks of himself as the guardian of rationality, the ascriber of rationality to others, and the prescriber of rationality to the social world" (Arrow, 1974: 16). Given this commitment, any assumption that appears to be at variance with rationality is apt to be dismissed out of hand. If it is not rational, it must be nonrational or irrational, and these are matters for other social sciences to grapple with.

As Herbert Simon has pointed out, however, economists exaggerate the extent to which nonrationality is emphasized by other social sciences. Although economists are the only social scientists who invoke hyperrationality assumptions, rationality is nevertheless a common theme throughout all of the social sciences (Simon, 1978: 2–4). The issue thus is not whether human agents are rational or not. Rather the question is whether the assumption of hyperrationality is needed or if weaker rationality assumptions will suffice.

Partly this is a matter of taste in choosing between strong and weak assumptions where both yield the same implications (Simon, 1978: 8). But there is more to it than tastes. Conceptualizing a problem one way rather than another can have a profound effect on the follow-up research agenda. Thus organization structure is of little import and hence can be disregarded if hyperrationality assumptions are maintained, which explains why the neoclassical theory of the firm describes the organization as a production function rather than a complex hierarchy. The opposite assumption, that human agents are so overwhelmed by complexity that they are incapable of planning, likewise reduces the study of organizational design to insignificance. This appears to be close to the view of March and Olsen (1976) and Mintzberg (1973).

The Markets and Hierarchies approach avoids both of these extremes. An intermediate degree of bounded rationality is attributed to human agents. Organizational design takes on economic significance precisely because the productive utilization of this intermediate capability is of crucial importance. But there is more to organizational design than economizing on bounded rationality. Issues of opportunism also arise and need to be addressed.

Opportunism extends the usual motivational assumption of self-interest seeking to include self-interest seeking with guile. Thus, whereas bounded rationality suggests decision making less complex than the usual assumption of hyperrationality, opportunism suggests calculating behavior more sophisticated than the usual assumption of simple self-interest. Opportunism refers to "making false or empty, that is, self-disbelieved threats or promises," cutting corners for undisclosed personal advantage, covering up tracks, and the like. Although it is a central behavioral assumption, it is not essential that all economic agents behave this way. What is crucial is that *some* agents behave in this fashion and that it is costly to sort out those who are opportunistic from those who are not.

Faced with bounded rationality on the one hand and the proclivity for some human agents to behave opportunistically on the other, the basic organizational design issue essentially reduces to this: organize transactions in such a way as to economize on bounded rationality while simultaneously safeguarding those transactions against the hazards of opportunism.

The Governance of Contractual Relations

The governance of contractual relations warrants careful attention in the degree to which economic agents are subject to bounded rationality and are given to opportunism. In the absence of either, the ubiquitous contracting model goes through.

Thus suppose the absence of bounded rationality among opportunistic agents. Mind-boggling though it is to contemplate, such agents will engage in "a single gigantic once-for-all forward 'higgle-haggle' in which all contingent goods and services (i.e., all goods and services at each possible time-cum-environmental condition) are bought and sold once and for all now for money payments made now" (Meade, 1971: 166). Propensities to behave opportunistically will simply be of no account.

Suppose alternatively that agents are subject to bounded rationality but are free of opportunism. Autonomous contracting again applies, though the reasons here are different. Since each party can depend on his or her opposite to honor the spirit as well as the letter of an agreement, successive adaptations can and will be implemented as contingencies unfold. Bridges are thus crossed when they arise, whereas the unbounded rationality model stipulates bridge crossings exhaustively in advance. Adaptive, sequential decision making by nonopportunistic parties will nevertheless reach the same joint profit optimizing result.

The fact is, however, that human agents are neither unboundedly rational nor reliably free of opportunism. Interesting transaction cost issues thereby arise, and organizational design is a relevant concern precisely for this reason. But a predictive theory of efficient organizational structure requires more than an acknowledgment that human actors are subject to bounded rationality and given to opportunism. A schema for framing the dimensions of transactions is needed and must be joined with a description of alternative modes for organizing transactions. In addition, a strategy for matching organizing modes (governance structures) to transactions needs to be devised.

The rudiments of such an approach have been set out elsewhere (Williamson, 1979c). The critical dimensions for describing transactions are (1) uncertainty, (2) the frequency with which transactions recur, and (3) the degree to which durable transaction-specific investments are required to realize least-cost supply. The main governance modes to which transactions need to be matched are (1) markets (with varying degrees of adjudicatory support); (2) internal organization; and (3) an intermediate form of bilateral exchange referred to as "obligational market contracting."

Our principal interest here is internal organization. Internal organization is well-suited to transactions that involve recurrent exchange in the face of a nontrivial degree of uncertainty and that incur transaction-specific investments. Since internal organization requires the development of specialized governance structure, the cost of which must be amortized across the transactions assigned to it, it is rarely economical to organize occasional transactions internally. Likewise, transactions for which uncertainty is low require little adaptation, hence little governance, and thus can organized by market contracting. Except, however, as transaction-specific investments are involved, neither frequency nor uncertainty—individually or in combination—justifies the creation of internal organization (with its associated transaction specific governance structure).

Considering the importance that we attach to transaction-specific investments, some explication is needed. The crucial issue is the degree to which durable, non-marketable expenses are incurred. Items that are unspecialized among users pose few hazards, since buyers in these circumstances can easily turn to alternative sources, and suppliers can sell output intended for one buyer to other buyers without difficulty. (The argument also turns on the degree to which inputs can be diverted from one use to another without loss of productivity.) Nonmarketability problems arise when the *specific identity of* the parties has important cost-bearing consequences. Transactions of this kind will be referred to as idiosyncratic.

Occasionally the identity of the parties is important from the outset, as when a buyer induces a supplier to invest in specialized physical capital of a transaction-specific kind. Inasmuch as the value of this capital in other uses is by definition much smaller than the specialized use for which it has been intended, the supplier is effectively "locked into" the transaction to a significant degree. This is symmetrical, moreover, in that the buyer cannot turn to alternative sources of supply and obtain the item on favorable terms, since the cost of supply from unspecialized capital is presumably great.[4] The buyer is thus committed to the transaction as well.

Ordinarily, however, there is more to idiosyncratic exchange than specialized physical capital. Human-capital investments that are transaction specific commonly occur as well. Specialized training and learning-by-doing economies in production operations are illustrations. Except when these investments are transferable to alternative suppliers at low cost, which is rare, the benefits of the set-up costs can be realized only so long as the relationship between the buyer and seller of the intermediate product is maintained.

Additional transaction-specific savings can accrue at the interface between supplier and buyer as contracts are successively adapted to unfolding events, and as periodic contract-renewal agreements are reached. Familiarity here permits communication economies to be realized: specialized language develops as experience accumulates and nuances are signaled and received in a sensitive way. Both institutional and personal trust relations evolve.

In consideration of the value placed upon economies of these kinds, agents who engage in recurring, uncertain, idiosyncratic transactions have a strong interest in preserving the exchange relation. Autonomous contracting modes give way to internal organization as the value associated with exchange continuity increases. The continuity advantages of internal organization over markets in these circumstances are attributable to its more sensitive governance characteristics and its stronger joint profit maximizing features.

Applications

A theory is judged to be more fruitful the "more precise the prediction, the wider the area within which the theory yields predictions, and the more additional lines of future research it suggests" (Friedman, 1953: 10). The basic exchange paradigm that was originally worked up to address the issue of vertical integration across successive manufacturing stages has proved to be remarkably robust. Although this was not evident at the outset, it quickly became apparent that any organizational relation that can be reformulated as a contracting problem can be addressed in substantially identical terms. Applications of the exchange paradigm include: assessments of the employment relation (Williamson, Wachter, and Harris, 1975; Hashimoto and Yu, 1979); franchise bidding for natural monopolies (Williamson, 1976); the efficacy of capital markets (Williamson, 1975: Chapter 9); oligopoly (Posner, 1969; Williamson, 1975: Chapter 12); vertical market restrictions (Williamson, 1979a); and aspects of inflation (Wachter and Williamson, 1978).

Other applications include: a restatement of contract law in transaction cost terms (Williamson, 1979c: 235–254); the uses of transaction cost reasoning by marketing specialists (Carman, 1979); possible applications to the study of comparative economic systems (Campbell, 1978); and uses of the exchange paradigm to examine noneconomic phenomena—family law being an example (Williamson, 1979c: 258). Of special interest here are the applications of the Markets and Hierarchies approach to matters of internal organization. These design issues are developed in the following section.

Empirical tests of three kinds have been used to assess predictions of the Markets and Hierarchies approach: cross-sectional studies, experimental studies, and case studies. The cross-sectional studies that have been performed test what is referred to as the multidivisional form hypothesis (Williamson, 1975: 150).

The organization and operation of the large enterprise along the lines of the M-form favors goal pursuit and least-cost behavior more nearly associated with the neoclassical profit maximization hypothesis than does the U-form organizational alternative.

Three studies have been done in which organization form is used as an explanatory variable in studies of business performance. The studies by Peter Steer and John Cable (1978) of British firms and by Henry Armour and David Teece (1978) of U.S. petroleum corporations both confirm the importance of organization form. Teece has since extended the analysis from petroleum firms to assess the ramifications of organization form differences among the principal firms in 15 industries and obtains results that confirm the hypothesis (Teece, 1979).

Richard Burton and Borge Obel (1980) have tested the M-form hypothesis by examining the ramifications of organizational design for profitability in the context of a linear programming model of the firm in which the Danzig-Wolf decomposition algorithm was used. Two different technologies, one more decomposable than the other, were studied. The M-form hypothesis is confirmed for both technologies, the profit difference being greater for the more decomposable technology—which is also an implication of the theory.

Case studies of several kinds have been performed. The most complete of these involves an assessment of franchise bidding for natural monopolies. Demsetz (1968), Posner (1972), and Stigler (1968: 18–19) have argued that franchise bidding is an attractive alternative to rate-of-return regulation in dealing with natural monopolies. An abstract assessment of the contracting ramifications of franchise bidding discloses, however, that the purported benefits of franchise bidding are suspect where market and technological uncertainty are great and incumbent suppliers invest in specialized, long-lived equipment and acquire idiosyncratic skills (Williamson, 1976).

A case study of franchise bidding for CATV in Oakland, California, confirmed this. Not only were general ramifications of the contracting approach borne out by the study, but the study corroborated contracting details as well.

Organizational Design

Consistent with the general thrust of the Markets and Hierarchies approach, organization design is addressed as a transaction cost issue, and economizing purposes are emphasized. The general argument is this: except when there are perversities associated with the funding process, or when strategically situated members of an organization are unable to participate in the prospective gains, unrealized efficiency opportunities always offer an incentive to reorganize.

Inasmuch as these perversities are more common in noncommercial than in commercial enterprises, the argument has stronger predictive force for the latter. Indeed our attention in this section is restricted entirely to the commercial sector. We nevertheless believe that the spirit of the analysis carries over to nonprofit enterprises and government bureaus, which we include in our discussion of the research agenda.

Although the main organizational design "action" entails economizing on transaction costs, this is not to say that technology is irrelevant. But technology by itself rarely has determinative organizational consequences for more than a small group of highly interdependent workers. Indeed, except when the transaction costs of adapting interfaces between technologically separable work stations are great, markets will be the governance mode by which the exchange of intermediate product is accomplished. Internal organization not only has little to offer in these circumstances but incurs unneeded costs.

However, in circumstances in which autonomous contracting is costly and hazardous, governance structures of an internal organizational kind arise. Three applications of this general argument follow, after which we summarize the implications and go on briefly to consider other organizational design traditions and contrast them with the approach favored here.

Vertical Integration[5]

The . . . monograph by Alfred Chandler, Jr. (1977), describing marketing developments during the late nineteenth century provides strong support for the proposition that transaction costs are sufficiently significant to affect the structure of industries sometimes motivating firms to integrate forward from manufacturing into the distribution stage.

Chandler's Findings. Chandler's description of forward integration into distribution by American manufacturers distinguishes between the developments of infrastructure and the induced distributional response. The appearance of the railroads and the telegraph and telephone systems in the latter part of the nineteenth century permitted wider geographic areas to be served in a reliable and timely way. The "reliability and speed of the new transportation and communication" permitted greater economies of scale to be realized in factory organization (Chandler, 1977: 245). These economies of scale at the factory level were latent, in the sense that the technology was there waiting to be exploited. Because it is not manufacturing cost but delivered cost that matters, however, it became profitable to realize these scale economies only when a low-cost distribution system appeared. That is, so long as transportation expenses were great, the most efficient way to serve markets was by dispersing factories.

Once the new transportation and communication infrastructure was in place, the stage was set for the distributional response. A crucial question was how to devise a coordinated manufacturing-distribution response. In principle, both stages could have remained autonomous: manufacturers could have remained specialized and built larger-scale plants while specialized distributors could have responded simultaneously, either on their own initiative or by contract, by assembling the requisite distribution network. In many industries, however, "existing marketers were unable to sell and distribute products in the volume they were produced. . . . Once the inadequacies of existing marketers became clear, manufacturers integrated forward into marketing" (Chandler, 1977: 287). An administrative override was evidently needed.

Not all industries integrated forward, however, and when they did it was not to the same extent. Some industries linked manufacturing only with advertising and wholesaling; retail integration was not attempted. Nondurable industries that had recently adopted continuous process machinery—cigarettes, matches, cereals, and canned goods are examples—were in this category (Chandler, 1977: 287). More ambitious and interesting were producer and consumer durables that required "specialized marketing services demonstration, installation, consumer credit, after-sales service and repair," services that existing middlemen "had neither the interest nor facilities to provide" (Chandler, 1977: 288). Examples here included sewing machines, farm machinery, office machines, and heavy electrical equipment.

A Transaction Cost Interpretation. The new transportation and communication infrastructure permitted manufacturers to serve larger markets in a low-cost way. The effects of these infrastructural developments on plant size are displayed in Figure 14.2. (On the motivation for this, see Scherer, Beckenstein, Kaufer, and Murphy, 1975.)

The *APC* curve shows the average cost of production as plant size increases. These average costs decrease over a wide range due to assumed economies of scale. The curve ADC_1 shows the original average distribution cost of delivering products from a plant. This curve increases throughput because greater sales require marketing to a larger geographic region. The curve ADC_2 shows the average distribution cost after the new infrastructure is put in place. It is consistently lower than ADC_1 but also rises throughout. ATC_1, and ATC_2 are average total cost curves that are given by the vertical summation of *APC* with ADC_1, and ADC_2, respectively. Average total costs reach a minimum at Q_1^* and Q_2^*, where Q_2^* is necessarily larger than Q_1^*, given the stipulated shift in average distribution costs. An increase in plant scale and the extension of service to larger geographic markets are thus indicated.

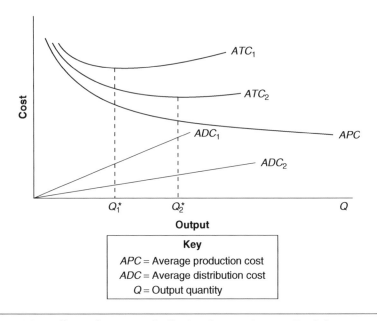

Figure 14.2 Effects of Average Distribution Cost on Average Total Cost

Problems of implementation, however, are not addressed by this cost curve apparatus. How are the linkages between manufacturing and distribution to be forged? They are not created automatically. If existing middlemen respond in a slow and faltering way to the opportunities that the new transportation and communication infrastructures afford, the stage is set for someone, in this instance the manufacturers, to experiment with new organizational structures.

The issues here are of a transaction cost rather than of a production cost kind. Although a definitive analysis of the "inadequacies of existing marketers" reported by Chandler (1977: 287) would require further research, we conjecture that these distributional difficulties are due to goal incongruence coupled with the hazards posed by small numbers supply relations between autonomous parties. It was difficult for marketers who were accustomed to operating in a local market regime to perceive the opportunities that awaited them. And there was no obvious way to signal these opportunities by relying upon decentralized pricing (Malmgren, 1961). Moreover, even if manufacturers and distributors both perceived the opportunities that the new transportation and communication infrastructure afforded, and if each responded independently in reliance upon the other, problems of divergence would arise if each recorded or interpreted the data differently. Such goal incongruence would exist, moreover, at both an aggregate and a disaggregate level.

In principle, manufacturers could have taken the initiative and effected goal congruence by contract. Coordination by contract is costly, however, where the two parties are bargaining in an unfamiliar situation and the hazards of contracting are great. The hazards to which we refer have been discussed elsewhere in the context of idiosyncratic exchange. Such problems arise when investments in specialized human or physical assets are required in order to complete the transaction in an economical way. With respect to the issues of concern to Chandler, the problems were especially severe when the mass production and sale of consumer or producer durables were contemplated. Distributors here would have to be induced to make specialized (product-and-brand specific) investments and, once these investments were made, manufacturers and distributors would thereafter often be dealing with each other in what essentially was a bilateral exchange arrangement. Given the hazards of opportunism that arise in such circumstances, both parties were reluctant to rely on autonomous contracting.

Note in this connection that Chandler did not observe vertical integration occurring in uniform degree in all industries. This is precisely what one would anticipate when vertical integration is assessed in transaction cost terms. Thus vertical integration into distribution was negligible in some industries—standardized nuts and bolts being an example. In others, integration involved advertising and wholesaling but not retailing—branded consumer nondurables being in this category. In still others, integration included retailing and related support services—certain branded nondurables being among these. This progression is marked by the degree of transaction-specific investment, which is an implication of transaction cost theory. Other theories of vertical integration, by contrast, are silent on these matters.

This substitution of bureaucratic for market governance occurred in response to profit opportunities. But social cost savings also resulted. In the absence of other factors, net social as well as net private gains accrue when such organizational innovations appear.

Becoming Multidivisional. The transformation of the modern corporation from a functional to a multidivisional structure has been documented in Chandler.[6] This transformation is treated prominently in the *Markets and Hierarchies* volume (Williamson, 1975: Chapters 8–9). Only a few comments are offered here.

Chandler characterizes the reasons for the success of the multidivision structure thus:

> The basic reasons for its success was simply that it clearly removed the executives responsible for the destiny of the entire enterprise from the more routine operational activities, and so gave them the time, information, and even psychological commitment for long-term planning and appraisal. . . .
>
> [The] new structure left the broad strategic decisions as to the allocation of existing resources and the acquisition of new ones in the hands of a top team of generalists. Relieved of operating duties and tactical decisions, a general executive was less likely to reflect the position of just one part of the whole. (Chandler, 1966: 382–383)

If Chandler is correct, this organizational change from a functional to a multidivisional structure served both to economize on bounded rationality, by relieving top executives of the more routine operational activities, and simultaneously to reduce subgoal pursuit, which is a manifestation of opportunism. Inasmuch as most institutional choices involve trade-offs rather than Pareto superior moves, this is surely quite remarkable. How was this accomplished?

The difficulties that the functionally organized firm encountered as it grew in size and diversity were attributable to diseconomies of agglomeration. The centralization of what are effectively decomposable parts has adverse operating consequences of three kinds. First, attempts to achieve unneeded coordination generate overhead costs. Second, forced interdependencies give rise to congestion and other spillover costs. Third, opportunistic subgoal pursuit is more difficult to detect and control as the degree of interconnectedness increases. Operating cost increases thus arise out of a failure to recognize essential decomposability. But the deficiencies of the functional structure went beyond these operating cost features. The functional form also served to confuse organizational purpose by failure to separate strategic from operating decision making.

Although becoming multidivisional would not have been feasible without decomposability, the benefits of reorganization required more than an assignment of semiautonomous standing to natural subunits within the firm. Becoming multidivisional further required the development of a strategic decision-making capability in the central office—indeed would have been hazardous to implement without this capability. The assignment of investment resources to high yield uses could be reliably accomplished only as the general office (1) had a sense of direction, (2) was able to evaluate the merits of investment proposals originated by the operating divisions, and (3) had the capacity to audit and assess operating division performance.

Removing top management from the operating affairs of the enterprise meant that, whereas bureaucratic control processes had governed previously, operating divisions were now governed in quasi-market fashion. Thus divisions were assigned the status of quasi firms, and the central office assumed functions of review and resource allocation ordinarily associated with the capital market. As a consequence of these changes the goal confusion (or incongruence) that had previously reigned was supplanted by subgoal clarity that was meaningfully related to enterprise objectives. The self-interest seeking that, when coupled with goal incongruence, had once drained the energies of the enterprise was now turned to productive purposes.

It is noteworthy that the transformation of the functional to the multidivisional form had little if any relation to technology. Organizational structure was altered, but the underlying technology remained the same in most instances. Thus although efficiency purposes were served, the economies driving the change and the economies that were realized were of a transaction cost rather than technological kind.

Bureaucracies and Clans

The shift from functional to divisional structure has for the most part been completed in large U.S. corporations (Teece, 1979) and has been proceeding rapidly in Europe (Franko, 1972). But a further question is what management "style" ought to be practiced in the large multidivisional enterprise. Issues relating to the "economics of atmosphere" (Williamson, 1975: 37–39) arise in this connection. Ouchi has addressed the merits of bureaucratic versus clan type management styles in a series of . . . papers on this subject (Ouchi, 1978, 1979, 1980).

To put the issue one way: What form of contracting ought to prevail within an organization? As with market modes of contracting, there are two general options, which we designate as "hard" and "soft" contracting, respectively. Under hard contracting, the parties remain relatively autonomous, each is expected to press his or her interests vigorously, and contracting is relatively complete. Soft contracting, by contrast, presumes much closer identity of interests between the parties, and formal contracts are much less complete. This is the clan-type management style.

Although contract law specialists, sociologists, and others have long recognized soft contracting practices, the study of soft contracting has only recently come under scrutiny. Ian Macneil's (1974, 1978) work on "relational contracting" is especially instructive. While it is beyond the scope of this paper to review the literature here, we nonetheless think it important to elaborate on the special problems that soft contracting encounters if it is introduced in an alien culture.

The basic argument is this: Soft contracting, to be viable, needs to be supported by a more elaborate informal governance apparatus than is associated with hard contracting. Thus, whereas the latter relies heavily on legal and economic sanctions, the former rests much more on social controls. As compared with hard contracting, soft contracting appeals more to the spirit than to the letter of the agreement.

Four points are relevant in this regard. First, not all transactions need the additional supports afforded by soft contracting. Economizing considerations would dictate that a distinction be made between those that do and that do not, and that each be organized appropriately. Second, the immediate parties to soft contracts are the ones who stand most to benefit from preserving the exchange. Accordingly, they have incentives to develop a bilateral (transaction-specific) trust relation. Third, the institutional infrastructure within which soft contracts are embedded also influences the viability of this type of exchange. And fourth, the design of transactions is a decision variable: Depending on their confidence in the trading relation, parties will vary the degree to which trading hazards are introduced.

Trading hazards differ with the degree of transaction-specific investment and with uncertainty. The first of these hazards is obvious: Where investments are of a transaction-specific kind, parties will be unable to divert these assets to alternative uses of an equally productive kind. Accordingly, as the degree of asset specificity increases, additional governance supports are needed. The same applies as uncertainty is increased. The argument here is that the occasions to adapt the transaction to new circumstances increase as the degree of uncertainty increases. Since the incentive to defect from the spirit of the agreement increases as the frequency and magnitude of the indicated adaptations are increased, greater hazards are thereby posed.

Although the degree of uncertainty is commonly beyond the control of the parties, the degree of asset specificity is often theirs to determine. Thus, assume that a particular transaction is subject to an intermediate degree of uncertainty and the parties are attempting to optimize with respect to its transaction-specific features. Specifically, assume the following:

1. The transaction in question involves an employment relation.

2. Two different job designs are under consideration, one of a hard contracting and the other of a soft contracting kind.

3. Human capital skill acquisitions are involved for each job design: Under hard contracting the skills acquired are of a general purpose kind, while under soft contracting they are of a special kind.

4. Physical capital expenditures are identical whichever job design is adopted.

5. Assuming contractual continuity, the more productive job design is the one that involves special-purpose skill acquisition.

Whether this more productive job design is adopted, however, is problematical. In contrast to employees with general-purpose skills, employees who have acquired task-specific skills will be able to move to alternative employment only by experiencing a nontrivial productivity sacrifice in the process. In consideration of these added hazards, employers will be successful in inducing employees to acquire specialized skills only when the workers are either adequately compensated in advance for the hazards or when the job is adequately protected against opportunism during the course of task execution.

Holding governance structures constant, the wage premium needed to compensate workers against the added hazards may easily render the task specific job design competitively nonviable, especially if workers are risk averse. The question then is whether this potentially more productive job design can be salvaged by surrounding it with transactional safeguards. This brings us back to the matter of bilateral trading relations and the institutional matrix within which trading takes place.

The "special problems" of soft contracting to which we referred earlier are particularly great when soft contracting is introduced into an alien culture. The reason for this is that the entire burden of providing contractual safeguards falls entirely on the immediate parties to the transaction if background cultural supports are missing. Should one of the parties choose to defect, there is no further support for sustaining the transaction to which either can appeal. In contrast, where individual soft contracts are embedded in a soft contracting trading culture, defection is subject to added sanctions. The incentives to defect are accordingly reduced.

To some extent, the parties to the transaction may be able to devise procedural safeguards themselves. One example is the development of "internal labor markets" whereby wages are assigned to jobs rather than to individuals, promotion ladders are defined, a sensitive grievance structure is devised, and so on (Doeringer and Piore, 1971; Williamson, Wachter, and Harris, 1975). But societal safeguards may provide additional security. This varies among economic systems. The "clan" form of organization that Ouchi (1978, 1979) has studied is much more viable in some cultures (e.g., Japanese) than in others (e.g., American).

The limitations of hard contracting are nevertheless great as the need progressively increases for successive adaptations to be made in response to uncertainty. Contracts simply fail to provide adequately for the appropriate responses in advance, and employees may engage in strategic bargaining. The more cooperative work relations associated with soft contracting have a clear advantage in these circumstances. The problem then is how to bring this off. This is a matter for which future research is plainly needed.

Other Organizational Design Traditions

The literature on organizational design is vast, and we address only a small part of it here. Jeffrey Pfeffer's (1978) . . . book on this subject distinguishes between longitudinal studies, managerial studies, and the power approach. He observes that most of the longitudinal studies have been preoccupied with measurement to the exclusion of theory (Pfeffer, 1978: xiv). The work of Jay Galbraith (1973) and of Paul Lawrence and Jay Lorsch (1967) is in the managerial tradition. Pfeffer contends that this work is preoccupied with efficiency and effectiveness and neglects power and influence (Pfeffer, 1978: xv). Pfeffer's preferred approach is to regard organizations "as coalitions with ill-defined and inconsistent preferences" (Pfeffer, 1978: xvi), a tradition that he associates with Cyert and March (1963), Karl Weick (1969), and March and Olsen (1976). Organizational design issues are then addressed in terms of control, influence, and power.

Other organizational design approaches that go unmentioned by Pfeffer are the organizational ecology approach (Hannan and Freeman, 1977; Aldrich, 1979) and the theory of organizational structures advanced by Kenneth Mackenzie (1978). Inasmuch as efficiency figures prominently in both of these last two approaches, both are complementary to the Markets and Hierarchies approach. The power approach to organizational design, by contrast, is a very different tradition.

The neglect of power by the M&H approach is not to suggest that power is either uninteresting or unimportant. We submit, however, that power considerations will usually give way to efficiency—at least in profit-making enterprises, if observations are taken at sufficiently long intervals, say a decade. Thus the powers of heads of functional divisions and of their subordinates were vastly altered when functionally organized firms shifted to a multidivisional structure. Were power the only or the main organizational design factor, it is difficult to believe that large American and subsequently European businesses would have undergone such a vast organizational transformation over the past thirty years. From transaction cost and ecological points of view, however, the transformation, once started, was predictable.

Or consider Pfeffer's assertion that if "the chief executive in a corporation always comes from marketing . . . there is a clue about power in the organization" (Pfeffer, 1978: 23). Viewed from a power perspective, the argument evidently is that the marketing people in this corporation have "possession of control over critical resources," have preferential access to information, and are strategically located to cope with "critical organizational uncertainty" (Pfeffer, 1978: 17–28). We do not disagree with any of this but would make the more straightforward argument that the marketing function in this organization is especially critical to competitive viability.

Thus our position is that those parts of the enterprise that are most critical to organizational viability will be *assigned* possession of control over critical resources, will *have* preferential access to information, and will be *dealing with* critical organizational uncertainties. In some organizations this may be marketing, in others it may be R&D, and in still others it may be production. Failure to assign control to that part of the enterprise on which viability turns would contradict the efficiency hypothesis but would presumably be explained as a power outcome.[7]

Inasmuch as power is very vague and has resisted successive efforts to make it operational, whereas efficiency is much more clearly specified and the plausibility of an efficiency hypothesis is buttressed by ecological survival tests, we urge that efficiency analysis be made the centerpiece of the study of organizational design. This does not imply that power has no role to play, but we think it invites confusion to explain organizational results that are predicted by the efficiency hypothesis in terms of power. Rather, power explains results when the organization sacrifices efficiency to serve special interests. We concede that this occurs. But we do not believe that major organizational changes in the commercial sector are explained in these terms. The evidence is all to the contrary.

The Research Agenda

The Markets and Hierarchies approach to the study of organizational issues is relatively new as compared with other research traditions. Neither its power nor its limits have been fully established. Applications to date, however, have been numerous and mainly encouraging. Our discussion here merely suggests additional theoretical, empirical, and public policy applications.

General

As noted earlier, any problem that arises as a contracting problem or can be recast as one can usefully be examined in Markets and Hierarchies terms. This is not to suggest that the contracting paradigm should be applied to the exclusion of other research traditions. We nevertheless believe that insights not easily derived from alternative approaches can often be obtained by assessing transaction cost features. While sometimes these insights may be of a fragmentary kind, often they relate to core issues.

Inasmuch as transaction costs have reference to the costs of running the economic system, the useful comparisons are between alternative modes rather than between a proposed mode and a frictionless ideal. Given that an explicit or implicit exchange is to be accomplished or a coordinated adaptation is to be affected, how should the transaction be organized? For many purposes, the analysis can be thought of as interface management. This applies within and between markets and firms.

Some Specifics

Business History: Markets to Hierarchies. Transaction cost economics can be applied advantageously to the study of changing organizational structures through time. This is true both of organizational changes since the industrial revolution (Chandler, 1966, 1977) and also preindustrial changes (North, 1978). A richer understanding of the economics of institutions is sure to emerge as business historians, industrial organization specialists, economic theorists, and organization theorists apply their collective talents to the systematic study of institutional issues.

Transaction cost economizing is, we submit, the driving force that is responsible for the main institutional changes (for an interpretation of Chandler's recent book in transaction cost terms, see Williamson, 1980). Applications will include product market organization and also changing labor and capital market forms of organization through time.

Bureaucracies. Applications of Markets and Hierarchies to commercial bureaucracies will be concerned with interface governance. Specific organizational design applications (possibly with special reference to particular functions such as research and development) as well as general applications (again, the matrix form is in need of interpretation) should be possible. Additional empirical tests of the M-form of other hypotheses can also be anticipated. Perhaps most important, the limits of internal organization are poorly understood in relation to the limits of markets. The transaction cost approach appears to have much to offer for such an assessment. The ramifications are of interest both to worker-managed and to capitalist enterprises (Fitzroy and Mueller, 1978). Whether recent developments involving employee participation in Europe constitute a contradiction to the efficiency hypothesis also warrants scrutiny.

Clans. The organization of economic activity by greater reliance on clan type structures requires study. Both the limitations of clans as well as the discriminating application of clan forms of organization deserve attention. As between alternative forms of internal organization, the clan appears to realize greater advantage in circumstances in which uncertainty is great. The argument needs to be elaborated and specific applications attempted, to service industries, high technology industries, and others characterized by extreme performance ambiguity.

The proposition that clan forms join high productivity with emotional well-being (low levels of alienation) deserves further scrutiny. As with other organizational panaceas, we believe that this is too simplistic. Rather the argument needs to be made in a more discriminating way that recognizes transaction cost distinctions. The proposition that defection hazards are greater for clan forms, and that such forms are viable only when accompanied by additional governance supports, also warrants further study. Comparative international studies, in which hard versus soft contracting cultures are scrutinized, may be useful.

Public Policy Toward Business. Public policy applications will also continue. This includes both antitrust and regulation. In the antitrust area, issues of strategic behavior and fairness will come under special scrutiny. What has been referred to as the Decision Process Approach, which makes operational "procedural rationality" (Simon, 1978), would appear to hold promise for the microanalytic study of regulatory issues (Williamson, 1979b).

Nonprofit Organizations. The organization of nonprofit enterprises, which are growing in economic importance (Weisbrod, 1979), is intriguing and has hitherto evaded explanation of more than a partial or ad hoc kind. Whether the transaction cost approach will be illuminating remains to be seen. One of the problems, with transactions in many nonprofit organizations, as in service businesses, is that they are amorphous. Also the viability tests for nonprofit organizations are often much weaker—partly because product market competition is weak, but also because an effective capital market displacement mechanism (takeover) is missing.

The study of government bureaus suffers from many of these same limitations. Once progress is made in studying nonprofit organizations from a transaction cost (or any other) point of view, follow-up applications to government bureaus should be easy.

Conclusion

The Markets and Hierarchies program of research is relatively young in comparison with other research traditions in organization theory. Being young, it has its skeptics. We would not have it otherwise.

For one thing, we are inclined to be eclectic. No single approach applies equally well to all problems, and some issues are usefully addressed from several points of view. For another, we believe that most of the challenges can be met. Sometimes this may require extending the theory to apply to new circumstances. Sometimes it will require sharpening or qualifying parts of the argument. Formalizing aspects of the argument may sometimes be needed and appears to be feasible. (See the paper by Hashimoto and Yu, 1980, for developments of this last kind.)

The distinctive powers of the approach are attributable to its reliance on transaction cost reasoning and its unremitting emphasis on efficiency. While the particulars differ, the same approach to the study of transactions applies quite generally. The core methodological properties are these:

The transaction is the basic unit of analysis.

Human agents are subject to bounded rationality and self-interest.

The critical dimensions for describing transactions are frequency, uncertainty, and transaction-specific investments.

Economizing on transaction costs is the principal factor that explains viable modes of contracting; it is the main issue with which organizational design ought to be concerned.

Assessing transaction cost differences is a comparative institutional exercise.

The approach is able to deal symmetrically with market and nonmarket modes of organization and has successfully addressed a wide variety of organizational issues in a coherent way.

Those who prefer methodology and those who are averse to efficiency analysis will insist, with cause, that there is more to organization theory than economizing on transaction costs. We agree. We submit, however, that efficiency analysis is important to the study of all forms of organization and is absolutely crucial to the study of commercial organizations. And we furthermore contend that the main test of a theory is its implications. So long as alternative theories are evaluated on this standard, we are confident that the Markets and Hierarchies approach will fare well in the comparison.

Notes

1. Reprinted by permission of the authors and the publisher from *Perspectives on Organization Design and Behavior*, by A. van de Ven and W. Joyce, 1981, New York: Wiley.

2. J. R. Commons (1934) had urged such an approach much earlier, but both his efforts and those of other institutionalists were outside the mainstream of economic analysis and, except as they are dealt with in the study of economic thought, have been neglected.

3. This was economics of a nontraditional kind. An efficiency orientation was maintained, but attention shifted from neoclassical production function issues to the study of transaction costs, in the spirit of J. R. Commons (1934), R. H. Coase (1937), and K. J. Arrow (1969).

4. This assumes that it is costly for the incumbent supplier to transfer specialized physical assets to new suppliers. On this, see Williamson (1976).

5. The argument here follows Williamson (1979a, pp. 968–972).

6. The path-breaking book here is Chandler's *Strategy and Structure* (1966). Williamson's shift of emphasis from the factors that were responsible for managerial discretion to the factors, including especially internal organization, that served to attenuate managerial discretion was much influenced by this book.

7. Thus suppose that, from a competitive effectiveness viewpoint, marketing is the most important functional area. Suppose further that the founder and his progeny are engineers, and that each has worked his way up through manufacturing. Inasmuch as they have an ownership lock (power) on the system, the chief executive and his principal aides are appointed from these ranks. Although this has the efficiency benefit of coupling ownership and control, the firm may be vulnerable to market developments in relation to its rivals. Power explains the inefficiency (vulnerability) condition.

PART VI

Open System Natural Models

I f closed system rational models are the things of management, focusing on increasing firm performance, then open system rational models are the things of sociologists, and they differ in an important way from sociologists of earlier eras. The early works of Mayo (1945) and Roethlisberger and Dixon (1945) at Western Electric, Barnard (1938), Gouldner (1954), and Blau (1972) were concerned, as were the classical theorists, with the implications of their findings for organizations effectiveness (Meyer, 1999). By the end of the 1960s, rationality as a theme in the design of organizations was confronted by the emergence of *institutional* and *ecological models*, theoretical approaches that place a much stronger emphasis on the environmental context in which the organization exists and much less emphasis on the issue of firm performance. As Meyer says, "To characterize [these two approaches], population ecology was concerned with competition, but not the kinds of performance that most people were interested in, while institutional theory denied the relevance of both competition and performance" (p. 509).

Ecology models, unlike most other theories that focus on the analysis of single organizations, direct their analysis toward populations, or clusters, of similar organizations. Additionally, they also tell us something about the processes by which organizations are selected by the environments in which they operate. While Hannan and Freeman (1977) in their original paper recognize that managers may make choices about how to adapt to changing environments, they argue that structural inertia may limit the adaptation process. That is, this inertia may arise from internal and external sources. Internal forces, for example, are sunk costs in investment and human resource, lack of information, internal political matters, and the organization's own history. External forces, for example, may be legal and fiscal barriers to entering and exiting markets, the inability to obtain information about the environment itself, and the legitimacy of adaptive choices to important external constituent sectors. Such factors lead to a reluctance of the dominant coalition in an organization to change, which increases its vulnerability. The effect, therefore, is that the organization that does not fit well with the environmental demands will be selected out and die.

Institutional theories seek to show how organizations are socially constrained to act in similar ways instead of differing "themselves from one another, compete, and hence perform more or less effectively" (Meyer, 1999, p. 509). Selznick (1949), generally considered to be a pioneering institutional theorist, showed how organizations, specifically the Tennessee Valley Authority, adapted their organizational structures (the technical system) to the demands of external pressures from those communities affected by them. His contribution is that he "distinguished between organizations as technically devised instruments, as mechanical and disposable tools, and organizations that have become institutionalized, becoming valued, natural communities concerned with their own self-maintenance as ends in themselves" (Scott, 1987b).

While there are several variants of institutional theory, there are two core concepts that pervade all of them: *institution* and *institutionalization* (Haveman, 2000). Key constructs in these theories have focused on the broad contexts in which organizations exist as well as the mechanisms that result in institutionalization.

I have included three selections from this class of models. The first is the institutional approach of Phillip Selznick (1949). In his study of the development of the Tennessee Valley Authority that was reported in *TVA and the Grass Roots*, he described how the structure of an organization is affected by outside restraints, so that the organization develops both formal and informal systems that help it to adapt to the outside environment and thus survive.

A second piece, by W. Richard Scott (1987a), elaborates on the more recent developments in institutional theory. In it he discusses different institutional approaches and their strengths and weaknesses, providing a very useful overview of the state of the field.

The third selection is the classic paper on organization ecology by Hannan and Freeman (1977), in which they set forth a Darwinist perspective on the survival of organizations. The central idea of ecological models is that a natural selection process operates such that "environments differentially select organizations for survival on the basis of fit between organizational forms and environmental characteristics" (Scott, 2003, p. 117).

CHAPTER 15

Selznick's *TVA and the Grass Roots**

Henry L. Tosi

Selznick's basic aim in *TVA and the Grass Roots* is to present an approach to analyzing organizations. He is concerned with behavior that is internally relevant to them, and he attempts to examine structural conditions that influence that behavior.

The organization is an adaptive social structure. It is a technical instrument for mobilizing human energies and directing them toward set aims. It is a mechanism that adapts to its environment. It is molded by forces tangential to its rational, ordered structure, and stated goals. The organization may be viewed as a dynamic conditioning field that shapes the behavior of those at its helm (and implicitly other members). It is a tool that has a life of its own separate from that of the members, yet it mobilizes units that must come to terms with the environment. Organization behavior can best be understood when it is traced to the needs and structure of the organization as a living social institution.

Organizations have certain needs generated by the organization itself that command the attention and the decisions of those in power. To satisfy these needs, the organization must adapt to the environment in which it operates. These needs are as follows:

1. The security of the organization in the social environment—this requires some continuity of policy and leadership.

2. Maintenance of the stability of lines of communication and authority.

*Summarized from *TVA and the Grass Roots*, by P. Selznick, 1949, Berkeley: University of California Press. I assume full responsibility for the interpretation herein.

3. A homogeneous outlook of participants regarding the meaning and role of the organization.

4. The achievement of continuous support and participation on the part of the members.

5. The stability of informal relations within the organization.

The formal and informal structure of activities within the organization develops in response to these needs. The organization can continue to exist only when it satisfies these needs and comes to terms with the environment. An informal structure develops within the formal structure of the organization. This informal structure reflects attempts of individuals and subgroups to control the conditions of their existence. It contains an informal control and communications mechanism, or system. This informal structure may be useful to the formal leadership as a communication device, but it extracts a cost for its existence; some power is taken from the formal system.

External Organizations

The characteristics of the organization may be determined by the constraints of other organizations in the environment. External organizations or groups sometimes have a special relationship to the organization. This may require that both the organization and the external body support each other in some way. The organization may have some responsibility to the external units, such as clients, customers, or the public. The character of this external group tends to define and shape the character of the organization. Somehow, it must be represented. It may be formally represented. The organization may recruit external unit members as organization members. They may also absorb them into the leadership structure of the organization. When the outside organization is not formally represented, it must rely on the ideology (to be discussed later) or some other mechanism to maintain the relationship. These external relationships affect the character and policy of the organization since adjustment to them is required.

Cooptation

One way that the organization comes to terms with the environment it through the mechanism of cooptation. Cooptation is an adjustment, or coping, mechanism that enhances the chances of survival of the organization. It is needed when formal authority is out of balance with the institutional environment. It is the process of absorbing new elements into the leadership or policy-determining structure of the organization as a means of averting threats to the organization's stability and existence. It is an attempt to accommodate to the existing environment. In effect, power is shared with other interested groups.

Cooptation may be viewed in both formal and informal dimensions. Formal cooptation occurs when those absorbed into the policymaking and leadership structure share in the power as well as the burdens of administration. This happens when the organization publicly absorbs new elements. It is required when it is necessary to enhance or increase the legitimacy of the governing group, or where there is need for self-government within the organization.

Cooptation may be, however, a response to specific power centers. Informal cooptation is an internal response to the specific pressures of power within the community or the organization. In this case, the coopted elements share only in the power. It is an internal adaptation of the system when the formal authority structure is threatened. The power nucleus of affected groups may be absorbed into the organization to appease or reduce the opposition of other groups. Informal cooptation is a recognition of and a concession to the human resources in the organization. This type of cooptation may *not* be formally acknowledged.

Cooptation reflects the existing tension between social power and formal authority. When formal authority and social power exist together, there is no need for it. Cooptation broadens the leadership and has an important effect on the governing body. It restricts alternatives available to them. There is a need to accommodate the organization to those who have been coopted.

Cooptation is, in fact, a form of delegation. Those who coopt (the leaders) must be concerned with objectives and the means for achieving them. But they must also be concerned with those whom the organization affects. When either formal or informal cooptation occurs, the organization commits itself to activities supported and reinforced by the coopted elements. Thus, it must reach an equilibrium with those coopted, the objectives, the means of achieving them, and the environment. Thus cooptation, even though relatively slight, exerts pressure throughout the organization.

As a result of cooptation, a flow of information may be provided to those who have been coopted. Additionally, the organization is provided with the group resources of those coopted members. Cooptation also allows adaptation of decisions to lower, or local, levels of the organization. Therefore, other organizations within the environment that have been coopted shape the characteristics and the nature of the coopting organization.

Ideology

Organizations are like people, searching for stability and meaning. Instability in the environment results in the development of a sustaining ideology, especially when the organization is threatened by the surrounding environment. It is necessary that this ideology be based on accepted political and moral values. The organization ideology serves as a parameter for decisions.

Ideology, or doctrine, arises as a special need of the organization. The source of ideology in the organization may be (a) from the influence of other institutions, and/or (b) the result of the need for internal communications to develop stability and homogeneity of attitudes.

Ideology facilitates the decentralization of management to lower levels. It shapes the views of new members as well as uniting technical experts within the bounds of the organization rather than toward their professions. Ideology may also emerge as organization members defend it against outsiders. Thus, doctrine, or ideology, satisfies internal needs but also provides an adjustment mechanism for the organization through which it can interact with other segments of the environment. It does not, however, provide a complete adjustment mechanism.

Ideology most probably is stated in language that is ambiguous to the members. The meanings of concepts included in it may be different for different members. For instance, the concept of "increased effectiveness" might suggest reduced operating costs to a production foreman, while it may mean a more restrictive quality-control policy to the quality-control staff executive. These ambiguities, however, mean something to members in terms of the specific activity in which they engage. The diverse meanings of ideology begin to take shape and become concrete through administrative decisions. Decisions must be made within discretionary bounds of the executive. Discretion has to do with the selection of alternatives. When it is used it involves, in some cases, intervention in the activities of other people. It is necessary therefore to consider the interests of those whom the decisions affect.

Decisions must be made within "ideology." The existence and use of abstract philosophies and ideologies to control organization result in problems. Ideology is abstract and action is specific. The resolution of this dilemma is an ongoing activity, and specific action programs must be developed to achieve these abstractions. The activities generally required to achieve abstractions may in practice be difficult to implement. Additionally, the delegation process separates planning functions (which may be derived from the philosophy or ideology) from the operating or specific activity.

Decisions made within the discretion bounds are inhibited by pressure groups within and outside the organization. Some policies may be highly dependent on the connection the organization has with external organizations. For instance, the return goods policy of industrial manufacturers may be a function of "real control" that the buyer has over the seller.

Unanticipated Consequences

Lower-level officials of the organization must make decisions. In some cases, when there is ambiguity regarding the job content of these lower-level officials, their decisions may be based on their own values and norms. These may be inconsistent with, or different from, those of others in the organization. They may also be inconsistent with or different from the objectives of the organization. Policy and doctrine attempt to generate action that is intended to be rational. Decisions within the discretion boundaries of administrators, however, require that they act selectively within their environment, which is conditioned by their own interests, values, or internalized norms. These decisions may yield results other than those intended within the concept of the ideology.

There are several reasons why these unanticipated consequences may occur. First, the individual may have commitments to other places or other organizational units that exert pressures contrary to the ideology. The external commitments of groups or members (basic values, norms, and loyalties) may result in the inability of that organizational component to adjust to other aspects of the organization and to the organization's structure. This is most likely when these various commitments and norms are divergent.

Decisions made by higher-level organization members may commit lower levels to specific actions that the lower levels may not deem desirable. The interests of subgroups or departments must be viewed in light of the social situations within which their activities are carried on and the long-run consequences to the organization. Some activities necessary to maintain the organization may have, then, undesirable consequences for subordinate units. Some acts are simply required, such as procedures, which may become ends in themselves to these lower-level units. When this happens the unit may become more concerned with the performance of the function rather than the end that is desired as a result of performance. This preoccupation with means rather than ends may be harmful to the organization, yet these commitments may be enforced by the social environment and institutionalization.

The individual's personality also must be considered in obtaining unanticipated results. His or her needs, personal history, and experiences may result in a personality that rejects the demands of others, yet he must conform to some degree. Resistance to change and conflict may develop.

The organization strives, however, for a unified pattern of responses. This requires unity, or homogeneity, of outlook of members. As unity is approximated, the organizational character emerges. This may be essentially described as the way people live together in an organization. Those who cannot tolerate this character leave the organization.

The discretion of an executive is related to the organization character in the following manner. By increasing and integrating the many responses within an organization, it can be invested with a character. Precedent and custom then tend to preserve this character. When organizational conflict exists, the process of decisions, or the use of discretion, will be closely scrutinized. The administrator's decision will be infused with a high degree of self-consciousness.

The internal pressures toward unity are generated by the interests, values, and ideas that characterize the social environment of the organization. Once the organization has selected from the many alternative philosophies and values available, the organization reflects on its own character and sentiment to which it becomes aligned. These philosophies and values are available in the social environment, or context, within which the organization operates.

Additionally, different philosophies and values may be representative of various groups within the organization. This may be an unanticipated result of cooptation of members with divergent views. As each group attempts to make its basic philosophy predominant, a struggle for influence may ensue. The internal struggle between these groups is important in the concept of organizational leadership. The struggle results in the evolution of "organization character." This means that if the organization character changes, the leadership that stands for those ideals may be placed in a power position. Or leadership may change the character of the organization by gaining unity of thought regarding a particular ideology.

Another paradox for leadership in an organization should be considered. Leadership, by its nature, is involved with conflicting goals and problems. If it ignores the participation of the members, then the cooperation level may be threatened. If it encourages participation, however, its leadership position may be threatened by the acceptance of another ideology by other organization members.

CHAPTER 16

The Population Ecology of Organizations[1]

Michael T. Hannan

John Freeman

I. Introduction

Analysis of the effects of environment on organizational structure has moved to a central place in organizations theory and research in recent years. This shift has opened a number of exciting possibilities. As yet nothing like the full promise of the shift has been realized. We believe that the lack of development is due in part to a failure to bring ecological models to bear on questions that are preeminently ecological. We argue for a reformulation of the problem in population ecology terms.

Although there is a wide variety of ecological perspectives, they all focus on selection. That is, they attribute patterns in nature to the action of selection processes. The bulk of the literature on organizations subscribes to a different view, which we call the adaptation perspective.[2] According to the adaptation perspective, subunits of the organization, usually managers or dominant coalitions, scan the relevant environment for opportunities and threats, formulate strategic responses, and adjust organizational structure appropriately. The adaptation perspective is seen most clearly in the literature on management. Contributors to it usually assume a hierarchy of authority and control that locates decisions concerning the organization as a whole at the top. It follows, then, that organizations are affected by their environments according to the ways in which managers or leaders formulate strategies, make decisions, and implement them. Particularly successful managers are able either to buffer their organizations from environmental disturbances or to arrange smooth adjustments that require minimal disruption of organizational structure.

Clearly, leaders of organizations do formulate strategies and organizations do adapt to environmental contingencies. As a result at least some of the relationship between structure and environment must reflect adaptive behavior or learning. But there is no reason to presume that the great structural variability among organizations reflects only or even primarily adaptation.

There are a number of obvious limitations on the ability of organizations to adapt. That is, there are a number of processes that generate structural inertia. The stronger the pressures, the lower the organization's adaptive flexibility, and the more likely that the logic of environmental selection is appropriate. As a consequence, the issue of structural inertia is central to the choice between adaptation and selection models.

The possibility that organization structure contains a large inertial component was suggested by Burns and Stalker (1961) and Stinchcombe (1965). But, on the whole the subject has been ignored. A number of relevant propositions can be found in the organizations literature, however.

Inertial pressures arise from both internal structural arrangements and environmental constraints. A minimal list of the constraints arising from internal considerations follows.

1. An organization's investment in plant, equipment, and specialized personnel constitutes assets that are not easily transferable to other tasks or functions. The ways in which such sunk costs constrain adaptation options are so obvious that they need not be discussed further.

2. Organizational decision makers also face constraints on the information they receive. Much of what we know about the flow of information through organizational structures tells us that leaders do not obtain anything close to full information on activities within the organization and environmental contingencies facing the subunits.

3. Internal political constraints are even more important. When organizations alter structure, political equilibria are disturbed. As long as the pool of resources is fixed, structural change almost always involves redistribution of resources across subunits. Such redistribution upsets the prevailing system of exchange among subunits (or subunit leaders). So at least some subunits are likely to resist any proposed reorganization. Moreover, the benefits of structural reorganization are likely to be both generalized (designed to benefit the organization as a whole) and long-run. Any negative political response will tend to generate short-run costs that are high enough that organizational leaders will forego the planned reorganization. (For a more extensive discussion of the ways in which the internal political economy of organizations impedes change or adaptation, see Downs [1967] and Zald [1970].)

4. Finally, organizations face constraints generated by their own history. Once standards of procedure and the allocation of tasks and authority have become the subject of normative agreement, the costs of change are greatly increased. Normative agreements constrain adaptation in at least two ways. First, they provide a justification and an organizing principle for those elements that wish to resist

reorganization (i.e., they can resist in terms of a shared principle). Second, normative agreements preclude the serious consideration of many alternative responses. For example, few research-oriented universities seriously consider adapting to declining enrollments by eliminating the teaching function. To entertain this option would be to challenge central organizational norms.[3]

The external pressures toward inertia seem to be at least as strong. They include at least the following factors.

1. Legal and fiscal barriers to entry and exit from markets (broadly defined) are numerous. Discussions of organizational behavior typically emphasize barriers to entry (state licensed monopoly positions, etc.). Barriers to exit are equally interesting. There are an increasing number of instances in which political decisions prevent firms from abandoning certain activities. All such constraints on entry and exit limit the breadth of adaptation possibilities.

2. Internal constraints upon the availability of information are paralleled by external constraints. The acquisition of information about relevant environments is costly particularly in turbulent situations where the information is most essential. In addition, the type of specialists employed by the organization constrains both the nature of the information it is likely to obtain (see Granovetter, 1973) and the kind of specialized information it can process and utilize.

3. Legitimacy constraints also emanate from the environment. Any legitimacy an organization has been able to generate constitutes an asset in manipulating the environment. To the extent that adaptation (e.g., eliminating undergraduate instruction in public universities) violates the legitimacy claims, it incurs considerable costs. So external legitimacy considerations also tend to limit adaptation.

4. Finally, there is the collective rationality problem. One of the most difficult issues in contemporary economics concerns general equilibria. If one can find an optimal strategy for some individual buyer or seller in a competitive market, it does not necessarily follow that there is a general equilibrium once all players start trading. More generally, it is difficult to establish that a strategy that is rational for a single decision maker will be rational if adopted by a large number of decision makers. A number of solutions to this problem have been proposed in competitive market theory, but we know of no treatment of the problem for organizations generally. Until such a treatment is established we should not presume that a course of action that is adaptive for a single organization facing some changing environment will be adaptive for many competing organizations adopting a similar strategy.

A number of these inertial pressures can be accommodated within the adaptation framework. That is, one can modify and limit the perspective in order to consider choices within the constrained set of alternatives. But to do so greatly limits the scope of one's investigation. We argue that in order to deal with the various inertial pressures the adaptation perspective must be supplemented with a selection orientation.

We consider first two broad issues that are preliminary to ecological modeling. The first concerns appropriate units of analysis. Typical analyses of the relation of organizations to environments take the point of view of a single organization facing an environment. We argue for an explicit focus on populations of organizations. The second broad issue concerns the applicability of population ecology models to the study of human social organization. . . .

II. Population Thinking in the Study of Organization-Environment Relations

Little attention is paid in the organizations literature to issues concerning proper units of analysis (Freeman, 1975). In fact, choice of unit is treated so casually as to suggest that it is not an issue. We suspect that the opposite is true, that the choice of unit involves subtle issues and has far-reaching consequences for research activity. For instance, in the case at hand, it determines which of several ecological literatures can be brought to bear on the study of organization-environment relations.

The comparison of unit choice facing the organizational analyst with that facing the bioecologist is instructive. To oversimplify somewhat, ecological analysis is conducted at three levels: individual, population, and community. Events at one level almost always have consequences at other levels. Despite this interdependence, population events cannot be reduced to individual events (since individuals do not reflect the full genetic variability of the population) and community events cannot be simply reduced to population events. Both the latter employ a population perspective which is not appropriate at the individual level.

We use the term population . . . to refer to aggregates of organizations rather than members. Populations of organizations must be alike in some respect, that is, they must have some unit character. Unfortunately, identifying a population of organizations is no simple matter. The ecological approach suggests that one focus on common fate with respect to environmental variations. Since all organizations are distinctive, no two are affected identically by any given exogenous shock. Nevertheless, we can identify classes of organizations which are relatively homogeneous in terms of environmental vulnerability. Notice that the populations of interest may change somewhat from investigation to investigation depending on the analyst's concern. Populations of organizations referred to are not immutable objects in nature but are abstractions useful for theoretical purposes.

If we are to follow the lead of population biologists, we must identify an analogue to the biologist's notion of species. Various species are defined ultimately in terms of genetic structure. As Monod (1971) indicates it is useful to think of the genetic content of any species as a blueprint.

Consequently, all of the adaptive capacity of a species is summarized in the blueprint. If we are to identify a species analogue for organizations, we must search for such blueprints. These will consist of rules or procedures for obtaining and acting upon inputs in order to produce an organizational product or response.

So for us, an organizational form is a blueprint for organizational action, for transforming inputs into outputs. The blueprint can usually be inferred, albeit in somewhat different ways, by examining any of the following: (1) the formal structure of the organization in the narrow sense—tables of organization, written rules of operation, etc.; (2) the patterns of activity within the organization—what actually gets done by whom; or (3) the normative order—the ways of organizing that are defined as right and proper by both members and relevant sectors of the environment.

To complete the species analogue, we must search for qualitative differences among forms. . . .

[Organizations] are usually defined by geography, by political boundaries, by market or product considerations, etc. Given a systems definition, a population of organizations consists[4] of all the organizations within a particular boundary that have a common form. That is, the population is the form as it exists or is realized within a specified system.

Finally, we would like to identify the properties of populations most interesting to population ecologists. The main concern in this regard was expressed clearly by Elton (1927): "In solving ecological problems we are concerned with *what animals do* in their capacity as whole, living animals, not as dead animals or as a series of parts of animals. We have next to study the circumstances under which they do those things, and, most important of all, the limiting factors which prevent them from doing certain other things. By solving these questions it is possible to discover the reasons for *the distribution and numbers of animals in nature*." Hutchinson (1959) in the subtitle to his famous essay, "Homage to Santa Rosalia," expressed the main focus even more succinctly: "Why Are There So Many Kinds of Animals?" Taking our lead from these distinguished ecologists, we suggest that a population ecology of organizations must seek to understand the distributions of organizations across environmental conditions and the limitations on organizational structures in different environments, and more generally seek to answer the question, Why are there so many kinds of organizations?

III. Discontinuities in Ecological Analysis

. . . The adaptiveness of structure can be unambiguously identified with net reproduction rates. When a population with given properties increases its net reproduction rate following an environmental change, it follows that it is being selected for. This is why modern biologists have narrowed the definition of fitness to the net reproductive rate of population.

Human social organization presumably reflects a greater degree of learning or adaptation. As a result it is more difficult to define fitness in a precise way. Under at least some conditions, organizations may undergo such extreme structural change that they shift from one form to another. As a result, extreme adaptation may give rise to observed changes that mimic selection. This is particularly problematic when the various organizational forms are similar on many dimensions.

We have argued previously (Hannan and Freeman, 1974) for a composite measure of fitness that includes both selection (actual loss of organizations) and mobility among forms (extreme adaptation). Fitness would then be defined as the probability that a given form of organization would persist in a certain environment. We continue to believe that such an approach has value, but we now believe that it is premature to combine adaptation and selection processes. The first order of business is to study selection processes for those situations in which inertial pressures are sufficiently strong that mobility among forms is unlikely.

Furthermore, it is worth noting that the capacity to adapt is itself subject to evolution (i.e., to systematic selection). As we argue below, organizations develop the capacity to adapt at the cost of lowered performance levels in stable environments. Whether or not such adaptable organizational forms will survive (i.e., resist selection) depends on the nature of the environment and the competitive situation. Therefore, a selection point of view treats high levels of adaptability as particular evolutionary outcomes.

IV. The Principle of Isomorphism

There are at least two respects in which the isomorphism formulation [from biology] must be modified and extended if it is to provide satisfactory answers to the question posed. The first modification concerns the mechanism or mechanisms responsible for equilibrium. In this respect, the principle of isomorphism must be supplemented by a criterion of selection and a competition theory. The second modification deals with the fact that the principle of isomorphism neither speaks to issues of optimum adaptation to changing environments nor recognizes that populations of organizations often face multiple environments which impose somewhat inconsistent demands. An understanding of the constraints on organizational forms seems to require modeling of multiple, dynamic environments. . . .

V. Competition Theory

The first of the needed extensions is a specification of the optimization process responsible for isomorphism. We have already discussed two mechanisms: selection and adaptive learning. Isomorphism can result either because nonoptimal forms are selected out of a community of organizations or because organizational decision makers learn optimal responses and adjust organizational behavior accordingly. We continue to focus on the first of these processes: selection. . . .

A focus on selection invites an emphasis on competition. Organizational forms presumably fail to flourish in certain environmental circumstances because other forms successfully compete with them for essential resources. As long as the resources which sustain organizations are finite and populations have unlimited capacity to expand, competition must ensue.

We propose . . . an explicit focus on competition as a mechanism producing isomorphism.[5] In so doing, we can bring a rich set of formal models to bear on the problem. For the case of human social organization, one might argue that selection optimizes the utilization of a specific set of resources including but not restricted to the power and the time of members.

VI. Niche Theory

The principle of isomorphism implies that social organizations in equilibrium will exhibit structural features that are specialized to salient features of the resource environment. As long as the environment is stable and certain, we see no difficulty with this proposition. But does it hold when the environment shifts either predictably or unpredictably among several alternative configurations? Though the issues raised by attempting to answer this question are complex, doing so is crucial to developing adequate models of organizational-environment relations.

Intuition suggests that isomorphism holds as a good approximation only in stable environments. Faced with unstable environments, organizations ought to develop a generalist structure that is not optimally adapted to any single environmental configuration but is optimal over an entire set of configurations. In other words, we ought to find specialized organizations in stable and certain environments and generalist organizations in unstable and uncertain environments. Whether or not this simple proposition holds for social organizations, only empirical research will tell. However, a variety of population ecology models suggests that it is too simplistic. We cannot hope in one paper to develop fully the arguments involved. Instead we indicate the main lines of development with reference to one rather evocative perspective developed by Levins (1962, 1968): the theory of niche width. . . .

In essence, the distinction between specialism and generalism refers to whether a population of organizations flourishes because it maximizes its exploitation of the environment and accepts the risk of having that environment change or because it accepts a lower level of exploitation in return for greater security. Whether or not the equilibrium distribution of organizational forms is dominated by the specialist depends . . . on the shape of the fitness [characteristics] and on properties of the environment. . . .

Part of the efficiency resulting from specialism is derived from the lower requirements for excess capacity. Given some uncertainty, most organizations maintain some excess capacity to ensure the reliability of performance. In a rapidly changing environment, the definition of excess capacity is likely to change frequently. What is used today may become excess tomorrow, and what is excess today may be crucial tomorrow. Organizations operating in environments where the transition from state to state is less frequent will (in equilibrium) have to maintain excess capacity in a given allocational pattern for longer periods of time; whereas those charged with assessing performance will be tempted to view such allocations as wasteful, they may be essential for survival. Thompson (1967) has argued that organizations allocate resources to units charged with the function of insulating core technology from environmentally induced disruption. So, for example, manufacturing firms may retain or employ legal staffs even when they are not currently facing litigation.

The importance of excess capacity is not completely bound up with the issue of how much excess capacity will be maintained. It also involves the manner in which it is used. Organizations may ensure reliable performance by creating specialized units, as Thompson (1967) suggests, or they may allocate excess capacity to organizational roles, by employing personnel with skills and abilities which exceed the routine requirements for using professionals of their jobs.

The point here is that populations of organizational forms will be selected for or against depending upon the amount of excess capacity they maintain and how they allocate it. It may or may not be rational for any particular organization to adopt one pattern or another. What would seem like waste to anyone assessing performance at one time may be the difference between survival and failure later. Similarly, organizations may survive because high levels of professionalization produce coordination by mutual adjustment despite a somewhat chaotic appearance. Others, in which everyone seems to know precisely what he is doing at all times, may fail. Under a given set of environmental circumstances the fundamental ecological question is: which forms thrive and which forms disappear?

Generalism may be observed in a population of organizations, then, either in its reliance upon a wide variety of resources simultaneously or in its maintenance of excess capacity at any given time. This excess capacity allows such organizations to change in order to take advantage of resources which become more readily available. Corporations which maintain an unusually large proportion of their total assets in fluid form ("slack," in terms of theory of the firm; Penrose, 1959; Cyert and March, 1963) are generalizing. In either case, generalism is costly. Under stable environmental circumstances, generalists will be outcompeted by specialists. And at any given point in time, a static analysis will reveal excess capacity. An implication—shifting our focus to individual generalists—is that outside agents will often mistake excess capacity for waste.

[We] introduce a further distinction. Ecologists have found it useful to distinguish both spatial and temporal environmental variation according to grain. Environmental variation is said to be fine-grained when a typical element (organization) encounters many units or replications. From a temporal perspective, variation is fine-grained when typical durations in states are short relative to the lifetime of organizations. Otherwise, the environment is said to be coarse-grained. Demand for products or services is often characterized by fine-grained variation whereas changes in legal structures are more typically coarse-grained.

The essential difference between the two types of environmental variation is the cost of suboptimal strategies. The problem of ecological adaptation can be considered a game of chance in which the population chooses a strategy (specialism or generalism) and then the environment chooses an outcome (by, say, flipping a coin). If the environment "comes up" in a state favorable to the organizational form, it prospers; otherwise, it declines. However, if the variation is fine-grained (durations are short), each population of organizations experiences a great many trials and environment is experienced as an average. When variation is coarse-grained, however, the period of decline stemming from a wrong choice may exceed the organizational capacity to sustain itself under unfavorable conditions. . . .

Consider first the cases in which the environment is stable. . . . Not surprisingly, specialism is optimal. The results for unstable environments diverge. When . . . the demands of the different environmental states are similar and/or complementary, generalism is optimal. But when the environmental demands differ . . . , specialism is optimal. This is not as strange a result as it first appears. When the environment changes rapidly among quite different states, the cost of generalism is high. Since the demands in the different states are dissimilar, considerable structural management is required of generalists. But since the environment changes rapidly, these organizations will spend most of their time and energies adjusting structure. It is apparently better under such conditions to adopt a specialized structure and "ride out" the adverse environments.

The case of coarse-grained environments is somewhat more complex. Our intuitive understanding is that since the duration of an environmental state is long, maladaptation ought to be given greater weight. That is, the costs of maladaptation greatly outweigh any advantage incurred by the correct choice. . . . We saw above that when such variation is fine-grained, it is better to specialize. When the duration of environmental states is long, however, the costs of this strategy are great. Long periods of nonadaptation will threaten the survival of the organization. In addition, the fact that the environment changes less often means that generalists need not spend most of their time and energies altering structure. Thus generalism is the optimal strategy. . . .

Coarse-grained and uncertain variation favors a distinct form of generalism: polymorphism. We do not have to search very far to find an analogous outcome. Organizations may federate in such a way that supraorganizations consisting of heterogeneous collections of specialist organizations pool resources. When the environment is uncertain and coarse-grained and subunits difficult to set up and tear down, the costs of maintaining the unwieldy structure imposed by federation may be more than offset by the fact that at least a portion of the amalgamated organization will do well no matter what the state of the environment. In terms of the model suggested above there are no other situations in which such federated organizations have a competitive advantage. And even in this case, the only time during which they have such an advantage is when coarse-grained variation is uncertain. . . .

Such an amalgamated "holding company" pattern may be observed in modern universities. Enrollment and research support wax and wane over time as do the yield on invested endowment securities and the beneficence of legislatures. Some of these resources follow predictable cycles. Others do not. But it is extremely expensive to build up and dismantle academic units. It is costly not only in money but also in the energies consumed by political conflict. Consequently, universities are constantly "taxing" subunits with plentiful environments to subsidize less fortunate subunits. It is common, for instance, for universities to allocate faculty positions according to some fixed master plan, under-supporting the rapidly growing departments and maintaining excess faculty in others. This partial explanation of the unwieldy structures that encompass liberal arts departments, professional schools, research laboratories, etc. is at least as persuasive as explanations that emphasize intellectual interdependence among units.

Much more can be said concerning applications of niche theory to organization-environment relations. We have focused on a simple version highlighting the interplay between competition and environmental variation in the determination of optimal adaptive structure in order to show that the principle of isomorphism needs considerable expansion to deal with multiple environmental outcomes and their associated uncertainty. The literature in ecology to which we have made reference is growing exponentially at the moment and new results and models are appearing monthly. The products of these developments provide students of organizations with a rich potential for the study of organization-environment relations.

Consider an example. In his analysis of bureaucratic and craft administration or production, Stinchcombe (1959) argued that construction firms do not rely upon bureaucratically organized administrative staffs because of seasonal fluctuations in demand. Administrative staffs constitute an overhead cost which remains roughly constant over the year. The advantage of the otherwise costly (in terms of salaries) craft administration is that coordination of work is accomplished through a reliance upon prior socialization of craftsmen and upon organization. Since employment levels can more easily be increased or decreased with demand under a craft system, administrative costs are more easily altered to meet demand.

The fundamental source of this pattern is the seasonal variation in construction. In ecological terms, the demand environment is coarse-grained. In addition, the two states defined by season are quite different, resulting in a concave fitness curve. Craft-administered housing construction firms are probably quite inefficient when demand is at its peak and when the kind of housing under construction is standardized. In such situations, we would expect this form of organization to face stiff competition from other firms. For instance, in regions where housing construction is less seasonal, modular housing, mobile homes, and prefabricated housing are more likely to flourish and we would expect the construction business to be more highly bureaucratized.

Another variation in demand is to be found in the business cycle. While seasonal fluctuations are stable (uncertainty is low), interest rates, labor relations, and materials costs are more difficult to predict. Variations of this sort should favor a generalist mode of adaptation. That is, when environments are coarse-grained . . . and uncertain, populations of organizations will be more likely to survive if they hedge their bets by seeking a wider variety of resource bases. For this reason, we think, craft-administered construction organizations are frequently general contractors who not only build houses but engage in other kinds of construction as well (shopping plazas, office buildings, etc.). In comparison, modular housing is cheaper and the units are installed on rented space. Consequently, interest rates are less important. Since organizations producing this kind of housing do not employ craftsmen but use the cheapest and least skilled labor they can obtain, labor relations are less problematical. It may also be that their reliance on different materials (e.g., sheet aluminum) contributes to a lower level of uncertainty. In consequence, we would expect this form of organization to be more highly specialized in its adaptation (of course there are technical factors which contribute to this as well).

Craft-administered construction firms are set up in such a way that they can adapt rapidly to changes in demand, and they can adapt to different construction problems by varying the mix of skills represented in their work force. Bureaucratically administered construction firms are more specialized and as a result they are efficient only when demand is high, and very inefficient when it is low. We also believe that they tend to be more specialized with regard to type of construction. Craft-administered organizations sacrifice efficient exploitation of their niche for flexibility. Bureaucratic organizations choose the opposite strategy. This formulation is an extension of Stinchcombe's and serves to show that his argument is essentially ecological.

VII. Discussion

Our aim in this paper has been to move toward an application of modern population ecology theory to the study of organization-environment relations. For us, the central question is, why are there so many kinds of organizations? Phrasing the question in this way opens the possibility of applying a rich variety of formal models to the analysis of the effects of environmental variations on organizational structure.

We begin with Hawley's classic formulation of human ecology. . . . In particular we concentrate on the principle of isomorphism. This principle asserts that there is a one-to-one correspondence between structural elements of social organization and those units that mediate flows of essential resources into the system. It explains the variations in organizational forms in equilibrium. But any observed isomorphism can arise from purposeful adaptation of organizations to the common constraints they face or because nonisomorphic organizations are selected against. Surely both processes are at work in most social systems. We believe that the organizations literature has emphasized the former to the exclusion of the latter.

We suspect that careful empirical research will reveal that for wide classes of organizations there are very strong inertial pressures on structure arising both from internal arrangements (e.g., internal politics) and the environment (e.g., public legitimation of organizational activity). To claim otherwise is to ignore the most obvious feature of organizational life. Failing churches do not become retail stores; nor do firms transform themselves into churches. Even within broad areas of organizational action, such as higher education and labor union activity, there appear to be substantial obstacles to fundamental structural change. Research is needed on this issue. But until we see evidence to the contrary, we will continue to doubt that the major features of the world of organizations arise through learning or adaptation. Given these doubts, it is important to explore an evolutionary explanation of the principle of isomorphism. That is, we wish to embed the principle of isomorphism within an explicit selection framework.

In order to add selection processes we propose a competition theory [that] . . . relies on growth models that appear suitable for representing both organizational development and the growth of populations of organizations. Recent work by bioecologists . . . yields propositions that have immediate relevance for the study of organization-environment relations. These results concern the effects of changes in the number and mixture of constraints upon systems with regard to the upper bound of the diversity of forms of organization. We propose that such propositions can be tested by examining the impact of varieties of state regulation both on size distributions and on the diversity of organizational forms within broadly defined areas of activity (e.g., medical care, higher education, and newspaper publishing).

A more important extension of Hawley's work introduces dynamic considerations. The fundamental issue here concerns the meaning of isomorphism in situations in which the environment to which units are adapted is changing and uncertain. Should "rational" organizations attempt to develop specialized isomorphic structural relations with one of the possible environmental states? Or should they adopt a more plastic strategy and institute more generalized structural features? The isomorphism principle does not speak to these issues.

We suggest that the concrete implication of generalism for organizations is the accumulation and retention of varieties of excess capacity. To retain the flexibility of structure required for adaptation to different environmental outcomes requires that some capacities be held in reserve and not committed to action. Generalists will always be outperformed by specialists who, with the same levels of resources, happen to have hit upon their optimal environment. Consequently, in any cross-section the generalists will appear inefficient because excess capacity will often be judged waste. Nonetheless, organizational slack is a pervasive feature of many types of organizations. The question then arises: what types of environments favor generalists? Answering this question comprehensively takes one a long way toward understanding the dynamic of organization environment relations.

We begin addressing this question in the suggestive framework of Levins's (1962, 1968) fitness-set theory. This is one of a class of recent theories that relates the nature of environmental uncertainty to optimal levels of structural specialism. Levins argues that along with uncertainty one must consider the grain of the environment or the lumpiness of environmental outcomes. The theory indicates that specialism is always favored in stable or certain environments. This is no surprise. But contrary to the view widely held in the organizations literature, the theory also indicates that generalism is not always optimal in uncertain environments. When the environment shifts uncertainly among states that place very different demands on the organization, and the duration of environmental states is short relative to the life of the organization (variation is fine-grained), populations of organizations that specialize will be favored over those that generalize. This is because organizations that attempt to adapt to each environmental outcome will spend most of their time adjusting structure and very little time in organizational action directed at other ends.

Stated in these terms, the proposition appears obvious. However, when one reads the literature on organization-environment relations, one finds that it was not so obvious. Most important, the proposition follows from a simple explicit model that has the capacity to unify a wide variety of propositions relating environmental variations to organizational structure.

Notes

1. From "The Population Ecology of Organizations," by M. Hannan and J. Freeman, 1977, *American Journal of Sociology, 82*(3), pp. 929–964.

2. There is a subtle relationship between selection and adaptation. Adaptive learning for individuals usually consists of selection among behavioral responses. Adaptation for a population involves selection among types of members. More generally, processes involving selection can usually be recast at a higher level of analysis as adaptation processes. However, once the unit of analysis is chosen there is no ambiguity in distinguishing selection from adaptation. Organizations often adapt to environmental conditions in concert and this suggests a systems effect. Though few theorists would deny the existence of such systems effects, most do not make them a subject of central concern. It is important to notice that, from the point of view embraced by sociologists whose interests focus on the broader social system, selection in favor of organizations with one set of properties to the disfavor of those with others is often an adaptive process. Societies and communities which consist in part of formal organizations adapt partly through processes that adjust the mixture of various kinds of organizations found within them. Whereas a complete theory of organization and environment would have to consider both adaptation and selection, recognizing that they are complementary processes, our purpose here is to show what can be learned from studying selection alone (see Aldrich and Pfeffer [1976] for a synthetic review of the literature focusing on these different perspectives).

3. Meyer's (1970) discussion of an organization's charter adds further support to the argument that normative agreements arrived at early in an organization's history constrain greatly the organization's range of adaptation to environmental constraints.

4. The term "organizational form" is used widely in the sociological literature (see Stinchcombe [1965]).

5. We include only the first and third of Hawley's stages in our model of competition. We prefer to treat uniformity of response and community diversity as consequences of combinations of certain competitive processes and environmental features.

CHAPTER 17

The Adolescence of Institutional Theory

W. Richard Scott

After a period of rapid growth and high creative energy, institutional theory in organizations has apparently entered a phase of more deliberate development, accompanied by efforts aimed at self-assessment and consolidation. Recently, several prominent institutional theorists—including DiMaggio (1988) and Zucker (1987)—have momentarily suspended their efforts to expand the variety and scope of institutional arguments and/or devise new data sets and tests, in order to step back and take stock of the progress of this new perspective to date. This paper is in that same contemplative and critical vein.

To examine contemporary institutional analysis, I review both influential theoretical statements and recent empirical work. The latter is surveyed in order to gather more inductive evidence about the types of arguments that are currently being made in linking institutional factors to organizational structure and performance.

The Many Faces of Institutional Theory

The concepts of institution and institutionalization have been defined in diverse ways, with substantial variation among approaches. Thus, the beginning of wisdom in approaching institutional theory is to recognize at the outset that there is not one but several variants. Some versions are much more carefully defined and explicit about their definitions and referents, while others are less clear in conceptualization. Although there seems to be an underlying similarity in the various approaches, there is little agreement on specifics.

*From "The Adolescence of Institutional Theory," by W. R. Scott, 1987, *Administrative Science Quarterly*, 32(4), pp. 493–511.

Without claiming to be definitive or exhaustive, but rather as a way of illustrating the present variety of offerings available to scholars of organizations, I briefly review four sociological formulations all claiming an institutional focus.[1] The review proceeds generally from the earlier to the more recent conceptions.

Institutionalization as a Process of Instilling Value

One of the earliest and most influential versions of institutional theory in organizations remains that associated with the work of Philip Selznick and his students. Seznick borrowed from Michels and Barnard in creating his somewhat distinctive model of institutional theory (Scott, 1987: 51–68). He viewed organizational structure as an adaptive vehicle shaped in reaction to the characteristics and commitments of participants as well as to influences and constraints from the external environment. Institutionalization refers to this adaptive process: "In what is perhaps its most significant meaning, 'to institutionalize' is to *infuse with value* beyond the technical requirements of the task at hand" (Selznick, 1957: 17). Anticipating later work, Selznick distinguished between organizations as technically devised instruments, as mechanical and disposable tools, and organizations that have become institutionalized, becoming valued, natural communities concerned with their own self-maintenance as ends in themselves:

> . . . organizations are technical instruments, designed as means to definite goals. They are judged on engineering premises; they are expendable. Institutions, whether conceived as groups or practices, may be partly engineered, but they also have a "natural" dimension. They are products of interaction and adaptation; they become the receptacles of group idealism; they are less readily expendable. (Selznick, 1957: 21–22)

Selznick's institutional approach also emphasized the importance of history—the "natural history" of the evolution of a living form that is adaptively changing over time, and he stressed a holistic and contextual approach. As Perrow (1986: 157–158) noted:

> For institutional analysis, the injunction is to analyze the whole organization. To see it as a whole is to do justice to its "organic" character. Specific processes are, of course, analyzed in detail, but it is the nesting of these processes into the whole that gives them meaning.

Selznick's distinctive brand of institutional theory was applied by him to the analysis of the Tennessee Valley Authority public corporation and by his students—including, most notably, Burton Clark, Charles Perrow, and Mayer Zald—to a number of educational, service, and voluntary organizations. The typical research methodology is that of the case study, with an emphasis on adaptive change.

At the risk of oversimplifying Selznick's rather complex views, his primary emphasis appears to have been on institutionalization as a means of instilling value, supplying intrinsic worth to a structure or process that, before institutionalization, had only instrumental utility. By instilling value, institutionalization promotes stability: persistence of the structure over time.

Selznick (1957: 16) clearly viewed institutionalization as a "process," as something "that happens to the organization over time." He observed the extent of institutionalization to vary across organizations—for example, those with more specific goals and those more specialized and technical in operation were seen to be less subject to becoming institutionalized than those lacking these features. In his early, more descriptive work, Selznick emphasized the cressive . . . , unplanned, and unintended nature of institutional processes (e.g., Selznick, 1949). By contrast, in his later, more prescriptive writings, following the lead of Barnard (1938), he embraced an "enacted" conception, emphasizing that effective leaders are able to define and defend the organization's institutional values—its distinctive mission (e.g., Selznick, 1957). The institutionalization process was viewed as being subject to conscious design and intervention.

Nevertheless, Selznick's conception remains largely definitional rather than explanatory: he defined and described the process but did not explicitly account for it. His treatment of institutionalization informs us *that* values are instilled; not *how* this occurs.

Institutionalization as a Process of Creating Reality

Both the second and the third versions of institutional theory are heavily indebted to the work of Peter Berger in the sociology of knowledge. This work is based on philosophical underpinnings established by German idealists and phenomenologists such as Dilthey and Husserl and strongly shaped by the ideas of Alfred Schutz (1962). The most complete and influential statement of Berger's ideas on institutionalization is to be found in the work coauthored with Luckmann in which the central question addressed is, What is the nature and origin of social order?

The argument is that social order is based fundamentally on a shared social reality which, in turn, is a human construction, being created in social interaction. It is recognized that man or woman as a biological organism confronts few limits or constraints in the form of instinctual patterns, yet constraints develop in the form of a social order. Berger and Luckmann (1967: 52) argued that this order "is a human product, or, more precisely, an ongoing human production. It is produced by man in the course of his ongoing externalization. . . . Social order exists only as a product of human activity." Social order comes into being as individuals take action, interpret that action, and share with others their interpretations. These interpretations, or "typifications," are attempts to classify the behavior into categories that will enable the actors to respond to it in a similar fashion. The process by which actions become repeated over time and are assigned similar meanings by self and others is defined as institutionalization: "Institutionalization occurs whenever there is a reciprocal typification of habitualized actions by types of actors" (Berger and Luckmann, 1967: 54). Both actions and actors are typed: certain forms of actions come to be associated with certain classes of actors; e.g., supervisors give orders, workers follow them.

Like Selznick, Berger and Luckmann (1967: 54–55) emphasized the necessity of employing an historical approach:

> Reciprocal typifications of action are built up in the course of a shared history. They cannot be created instantaneously. Institutions always have a history, of which they are the products. It is impossible to understand an institution adequately without an understanding of the historical process in which it was produced.

As explicated by Berger and Luckmann, institutionalization involves three phases, or "moments": externalization, objectivation, and internalization. We and our associates take action (externalization), but we together interpret our actions as having an external reality separate from ourselves (objectivation); further, the objectivated world is internalized by us, coming to "determine the subjective structures of consciousness itself" (internalization) (Wuthnow et al., 1984: 39). Each moment corresponds to "an essential characterization of the social world. *Society is a human product. Society is an objective reality. Man is a social product*" (Berger and Luckmann, 1967: 61). Together they comprise the paradox "that man is capable of producing a world that he then experiences as something other than a human product" (Berger and Luckmann, 1967: 61).

This quite general conception serves as the foundation for the work of both Zucker and of Meyer and Rowan—theorists who have developed and applied these ideas to the analysis of organizational forms. Berger and Luckmann's formulation is clearly visible in the definitions they employ as the basis of their own work. Thus, Zucker (1977: 728) asserted that institutionalization is both a process and a property variable. It is the process by which individual actors transmit what is socially defined as real and, at the same time, at any point in the process the meaning of an act can be defined as more or less a taken-for-granted part of this social reality. Institutionalized acts, then, must be perceived as both *objective* and *exterior*.

Meyer and Rowan (1977: 341) in their influential article on institutionalized organizations also embraced Berger and Luckmann's conception:

> Institutionalized rules are classifications built into society as reciprocated typifications or interpretations (Berger and Luckmann, 1967, p. 54).... Institutionalization involves the processes by which social processes, obligations, or actualities come to take on a rulelike status in social thought and action.

The common feature in all of these definitions is that institutionalization is viewed as the social *process* by which individuals come to accept a shared definition of social reality—a conception whose validity is seen as independent of the actor's own views or actions but is taken for granted as defining the "way things are" and/or the "way things are to be done."

Still, these definitions are very general, pertaining to the construction of social reality—and, hence, stable social order—in all its various guises, not to features conducive to the rise of formal organizations in particular. In subsequent work, however, Berger and other collaborators attempted to characterize the distinctive set of beliefs associated with the development of societal modernization. In an important work that has not received the attention it merits, Berger, Berger, and Kellner (1973) argued that modern consciousness is shaped by the set of interconnected belief systems associated with the development of (1) technological production, (2) bureaucracies, and (3) the pluralization of life-worlds (e.g., the differentiation of public and private spheres). These belief systems and their associated cognitive styles both develop out of and independently cause the further spread of "rational" economic, political, and social organizations.

Zucker (1983: 1) echoed and elaborated this view of organization as an institutional form or, more compellingly, as "the preeminent institutional form in modern society." And Meyer and Rowan (1977) placed great emphasis on societal modernization as being accompanied by the growth of "rationalized institutional elements" or "rational myths" that give rise to an increasing number of organizations as well as to the elaboration of existing organizational forms.

In Zucker's work, the emphasis on institutionalization as process has continued to dominate. The force of these models is in the cognitive convictions they evoke:

> . . . institutionalization is rooted in conformity—not conformity engendered by sanctions (whether positive or negative), nor conformity resulting from a "black-box" internalization process, but conformity rooted in the taken-for-granted aspects of everyday life. . . . institutionalization operates to produce common understandings about what is appropriate and, fundamentally, meaningful behavior. (Zucker, 1983: 5)

Her empirical work includes laboratory research demonstrating that subjects' behavior is much more likely to be stable and conform to the requirements imposed by other actors if the latter are perceived to occupy a position in an organization: "Any act performed by the occupant of an office is seen as highly objectified and exterior" (Zucker, 1977: 728). It also includes field studies of the process by which civil service reforms were diffused through a set of municipal governments during the period 1880–1935 (Tolbert and Zucker, 1983). While early adopters of these reforms were argued to be acting in rational self-interest—city characteristics predicted early adoption—later adopters were argued to be acting in response to the established legitimacy of these institutional practices—reforms were adopted by more and more cities regardless of their specific demographic or political makeup.

In Zucker's approach, the focus is on a single pattern or mode of organizational behavior and the emphasis is placed on the rationale for or nature of the process underlying adoption of or conformity to the pattern. By contrast, the work of Meyer and his collaborators has evolved in a somewhat different direction. Beginning with his seminal article with Rowan (Meyer and Rowan, 1977), Meyer began to develop an alternative conception. From a primary focus on institutionalization as a distinctive process—whether stressing infusion with value or with taken-for-granted meaning—institutionalization began to be viewed as pertaining to a distinctive set of elements.[2]

Institutional Systems as a Class of Elements

In this version of institutional theory it is emphasized that institutionalized belief systems constitute a distinctive class of elements that can account for the existence and/or the elaboration of organizational structure. This emphasis can be dated from Meyer and Rowan's (1977) argument that the prevalence of organizational forms can be attributed not only to the complexity of "relational networks" and exchange processes but also to the existence of elaborated "rational myths" or shared belief systems. The emphasis shifts from the properties of generalized belief systems to the existence of a variety of sources or loci of "rationalized and impersonal prescriptions that identify various social purposes" and "specify in a rulelike way the appropriate means" to pursue them (Meyer and Rowan, 1977: 343). These sources are described as institutionalized in that their existence and efficacy is "in some measure beyond the discretion of any individual participant or organization" (Meyer and Rowan, 1977: 344).

A number of important changes are introduced by this shift in emphasis. First, the salient features of organizational environments are reconceptualized. In contrast to the prevailing theories of organizational environments—such as contingency theory or resource dependence—that call attention primarily to technical requirements, resource streams, information flows, and influence relations, the new formulation stresses the role played by cultural elements—symbols, cognitive systems, normative beliefs—and the sources of such elements. Institutional elements of environments begin to be defined in contrast to technical elements, and this definition becomes more explicit and pronounced over time. Thus, Scott and Meyer (1983: 140, 149) defined technical environments as "those within which a product or service is exchanged in a market such that organizations are rewarded for effective and efficient control of the work process," in contrast to institutional environments that "are characterized by the elaboration of rules and requirements to which individual organizations must conform if they are to receive support and legitimacy. . . ."

Second, it follows that there is less emphasis on institutionalization as a distinctive process. Organizations do not necessarily conform to a set of institutionalized beliefs because they "constitute reality" or are taken for granted, but often because they are rewarded for doing so through increased legitimacy, resources, and survival capabilities (Meyer and Rowan, 1977). Since the concept of institutionalization is not definitionally linked to a distinctive process, analysts begin to theorize more explicitly about the variety of types of processes that might cause an organization to change its structure in ways that make it conform to—become isomorphic with—an institutional pattern. The best-known classification of this type is that developed by DiMaggio and Powell (1983), who distinguished among coercive, memetic, and normative processes leading to conformity. None of these classes, however, is consistent with the previous process-based definition of institutionalization; that is, none focuses specifically on conformity based on the extent to which the model being adopted is taken for granted.

Third, with less attention devoted to process, more can be given to the nature of the belief systems themselves. In their formal propositions, Meyer and Rowan theorized about the general effects of rationalized institutional structure as though there were only one such structure, but with their concept of rational myths and through the use of many and diverse examples—public opinion, educational systems, laws, courts, professions, ideologies, regulatory structures, awards and prizes, certification and accreditation bodies, governmental endorsements and requirements— they underscored the multiplicity and diversity of institutional sources and belief systems found in modern societies. Following this insight, more recent work has moved away from a conception of the institutional environment to one of multiple institutional environments (DiMaggio and Powell, 1983; Meyer and Scott, 1983).

Fourth, there is the recognition that, in modern, rationalized societies, the forms and sources of social beliefs and other types of symbolic systems have themselves become more rationalized: folkways and traditions and customs give way to laws, rules, and regulations; and elders' councils and other forms of traditional authority are replaced by the nation-state, the professions, and rationalized systems of law. Thus, this version of institutional theory tends to shift attention away from such environmental elements as the market, the location of resources and customers, and the number and power of competitors, in order to call attention to the role of other types of actors, such as the state and professional associations, that shape organizational life both directly by imposing constraints and requirements and indirectly by creating and promulgating new rational myths.

Finally, with the shift to a focus on symbolic aspects of environments and their sources, this version of institutional theory has both contributed to and benefited from the resurgence of interest in culture. Thus, this institutional theory provides a bridge for students of organizations to link to the insightful work of Berger, Bourdieu, Douglas, Foucault, Geertz, and Wuthnow, to name only some of the leading contributors to the "new" cultural approaches.

Institutions as Distinct Societal Spheres

A fourth conception of institution embraces the idea just described of diversity among belief systems and links it with the early, traditional view of social institutions found in general sociology. As conventionally defined, social institutions refer to relatively enduring systems of social beliefs and socially organized practices associated with varying functional arenas within societal systems, e.g., religion, work, the family, politics. In most of these traditional definitions, social institutions are viewed as both symbolic—cognitive and normative—systems and behavioral systems, and strong emphasis is given to persistence and stability as a key defining characteristic. For example, in his early, influential discussion, Hughes (1939: 283–284) noted:

> More commonly the term *institution* is applied to those features of social life which outlast biological generations or survive drastic social changes that might have been expected to bring them to an end. . . . [There exists] a tendency of human beings to get set in their ways. Other animals undoubtedly show a similar tendency, but man alone transmits to future generations a great number of his acquired ways of behaving. He alone gives reasons for his ways, makes a virtue of them and glorifies them for their antiquity.

Hughes also anticipated Selznick's views on institutionalization as a source of value independent of instrumental utility:

> A ceremony may be celebrated by people who no longer know its origin and would repudiate its first meaning if they but knew it. A once technically useful means of achieving some known end persists as an accepted and even sacred practice after better technical devices have been invented. (Hughes, 1939: 283)

Hertzler's (1961: 81) discussion of social institutions has also had influence, and he stressed the theme of persistence in stating, "The institutions of a society have a high degree of stability and function as the major mechanisms for social continuity." Hertzler (1961: 84) also placed great importance on the external and overdetermined nature of institutional patterns:

> Especially important is the fact that they are organized, that is, established, regularized, chartered, endorsed, and enforced, and hence made predictable and effective in all of the common or recurrent relational-functional situations.

But finally, embedded in all of the early treatments, there was the structural-functional assumption that basic needs or survival requisites were set and that the differentiation of institutional spheres constituted an adaptive societal response to these requirements. Institutional analysis consisted of describing these different social structures—for example, much attention was given to the varying beliefs and practices in the conduct of family life as compared to economic pursuits and linking them to a specified set of social requirements. . . .

Friedland and Alford (1987) proposed that this relatively neglected conception of societal structure can usefully be revived, with some revision. As a starting point, they asserted that the notion of society comprising differentiated societal spheres containing different belief systems and defining different types of social relations is both correct and useful. Moreover, they insisted that it is essential to introduce substantive content into any discussion of institutions. Different institutional spheres call up different belief systems. For example, the institutional logic of capitalism is accumulation and the commodification of human activity. That of the state is rationalization and the regulation of human activity by legal and bureaucratic hierarchies. . . . That of the family is community and the motivation of human activity by unconditional loyalty to its members and their welfare . . . (Friedland and Alford, 1987: 36). Friedland and Alford emphasized the importance of differentiated institutional spheres with varying substantive content but did not take on the question as to why such differentiation occurs.

The aspect of early institutional arguments to which Friedland and Alford took exception is the assumption—one that frequently accompanies such functionalist models—of normative integration or institutional coherence. They suggested that there is no necessary harmony among various institutional complexes. Moreover, there may not be consensus within a given society regarding which beliefs are appropriate for what types of activities. Any given activity—the carrying on of productive work, the attempt to govern—can have multiple meanings and can be the focus of conflicting and contradictory institutional definitions and demands:

> Some of the most important struggles between groups, organizations and classes are over the appropriate relation between institutions, and by which institutional logic different activities should be regulated and to which categories of persons they apply. Are access to housing and health to be regulated by the market or by the state? Are families, churches or states to control education? Should reproduction be regulated by state, family or church? (Friedland and Alford, 1987: 32–33)

Thus, this version of institutional theory focuses attention on the existence of a set of differentiated and specialized cognitive and normative systems—institutional logics—and patterned human activities that arise and tend to persist, in varying form and content, in all societies. These logics and behaviors constitute repertoires that are available to individuals and organizations to employ in pursuit of their own interests (cf. Swidler, 1986). In this view, an important part of the social analyst's agenda is not only to determine which organizations come to adopt which beliefs and practices but also "to study why the institutional arenas are patterned in the way that they are or the conditions under which new institutional forms develop" (Friedland and Alford, 1987: 18).

To approach the latter issue requires both a greater attention to content—to examining the varying substantive beliefs and behaviors associated with different institutional spheres—as well as the explicit adoption of a societal level of analysis to supplement the current work now underway at the organizational level of analysis (for a related analytical framework and agenda, cf. Burns and Flam, 1986).

It should be clear from the four versions of institutional theory reviewed that while there are some basic recurring themes, there nevertheless exists much variation among contemporary institutional theories of organizations. When someone announces that he or she is conducting an institutional analysis, the next question should be, using which version?

The Multiple Forms of Institutional Explanation

In recent empirical studies, organizational investigators have invoked institutional arguments in order to explain features of organizational structure. While there is little disagreement among such analysts that institutional elements affect the structural characteristics of organizations, a review of the current literature suggests that there is little agreement as to how and why and where—in what parts of the structure such effects occur. While I did not attempt to conduct a comprehensive survey or construct a complete listing, my reading of the recent empirical studies has identified seven different accounts of structural influence. The accounts vary in one or more respects: (1) what types of institutional elements are singled out for attention; (2) what influence or causal mechanisms are identified; and (3) what aspects of organizational structure are affected. My categorization scheme placed major emphasis on the causal arguments. My object is not to determine which of these accounts is more or less "institutional" in character but only to call attention to the fact that, at least at present, institutional explanations are not all of a piece.

The Imposition of Organizational Structure

Some institutional sectors or fields contain environmental agents that are sufficiently powerful to impose structural forms and/or practices on subordinate organizational units. Nation-states do this when mandating by law changes in existing organizational forms or when creating a new class of administrative agencies. Corporations routinely do this, for example, when structural changes are imposed on companies that have been acquired or when existing subsidiaries are reorganized. DiMaggio and Powell (1983) referred to this type of influence as coercive, but it may be useful to employ more fine-grained distinctions. For example, under the category of imposition, it seems useful to distinguish between two subtypes: imposition by means of authority vs. imposition by means of coercive power. We would expect changes in structural forms imposed by authority to meet with less resistance, to occur more rapidly (see Tolbert and Zucker, 1983, on the diffusion of municipal reforms in those states that adopted them for all cities), and to be associated with higher levels of compliance and stability than those imposed by force. The structural changes should also be less superficial and loosely coupled to participants' activities than those imposed by coercive power.

While institutionalists share with others—e.g., resource dependency theorists—an interest in power processes, an institutional perspective gives special emphasis to authority relations: the ability of organizations, especially public organizations, to rely on legitimate coercion (cf. Streeck and Schmitter, 1985).

The Authorization of Organizational Structure

A related but distinct type of institutional mechanism involves the authorization or legitimation of the structural features or qualities of a local organizational form by a superordinate unit. The feature that distinguishes this mode from the case of imposition is that the subordinate unit is not compelled to conform but voluntarily seeks out the attention and approval of the authorizing agent. As DiMaggio and Powell (1983) noted, this type of normative pressure is especially likely to be found in professional sectors and organizations. Thus, voluntary hospitals in the U.S. are not required as a condition of their operation to receive accreditation from the Joint Commission on Accreditation of Hospitals, but most find it in their own interests to seek out such legitimation. In their study of the population of voluntary social service agencies operating in Toronto, Canada, during the period 1970–1980, Singh, Tucker, and House (1986) measured such authorization mechanisms as being listed in the *Community Directory of Metropolitan Toronto* and receipt of a charitable registration number issued by Revenue Canada. Such voluntarily sought indicators were treated as signifying "external legitimacy"—as indicating that the organizations listed had been "endorsed by powerful external collective actors" (Singh, Tucker, and House, 1986: 176). Their analyses provide strong evidence that the receipt of such endorsements was associated with improved life chances: listed organizations showed significantly higher survival rates than those that were unlisted over the period surveyed.

I use the term "authorization" in this context in order to connect this mechanism directly with an earlier treatment of authority norms. In discussing the sources of authority, Dornbusch and Scott (1975: 56–63) defined "authorization" as the process by which norms supporting the exercise of authority by a given agent are defined and enforced by a superordinate unit. Authority is legitimated power; legitimated power is normatively regulated power. When an organization's power is "authorized" it is, presumptively, supported and constrained by the actions of officials superior to it and in a position to oversee its appropriate use.

In many arenas there are multiple possible sources of authorization. Organizations must determine to which, if any, external sponsors to connect. There are often costs as well as gains associated with such choices. Organizations may have to modify their structures and/or activities in various ways in order to acquire and maintain the support of external agents; and, at a minimum, they must provide information and access to the representatives of these bodies. The frequent occurrence of authorization processes across a wide variety of sectors, however, suggests that, for many types of organizations, the gains associated with these external connections far outweigh the costs.

The Inducement of Organizational Structure

Many institutional sectors lack agents with power or authority to impose their own structural definitions on local organizational forms, but they may be in a position to provide strong inducements to organizations that conform to their wishes. Relatively weak nation-states, like the U.S., often resort to such market-like control tactics because they lack the authority to impose their programs on subordinate units, especially when the subordinate units are lodged in a different tier of the federalist "cake" from the control agent. For example, the U.S. government frequently is able to obtain control over funding streams within a given societal sector such as education or health care but lacks authority over programmatic elements, which remain under the control of local organizational officials or assorted professions (Scott, 1982; Meyer, 1983; Scott and Meyer, 1983).

Inducement strategies create structural changes in organizations and organizational fields by providing incentives to organizations that are willing to conform to the agent's conditions. Typically, the funding agent specifies conditions for remaining eligible for continuation of funding or reimbursement for work performed. Usually the recipient organization must provide detailed evidence concerning continuing structural or procedural conformity to requirements—accounts of who performed the work; how the work was performed; on whom the work was performed—in the form of periodic reports. Complex accounting control systems are employed because more straightforward command-and-compliance authority is lacking.

DiMaggio's (1983) study of the effects of controls exercised by the National Endowment for the Arts (NEA) provides a carefully researched example of this type of influence strategy. This study, along with a second conducted by Meyer, Scott, and Strang (1987) on federal funding of educational programs, points to important effects of this approach, in particular, to *where* the structural changes are most likely to occur. Inducement strategies create increased organizational isomorphism (structural similarity), but more so at the intermediate than the operative organizational field level. The major effects reported by DiMaggio were on the states' arts councils—their existence, form, and functions being specified by NEA as a condition for eligibility of states for funding rather than on the arts organizations themselves. Similarly, the major effects of federally funded programs we observed in our research on educational systems were to be found at the level of the several states' educational agencies and the district office level rather than at the level of the local school—although such programs were designed to influence the behavior of school teachers, not district and state administrators (Meyer, Scott, and Strang, 1987).

For a great many reasons, organizational structures created by inducements are unlikely to have strong or lasting effects on the organizational performance they are intended to affect. Usually, they constitute only one of many funding streams on which the organization relies to sustain its performance, and organizational participants seem to have a strong aptitude for co-mingling funds from various sources in carrying on their operations in pursuit of organizationally defined purposes (Sproull, 1981). The funding agent's distinctive purposes are more likely to be reflected in the preparation of organizational "accounts"—both fiscal and retrospective reporting—than in the performance of workers. An additional explanation of the weakness of inducement strategies is suggested by the social psychological literature that reports that internal motivation and commitment are weakened, not reinforced, by the use of external incentives (Deci, 1971; Staw et al., 1980).

Like imposition, the utility of inducement processes is emphasized by a variety of organizational theories. Institutional theorists differ primarily in stressing the somewhat unexpected importance of these mechanisms for governmental units.

The Acquisition of Organizational Structure

Probably the influence process most widely studied by institutional analysts has involved the acquisition—the deliberate choosing—of structural models by organizational actors. Whether because of memetic or normative mechanisms (DiMaggio and Powell, 1983), organizational decision makers have been shown to adopt institutional designs and attempt to model their own structures on patterns thought to be, variously, more modern, appropriate, or professional.

In analyses by Tolbert and Zucker (1983) of municipal agencies' adoption of civil service reforms and by Fligstein (1985) of the spread of multidivisional forms among large U.S. corporations, the diffusion of a novel organizational pattern is shown to spread across a field of similar, autonomous organizations. When a new structural pattern is voluntarily adopted by organizational managers—in contrast to the situations described above in which the major impetus for the change comes from outside the organization—then analysts must attempt to rule out an obvious competing explanation: that the changes are embraced for efficiency reasons—because they are expected to improve technical performance. This is easier said than done. The approaches employed to date are indirect, and the results are subject to varying interpretations. For example, as noted above, Tolbert and Zucker argued that "internal," e.g., demographic, characteristics of cities predicted adoption of civil service reforms in earlier but not later periods, asserting that the former officials were driven by rational motives (an interest in excluding immigrants and improving control), while later adopters were motivated by conformity pressures or a concern to appear up-to-date. However, it could well be that later city officials confronted different types of governance issues—giving rise to a different set of internal problems—to which civil service reform was viewed as a rational solution.

In comparison with imposed or induced structural changes, one would expect acquired changes to be less superficial. Organizational managers should be more committed to them and in a better position than external agents to encourage their adoption and implementation or, if necessary, to inspect and enforce conformity to them.

The Imprinting of Organizational Structure

While there have been relatively few empirical studies of imprinting—the process by which new organizational forms acquire characteristics at the time of their founding that they tend to retain into the future—this phenomenon has been much discussed since it was first described by Stinchcombe (1965).

In his original essay, Stinchcombe (1965: 153–164) offered illustrative evidence concerning the imprinting process by noting how the basic features of various industries—the characteristics of the labor force, establishment size, capital intensity, relative size of the administrative bureaucracy, relative size of staff vs. line personnel, and proportion of professionals within the administration—varied systematically by time of founding. In a later study, Kimberly (1975) showed that the type of program, staffing, and structures employed within a population of rehabilitation organizations varied according to when the units were created.

The mechanism posited to account for these results seems highly consistent with the views of those theorists who see institutionalization as a process entailing the creation of reality. It embodies their central argument that organizations acquire certain structural features not by rational decision or design but because they are taken for granted as "the way these things are done." That this form is taken for granted is then argued to be an important basis for its persistence over time.

The Incorporation of Organizational Structure

In their own broad version of "neo-institutional" theory, March and Olsen (1984) pointed out that everything that happens is not necessarily intended, that every outcome is not the result of a conscious decision process. This general argument helps to account for some of the effects of institutional environments I and my colleagues have attempted to describe in a number of recent studies (Meyer and Scott, 1983; Scott and Meyer, 1987; Meyer et al., 1988).

It is a well-known proposition in open systems theory that organizations will tend to map the complexity of environmental elements into their own structures (Buckley, 1967). We have pursued empirically a specific instance of this prediction: that "organizations operating in more complex and conflicted environments will exhibit greater administrative complexity and reduced program coherence" (Scott and Meyer, 1987: 129). To test this argument, we have focused research attention on the organization of societal sectors that are both centralized and fragmented—a situation, we argue, that creates disproportional administrative complexity in local organizations attempting to relate to them (see also Meyer and Scott, 1983).

The argument here is not that environmental agents, by power and/or authority, always require administrative development, nor is it that environmental agents necessarily provide incentives for administrative elaboration, nor is it that organizational managers always consciously decide to add more effectively with a differentiated environment, although any or all of these processes may be involved. Rather, it is that via a broad array of adaptive mechanisms occurring over a period of time and ranging from co-optation of the representatives of relevant environmental elements to the evolution of specialized boundary roles to deal with strategic contingencies, organizations come to mirror or replicate salient aspects of environmental differentiation in their own structures. They incorporate environmental structure.

This type of institutionalization process, in which organizational structure evolves over time through an adaptive, largely unplanned, historically dependent process, is perhaps most consistent with Selznick's version of institutionalization theory.

The Bypassing of Organizational Structure

Yet another view of the relation between institutional environments and organizational structure developed out of our research on schools. We have proposed that, in important respects, much of the orderliness and coherence present in American schools is based on institutionally defined beliefs rather than on organizational structures (Meyer, Scott, and Deal, 1981).

Of course, it is the case for schools, as virtually all of the arguments summarized up to this point assert, that institutional beliefs, rules, and roles come to be coded into the structure of educational organizations. Thus, as Meyer and Rowan (1977: 96) argued:

> In modern society . . . educational organizations have good reasons to tightly control properties defined by the wider social order. By incorporating externally defined types of instruction, teachers, and students into their formal structure, schools avoid illegitimacy and discreditation.

But in later, related research on the belief systems and the existence of rules reported by various classes of school participants—superintendents, principals, teachers—we discovered a good deal of consensus across these role groups on the extent of educational policy on curricular materials, grades, student conduct, and similar matters. However, such agreements were little affected by organizational boundaries: teachers and principals within the same school as well as teachers, principals, and superintendents in the same district did not show higher levels of consensus on educational policies than that present across the role groups generally—groups whose members were selected from a diverse sample of schools in an urban metropolitan area.

We proposed that the high level of "overall agreement about the extent of formal policies and the areas to which they apply" was the result not of organizational but of institutional processes:

> According to this view, agreements on the nature of the school system and the norms governing it are worked out at quite general collective levels (through political processes, the development of common symbols, occupational agreements). Each school and district—and each teacher, principal, and district officer—acquires an understanding of the educational process and division of labor, not from relating to others within the same organizational unit, but from participating in the same institutional environment, from sharing the same educational "culture." (Meyer, Scott, and Deal, 1981: 159–160)

Today I would amend the argument to include students and parents among the primary carriers of the cultural belief system. Such shared conceptions and symbols provide order not only by being mapped into organizational forms and procedures but also by their direct influence on the beliefs and behaviors of individual participants, the presence of which makes their organizational embodiment less essential. They are embedded in the cultural infrastructure. Organizational structures may only be required to support and supplement those cultural systems that exercise a direct influence on participants.

According to such an argument, the existence of strong institutional environments may, under some conditions, reduce rather than increase the amount or elaborateness of organizational structure. Cultural controls can substitute for structural controls. When beliefs are widely shared and categories and procedures are taken for granted, it is less essential that they be formally encoded in organizational structures.

As shown above, previous work has identified a variety of mechanisms and proposed a number of diverse arguments as to how institutional elements affect organizational structures. Since the arguments made are quite varied—and at least some of them make competing predictions—institutional analysts need to become more articulate about the alternative paths by which institutional processes exert their effects and the factors determining such paths. The seven specific mechanisms I have detected in the empirical literature may or may not hold up as distinct types of institutional pressures or forces. In any case, I would argue that sorting out and codifying these arguments is an essential accompaniment to the maturation of institutional theory.

Interests and Institutions

Organizations and Interests

The institutional features of environments are receiving increasing attention, in ways I have tried to document, as important determinants of the structure and functioning of organizations. Until the introduction of institutional conceptions, organizations were viewed primarily as production systems and/or exchange systems, and their structures were viewed as being shaped largely by their technologies, their transactions, or the power-dependency relations growing out of such interdependencies. Environments were conceived of as task environments: as stocks of resources, sources of information, or loci of competitors and exchange partners. While such views are not wrong, they are clearly incomplete.

Institutional theorists have directed attention to the importance of symbolic aspects of organizations and their environments. They reflect and advance a growing awareness that no organization is just a technical system and that many organizations are not primarily technical systems. All social systems—hence all organizations—exist in an institutional environment that defines and delimits social reality. And just as with technical environments, institutional environments are multiple, enormously diverse, and variable over time. To neglect their presence and power is to ignore significant causal factors shaping organizational structures and practices: to overlook these variables is to misspecify our causal models.

In his recent paper, DiMaggio (1988: 4–5) argued that institutional theory tends to "defocalize" interests in the explanation of human behavior. Rather than assuming the common utilitarian position that actors attempt to pursue their interests, he suggested, institutional arguments emphasize (1) factors such as norms or taken-for-granted assumptions "that make actors unlikely to recognize or to act upon their interests" and (2) circumstances such as behavioral constraints or cognitive limitations "that cause actors who do recognize and try to act upon their interests to be unable to do so effectively."

By contrast, based on the review reported above, it does not seem to me correct to conclude, as did DiMaggio, that most institutional arguments deny "the reality of purposive, interest-driven" behavior either on the part of organizations or their participants. Rather, institutional theory reminds us that interests are institutionally defined and shaped (cf. Friedland and Alford, 1987: 20). Institutional frameworks define the ends and shape the means by which interests are determined and pursued. Institutional factors determine that actors in one type of setting, called firms, pursue profits; that actors in another setting, called agencies, seek larger budgets; that actors in a third setting, called political parties, seek votes; and that actors in an even stranger setting, research universities, pursue publications.

Moreover, institutional theorists call attention to the truth that rules themselves are important types of resources and that those who can shape or influence them possess a valuable form of power. As Burns (1986: 28–29) noted:

Rule systems as important social technologies become resources and stakes in social interaction and the strategic structuring of social life. Thus, they cannot be viewed as simply "neutral" or "technical means" of realizing certain purposes. . . . [They constitute] a power resource which social agents utilize in their struggles and negotiations over alternative structural forms and development of social systems, serving their interests.

Institutional Actors and Interests

Shifting levels of analysis, institutional theorists can usefully not only inquire into the ways in which institutional features shape organizational structures but can also examine the determinants of institutional systems themselves. This is a broad and complex topic concerning which I offer here only a few general observations.

DiMaggio and Powell (1983: 147) correctly identified the nation-state and the professions as the primary modern shapers of institutional forms, as, in their terms, "the great rationalizers of the second half of the twentieth century." While both are forces for rationalization, that should not lead us to assume that they share the same interests or that they will necessarily espouse similar institutional forms. Given the power, state officials are more likely to create bureaucratic arrangements that centralize discretion at the top of the structure and allow relatively little autonomy to local managers and providers (Simon, 1983). Professional bodies, by contrast, will generally prefer weaker and more decentralized administrative structures that locate maximum discretion in the hands of individual practitioners. Both forms embody rational assumptions and modes of consciousness but posit different foci of discretion, giving rise to quite different structural arrangements (Scott, 1985).

The modes or mechanisms employed to disseminate structures are also expected to vary between the two classes of actors. State actors are more likely to employ coercion or inducement in pursuing their ends, and they are more likely to attempt to create a formal organizational network to carry out their purposes. The professions are expected to rely primarily on normative and/or memetic influences and to attempt to create cultural forms consistent with their own aims and beliefs. Of course, to the extent possible, they will enlist the backing of state authorities for their models. Whether or not state power is employed to support or undercut professional patterns will vary over time and place. The examination of these struggles and alliances is an important analytic key to understanding the shaping of contemporary institutional environments (see, e.g., Larson, 1977; Starr, 1982; Friedson, 1986).

Which environmental agents are able to define the reigning forms of institutional structure will be determined largely by political contests among competing interests. The term "political" as employed here should be interpreted in the broadest possible way, since outcomes will be influenced not only by differential resources and sanctioning facilities but will also be strongly shaped by the agents' differential ability to lay successful claim to the normative and cognitive facets of political processes: those identified by such concepts as authority, legitimacy, and sovereignty. Outcomes will also be influenced by the structure of the state itself and its relation to and penetration of society (see, e.g., Berger, 1981; Burawoy, 1985; Evans, Rueschemeyer, and Skocpol, 1985).

To pursue these matters, organizational scholars must increasingly link their energies and interests with those of the new breed of political scientist/sociologist, who is not only "bringing the state back in" as an important institutional actor in its own right but reconceptualizing political systems in ways that reveal the varied role that political and legal structures play in shaping the institutional frameworks within which organizations of varying types operate. As with the introduction of cultural interests, institutional theorists are well situated to provide a vital bridge to bring these insights into the domain of organization theory.

Conclusion

A review of both institutional theories and recent empirical studies employing institutional arguments reveals much diversity. Different definitions are employed and a variety of causal arguments are subsumed under this general perspective. I identified these differences not to enshrine or condemn them but to facilitate clarification and orderly development. I have also suggested that institutional arguments need not be formulated in opposition to rational or efficiency arguments but are better seen as complementing and contextualizing them.

Throughout, I have attempted to sound an optimistic note. Institutional theory is at an early stage of development. Adolescents have their awkwardness and their acne, but they also embody energy and promise. They require encouragement as well as criticism if they are to channel their energies in productive directions and achieve their promise.

Notes

1. Excluded in this review are related developments in political science (e.g., March and Olsen, 1976) and economics (e.g., Williamson, 1981, 1985). These variants depart from sociological works in ways too complex to consider in this essay.

2. For a thoughtful and forceful discussion of the virtues of process/property conception of institutionalization/institution, see Jepperson (1987).

PART VII

Critical Theory and Postmodernism

To this point, the theories included in this book have been models that seek to explain something about how organizations work and how they might be made to work better. The constructs in them deal with organizational characteristics and organizational processes. For example, rational models articulate ways to manage organizations more effectively, while natural models focus on how organizations adapt to internal and external pressures. They are theories, as noted in an earlier chapter, that take a natural science approach to studying and understanding organizations.

The papers in this section depart from that approach and set forth some basic ideas from the critical theory of organization and postmodern approaches. They are critiques of the conventional approaches of the other models in this book. Essentially, these two papers argue that the models of organization that are extant in the field are a result of underlying biases and assumptions that shape them, and these biases and assumptions are not articulated in ways that allow readers to understand their implications.

Critical theory, as set forth in the selection by Jermier, is a normative theory that has its roots in the work of Karl Marx (Burrell & Morgan, 1979). Its proponents seek to reveal society for what it is, to unmask its essence and mode of operation, and to lay the foundations for emancipation through deep-seated social change. It is an overtly political philosophy (Burrell & Morgan, p. 284).

The fundamental premise is that organizations are control mechanisms that are designed to exploit those in the weaker sectors of a society, and this is reflected in the theoretical and empirical work. For example, leadership theory and research focuses on how leaders (managers) can be more effective in improving worker productivity, the field of organizational psychology seeks to fit people in organizations into existing hierarchical structures, and rational organization theory seeks to design procedures, policies, and structures to maximize performance.

Critical theorists argue that all of this intends to exploit those who work in the organization. This is clear in Jermier's chapter, as he argues that "no knowledge is neutral" and the dominant theme of more conventional organization theorizing is the domination of the working class by disguising control "in the rhetoric of emancipation" (Jermier, 1998). In the end, it seems that the question is not whether organizations are or are not control mechanisms but one of who controls the control mechanism.

The paper by Calas and Smircich (1999) describes a postmodern approach to organizations and its implications for the field of organization studies. Postmodernists in the field of organization studies argue that since conceptions of the world, and in our case, theories of organizations, are socially constructed, then the theoretical models themselves must be a function of cultural and symbolic elements that the theorist (as well as others who are part of the discipline) has experienced. As such, a person with different experiences would have a different view of the world, which may be equally valid, though significantly different. Thus, you can't really be sure what the theorist means, but rather the meaning is what the reader interprets it to be—which becomes the basis for the reader's meaning. This is what the term *deconstructionism,* a key concept of postmodernism, means. To the conventional theorist and researcher, deconstruction poses a serious problem for at least two reasons. First, if different people have different meanings for the same term (say, for example, "organizational structure") then they cannot meaningfully communicate about that concept. Second, having multiple meanings of the same term renders replication research virtually impossible, since replication requires that the same concepts be examined, something impossible when meaning is not clear.

CHAPTER 18

Critical Organizational Theory*

John M. Jermier

The field of Critical Management Studies (CMS) which emerged during the past 2 decades, offers a wide range of alternatives to mainstream organizational and management theory. With roots in Marxist theory, feminist theory, postmodern theory, postcolonial theory, poststructural theory, pragmatism and symbolic interactionism, environmentalism, and other critical approaches to understanding social life, CMS provides a growing but loosely organized movement in alternative scholarship, teaching, and practical change (Adler, Forbes, & Willmott, 2007).

One important segment of CMS, referred to as critical organizational theory (CritOT), is devoted to promoting understanding of attempts to organize and control human labor activity, particularly in capitalist societies where wage laborers are persuaded to produce enough value to maintain themselves, the owners of capital, and the enterprise in which they are employed. CritOT has three main purposes: (1) to guide systematic study of regimes and processes of organizational control, (2) to guide systematic study of the subjective worlds of workers and other actors struggling for control in organizational settings, and (3) to develop knowledge that exposes patterns of exploitation and oppression and that can serve as a resource in overcoming these patterns. The hallmark of CritOT is that it is conducted with the intent to aid in the emancipation of the downtrodden and eradicate mistreatment of human beings and the natural environment.

The purpose of this chapter is to introduce the reader to critical theory and to CritOT. The chapter includes a section on critical theory, one on the purposes and

---

*Prepared especially for this book by John J. Jermier, drawn from his 1998 paper "Critical Perspectives on Organizational Control," *Administrative Science Quarterly, 43*, pp. 235–256.

central concepts and relationships in CritOT, and one featuring a research article that illustrates processes of organizational control and deep subjectivity through the lens of CritOT.

What Is Critical Theory?

Foundational Works

Most academic scholars think their work is critical because the topics they study are important and because they "criticize" other research. Critical theory, however, denotes a more specific and distinctive approach to analyzing social relations. Karl Marx is often thought to be the first critical theorist. His analyses of capitalism, in particular volume 1 of *Capital* (Marx, 1867/1972), are the basic reference points for much contemporary critical theory. Another basic reference point is Max Weber's (1922/1978) theses on societal rationalization. Some scholars limit the use of the term *critical theory* to the neo-Marxist theorists of the Frankfurt School—Max Horkheimer, Theodore Adorno, and Herbert Marcuse. The Frankfurt School theorists developed a vast body of critical work focused on how enlightenment rationality was perverted in the building of "totally administered societies" (see Habermas, 1987). The impact of the Frankfurt School on the development of critical theory has been well chronicled (see Kellner, 1989; Agger, 1991). My use of the term *critical theory* is not harnessed to that of the Frankfurt School, but I do find their emphasis on over-organization and totalitarian control, as well as their work on epistemology, to be highly relevant to my purposes here. Critical theory requires thoughtful examination of the structures of control in society and of the political implications of academic work.

The "Critical" Attitude

With this reference to politics, some readers may assume there is a "party line" by which critical theorists think, work, and live. On occasion, those hostile to the aims of critical theory have been known to reduce it to associations with rigid Marxism and communist dictatorships, feminist separatism, ecofascism, or other houses of straw that they find easy to disperse. To be sure, most critical theorists adopt a perspective that somehow challenges the status quo and usually one that is skeptical of piecemeal, liberal reformism (see Best & Kellner, 1991; Calhoun, 1995). But, beyond general agreement on the aims of critical theory, scholars subscribe to diverse and even irreconcilable points of view.

 What critical theorists do tend to agree on is that no knowledge is neutral. Even science is an integral part of society and cannot be insulated from broader struggles for control. These struggles shape scientific activity, and, in turn, scientific activity plays a role in shaping how the struggles unfold. Critical theorists maintain that social scientists in particular serve interests and take sides on important issues, even when they strive for impartiality and aspire to serve the public good. This stance goes to the heart of the distinction between all forms of traditional and critical social theory: The former assist (often unwittingly) in the process of social reproduction, while the latter consciously aspire to subvert it. Since scholars cannot rid their theories and empirical inquiries of normative content and partisan consequences, critical theorists maintain that it is best to acknowledge one's partiality openly. Thus, the inescapable question for a critical theorist is, "Whose side are you on?"

One classic answer to this fundamental question appeared in a series of essays on capitalism written by Max Horkheimer (1933, 1937, 1939) whose work is widely regarded as foundational by critical scholars. As an adversary of scientism, Horkheimer formulated an alternative epistemology for social theory, which advocated that social scientists adopt "*the critical attitude*" (1937, p. 207). For Horkheimer, the critical attitude entailed rejecting conventional images of scientific conduct that portrayed sequestered intellectuals pursuing disinterested inquiry. He recommended, instead, that scholars drop the pretense of being disinterested and engage (through their research and writing) in conscious opposition to the class-based, commodified, and programmed society. This includes opposing all forms of totalitarianism, including those "softer" forms that subtly enslave people while appearing to enrich life and enhance freedom of choice (e.g., consumerism). Furthermore, scholars ought not to strive to eliminate one isolated abuse or another but instead should work to transform radically the whole interrelated system of abusive and dominating relations (cf. Horkheimer, 1939).

For Horkheimer (1937), the project of the critical theorist is to think in the service of exploited and oppressed humanity and to work for the abolition of social injustice.

Given that distributions of privilege and pain in capitalist societies are based on class and that many people in such societies accept asymmetrical class structures as inevitable (or even as necessary or desirable), Horkheimer specifically recommended that critical theorists align with the working class. He advocated that theory be developed for those who suffer most (the working class) and in solidarity with actors and parties committed to eliminating suffering. Thus, he envisioned an emancipatory theory that would stand in self-reflexive opposition to traditional theories and in opposition to further development of the "commodity economy," which he believed was "driving humanity into a new barbarism" (1937, p. 227).

Currently, critical theorists are beginning to think more abstractly about the general social processes that lead to mistreatment of the less powerful and about similarities in the situations of those who experience deprivation. This has led to the development of forms of critical theory that advocate multiple perspectives (e.g., Kellner, 1989), that emphasize new social movements (see Pichardo, 1997), and that present hybrid frameworks (e.g., Salleh, 1997). Nevertheless, most contemporary applications of the critical attitude at least implicitly endorse the wisdom of Horkheimer's (1937) manifesto: "[form] a dynamic unity with the oppressed class" (p. 213). In general, they retain his emphasis on (a) describing and criticizing exploitation, oppression, and social injustice, on (b) the impossibility of a disinterested social science, and on (c) the desirability of uniting theory with struggles for emancipatory social change.

Critical Organizational Theory (CritOT)

Although CritOT has deep roots in Marxist theory, its focus on *organizations* and *systems of organizational control* separates it to some degree from classical Marxism (which understandably had little to say about organizations during early capitalism) and from contemporary sociological research aimed at identifying broader mechanisms of social control. Like Marxist theory, however, the key concepts in CritOT underscore the plight of working people and other oppressed subjects, illuminate the mechanisms through which systems of control create advantage for the few and disadvantage for the many, and depict the subjective worlds of workers and other actors struggling for control in organizational settings.

Mistreatment

Critical organizational theorists maintain that in stratified and divided societies, more powerful groups and individuals reap the benefits of participating in processes through which less powerful people and the natural environment are mistreated. This belief is derived from many different sources including careful study of empirical data on earnings, health and safety, life satisfaction, subjective wellbeing, and other outcomes. It is also derived from careful study of processes of organizational control that point to, for example, harsh and difficult circumstances as well as situations that lead to overwork, oppression through teamwork, misguided trust in management, blind organizational commitment, and exploitation of all resources.

Mistreatment is classically theorized with the Marxist concept of exploitation and refers to the process in capitalist societies through which wealth is unjustly taken from the workers who produce it. Marx (1867/1972) laid the foundation for thinking systematically about mistreatment. As the passage below suggests, he was a passionate critic of the abuses he saw in early capitalist systems of production:

> [W]ithin the capitalist system all the methods for increasing the social productiveness of labour are carried out at the cost of the individual worker: . . . [the methods] mutilate the worker into a fragment of a human being, degrade him to become a mere appurtenance of the machine, make his work such a torment that its essential meaning is destroyed; . . . [they] distort the conditions under which he works, subjecting him, during the labour-process, to a despotism . . . all the more hateful because of its pettiness; . . . they transform his whole life into working time, and drag his wife and children beneath the Juggernaut wheels of capital's car. . . ." (pp. 713–714)

In contemporary CritOT, mistreatment is often conceived with terms that are not as narrow as exploitation. The critique has been expanded beyond the metaphysic of labor and is represented with concepts such as oppression, social injustice, and corrosion (cf. Sennett, 1998).

Mistreatment can result in palpable pain and suffering, which sometimes leads to conflict. In such instances, members of various groups may struggle openly over issues ranging from economic wellbeing to life and death. Alternatively, a culture may promote practices and systems of belief that limit awareness of deprivation, fostering a general aura of contentment and stability without changing material or structural inequities. Under such conditions, subjugated groups may perceive their mistreatment to be natural and inevitable.

Indeed, critical organizational theorists are acutely sensitive to both the long history of inhumanity and to the astonishingly adaptive capabilities of human beings. Part of their view of inhumanity is derived from 20th-century totalitarianism, but many are equally concerned about the regimes of comprehensive, detailed control that are possible for the first time today. Their concerns echo cautions issued over 4 decades ago by critical theorist Herbert Marcuse (1964/1966), who highlighted subtle, new forms of control in advanced industrial civilization. Marcuse warned that "a comfortable, smooth, reasonable democratic unfreedom prevails" (p. 1) and that by "virtue of the way it has organized its technological base, contemporary industrial society tends to be totalitarian" (p. 3).

Critical organizational theory also has a normative component. It stresses not what is but what could be or should be. That is, it encourages reflection on the possibilities of an idealized society and cultivates the utopian imagination. This is important because utopian images are the foundations of critique; they shape social definitions of mistreatment. It is also important because part of the CritOT project involves working toward utopian states that are free from exploitation, oppression, and social injustice. Utopian thinking can provide useful blueprints, although some critical organizational theorists, following Habermas (1984, 1987), place more trust in building processes of idealized human communication than they do in envisioning utopian end-states.

Regimes and Processes of Organizational Control

Creating a regime of organizational control is a trend that characterizes the predominant macro system that elites use to try to extract desired work behavior and productivity from employees (Edwards, 1979). A process of organizational control is a more micro phenomenon that involves struggles for control between and among various actors in an organizational setting. Struggles center on control of the performance of labor and other work activity, governance, and relations with external agents and stakeholders.

In an interesting way, the emphasis in CritOT on organizational control parallels great works by literary critics and dystopian satirists George Orwell (1949/1981) and Aldous Huxley (1932/1969). Orwell and Huxley addressed hierarchical control in the contemporary social world, focusing, respectively, on control that is coercive and brutal and on control that is subtle and refined. What do critical organizational theorists make of the sinister forms of control that so concerned Orwell and Huxley? Do CritOT scholars contend that control in the contemporary world is exercised more frequently with boot-on-the-face force, yielding resentful compliance, or with siren-song civility through which psychic prisons of consent may be manufactured? Has the iron fist of power—naked and obscene, loathsome and abhorrent—disappeared completely? Has the velvet glove of power replaced it—camouflaged and subtle, unobtrusive and obscure—working its magic mostly in the shadows? Or, do contemporary configurations of control defy neat categorization along the lines suggested above?

Questions of this kind have long exercised the minds of critical organizational theorists, many of whom have been concerned with *creeping totalitarianism* in the organizations and fields of organizations, which are its primary purveyors. One of the earliest statements of concern about totalitarian tendencies of large-scale organizations and their threat to democratic institutions was issued by the radical Weberian, Nicos Mouzelis (1967). In his text, *Organization and Bureaucracy*, which was one of the first forays into critical theory by an organizational theorist (see Burrell & Morgan, 1979), Mouzelis echoed Huxley's (1958) sentiments about "over-organization":

> The crucial problem today is not so much how to increase . . . the functional rationality of modern bureaucracies but rather how to safeguard . . . a minimum of substantive rationality and individual initiative; not how to make people more contented and cooperative with management but rather how to prevent them from becoming happy automatons in a "brave new world." (pp. 173–174)

Concern with the insidiousness of bureaucratic mechanisms of control (and the threat they pose to democracy and freedom) launched CritOT (e.g., Blau & Schoenherr, 1971; Braverman, 1974; Goldman & Van Houten, 1977; Salaman, 1978), sustained it in large part for nearly 4 decades, and remains highly relevant today given the master trend of the McDonaldization of contemporary organizations (Ritzer, 2004). But from its inception, CritOT has also unraveled the velvet glove to reveal the mettle of well-hyped, "humanistic" strategies (e.g., Nord, 1974; Zimbalist, 1975; Marglin, 1977; Friedman, 1977; Salaman, 1979; Clegg, 1979). Importantly, CritOT focuses on the totalitarian tendencies intrinsic to various systems of organizational control, whether those systems rely on the iron fist or the velvet glove of power.

Although all functioning organizations employ a mix of strategies of control, several scholars have argued that specific strategies have been more prominent or popular during particular historical eras (e.g., Perrow, 1972; Edwards, 1979; Clawson, 1980; Barley & Kunda, 1992; Jermier, 1998; Strang & Macy, 2001; Willmott, 2005). Edwards, for example, argued that managerial practices moved away from widespread reliance on coercive control in the late 19th century toward technological control (such as the assembly line) and then, by the mid-20th century, to bureaucratic forms of control. He also contended that each shift was precipitated by changes in the nature of work and the climate of labor relations. In recent years, critical organizational theorists have suggested that contemporary organizations are making more use of "post-bureaucratic" systems of control. These systems rely heavily on advanced technology and on the inculcation of emotions, values, and worldviews congruent with the interests of the more powerful actors (e.g., Burris, 1989; Sturdy, Knights, & Willmott, 1992; Barker, 1993; Wilkinson & Willmott, 1995; Casey, 1999; Maravelias, 2003).

It is unclear whether contemporary organizations are relying more heavily on post-bureaucratic systems of control. Evidence can be marshaled pro and con (see McSweeney, 2006). Few doubt that team-based organization is more prevalent today or that increased attention has been placed on engineering high-commitment cultures at work or that positive emotional responses from employees are being cajoled with greater skill than ever. Yet, at the same time, organizations continue to rely heavily on more conventional forms of control, including coercion. For instance, Burawoy's (1985) concept of "hegemonic despotism," which he used to represent new regimes of control anchored in threats of outsourcing, plant closure, and other types of capital flight, still seems especially relevant today. And, it is clear that many organizations are still characterized to some extent by McDonaldized and hazardous work, employment-at-will arrangements, forced overtime, and other involuntary forms of overworking, child labor, racial and sexual harassment and discrimination, organizational misconduct resulting in environmental degradation, and routine decision making that sacrifices the quality of life of children and future generations for present, garish material prosperity.

In summary, critical organizational theorists contend that many organizational systems are managed not to maximize efficiency or effectiveness but to stabilize modes of asymmetrical control and preserve the prerogatives of powerful actors (cf. Adler et al., 2007). They question the rationality of such practices and demystify thinking that tries to justify excessive control through fallacious arguments that systems of control are natural, God-given, or inevitable. From a normative angle, they challenge conventional organizational theorists to examine the ethical and other pragmatic implications of disregarding the effects of disproportionate control. They point to the deleterious effects of existing systems on employees, communities, the natural environment, and other stakeholders and ask why conventional organizational theorists tend to be silent on these issues. Critical organizational theorists are sympathetic to those who suffer as a result of pernicious organizational systems but they do not dismiss all workers and other agents as passive, even in the face of crushing force.

If at least some individual subjects are not passive in relation to regimes and processes of organizational control, how does CritOT represent active, lived experiences? In the section below, I turn to the concepts of subjectivity, consciousness and resistance to shed light on debates about how individual and collective ways of being can be best represented.

Subjectivity, Consciousness, and Resistance

Critical organizational theorists who work in the tradition of labor process studies and related fields have conducted a detailed debate on the individual (see McCabe, 2007).

The fundamental question addressed by scholars in this tradition has to do with the relationship between structures of control and the subjective, meaning imbued, lived experiences of actors in these systems (subjectivity). A key factor that separates CritOT from conventional studies of individuals in the workplace is that

CritOT attempts to portray the deeper realms of being of individuals and critiques studies focused on more superficial indicators of experience, such as attitudes. Also, critical organizational theorists emphasize that subjectivity is largely constituted (constructed) by relations of power and systems of control and is not freely chosen by individuals seeking a meaningful life.

A central dimension of subjectivity has to do with the way participants struggle with and negotiate structures of control, or as more commonly expressed, the forms of resistance (or lack thereof) practiced by subjects. Resistance flows from consciousness, but in this literature subjectivity is not reducible to a particular form of consciousness or to resistance itself:

> [It] is the culmination of various power relations and the reciprocal interpreta-
> tions, reflexivity and actions of an individual at any given moment. It is the way
> in which we understand and interpret the world and ourselves. Although sub-
> jectivity refers to the lived experience of individual subjects, this does not mean
> that the individual is separate from groups, collectives or society, or that one
> necessarily embraces individualism [as an ideology]. (McCabe, 2007, p. 245)

According to CritOT, individuals are not completely programmed by any single social force and they are able to resist their own subjectivity to some degree by look-ing back at how they were constituted and by developing a critical awareness of the sources of control in their environment.

Marx and Subjectivity

Marx did not theorize subjectivity per se but did develop a philosophical anthro-pology of human nature in his early work and also provided insights into states of consciousness and resistance. For Marx (1867/1972), "real" resistance in and around capitalist work organizations could take many forms. But it would derive from only one source: *revolutionary class consciousness.* Thus, the meaning of sub-jectivity was straightforward and was to be interpreted as forms of struggle against the fundamental defining feature of the capitalist mode of production—exploitation of labor through the generation and extraction of surplus value. Importantly, Marx recognized that one source of surplus value was hidden in cooperative labor. He understood exploitation primarily at the supra-individual level: "What the capital-ist pays is the value of the separate labor powers of a hundred individuals, not the value of their combined labor power" (p. 349). In his view, the severity of the prob-lem of exploitation was complicated and compounded by its collective nature.

Marx's (1867/1972) essentialist view of human nature led him to propose an "inevitable antagonism between the exploiter and the living raw material he exploits" (p. 348). Alienated laborers, separated from ownership of the means and ends of their production, dominated by their output, experience themselves (and all human beings) as inhuman:

> In its blind, unbridled passion, its werewolf hunger for surplus labor, capital is
> not content to overstep the moral restrictions upon the length of the working
> day. It oversteps the purely physical limitations as well. It usurps the time

needed for the growth, the development, and the healthy maintenance of the body. . . . It causes the premature exhaustion and death of labor power. (Marx, 1867/1972, p. 269)

Marx believed that to overcome alienation, citizens must abolish private ownership of production, which involves building labor solidarity and engaging in class-based resistance.

According to Marx, however, class-conscious radicalism is not inevitable or predetermined. There is merely a *tendency* for this to occur. Because of "all the mystifications of the capitalist method of production [and] all its illusions of freedom . . ." (p. 589), the fundamental source of alienation might be obscured, leaving laborers and owners of capital unable to engage in 'real resistance.'"

This is, of course, where some understanding of subjectivity becomes important because attitudes may emerge reflecting the idea that it is "better to live with the devil you know." This may readily weaken strategies of resistance. The divisive and individualizing effects of capitalism may further weaken class and other collective forms of subjectivity, limiting the potential for resistance even more. This may be what Marx had in mind when he stated that "The organization of the fully developed capitalist process of production breaks down all resistance" (p. 817).

Many critical organizational theorists think this position is too fatalistic and that Marx went too far in his analysis condemning the capitalist mode of production, organization, and control. An all-or-nothing conception of subjectivity and resistance is probably wide of the mark, even at the point of large-scale revolutions. Relations of control and resistance operate in more complex ways than can be depicted in simple all-or-nothing polarities.

In several sections of *Capital*, Marx indicated an awareness of resistance practices. He explained why workers might engage in class struggle and class-conscious revolutionary action, but he did not elaborate on the meaning of resistance by alienated ("falsely conscious," not class-conscious) subjects, and he did not develop a theory of everyday resistance to capitalist control. Thus, his approach to subjectivity can be seen as important but limited primarily to the case where workers and other disenfranchised employees understand their historic role as class actors transforming capitalism.

Braverman and Subjectivity

In his foundational work on changes in the control of the labor process in the 20th century, Marxist scholar Harry Braverman (1974) also made several simplifying assumptions about subjectivity, primarily to distance his position on class consciousness from the "superficial, remote, and mechanistic" (p. 29) approaches of empirical social scientists studying job satisfaction and class identification. He was not specifically opposed to accepting premises about human nature or to conducting studies into the meaning of worker subjectivities. What he did oppose was managerialist social research that reduced the subjectivity of workers to statements of job satisfaction or dissatisfaction or that took at face value questionnaire reports of class identifications.

Braverman's research strategy provoked much criticism and discussion among critical organizational theorists, but it can be argued that he was working with a sophisticated, critical understanding of subjectivity. When he chose to write beyond his simplifying assumptions about "objective" forces in the labor process (such as deskilling, the intensification of labor, and management control), Braverman displayed penetrating insight. For example, his conceptualization of class consciousness probed critically into the realm of the subjective as he wrote about the way "changes in mood draw upon and give expression to the underlying reservoir of class attitudes . . . [existing] deep below the surface" (p. 30). His concern with "apparent" habituation (p. 151) was brilliantly incisive and laid groundwork for the analysis of deeper subjectivity. Similarly, his criticism of subjectivist managerial sociology was well constructed and filled an important gap in the critical literature on job satisfaction and studies of other employment attitudes, pushing researchers to probe deeper in their analysis of subjectivity. Perhaps most significantly for critical studies of subjectivity, Braverman's neglect of resistance was not as great as some critics have claimed. For example, his conclusion to the chapter on the habituation of the worker to the capitalist mode of production makes it clear, contrary to his critics, that he was fully aware of worker resistance. It can be seen in this chapter that he understood that habituated, alienated workers, naïve to the historic role of the working class, would still have occasion to enact resistance. It would, however, manifest in the crawlspaces of work settings rather than out in the open:

> But, beneath this apparent habituation, the hostility of workers to the degenerated forms of work which are forced upon them continues as a subterranean stream that makes its way to the surface when employment conditions permit, or when the capitalist drive for a greater intensity of labour oversteps the bounds of physical and mental capacity. (p. 151)

The philosophical anthropology underlying Marx's and Braverman's views on the subjective worlds of workers and other employees has been discussed frequently. Their approach begins with a fixed, universal human nature, from which laborers attempt to develop themselves in ways that fulfill their (latent) destiny as class-conscious revolutionaries. These assumptions can easily lead to theorizing subjectivity in a way that relies on concepts of false consciousness or reification. A result is that sharp distinctions between "real" or "genuine" (class-conscious) resistance and everyday forms of resistance are drawn that are not only epistemologically problematic but also undermine subjects by representing them as naïve and unenlightened. Marx and Braverman were aware of the importance of subjective consciousness and the part it plays in resistance to capitalist control. Neither could escape these issues, even when their work consciously attempted to limit the scope of analysis to a more "objectivist" realm. However, neither chose to theorize subjectivity and resistance in any acceptable detail, leaving scope for critical organizational theorists to develop the link between subjectivity and systems of organizational control.

Post-Braverman and Subjectivity

Post-Braverman studies of subjectivity have been far-reaching. Consistently they have included calls to redress the relative neglect of resistance. Equally importantly, they have undertaken close examination of what may appear to be employee *cooperation and the giving of consent.* For example, in what is now regarded as a landmark study of subjectivity, Burawoy (1979) focused on aspects of the development of consent among shop floor factory workers engaged in the "game" of "making-out" (maximizing bonus pay in piece-rate work). He was able to explore, through participant observation on the shop floor, the way playing the game of "making-out" created workers as competitive *individuals*, masking their "common membership in a class of agents of production who sell their labor power for a wage" (p. 81). Thus, from the realm of subjective experience, Burawoy provided an interpretation of traditional Marxist processes of securing and obscuring surplus value. He did not draw implications for understanding shop floor resistance from this analysis, but it is clear that to the extent playing the game becomes an arena for self-esteem testing, factory workers can become locked, unwittingly, into practices that reproduce conditions of exploitation and subordination. That is, absorption in the game at a level where workers' deeper subjectivity is affected can have profound negative implications for meaningful resistance.

Critical organizational theorists have critiqued Burawoy's (1979) account of game playing and worker subjectivity in considerable detail. As one of the earliest attempts to reinsert subjectivity into processes of organizational control, his work has been praised. The consensus of opinion, however, seems to be that Burawoy did not investigate workplace subjectivity completely enough, leaving out some crucial dimensions of subjective experience. For example, several critics have pointed out his failure to explain exactly how individualizing tendencies in capitalist labor processes lead to fragmented and atomized subjects. Others have noted how his neglect of gender and sexual identity led to a somewhat superficial analysis of the way subjectivity is constructed.

CritOT has made considerable progress since Burawoy's classic analysis of worker subjectivity in heightening appreciation of the significance of subjective phenomena and in elaborating their properties. During the past 25 years, extensive research has been conducted on consent, compliance, and both individual and collective resistance in struggles for control. With this research, scholars have established the analytical importance of subjectivity in developing understanding of micro-struggles for control in the workplace. This emphasis on micro-struggles has diverted attention away from the grand narratives of class conflict and revolutionary struggle in favor of a focus on more complex, localized forms of subjectivity and resistance (e.g., Knights & Collinson, 1985; Jermier, 1988; Willmott, 1993; Gottfried, 1994; Gabriel, 1999; Fleming & Sewell, 2002; Fleming & Spicer, 2003; McCabe, 2007). It paints a picture of a contemporary era characterized more by compliance, consent, and subjugation than revolutionary class consciousness as even trade union consciousness and collective militancy have been documented relatively rarely (see Knights & Willmott, 1989; Collinson, 1994; Ezzamel & Willmott, 1998; Ezzy, 2001; Fleming, 2003; Thomas & Davies, 2005; McCabe, 2007). Marx anticipated class-conscious resistance among capitalist workers but theorized this only as a tendency not as a certainty. CritOT still does not provide a fully developed theory of workplace subjectivity, but it has generated a relatively rich understanding of how subjectivity intertwines with normative (velvet glove type) approaches to organizational control.

More research is needed to describe and explain the subjective worlds of employees embedded in coercive (iron fist type) systems of organizational control. While there is widespread recognition among scholars that most employees in advanced capitalist societies are neither class-conscious revolutionaries nor passive, docile automatons, further theoretical and empirical work is necessary to clarify the way control shapes subjectivity and to represent deeper realms of subjectivity.

Deep Subjectivity and Organizational Control Through the Lens of CritOT

In one of the earliest CritOT studies of alienation at work, I identify two types of deep subjectivity—reified consciousness and reflective militancy. Based on concepts drawn from critical theory and fieldwork in a large phosphate plant, I illustrate how these contrasting subjectivities shape the actions and lived experience of a skilled operator in the phosphate plant. The story contrasts the two forms of alienated consciousness with class-conscious radicalism and with ideas about humanistic management derived from managerial psychology.

"When the Sleeper Wakes"

A Short Story Extending Themes in Radical Organization Theory

This is a short story about the two minds of Mike Armstrong, dialectical Marxist theory's romantic "everyman" and critical theory's "antihero." The story contrasts day and night versions of Armstrong's worklife as a skilled operator in the control room of a large phosphate plant located in Tampa, Florida. The two versions are presented to illustrate theoretical descriptions of psychic processes engaged when human actors confront an alien world and make sense of it. Alternative forms of subjective alienation, reified consciousness (drawn from critical theory), and reflective militancy (drawn from dialectical Marxism) are developed as deep psychic states through which meaning is constructed in the world. It is proposed that subjective alienation is shaped by mythical forces in the broader symbolic environment and that it profoundly conditions actions and attitudes. Its importance in understanding organizational behavior and the practice of humanistic management is discussed in terms of human meaning-making processes.

Within each of us there is another whom we do not know. He speaks to us in dreams and tells us how differently he sees us from how we see ourselves.

—Jung, 1970

The Dream

5:28 A.M.
Thursday, May 2, 1985
Tampa, Florida

"I'll shut it off now," thought Mike, lying in the king-size waterbed of his condominium at Palm Court Village. He could always wake up a few minutes before the alarm rang, a command of time he considered remarkable. He had so much confidence in it that he occasionally did not set the alarm, challenging himself to get to the phosphate plant before the 7 o'clock whistle. "I'm in touch with nature," Mike reasoned.

He got out of bed, shut off the cosmo-time clock, and thought, "No chances today though—I have to meet with Phil and the guys and the OSHA official about the new safety regulations."

As Mike stepped into the warm shower and adjusted the steam mist massager, he focused on last night's game. "A three-run triple in the bottom of the thirteenth. Fantastic! That moves the Braves into first place. Wish they had better relief pitching, but what power hitters. God, cable! I can watch a different game every night!"

Mike realized it was approaching 6:40. He hurriedly dragged a comb across his head, grabbed a high-protein, instant breakfast and mixed it with low-fat milk. He had a great sense of well-being when he ate right.

The Z290 turned over right away. Mike adjusted the air conditioning and eased the plush seat back. The thirteen-minute drive to work was always soothing. Mike drowsily switched on the digital FM radio.

"That's 'Survivor' on 95 YNF, Tampa's home of rock 'n' roll. This is the 'Breakfast Flakes' bringing you the finest in rock programming in the Bay area. It's 78 degrees under brilliant blue skies, and there's no chance of rain today."

On a dark desert highway, cool wind in my hair, warm smell of colitas rising up through the air. Up ahead in the distance, I saw a shimmering light. My head grew heavy and my sight grew dim. I had to stop for the night . . .

"'Hotel California'! What a classic! The guitars sound awesome through these speakers." Mike drifted back to the song's lyrics:

Mirrors on the ceiling, pink champagne on ice, and she said, "We are all just prisoners here of our own device." . . . Last thing I remember I was running for the door. I had to find the passage back to the place I was before. "Relax," said the nightman, "we are programmed to receive. You can check out anytime you like, but you can never leave."

Immediately, the screaming guitars captured Mike's attention and drove the lyrics from his mind. After a couple of minutes, he remembered his destination:

"Wow! I almost missed the turn."

In the distance was the small pond with palm trees and flowers surrounding it and the attractive Thomas Industries sign. As Mike waved to the security guard, he gazed at the gargantuan structure of brick and steel, high voltage lines, cranes, railroad cars, machinery, storage bins, smokestacks, and iron walkways, all semi-enclosed by a great wall of gypsum. On the night shift, when the plant was well lit, Mike likened it to an alien spaceship, ready to take off, or just landing. Even by day, Mike thought the structure looked extraterrestrial. "Makes me feel kind of like I do when I'm in the St. Augustine Cathedral," he observed.

It was 6:59 A.M. when Mike punched the clock outside the sulphuric acid reactor complex. A few workers, gathered around Phil, the foreman, were talking about an article in the *Tribune* having to do with dangers to the ground water posed by phosphate plants.

There was some concern that low-level radioactivity, often present in the gypsum byproduct, would transfer to rain water as it seeped into the aquifer. Mike heard one of the new employees say, "According to the article, the fluoride gas produced is a health hazard to us, too."

Before he finished his sentence, Phil responded: "What we produce here isn't really hazardous. Why do you think we pay the lab group to work around the clock? They have to keep records for the county, the state and the feds. Remember in '79 when EPA was investigating us? They couldn't pin a *thing* on us. If you think that gypsum pile is contaminating the water in this area, how do you explain all the wildlife in the front pond? There's fish, frogs—why, even ducks . . . they're growing and multiplying faster than anywhere else in the county. No, sir! We can be proud of what we produce here! Without fertilizer, half the crops in this country wouldn't be harvested. If God intended us to live without fertilizer, he wouldn't have given us the brains to mine the wet rock and mix it with acid."

Mike responded: "I read that article. It wasn't a headline story or anything. I think it was one column in the Metro section—mostly positive stuff."

At that moment, the plant manager and a stranger wearing a blue suit and a visitor's tag walked by silently. The group began to move to the Personnel Auditorium, about 100 yards from the sulphuric acid reactor complex.

After a brief introduction, Byron Johannsen of OSHA said, "Good morning, gentlemen. I'll be brief and to the point. We've been spotchecking the plant and have noticed a couple of problems. Most of you aren't wearing hard hats and safety glasses. This is a must in all industrial plants, and we need to bring this one up to standards. Second, the masks the company bought two years ago to protect you from dust in the dry-side storage areas and to prevent you from breathing fluoride gas don't fit properly over beards or long hair. So we're ordering management to begin enforcing the safety rules and see that the masks fit. We can't allow the plant to operate with these health risks."

"We're cooperating with OSHA one hundred percent with this," the plant manager hastily added. "Any of you with beards or hair that keep those masks from fitting right have to clean up your act, right away. Any questions?"

Mike quickly scanned the room and broke the lengthy silence: "Does that mean nothing can be done about the dust and vapors, or . . ."

Before he could finish, the manager began the answer Mike himself knew only too well: "My God, all phosphate plants have some dust and vapors because of the process we use. We can't tinker with the process—it's the most rational way to make triple, and it's the triple that keeps us in business. It's out of our hands here. Engineers have studied this, and you know they have to design the process to run as efficiently as possible. There's a very delicate, natural balance among the parts of this plant. It's nothing personal—simply technical requirements and decisions."

Mike noticed himself nodding to the technological tempo of the manager's speech, as were others in the room. While walking back to the reactor complex, Mike thought about shaving his beard: "Small thing, really. I'm still free to dress as I like . . . free to buy what I need . . . free to think."

The day passed quickly. According to Mike's digital wristwatch, it was 3:04 P.M. Phil's face looked strained as he approached Mike's station: "Bad news, Mike. I had to bust Larry Jones and Randy Markus in Granulating—walked in and caught them smoking dope. I guess it was hash. I had to call Security to have their stuff searched. They found more in Jones's car. We'll probably have to let them go—they're up in Personnel now." Phil anticipated Mike's question:

"Mike, I *had* to do it. That drug rule has been on the books for years. It's there for a rea-son. We can't have *anybody* in this plant acting dreamy. It's full of hazards—heavy machin-ery, steam lines, acid lines, slurry lines. And you know how expensive the equipment is."

Although Mike appreciated the freedom drugs gave him, he tightened his lips, nodded slowly, and said, "It's not your fault, Phil. We knew the rule would have to be enforced sometime or it wouldn't be there. I know it's nothing personal; you're just doing your job. Rules are tools, like knives. They're not always razor sharp, but they serve a purpose. We need to stay in touch with what's real here." A state of calm engulfed Mike as he experi-enced what he thought was the reasonableness of his statements.

It was 3:50 P.M. as Mike walked into his living room and switched on the widescreen tele-vision to watch the ballgame. His thoughts drifted to the workday: "I wonder why Randy was so careless at work? He was never in trouble in high school. He could have hidden it, like everyone else. Granulating work is . . ." Mike's attention was abruptly drawn back to the screen: "Stupid commercial," he muttered. "I buy light beer because I want to drink light beer. I don't care if it's less filling." He sprawled on the couch and was soon dozing.

Mike's nap was disturbed by the front door opening. It was Sarah. "Sell any houses?" he inquired groggily.

"Yes," Sarah replied.

Mike grabbed a light beer. As he began drinking it, he turned down the volume on the television and put a cassette in the remote-controlled tape deck. "Sarah, there's a song I'd like you to listen to," Mike said, replaying "Hotel California." He drew two lines of cocaine on the table. The world was soft and warm and mellow and . . .

When the Sleeper Wakes . . . The Nightmare

6:15 A.M.
Thursday, May 2, 1985
Tampa, Florida

Sarah's grating voice heralded another dreary day: " . . . and grab your shirt. Mike! Mike! Rise and shine, Mike."

He rolled over, looked at her, and wished she were the dream mate her voice had just banished. He wiggled his shoulder to rearrange the pillow under his head.

"You're going to be late," she cautioned. "It's six fifteen."

"Another minute," he pleaded. "I was dreaming . . . I was in tune and in time with life . . . everything went right . . . nothing bothered me . . . it was *so* smooth."

"That was a dream all right," Sarah said sarcastically. "Charlie called. He'll be here at six thirty. Why is he picking you up? I thought you weren't all that friendly with the people at work."

"The company's changing some rules . . . we heard they're going to try to make us shave every day and cut our hair. Charlie and Randy and I are talking it over before work."

Mike rolled out of bed and flipped on the stereo. On the way to the shower, he stum-bled over Gypsum, his miniature silver poodle. "Dammit, Gyp! One of these days you're going to kill me."

Brooding, he turned on the water and waited for it to warm up. "They can't make me shave," he muttered as he stepped into the shooting shower. "I've had my beard since I was twenty-one. No company should be able to dictate that."

Mike realized it was getting late. "Hell-fire! Someone else's time is always on my mind. Whose life is this?"

A horn blasted outside the condominium as Mike rushed to get dressed. Climbing into Charlie's new Cutlass Supreme, he noticed Randy had on a gold chain heavy enough to anchor the *Queen Mary*.

"Morning, Mike," Charlie said grimly.

"Hi, Charlie, Randy. I've been thinking about the masks. We need to push Barkley to get us some that fit, if we have to wear them. It's the plant manager's decision."

"Mike, you know they aren't going to re-outfit the whole plant with new masks. They'll say it's too expensive," Randy said.

"Randy, let's not make it easy. . . . Make *them* say that. Let's not defeat *ourselves*," said Charlie.

Mike angrily agreed: "Right! Why do we have to work in dust and vapors in the first place? That's the *real* issue. Let's stick together on this. First, we tell them to get rid of the problems. If that fails, we push for better equipment. But, let's *not* let them tell us how to look!"

"Okay, okay," Randy responded. "Turn up the radio—I like this song." Charlie did so.

On a dark desert highway, cool wind in my hair, warm smell of colitas, rising up through the air. . . . Mirrors on the ceiling, pink champagne on ice, and she said, "We are all just prisoners here, of our own device." . . . "Relax," said the nightman, "we are programmed to receive. You can check out anytime you like, but you can never leave."

"The perfect description of Thomas Industries," Mike exclaimed. "We help lay the traps. We punch out, but don't stop working. It shows on our faces. Our minds are *crippled!*" Charlie and Randy nodded. "The noise from the control room, that damn Thomas Industries sign, the gyp mountain, smokestacks . . . every night this mess is with me before I go to sleep." Charlie and Randy were silent.

They arrived just in time to punch in before the 7 o'clock whistle. "Goddamn whistles," Mike grumbled. "Remind me of grade school." As he grabbed his time card, he thought of the Woody Guthrie cartoon poster of the worker punching out, with a punishing right, the horrified face on a time clock. He smirked.

Ever since whistles were installed, Mike tried to avoid his work station until at least 7:15. As he entered the sulphuric acid reactor complex, he heard Phil say, "If God intended us to live without fertilizer, he wouldn't have given us the brains and machinery to mine the wet rock and mix it with acid." Mike noticed Phil glancing at him disapprovingly.

Indignation always gripped Mike when Phil used religion to defend the industry. He thought, "Phil, you, I, Barkley, and every other employee here knows that gypsum pile is hot. Do we need a Karen Silkwood scene to shake it up? There's too much fluoride gas in the plant. There aren't enough safety checks made on the power and steam lines, heavy machinery, or storage bins. Every year there's less money for product testing, safety, and environmental stuff. Who do you think you're kidding?"

Mike knew it was a mistake to openly challenge Phil. He walked away resolutely. The group began moving toward the Personnel Auditorium. Mike motioned to his coworkers to pick up the slack while he was gone and followed the group.

Following a short speech by Byron Johannsen from OSHA on safety violations in the plant, Jack Barkley began talking: "We're cooperating with OSHA one hundred percent on this . . . Any of you with beards or hair that keep those masks from fitting right have to clean up your act, right away. Any questions?"

Mike probed: "Does that mean nothing can be done about the dust and vapors, or . . ." Before Mike could finish, Barkley began the answer Mike knew his question would provoke: ". . . . We can't tinker with the process—it's the most rational way to make triple. . . . Engineers have studied this. . . . There's a very delicate natural balance among the parts."

Mike whispered acrimoniously to Charlie: "Why do *we* have to make all the adjustments? They should clean this warzone up—spray the dry-side more, get rid of the vapor leaks, check the uranium dumps! Man! We shouldn't have to take this."

Barkley looked directly at Mike and said calmly: "If you have a problem with that, it's because you're not thinking straight. Talk to a technician if it don't make sense to you. *All* this benefits *you!* Besides, it's OSHA that forced these issues. Ask Johannsen!"

"Men," said Johannsen reluctantly as everyone's eyes turned toward him, "our job is to protect your health. At this point, we can't make the company eliminate dust and fumes. We know the face masks are uncomfortable, but they *will* fit. It's the best we can do, now. We think they will protect you."

Mike's sense of frustration multiplied as Johannsen spoke, but he knew it was unwise to provoke Barkley further. He nodded his head in mock acquiescence. "Being rational doesn't just mean following *production* logic," thought Mike, as he walked back to his station. "These guys may *look* easy, but I bet they'll find a way to get back at the company for this. I sure have!"

Phil unexpectedly walked into the control room. Mike was beginning final checks before shift change. "Bad news, Mike, I had to bust Larry Jones and Randy Markus in Granulating. . . . We'll probably have to let them go."

Mike viewed drug-taking as a crutch, never accepting it as a liberating act, but was furious on principle: "Phil! That rule hasn't been enforced in over three years. Why the hell now? And why in Granulating? The work there is the worst in the plant—it's hot and dirty and *boring!* Everybody on nights is high or low. The work gets done. You're trying to get back at Randy for filing against you!"

Phil stared mutely at Mike and then started to walk away. He turned, and angrily but deliberately responded: "Mike, if the rules are too tough here, I'm sure you can find other work."

Mike called the threat: "Don't push me, Phil. That's on my mind every day—and everyone else's, too."

Phil shouted as he left the room, "Let me know when!"

Mike recalled all the layoffs last year and thought, "I'm an idiot! I let him get to me. I should know better than to go one-on-one with a supervisor. There are so many other ways to fight back."

Mike left the control room to find Randy and met him and Charlie walking toward the time clock. Randy looked ragged and resigned. Mike embraced him compassionately and said, "The whole plant's in an uproar. We'll find a way for you to keep your job—you can count on that. Let's go to the Sunset and have a drink."

In the parking lot, Mike glanced back at the plant and thought resentfully, "You can check out any time you like, but you can never leave . . ."

Reprise

Like Graham, the central character in H. G. Wells' anti-utopian novel, *When the Sleeper Wakes*, this story's main figure, Mike Armstrong, encountered a nightmare world upon awakening from a deep sleep. However, it was not the dramatically inhuman, mechanical-urban world of the 22nd century which Armstrong encountered. This was not a story about dark, dusty, subterranean factories, blue-uniformed workers pale and disfigured from their labor but automatonically punctual, or brutal state police who coerce laborers. Instead, it was a story about alienated life in and around a modern, urban factory where the mechanisms of administrative control are subtle, complicated, and not encompassed by the plant gates.

Armstrong experienced these events first during a dream state and then again while awake. This literary device was used to compare and contrast two radical descriptions of subjective alienation, reified consciousness, and reflective militancy, and to illustrate the power of mythical forces in organizational settings. The main character's dual states of mind and action dramatize the existential moments of personal alienation (Laing, 1965) and symbolize the self-contradictory aspects of capitalist systems.

SOURCE: Adapted for use in this paper from *When the Sleeper Wakes*, by H. G. Wells, 1960, in E. F. Bleiler (Ed.), *Three Prophetic Novels of H. G. Wells*, New York: Dover.

This study is primarily a theoretical analysis that uses typical cases to illustrate positions. The method is subjectivist (Morgan & Smircich, 1980; Poole, 1972) because the realities probed are psychic and differs from purely fictional expression in that the characters' lives are created from actual fieldwork and theoretical description.

The sections below briefly recast the theoretical issues and concepts relevant to the study and develop some of its implications.

Worker Cognitions and Organization Theory

Most contemporary theories of organization contain descriptions of worker characteristics that mediate organizational events and worker reactions. Included are those that are relatively objective, such as age, sex, race, or need states, and those which are relatively subjective, such as preferences, values, and belief systems. In fusing cognitive theory and organization theory, Weick (1979) extended inquiry on employee cognitions into the deeply subjective, into the inner frameworks through which people select, organize, and interpret sensory impressions to make meaning in their world. The concept of schema is crucial in understanding these cognitive processes. Schemata are abstract, psychic frameworks of organized past experiences that establish relations among specific events and entities (cf. Bartlett, 1932; Hastie, 1981).

Worker Consciousness and Organization Theory

With the emergence of radical organization theory, many traditional and neo-Marxist concepts have been applied in studies of workplace dynamics (see Goldman, 1985, for review). However, a specific type of schema, studied extensively in Marxist analyses of the worker, remains unfamiliar to most organization theorists. One of the purposes of this study was to integrate concepts of class consciousness, defined as the extent of workers' awareness of their emancipatory role in history (cf. Mann, 1973), into the writings on organizations. These concepts are developed in terms of the subjective alienation literature and are proposed as active, psychic forces that serve the worker in selecting, organizing, and making meaning from impressions associated with capitalist power dynamics.

Moments of Subjective Alienation

In Marx's (1932/1964) early philosophical writing, worker alienation is presented as an historically necessary result of the tension generated between the contradictory social forces of production and the private appropriation of capital. Workers are legally separated from ownership of the means and product of their labor (objective alienation) and comprehend, in a shared way, their position in oppressive, class-based production systems (cf. Bramel & Friend, 1981; Nord, 1977). Thus, while objectively alienated, awareness of class oppression and the transformative historical mission prevents separation from true self.

Neo-Marxist formulations of alienation, originating with Lukacs's (1923/1971) classic essay, attempted to describe and explain the lack of awareness of classbased oppression on the part of workers. Concepts of subjective alienation were developed to represent mystified psychic states where workers misconstrue the reality of class-based oppression for freedom (Jermier, 1982).

Table 18.1 presents elements of two prominent humanistic Marxist theories of subjective alienation, critical theory and dialectical Marxism, and contrasts these with humanistic organization theory's self-actualizing worker. The table was constructed to summarize differences in perspectives on subjective alienation illustrated in the story and discussed below.

Central to critical theory formulations of worker consciousness and alienation (represented in "The Dream") is the concept of reification. In capitalist market systems, workers must sell their labor power and thus become semihuman objects of exchange, commodities, things (Israel, 1975). Reification is the "moment in the process of alienation in which the characteristic of thinghood becomes the standard of objective reality" (Berger & Pullman, 1965, p. 198). Reified consciousness is characterized by a *deprivation of awareness* that prevents realization that the world is socially constructed and can be remade. There is a concretizing and *naturalizing* (or *supernaturalizing*) of existing technical processes, social relations, concepts of reason, meanings of time, and definitions of adjustment (see Horkheimer, 1947/1974; Horkheimer & Adorno, 1944/1972). Only those momentarily not under "the spell" (Adorno, 1966/1973, p. 312) resist absolute integration or reject the benefits of the status quo.

The power of reification in rationalizing existing conditions of employment for workers is supplemented by the "culture industry" (Horkheimer & Adorno, 1944/1972), which is at once ideological and diversionary. Marx used the term "camera obscura" in *The German Ideology* to refer to the process whereby a distorted, upside-down version of the world (propagated by the privileged classes) becomes the standard of objective reality. The major institutions in society (schools, churches, the family, advertising and entertainment, etc.) act in harmony to present a version of the worker in society that denies oppressive realities. Cultural domination is completed when consumption is manipulated so thoroughly that

Table 18.1   Conceptions of the Worker in Humanistic Theories of Capitalist Organization

	Traditional Organization Theory's "Self Actualizer"	Critical Theory's "Antihero"	Dialectical Marxist Theory's "Everyman"
1. Objective Nature of Society:	Convergence of interests	Polarized, class-based, inherently contradictory due to legal relations of production	Polarized, class-based, inherently contradictory due to legal relations of production
2. Objective Features of Work Organizations:	Bureaucratic	Inequalitarian, unjust	Inequalitarian, unjust
3. Objective Nature of Work Settings:	Unfulfilling	Exploitative, oppressive, alienating	Exploitative, oppressive, alienating
4. Primary Analytical Category (Psychological):	Human need states	Human consciousness (interpretive schema)	Human consciousness (interpretive schema)
5. Description of Psychological State:	Frustration	Alienation: Reified Consciousness (deprivation of awareness)	Alienation: Reflective Militancy (awareness of deprivation, but not class conscious)
6. Behavioral Orientation:	Withdrawn; sometimes pointlessly aggressive	Passive, docile	Active, selectively militant
7. Role Played in Respective Theories:	Psychologically immature, unrevolutionary victim of industrial bureau-cratization	Unrevolutionary subject totally captivated by capitalist myths and meaning structures. Contributes to own exploitation through self-repression, reproduction of myths in social world, and frenetic consumption.	Sensitive, long-suffering, latently revolutionary victim of capitalist dynamics. Resists domination and constructs alternative realities through militant interpretation and selective protest.
8. Reflected in Short Story by:	Not represented in story	*Dream state* (Myths and consumerism captivate and insulate Mike from class-based injuries.)	*Nightmare State* (Myths obfuscate class basis of Mike's injuries which he makes sense of and reacts to from his own unique historicity.)
		a. Mike naturalizing industrial time.	a. Mike stumbling over Gypsum, his dog, who represents both affluence and the crippling effects of work.
		b. Mike consuming modern concepts of sport, nutrition, and transportation.	b. Mike resenting company's power over his appearance.
		c. Mike engaged by instrumental technique of music, not its critical message.	c. Mike understanding profound time consciousness as a form of enslavement.
		d. Mike supernaturalizing the plant and its setting.	

Traditional Organization Theory's "Self Actualizer"	Critical Theory's "Antihero"	Dialectical Marxist Theory's "Everyman"
	e. Mike endorsing Phil's supernaturalizing of the plant's products and dismissing the newspaper's warnings because of the story's length and placement.	d. Mike resisting self-repression and superficial definitions of safety issues.
	f. Mike accepting the (nameless) plant supervisor's definition of effectiveness in terms of efficiency and reasonableness in terms of technical rationality. Leads him to believe he needs to adjust since system cannot be changed.	e. Mike critically interpreting song.
		f. Mike symbolically connecting plant's whistles with management's view of workers.
	g. Mike embracing the illusion of freedom.	g. Mike using Guthrie cartoon as a critical psychological resource.
	h. Mike accepting the inevitability of living with capitalist rules—even bad ones—by likening them to knives (instruments). Takes ends for granted.	h. Mike's indignation over Phil's myth propagation.
	i. Mike's reflections on the workday aborted by the light-beer commercial which he thinks does not affect him.	i. Mike's dismissal of Barkley's definitions of effectiveness, rationality, and responsibility, and his vow to get back at the company.
	j. Mike completely turning his brain off for the night with in-vogue anesthetics: cocaine and rock music. Drugs and his possessions creating a padded, tranquilizing shell.	j. Mike's confrontation with Phil over arbitrary enforcement of rules.
		k. Mike reminding himself protest must be selective and creative.
		l. Mike using critical verse from song to symbolize work imprisonment
9. Classic Citations in the Literature:		
Argyris (1957)	Horkheimer & Adorno (1944/1972)	Sartre (1960/1963)
Maslow (1965)	Horkheimer (1947/1974)	Sartre (1960/1976)
	Marcuse (1964/1966)	Marcuse (1969)
	Adorno (1966/1973)	

(Continued)

Table 18.1 (Continued)

	Traditional Organization Theory's "Self Actualizer"	Critical Theory's "Antihero"	Dialectical Marxist Theory's "Everyman"
10. Management Portrayed as:	Anti-humanistic protagonist	Anti-humanistic protagonist	Anti-humanistic protagonist
11. Prescriptions:	Create new forms of organization (humanist bureaucracies) which facilitate healthy growth and development of workers	Promote democratic, revolutionary transformation of social and political-economic structures by raising consciousness of individual workers such that forms of oppression are revealed. This will facilitate free examination of alternative realities and healthy growth and development of human potentialities.	Promote democratic, revolutionary transformation of social and political-economic structures by connecting individual acts of self-emancipation with broader forms of class struggle. This will facilitate healthy growth and development of human potentialities.

consumers feel compelled to frenetically buy and use the culture industry's latest products, even though they see through them (Horkheimer & Adorno, 1944/1972). Workers are anesthetized by the persuasive rationalizations readily accessible in mythical structures and by manipulated, diversionary consumption, such that the injuries of class are neither perceived nor felt. Workers are viewed as eternal dreamers. Partly due to their programmed atomization, they are unable to transcend their entrancement.

The contemporary worker's subjective experience of alienation has also been addressed in the writings of New Left Marxists (e.g., Marcuse, 1969) and existential Marxists (e.g., Sartre, 1960/1963, 1960/1976). They are referred to here as dialectical Marxists (represented in "The Nightmare") because of their emphasis on the central role of the ultimately free individual in resisting class-based structures of domination. In rejecting both the class-conscious, collective subject of traditional Marxism and the totally dominated, individual subject of critical theory, dialectical Marxists characterize the ordinary worker as subjectively alienated (falsely conscious), but engaged in responsible, meaningful protest and new forms of class radicalism. Thus, workers are capable of understanding the actual operation of the system (Best & Connolly, 1979), and there is an awareness of deprivation and disadvantage, even though this awareness rarely fosters revolutionary motives. Individual workers are not psychologically dominated by property-based power dynamics to the point of mystification or resignation. They experience workplace events from reflectively militant schemata, usually rejecting simplistic and exploitative definitions of situations. Although the worker's world is full of oppressive realities, it is at the same time rich in critical resources; reflective interpretation mobilizes these resources. Each day, the worker resists domination; sometimes with overt and dramatic actions, more frequently with sensible, subterranean forms of sabotage (Ehrenreich & Ehrenreich, 1976). The injuries of class are internalized, cumulative, and latently explosive (Lefebvre, 1970).

At the extremes, states of subjective alienation may be personal and unique or intersubjective and common. The form of consciousness through which the world is comprehended results from a synthesis of myths in the broader cultural setting and active, personal reflection. Myths are culturally managed modes of explanation that account for social circumstances. If a myth denies or minimizes human agency or potentiality by casting class-based injuries as reasonable and inevitable, the myth is false and ideological (cf. Horkheimer & Adorno, 1944/1972). Myths of this kind permeate the broader symbolic environment and may "penetrate the innermost recesses of consciousness" (Gross, 1980, p. 259). They may account for social relations of production in society and may be applied to specific organizational settings, as meanings are constructed at that level. Theories of symbolic processes in organizations will eventually include explanations of the power of mythical forces. Critical theory and dialectical Marxist theory provide alternative perspectives on types of psychic domination resulting from symbolic constructions (cf. Morgan, Frost, & Pondy, 1983).

Implications

The divergent states of mind of Mike Armstrong illustrate the psychic processes engaged as human actors confront an alien world and make sense of it. The meaning experienced is a creative product of the properties of the alien world and the actor's psychic processes.

The psychic processes explored in this study differ from current approaches to conceptualizing characteristics of workers in several ways: (a) they are viewed as developing within objectively alienating and exploitative work settings and societal arrangements; (b) they may be isomorphic with or partially reflective of mythical forces in society; (c) they are deeply subjective, cognitive substances through which meaning is imposed upon the world; (d) they map domains of societal processes and represent collective phenomena in mental time and space; and (e) they are more fundamental and powerful mental forces than are expectations, beliefs, or even values and profoundly condition actions and attitudes.

The theoretical viewpoints on alienated consciousness illustrated here depict the effects of problematical organizational events on workers quite differently (Table 18.1). The anesthetized critical theory worker is so skilled at programmed rationalization and diversionary consumption that he or she barely notices the recurring surgery that separates and subjugates true self (cf. Laing, 1965). There is no counterforce or retaliation since this worker mistakes even capricious and surplus repression as natural and inevitable; there is no noticeable injury, hence no reprisal. The effects on the reflectively militant worker are poignant and potentially explosive. This worker cannot live at the level of ideology and therefore openly experiences the "buried features of working class life" (Matza & Wellman, 1980, p. 1). This creates feelings of incredulity, indignation, anger, horror, dread, fear, and loathing. The injuries are usually internalized, but their comprehension in a broader system of meaning creates an unexpected resiliency. It is the carefully timed and varied reprisals that generate managerial transformations and crises (cf. Morgan, 1984).

As Table 18.1 shows, concepts of humanistic management that are radically different from traditional organization theory derive from critical theory and dialectical Marxism. They emphasize the importance of the political–economic context in analyzing subjective states and propose macrolevel change strategies to eliminate alienation and humanize work (e.g., Jacoby, 1975; Nord, 1977). In this study, class-based workplace dynamics have been dramatized in relation to divergent forms of alienated consciousness to illustrate the importance of human meaning-making processes in understanding organizational behavior. Further theoretical analysis and research will clarify and assess the realism of these alternative viewpoints on the meaning of alienation in work.

CHAPTER 19

Past Postmodernism?

Reflections and Tentative Directions

Marta Calas

Linda Smircich

S ince the late 1970s, the social sciences, including organization studies, have been influenced by diverse theoretical perspectives calling for reflexivity toward the constitution of "theory" and the institutional, social, and political aspects of such constitution. "Postmodern" has been used to identify many of these perspectives, for they appear to share some features, including a concern for language and representation and a reconsideration of subjectivity and power.

More recently, the "postmodern turn" has come under increasing scrutiny, even by some of its advocates and supporters (e.g., Butler & Scott, 1992; Leitch, 1996). Insofar as postmodern perspectives allow for questioning conventional approaches to theory development, the argument goes, they provide incisive analyses showing the inner workings and assumptive basis of those theories. At the same time, however, the elusiveness of theory under postmodern premises prevents those who articulate postmodern perspectives from theorizing other, alternative views, because they do not have any "solid ground" from which to speak.

A typical response to an encounter with a poststructuralist analysis or a deconstructive reading in our field is "Yes, but. . . ." That is, "Yes, I see how the language in the text repeats what it seeks to suppress and excludes a devalued other" (upon reading Martin Kilduff's [1993] "Deconstructing Organizations"; Joanne Martin's [1990] "Deconstructing Organizational Taboos"; or Dennis Mumby and Linda Putnam's [1992] deconstructive readings of Simon's concept of bounded rationality),

*From "Past Postmodernism? Reflections and Tentative Directions," by M. B. Calas and L. Smircich, 1999, *Academy of Management Review, 24(4), 649–671.* Copyright 1999 by Academy of Management (NY). Reproduced with permission of Academy of Management.

or "Yes, I see how power/knowledge works in the unfolding of human resource management (HRM) practices and strategic management frameworks" (upon reading Barbara Townley's [1993] or David Knights' [1992] Foucauldian takes on HRM or strategic management, respectively). And then, "*But*, once you've deconstructed, then what? How can we reconstruct, or get anything positive from this?"

We are sympathetic to this reaction, coming as it typically does from a desire to make a difference with our scholarship. Yet, we would not share the sense of nothing "positive from this." Instead, we would emphasize the importance of the postmodern turn for transforming contemporary theorizing in the social sciences in general and organization studies in particular. That is, we wish to mark the importance for contemporary theorizing of having *gone through* these intellectual currents.

Thus, in this article we discuss the impact of postmodernism as a significant and positive contribution to organizational theorizing during the last 10 years or so. Its significance, we argue, resides in the opportunities it has offered for reflecting upon the production of theory as a genre and as an institutional and cultural activity. By calling attention to the textuality of organizational theories, postmodernism has opened a space for a different form of criticism (e.g., Fondas, 1997; Golden-Biddle & Locke, 1993; Van Maanen, 1988, 1995a, b). Viewing theory as a representational form places decisions regarding "for what" and "for whom" we are going to speak in the core of our scholarship (e.g., Deetz, 1996; Ferguson, 1994; Hatch, 1996; Putnam, 1996; Van Maanen, 1996; Wicks & Freeman, 1998). Questions such as "Who is the subject of organizational theories?" and "What is represented and what is not represented in organizational theorizing?" can now be asked as issues to be resolved in the textual configurations themselves (Mumby & Putnam, 1992; Nkomo, 1992). Perhaps more important, these questions have given way to different forms of writing theory and have allowed different theoretical "voices" to emerge. The postmodern turn has opened "the margins" of organization studies to be "written" by and for others whose theoretical voices have seldom been represented in our scholarship (Calas & Smircich, 1991; Shallenberger, 1994).

We expand the above reflections as follows. First, we locate the entrance of postmodern perspectives into organization studies during the late 1970s and early 1980s, connected to writings about the multiparadigmatic status of the field. Second, we review key preoccupations of postmodern theorizing and observe the ways in which they are evident in organization studies. By referring to several examples, we point to the contributions that postmodern and poststructuralist perspectives have brought to organization studies as the field stands today. Finally, we consider four contemporary approaches to organizational theorizing and their current and potential contributions to organization studies in light of the issues raised above: (1) feminist poststructuralist theorizing, (2) postcolonial analyses, (3) actor-network theory, and (4) narrative approaches to knowledge. These, we claim, may be considered as heirs (apparent) of the postmodern turn, each offering specific contributions to organizational theorizing after postmodernism and each not yet sufficiently materialized.

Before we proceed, we must acknowledge that we are writing from a North American and business school location. This placement no doubt influences how we understand some issues in organization studies. As well, as we write these lines and the rest of the article, we are struggling with the same problems of representation and form we discuss below as postmodern topics. At the most immediate level, writing this article as a commentary and a chronicle of some recent past and current issues in the field is writing in a modernist form that betrays our assumed location as postmodern intellectuals. As commentators, we are taking the authorial position as narrators of this "knowledge." We can also anticipate for our readers that we have not found a "way out" of these multiple contradictions, but, as postmodernists, we were certainly not expecting that we would.

Our modest hope is that, through this article, we will be able to sustain a conversation through a different kind of engagement that does not require arguing for the superiority of our views in relation to those of others. In Barbara Townley's words, following Foucault, some of what this entails is for authors to specify the aspects of the world with which they are trying to engage and why; to situate knowledge and so de-reify it; to speak in a way that takes ownership of their arguments; and to be accountable for the choices made. "It posits a different basis of engagement, one which is reciprocal not hierarchical. It is a call for writing in friendship" (Townley, 1994b: 28).

Postmodernism and Organizational Studies

Much has been written about postmodernism and poststructuralism in the social sciences (Bauman, 1992; Featherstone, 1988; Rose, 1991; Rosenau, 1992), and we cannot review it all here. Our aim, instead, is to highlight those arguments and issues, such as *the incredulity toward metanarratives, the undecidability of meaning, the crisis of representation, and the problematization of the subject and the author,* that were particularly influential in organizational theorizing as it turned into more reflective knowledge making.

A central concern of those who started to experiment with the postmodern turn in organization studies is what Lyotard identifies as "incredulity toward metanarratives" (1979, quoted here from English edition, 1984: xxiv). For Lyotard, the modernist view about the universality of the true, the good, and the beautiful is no longer tenable. Other competing views have appeared that question not only the veracity of the Enlightenment philosophies but also their "grand theory" style of theorizing that promotes a unitary vision of science and society.

Lyotard, following Wittgenstein, positions current conditions of knowledge as "language games." As long as these games are played with the intention of annihilation or cooptation, they force an agreement toward a dominant view where there can be none. Rather, Lyotard proposes, legitimate knowledge under postmodern conditions can only reside in "petit recits." Knowledge can only be produced in "small stories" or "modest narratives," mindful of their locality in space and time and capable of adapting or disappearing as needed. If recognized as the creation of small stories, *theorizing* thus becomes a temporary language game that assumes responsibility for its rules and its effects as power. Lyotard's "story" has an uncanny resemblance to how conditions of knowledge in organization studies were changing at the time. At about the time of his writing, early arguments appeared about the existence of multiple ontological and epistemological paradigms in organizational analysis (e.g., Astley & Van de Ven, 1983; Burrell & Morgan, 1979; Evered & Louis, 1981; Ritzer, 1975, 1981), and strong interest surfaced in organizational culture and symbolism, as well as qualitative research (e.g., *Administrative Science Quarterly,* 1979, 1983; Allaire & Firsirotu, 1984; Carter & Jackson, 1987; Frost, Moore, Louis, Lundberg, & Martin, 1985; Gray, Bougon, & Donnellon, 1985; *Journal of Management,* 1985; Pondy, Frost, Morgan, & Dandridge, 1983; Turner, 1986). The dominant paradigm—positivism, functionalism—was challenged by other language games: interpretive and critical perspectives.

Nonetheless, the appearance of competing paradigms, per se, does not change the conditions of knowledge from modern to postmodern. Insofar as each paradigm remains as a competing view in the search for foundational knowledge, it grounds a whole edifice of universal understanding that transcends culture and history (e.g., Bernstein, 1983; Chia, 1996). Multiparadigmatic awareness simply facilitates a still very modern, metatheoretical discussion around these issues: What philosophy of knowledge is behind "truthful knowledge"? Each paradigm is a foundational claim (a metatheory) about the possibility of true knowledge. Each offers a way toward a more complete understanding or explanation of the world in which we live. Each claims to be the best view of the world "out there." None accounts for the language game in which they all may be embedded.

Edging Toward Reflexivity

Yet, these shifting conditions in organizational knowledge anticipated the appearance of postmodern theorizing as several scholars in the field turned their gaze inward. Conversations about which paradigm was the most truthful or most legitimate transformed into a more reflective concern. What was the significance of having multiple paradigms in organization studies? As we see it, the importance of this turn is that it encouraged reflexivity regarding the "knowledge-making" enterprise itself (e.g., Whitley, 1984).

First, self-reflective awareness of the researcher/theoretician's complicity in the constitution of their objects of study started to appear. Kuhn's (1962) focus on scientific communities and changes in scientific paradigms became particularly influential. More important, organizational culture and symbolism research, with its phenomenological orientation, needed to account for the researched/researcher relationship, given its social constructionist ontological positioning (Mirvis & Louis, 1985; Peshkin, 1985; Van Maanen, 1988). Possibly, it was this scholarship that pointed most clearly at the constitutive character of the research activities in relation to the phenomena they were purported to study. Studies in the sociology of science also played an important role in this regard (e.g., Knorr-Cetina, 1981; Woolgar, 1988).

Second, arguments about the interested nature of knowledge making also surfaced (Connell & Nord, 1996; Rao & Pasmore, 1989; Stablein & Nord, 1985). The so-called paradigm wars is a good indication of these, for what is at stake is not simply the adequacy of particular theories but how the truthfulness behind those theories gets constituted by the different "contenders" (Donaldson, 1996; Hinings et al., 1988;

Martin & Frost, 1996; *Organization*, 1998). Further, the pragmatics behind reducing the number of "acceptable" paradigms has been debated. Notice, for instance, that recent writings by Pfeffer (1993, 1995), Van Maanen (1995a, b), and McKinley and Mone (1998), among others, are not so much about which paradigm is right. Rather, they are about why it is good for organization studies to limit—or not—their proliferation and how to do such a thing. All of these actions, and the writings that exemplify them, represent a reflexive understanding of theorizing in organization studies as a political process rather than merely as a neutral, truth-seeking operation (e.g., Cannella & Paetzold, 1994; Kaghan & Phillips, 1998; Martin & Frost, 1996; Scherer, 1998; Spender, 1998). Another reflexive concern appeared as well. How does the specific constitution of our writings—their textuality—define the nature of our knowledge? What are "the poetics" of knowledge making (e.g., Astley, 1985; Golden-Biddle & Locke, 1997; Hatch, 1997; Jermier, 1985; Martin, 1992; Martin & Frost, 1996; Mauws & Phillips, 1995; Van Maanen, 1988)? In our view, this latter concern completed the required cycle of reflection, but it was the emergence of all these reflections, taken together, that marked a radical departure in knowledge making within the field. An ontological/epistemological leap had happened which opened the space for postmodern "theorizing." Anyone interested in this leap could observe, for example, differences between the special forum on theory building in the *Academy of Management Review* of 1989 and the same journal's special issue on new intellectual currents in 1992. Organization studies was, indeed, experiencing "the postmodern condition."

From this perspective, postmodernism offered an important contribution from the humanities to contemporary social sciences and organization studies (Zald, 1996). The contribution was that of an occasion for reflexivity that allows for a critical examination of the way modern (paradigmatic or foundational) knowledge has been constituted, without needing to provide for an alternative knowledge.

Poststructuralism: "No Solid Grounds" for Knowledge?

Nonetheless, reflexivity alone may not change much, especially if the reflections are expressed unreflectively. That is, at the very moment the complicity of language in the constitution of knowledge becomes part of the "conversation," the "tone" of the conversation has to change. The issue becomes how to articulate the operations of modern knowledge without being caught in unreflective representational webs that hint of modernity. Poststructuralism provided approaches for such articulations. It is through the tenets of poststructuralism that organization studies, like many other social sciences, anthropology (Clifford & Marcus, 1986), sociology (Rosenau, 1992), psychology (Shotter & Gergen, 1989), political science (Connelly, 1993), and even economics (McCloskey, 1986) have been able to fully engage in the postmodern conversation.

Relationships between poststructuralism and postmodernism have been expressed in several different ways (see, for instance, Bauman, 1992, and Foster, 1983). For our purpose we prefer Huyssen's understanding of poststructuralism as a theory of modernism at the stage of its exhaustion:

> But if post structuralism can be seen as the revenant of modernism in the guise of theory, then that would also be precisely what makes it postmodern. It is a postmodernism that . . . in some cases, is fully aware of modernism's limitations and failed political ambitions. (1986: 209)

However, we would like to further specify the importance of the "post" in poststructuralism. Huyssen's reference to poststructuralism as a theory that highlights modernist exhaustion refers to expectations in French humanities and social theory that a new paradigm derived from structural linguistics—that is, structuralism—would provide the strong "scientific status" that the human sciences had lacked. This hope arose from the view of language offered by Saussurean linguistics (Saussure, 1916/1974; Gadet, 1989).

Semiology, as Saussure's science of signs became known, displaced linguistic approaches that focused on substance or meaning to focus on language as a structural system of relations and differences. Independence of structure from meaning while still accounting for their relationship became a general structuralist insight that transferred from linguistics to several other disciplines during the 1950s and 1960s. From anthropology (Levi-Strauss) to literature (Barthes) to philosophy (Althusser), structuralism offered a very specific response to the excessive subjectivism and intentionality of phenomenology and existentialism, as well as to the excessive social and economic determinism of conventional Marxism. However, the expectations of scientific legitimation to be achieved by structuralism in the human sciences were never fully realized. Scientific interest soon gave way to another understanding of structuralism, known as poststructuralism.

Poststructuralist analyses demonstrate how signification occurs through a constant deferral of meaning from one linguistic symbol to another. At its most basic, poststructuralist approaches suggest that there is no stable or original core of signification and, thus, no foundation, no grounding, and no stable structure on which meaning can rest. This insight affects, in particular, meanings that claim to be universal or that claim to be progressively moving toward universality, such as the Enlightenment conceptions of knowledge and science.

For example, consider searching for meaning in a dictionary that always refers you to another word, in a neverending movement from word to word and with no final meaning to be found to stop this process. From this example it is possible to rethink the common-sense understanding of a world of objects or notions existing independently of the linguistic symbol—signifiers—through which we address them. Rather, objects and notions—what we pay attention to—are always already mediated through signifiers and their capability to differentiate. There is no essence on which to ground meaning; there are only differences between meanings.

Quite profoundly, these ideas subvert all possibility of constituting legitimate knowledge in the modern (paradigmatic) sense. Modern knowledge (or theory) is presumed to represent some form of stable phenomena existing outside their representation. For instance, as we read a journal article, we assume that it represents phenomena that exist elsewhere, whether empirically observed or speculated upon. Yet, poststructuralist arguments contend that all we have as knowledge is the representation itself, such as the materiality of the text in which "knowledge" is written.

Further, textual representations have no fixed meanings. The text is constituted in signifiers whose referents could always slide to other referents. Words could always be reinterpreted through other words.

Modern knowledge also presupposes that even if disputes over interpretations occur, one always has recourse to the authority of the writer. One could always ask, "What were the author's intentions; what did he or she mean?" From a poststructuralist perspective, however, the notion of authorship is suspect as a repository of stable meanings. Authorship is suspect first on the matter of intention. Skepticism toward the author's intention derives from a postmodern critique of modern philosophy's notion of subjectivity. Modernist philosophy assumes that human beings are autonomous subjects, whose interests and desires are transparent to themselves and independent from the interests and desires of others. If one denies the autonomy of the "self," one may question whose intentions are represented in the author's text.

In poststructuralism "the author" is understood as embedded in a social context and in relation to others (e.g., a community of scholars). He or she is an "author-function" (Foucault, 1977), whose name merely operates to authorize another version of the tradition within that community. Thus, invoking "intention" mostly activates a chain of signifiers, which are the several authors and writings that stand behind that tradition. These signifiers, already interpreted and reinterpreted, may not have much to do with the actual body or possible intentions of "the author" that stands now as the end of the chain. Rather, these multiple interpretations have already constituted the author. To underscore this point, consider, for example, the function of citations in the constitution of theory and the multiple interpretations that have been imputed to the works of often-cited authors.

For poststructuralism, the position of the author is also in question in relationship to meaning. Insofar as the author is creating his or her work for others, the minute the work leaves the author's hands it becomes a public document whose status as work stands only in relationship to the possibility that it will be read. The document is meaningful only because it can be read by others, and once this happens, the author becomes just one interpreter among other readers. Even if the author were to converse with readers in order to clarify what he or she meant, that in itself would constitute another text—also subject to more interpretation. Think of the multiple texts that are produced by commentaries about any author's work, including the author's responses to those commentaries. Rather than putting an end to interpretation about the meaning of the original text, recourse to the author produces more and newer meanings.

Despite all these speculations, one may contend, we are surrounded by meaningful texts of knowledge, whose authors gain accolades for their ideas—ideas that may be put into practice in the "real world." How is this possible, if all that constitutes such knowledge is unstable language, illusory representations, and author-functions? This question brings us back to another issue regarding the operations by which signification is attained. As discussed above, the basic linguistic insight that gave way to structuralism, and later to poststructuralism, was that language is a system of differences. If we observe *how* we say what we say, we are always making choices between the words we write or speak and those we do not write or say but that are "the other" (i.e., the difference) of what we are saying. For instance, right now as we write these marks on the page, we are trying to construct something meaningful for a particular community of readers. We do this by leaving behind—by leaving unwritten—a series of other possible marks that may not (yet) belong to this community.

It is interesting to observe which marks become expressed and which do not. The unexpressed ones also constitute our text by their absence, since they make it possible to put a limit—to contain—what we are saying. In this way it is possible to consider how fixing signification occurs. Fixing signification—the operation that permits asserting the truthfulness of our expert texts and authors—occurs as what is said conceals its other—that is, what is not said. In other words, as we (any of us) write, we engage in a linguistic play that eventually constitutes a hierarchical arrangement: that which is visible (and that appears in the text as self-sustaining) and that which the visible makes invisible (but without which the visible cannot appear).

And so, as we make choices to render this text readable for a particular community, we are also not saying several other things that may make it unreadable for that community. As we suppress these words and use others, we contribute to the perpetuation of this cycle: we are closing the possible vocabulary of the field, and we are excluding other meanings. Thus, at the most basic and immediate, it is possible to see how the stabilization of meaning is constituted within a system of power relations—a system of inclusion and exclusion—which defines as acceptable or not the marks that will appear on the page as knowledge. We all, as we try to signify, participate in the activation of these power relations. Who we are, how we know ourselves, what we say to others, and so on—it is all the production and effects of power/knowledge.

In the paragraphs of the past few pages, we have been paraphrasing several themes that have become well known in the parlance of postmodernism and poststructuralism: the end of metanarratives, the undecidability of meaning, the crisis of representation, the problematization of the subject and the author. Each of them and their relationships to one another point to the operations of legitimating knowledge and theory, which are constituted through an unstable system of signification. Our "common sense" of knowledge production is no common sense at all, but a lot of hard work for controlling signification.

Equally important, and perhaps less frequently admitted, is that these issues are also linked with the institutional politics of knowledge making. As noted by Lyotard, the question of language in the constitution of knowledge is not only a question of aesthetics or epistemology. It is also a question of the relations between the institutions that define what knowledge is and the language through which knowledge gets made. The reflexivity over the constitution of knowledge that permeates the postmodern condition has helped to articulate these relationships. Poststructuralism has contributed to showing, however, that these relationships are neither determined by some structural imperative nor defined by some higher order of power or authority. Rather, they occur as we all continue to signify and resignify our social milieux—over and over again.

Poststructuralist writings bring forward these issues, not through commentary in "plain language," as we are doing (or trying to do) here, but, rather, by violating the norms and destabilizing how and what is possible to say. In Lyotard's words,

The text [the postmodern writer] writes, the work he [sic] produces, are not in principle governed by preestablished rules, and they cannot be judged . . . by applying familiar categories to the text or to the work. . . . Hence, the fact that work and text have the characters of an event. (1984: 81)

Postmodern Organization Theorizing

Postmodernism and poststructuralism are now well represented in organization studies. In several books, articles, and book chapters scholars describe these intellectual tendencies and discuss how they might perform and what might be the implications of their performance (e.g., Baack & Prasch, 1997; Boje, Gephart, & Thatchenkery, 1996; Burrell, 1988; Calas & Smircich, 1997a; Cooper, 1989; Cooper & Burrell, 1988; Hassard, 1993; Hassard & Parker, 1993; Jackson & Carter, 1992; Jeffcutt, 1993; Kilduff & Mehra, 1997; Kreiner, 1992; Letiche, 1992; Linstead, 1993; Schultz, 1992). As important as these are for familiarizing our scholarly community with the primary ideas behind the postmodern, we are particularly indebted to poststructuralist analyses—works and texts with the character of an event—for challenging the field to think and do differently. By way of illustration, we have selected articles that represent genealogical analyses, following Foucault's work (1979, 1980), and deconstructions, inspired by Derrida's work (1974, 1982), for these are the approaches that appear more often in organization studies. We will highlight how these examples perform as poststructuralist analytics within these two different approaches.

We are aware that we are walking a very thin line here. Singling out these "exemplar works" is also an exclusion of others that perform equally well. At the same time, we would be further "fixing signification" if our commentaries were to be read as making the case that these are examples to follow, rather than as encouragement for others to write outside the margins. Perhaps more dangerous, some may expect that we would articulate a "method": how to do genealogies or deconstructions. However, although there are certain aspects of these analyses that could be called methodological, the issue of method as a guarantee of getting the right data to prove a point is, precisely, part of the modernist logic that poststructuralism addresses. To clarify, the issue is not that in these analyses "anything goes," because they are indeed very carefully crafted textual arguments; rather, the issue is that these analyses are crafted in relation to the specific critique they want to raise, and, as such, they are exercises of the theoretical imagination. Common denominators, such as theory and method, conceptual or empirical, are not applicable to these kinds of writings. Thus, readers beware that we might not tell you what you might expect.

Genealogical analyses. Foucault's genealogies are a "history of the present," which traces connections among the arbitrary rather than the intentional, the accidental rather than the planned, in the historical constitution of contemporary practices. These connections denaturalize everyday activities and institutions that we take for granted. At the same time, the connections are not presented as determined by, say, the dominant over the dominated, as a critical theory analysis would do. Rather, they are presented as webs of practices, discourses, and institutions that have been adopted, imitated, and transformed to the point that they become knowledge and common sense and are repeated by many without recollection of their original purpose—thus, the notion of power/knowledge.

For instance, one may ask, "What do a prison observation tower and total quality management (TQM) practices have to do with one another?" (e.g., Sewell & Wilkinson, 1992). Or, one may ask, "What does a population census have to do with HRM practices?" (e.g., Townley, 1993). In both cases one may answer that the prison's tower and the census have contributed to the appearance of a particular kind of contemporary *subjectivity*. It is only because we, in our society, take for granted such understanding of "self" that it is conceivable to us that there is anything normal about HRM or TQM.

Sewell and Wilkinson (1992) retell the story of just-in-time (JIT) management and total quality control (TQC) management not as advanced development of more efficient production practices but in relation to the surveillance logic of Bentham's 1700s panopticon. Foucault (1979) describes the panopticon as a tower in the center of a prison, with cells built around it. From this tower the guard could always observe without being observed. Key here is that the cells would always be backlighted in relation to the tower so that prisoners would behave because they could not tell whether the guard was there or not. As Foucault notes, the panopticon was only a very concrete case among many others following the logic of surveillance, which encouraged people to exercise self-discipline, whether the disciplinarian was observing them or not.

Tracing this logic to contemporary organization practices that are claimed to give workers more control over their work, Sewell and Wilkinson argue that JIT and TQC make the workers more visible to the control of the organization, while making the mechanics of control more invisible. The more open architecture of the plant, the team work that creates a certain kind of peer pressure, the apparent decentralization that is at the same time displaced to more detailed instructions and computerized monitoring—all these have substituted for the hierarchy, the supervisor's gaze, and any buffering (e.g., inventories or down time) from or through which workers were once able to "hide." Throughout these changes, power also has become more dispersed and invisible.

But, aside from the panopticon, prisoners were also made docile through a more immediate disciplinary practice: a codification of knowledge that, like a census, permitted their distribution into classes, making them more governable by others and by themselves. Thus, a prisoner classified as more dangerous was likely to be subjected to more frequent observation and made more self-aware that such might be the case. In Foucault's words, "Disciplines characterize, classify, specialize; they distribute along a scale, along a norm, hierarchize [sic] individuals in relation to one another and, if necessary, disqualify and invalidate" (1979: 223; also quoted in Townley, 1993: 530).

Townley (1993) analyzes HRM from this perspective. Her work takes the reader on a tour of the common sense behind HRM (see also Townley, 1994a), emphasizing the connection between Foucault's investigations and HRM as an academic discipline and as a practice of power relations in the workplace. In very minute detail she provides a genealogy of the emergence and development of personnel practices as devices that, like the census, had no clear logic behind them, other than a belief in the *classificatory* and *normalizing power* of modem science.

Townley defamiliarizes HRM so that it can be observed as a very strange set of practices that simply accumulated over time, while becoming more *believable* as they became more specific regarding their ability to transform individuals—their minds and bodies—into "subjects of (the) discipline." Like the census, HRM makes us believe that we can be told apart, as well as believe in the possibility of being distributed to where each of us belongs. Because of these beliefs, we are willing to behave in certain ways and not others, and we hope that those behaviors will take us where we aspire to go. Like the prisoners, we are watching over "our selves" to ensure we are on our best behavior. This very short excursion into Foucaultian genealogies, via two organizational studies articles, also illustrates genealogy's relationship to poststructuralism, as discussed above. Genealogies destabilize meaning; they give us another way to think about our common sense without pretending that the genealogical story is the best story. As distinct from "history—a narrative of origin, cause, and effect with fairly clear directional arrows—genealogies show that history is possible only because we do not tell ourselves other stories that would make the logic of origin, cause, and effect suspect. Genealogies also decenter "the subject" that we believe "we are" in relation to our institutions. Rather than being the origin, our subjectivity is embedded as producer and effect of a complicated network of narratives and practices, sometimes more visible than others and always more unstable than we may think.

Other excellent examples of analyses inspired by Foucault's genealogies include Du Gay and Salaman (1992), on consumer culture; Sakolsky (1992), on labor processes; Pye (1988), Knights (1992), Willmott (1992), Jacques (1996), and Jacobson and Jacques (1997), on management knowledge and managerial practices; Fox (1989), on management learning; and Hollway (1991), on organizational behavior.

Deconstruction. Jacques Derrida's writings partake of poststructuralist sensibilities regarding meaning, representation, and authorship, as discussed before. However, his approach is quite different from Foucault's. The historiography that characterizes much of Foucault's work is not present in *deconstructions*. Rather, deconstructions are philosophical meditations delineated in very close readings of particular texts. These readings attend to the language in the text and to those areas where language betrays itself. For example, deconstruction often pays attention to what authors put "on the margin," such as footnotes that are set aside as not integral to the central point of the text. Yet, it is usual to find the main text contradicting its central points exactly on these marginal spaces. And, thus, in characteristic reversal, the margin becomes the center (of attention) in Derrida's analyses. At the same time, the style of deconstruction is not conventional criticism, since that would imply that the critic "knows better" (that he or she has foundational knowledge) than the writer whom the critic is criticizing. Rather, deconstruction disassembles textuality to show how, despite careful control of textual representations, language always exceeds the writer's control.

Deconstructive analyses follow certain general "rules." They identify areas of the text where a particular word or phrase is privileged as central to the meaning of the text. The analyst looks for "another term"—an opposite—the privileged term may have concealed, and brings that term to view. This operation decenters the supposedly self-sustaining central term. Eventually, the analyst makes both terms undecidable so that other meanings could be constituted over the text. For instance, we wrote in the first sentence of this section the word "partake." As we look for synonyms in our computer's thesaurus, we find that it means both share and divide. As we contemplate these two meanings, what is it that we are saying? That deconstruction comes together with others into the fold of poststructuralism to share with that intellectual community? Or that deconstruction disjoins the intellectual tendencies known as poststructuralism such that there are no common grounds to form a community? Or is it both?

Martin Kilduff's (1993) "Deconstructing *Organizations*" is an excellent and very sophisticated illustration of this approach in organization studies. His rereading of this famous book shows how the text works to position itself as filling a void in the literature. In this particular instance, the text registers complaints about Taylor's scientific management and claims to substitute the mindless mechanical worker with a rational decision maker. Yet, Kilduff soon focuses on the play of presence *and absence* identified by Derrida as a necessary operation in the composition of a credible text (whether literary, scientific, or any other genre). Kilduff shows how March and Simon exclude previous writing, such as the Hawthorne Studies, that offers other conceptions of working people. In Kilduff's words,

> *Organizations* makes no mention of Roethlisberger and Dickson's (1939) definitive account of 12 years of experimental work. To acknowledge the existence of this text would be tantamount to admitting that the gap MS claim that they are hoping to fill has already been plugged. (1993: 16)

Kilduff emphasizes how *Organizations* always returns to what it denies. The textual production of the rational decision maker is positioned as the opposite of Taylor's employee as machine. Yet, the deconstruction shows how the text both denounces and celebrates the machine model to finally reinscribe the hierarchical model of the organization. *Organizations'* move has been to simply substitute one mechanical notion of work with another, through the language of "programs," such that the worker continues to be represented as incapable of handling anything but simplification.

Although not as popular as the analyses based on Foucault's work, deconstructions have appeared in texts of accounting (Arrington & Francis, 1989; Cooper & Puxty, 1994; Nelson, 1993), information management (Beath & Orlikowski, 1994), marketing (Firat & Venkatesh, 1993; Fischer & Bristor, 1994), and organization theory, more generally (Boje, 1995; Calas, 1993; Calas & Smircich, 1991; Cooper, 1986, 1989; Gergen, 1992; Martin, 1990; Martin & Knopoff, 1997; Mumby & Putnam, 1992).

Now, what is the value of all this to organization studies? We argue that the problematization of foundational theorizing posed by poststructuralist analyses offers pause and a good space for reflecting over the constitution of knowledge in any disciplinary field. In particular, poststructuralist analytics permits us to think "the unthinkable," to move, as it were, "outside the limits," and to consider taken-for-granted knowledge-making operations under very different premises. At their most startling, these analyses promote a temporary state of "disbelief," which can make us conceive of knowledge and knowledge making as a very different enterprise alto-gether—"the end of innocence" in Flax's (1992: 445) words. Genealogical analyses, offering very detailed historical documentation of what otherwise may have become naturalized, offer important ways to rethink current issues in the organiza-tional literature. Genealogies will not result in better theories if judged under instrumental premises. What genealogies do best is to reposition conventional wis-dom and to show how what passes as knowledge is an entanglement of power rela-tions, in which many are implicated. From this perspective there is no way out of power/knowledge. That is, as we are all "effects" of the power of discourse, we all move from one discursive network to another, always producing power relations. Genealogies, nonetheless, do offer possibilities for *resisting* theories (i.e., not recog-nizing "our selves" in certain discourses of knowledge) and, thus, for reconceiving a theory or a research area in unexpected ways, bringing different insights into the field. Similarly, deconstructions, as close readings for understanding the constitution of textual knowledge, work on the blind spots that we all—readers and writers— are *unable to control* as we write theory. We may be surprised or irritated to read academic papers that, for example, analyze marketing's notion of exchange rela-tionships as pervaded by power relations and patriarchy (Fischer & Bristor, 1994); that demonstrate how charismatic leadership in organization studies is a surrogate for bureaucracy (Calas, 1993); that reveal how a systems development text ostensi-bly advocating user friendliness reinscribes relationships of control and depen-dency (Beath & Orlikowski, 1994); or that demonstrate the "great books" of the field of management to be complicit in exclusionary knowledge practices (e.g., Calas & Smircich, 1991; Martin & Knopoff, 1997). We might think these authors are excessive in their interpretations. Yet, deconstructive readings attend to language so carefully, it is hard not to read differently, or listen differently, after one's usual way of interpreting/reading has been so unsettled. The effectiveness of much of this work comes from *the effects* it has on us as we experience familiar language as unnatural. At a minimum, we would say, deconstructive writings provide an approach for learning and teaching the inner workings—the mode of existence— of conventional theorizing—historically, rhetorically, and politically—and for showing how we are all existing "inside" these.

In general, postmodern analyses help us to understand the exclusions on which writers need to rely in order to represent "positive knowledge." More important, they make us all more aware of those exclusions and of the possible consequences of apparently innocent textualizations. By decentering "true knowledge," these analyses can help us accept the possibility of "other knowledges," which otherwise may be ignored or deemed illegitimate—that is, "marginal." Further, a particularly important contribution of theorizing done in this fashion is that it provides a different language with which to address conventional issues (e.g., Gergen, 1992). As such, it makes it possible to "see" conventional theories in a different light and, further, to write knowledge in a different form.

On a more "practical" note, perhaps the most significant for us academics in the business of knowledge making, poststructuralist analyses can work directly on the taken for granted of the institutions in which we labor—that is, "the house of knowledge." Both historically and rhetorically, the arguments that we hear today about "the way it is" in the university (e.g., D'Aveni, 1996) require close analyses to show that "the way it is" is not necessarily so (e.g., Bensimon, 1994); "it" can be interpreted otherwise. We all, as organizational scholars, are in an excellent position to genealogize and deconstruct the "logics" of our institutions, for the construction of institutions is the primary object of our theories. In the process of doing so, all of us would be learning how to teach others to do the same for their own organizations: an immediate integration of theory and practice, if ever there was one.

In our view there is still much work to be done in organization studies through postmodern analytics, but perhaps it is now too late. Some commentators consider that postmodernism has become at least partially exhausted (e.g., Eco, 1992; Kaplan, 1988; Leitch, 1996; Parker, 1993). Thus, organizational studies may have gone past the "post," with very few achievements. Not too many writings in organization studies have actually engaged in the *serious play* intended by these analyses, especially when it comes to extending the consequences of the reflexivity so achieved. We even wonder up to what point the "post" has become a career maker for traditional knowledge-making bodies, and up to what point it has become a way to reclaim the field for marginal voices to speak. Still, the possibility of asking and trying to answer these questions could be an important legacy of the "post" for organization studies, as it seems to be for other fields. Further, it is conceivable that the major contribution of postmodernism is, precisely, that it has become partially exhausted, for this exhaustion has opened space for other theoretical approaches to appear.

Reclaiming Ground: After the "Post" in Organizational Theorizing

Despite concerns about unstable grounds for theory, or perhaps because of them, the postmodern turn has provoked new theoretical approaches in the social sciences and the humanities, such as feminist poststructuralist theorizing, postcolonial analyses, actor-network theory, and narrative approaches to knowledge. Some of these approaches are responses to limitations in postmodernism. Others, bearing a family resemblance and benefiting from the insights of poststructuralism, are reclaiming some "ground" on which to build their projects. Yet, most of these approaches are specific in their critiques of postmodern analyses for their lack of strong political engagement and for their remoteness from "the real world."

Be they in support of or distinct from postmodern analytics, these theoretical tendencies share the following concerns. First, they all emphasize the relationship between "power" and "knowledge" at the inception of "theory." That is, each of these approaches articulates relationships between those who do knowledge and the knowledge that gets made; each points at the subjectivities that get constituted through theory; and each takes seriously the politics of knowledge making and incorporates into their writings those reflective concerns. Second, they all share a preoccupation and an ambivalence about the way "other's knowledge/other knowledges" can be represented, while emphasizing the need to do so. The problems of representation and form—the poetics of knowledge making—become the focus of textual experiments.

Insofar as these are also concerns of poststructuralist writings, there may be not much difference between the "heirs" and their "parentage." However, here the family resemblance ends. These approaches also share ambivalence about the antiessentialist tenets of poststructuralism and the implications of these tenets for creating theories that could engage with the world "outside the text." Finally, each considers it necessary to adopt an ethical posture as part of the knowledge-making enterprise—as part of *writing* theory. At a minimum, they all ask, "Whose interests does theory serve? For whom is it good?" Such a posture would be difficult to sustain on more "shaky" poststructuralist grounds.

More generally, these theoretical tendencies create bridges between "the text" and "the world." However, the world they re-present may be very different from the one encountered by organization theory before postmodernism. Some of these writings may be classified as conceptual and others as empirical; however, these traditional definitions are difficult to maintain. Note that we continue to emphasize the term *analysis* since that is the focus of all these approaches. Their "evidence" may come from the words in another text, from a literature review, from ethnographic accounts, from questionnaires, from laboratory experiments, or from all of the above, and still others. Yet, they all use the evidence to produce interpretations and critical commentaries that denaturalize more conventional views and that may even bring about social activism. That is their theoretical posture. Below, we briefly review these approaches, emphasizing their current intersections with organizational theorizing.

Feminist Organizational Theorizing and Postmodernism

Ironically, feminist theorizing in organization studies may have gained momentum in the 1990s owing to the popularity, more generally, of poststructuralism (e.g., Calas & Smircich, 1992, 1997a; Calvert & Ramsey, 1992; Fondas, 1997; Hearn & Parkin, 1993; Martin & Knopoff, 1997; see also a new journal, entitled *Gender, Work & Organization*). Feminist theories are always political theories, regardless of the philosophies on which they stake their claims. Whether liberal, radical, Marxist, socialist, psychoanalytic, or so on, feminist theories have been mostly about how and why the exclusion or oppression of women happens and how to provide remedies for this situation (for recent reviews of this literature, see Alvesson & Billing, 1997, and Calas & Smircich, 1996). Several of these theories have been around for more than three decades without receiving much attention by organizational scholars. Specifically, despite the emphasis on gender in the women-in-management literature, most of this literature has skirted the issue of gender-specific theory development, and scholars have carried on their research agenda sustained by traditional organizational theories (Calas & Jacques, 1988).

Poststructuralism, however, opened the space for considering gender theoretically, independent from particular-sexed bodies. The linguistic turn moved the concerns of feminist theory from the body of women to the body of the text, and the effects of this change were felt in organization studies. For example, one could now ask, "How is gender written in organization theory?" (e.g., Calas & Smircich, 1992) and pay (deconstructive) attention to how the language of our theories would construct understandings of the world that represented the interests and concerns of certain populations and not others, despite organization theories' mantle of neutrality (e.g., Martin, 1990; Mumby & Putnam, 1992). Equally important, it became possible to theorize "gender relations," to observe how both men and women, together, constituted "gendered conditions" that produced very entangled webs of power/knowledge.

Organization studies scholars may have been more welcoming of feminist poststructuralist analyses than of other feminist theory tendencies, but many feminist scholars outside of organization studies were not so accepting of the conjunctions of feminism with poststructuralism. The separation of "sex"—a biological marker—from "gender"—a social, discursive, and institutional construction—became suspected of weakening any political agenda written on behalf of women. The gendering of theories could result in an interesting and sophisticated academic exercise, but how would this contribute to fighting the oppression of "real people"? Was this not another elitist posture more typical of "the patriarchs"? Some, even more defiant, questioned why poststructuralist approaches were gaining ascendancy at the same time more critical feminist theories were, at last, taken seriously in the academic milieux.

In summary, the relationship between feminist theories and postmodernism has been, at best, uneasy. Poststructuralist feminists accept the merits of deconstruction and genealogies because they make explicit the devaluation of the feminine in "universal" theories and in discursive practices (e.g., Flax, 1987). In particular, they appreciate the ways in which the margins interrogate "the center" through these analytical approaches. The critics, however, point at the depoliticizing effects of these antiessentialist approaches when it comes to claiming agency and empowering representation. The problematics of the subject and the undecidability of meaning stand in the way of positive political alliances (e.g., Alvesson & Deetz, 1996; Nicholson, 1990).

These issues have not escaped the notice of organizational scholars interested in feminism and postmodernism. In a very powerful argument that deconstructs "organizational taboos," Joanne Martin (1992) embraces the "linguistic turn" and produces an incisive analysis of the traps in the speech of a CEO who claims to be sensitive to female employees. At the same time, she notices the limitations of deconstruction, and even of her own "reconstructions," if she were to stay simply at the level of the text. Thus, she reconnects concrete organizational and social issues with the deconstructed text. She notices how task segregation and gender pay inequalities become reified rather than alleviated by small organizational reforms, and she calls for "a fundamental realignment of government policies concerning both the family and the marketplace" (1992: 356). Also, she notices the complicity of her analysis in silencing other voices in her text, for she privileges the story of a high-ranking female employee. Deconstruction alone is not sufficient for analyzing "the intersections of gender and class with race and ethnicity" (1992: 354).

Concerns of this kind, of which Martin's reflections are a good example, are now possible to address. Several processual approaches to feminist theorizing have emerged from the encounters of socialist feminist theories, black feminism, and poststructuralism. These approaches share the critique of subjectivity in poststructuralism but concede to a less dispersed, socially constituted "subject position," enacted through historical and cultural locations, as well as through power relations. In these approaches scholars have reconsidered the separation of sex from gender in theorizing, concluding that the antiessentialist posture also permits inclusion of other forms of social oppressions in the analyses.

The intersections of gender, ethnicity, race, class, and sexuality figure prominently (e.g., Hurtado, 1989). The emphasis here is not simply on the bodies that constitute these intersections but on the subjectivities that get formed and transformed within these social markers. Further, gender in these analyses is not about women anymore. One can now talk about "masculinities" or about "queer theory" as productive analytical approaches for understanding specific conditions of different people in the world (Butler, 1990; Graham, 1996). This also applies to the conditions we help create in the world with our scholarship. The more general questions these texts address are as follows. How would the analyses help us think differently about those with whom we relate? How would writing about these intersections contribute to better understanding and changing oppressive relationships? But asking these questions is not intended to provide permanent and universal answers. Instead, the answers are little narratives, intended as interventions for changing specific oppressive conditions that may be experienced by some at the present.

Organization studies have already been inspired by some of these theoretical intersections (e.g., Bell, Denton, & Nkomo, 1993, on race and gender; Calas & Smircich, 1993, on gender, race, class, and globalization; Calvert & Ramsey, 1995, on whiteness, privilege, and gender; Collinson and Hearn, 1994, on working-class men and masculinities; Nkomo, 1992, on the racialization of theory; Shallenberger, 1994, on professionalism and sexuality; see also *Organization,* 1996). Thus, as one may assess, feminist theories more generally, and feminist critiques of postmodernism in particular, have contributed strong interdisciplinary theories that lend multiple theoretical lenses and methodological approaches to the study of organizations.

Postcolonial Analyses

These theoretical tendencies, now represented both in the humanities and in the social sciences, emerged directly from Third World scholars extending the insights of poststructuralism to its logical consequences (e.g., Bhabha, 1988; Radhakrishnan, 1996; Said, 1989; Spivak, 1988). If Western modern knowledges (i.e., the Enlightenment notion of knowledge and science) have silenced the voices of "the marginal"—"the others"—what would happen if those others were to speak back as "knowledgeable"? More directly, poststructuralism is, in general, a critique of Western epistemology as a system of exclusions. But poststructuralist analyses are also critiques of modernity *in* the West *by* the West and, of necessity, themselves exclusionary of other forms of knowledge.

At their most immediate, postcolonial (or, according to some, neocolonial) analyses share with feminist poststructuralist theorizing objections about the decentering of subjectivity and the problems of representation. But, in response, they *pay* attention first to the ways in which Western scholarship creates categories of analysis that, even at their most critical, are blind to their own ethnocentrism (e.g., Chambers & Curti, 1996). For example, even critical categories, such as gender, race, and class, may assume an unproblematic universalism—often associated with the idea of "a core humanity." What if categories such as class have no counterpart in other societies? What if race as a social marker is irrelevant? What if gender stands for a universalized "woman" who only exists, conceptually, as the body of certain women from the West?

Postcolonial critiques also extend to narratives of "origins" in Western theories. They may retell the story of "the other," who was already there from "the beginning," and who might have been excluded or devalued in the Western version of the theoretical "tale" through such markers as "traditional," "primitive," or "less developed." At the same time, these are not nostalgic narratives of a return to a better primordial world. Rather, these are closer to Foucault's genealogies, which give us a different "history of the present" (and its configuration in power/knowledge), as particular relationships between "the West" and "the Rest."

Further, in postcolonial studies scholars analyze the intersections of Western theories and Western institutions as a politics of knowledge. Concepts such as, for instance, modernization processes conceal other social formations and issues of value for the populations that these concepts claim to represent. Postcolonial studies counter these conceptualizations by offering analytical categories and representational approaches for the others to represent themselves in "their own terms." For example, conceptual notions such as hybridity and hybridization (Garcia-Canclini, 1990; Pieterse, 1994) make both comprehensible and unique what "Western eyes" (Mohanty, 1991) often describe as "uneven development" or the "paradoxical modernization" of several Third World countries. "The border" and "borderlands," both as geography and as metaphor, have become productive spaces, rather than dividing lines, for theorizing complicated subjectivities and social relations in response to dominant ideologies (e.g., Anzaldua, 1987; Saldivar, 1997). And "diaspora" and "displacement" have become articulations of the experiences of immigrants from "the rest to the West" and of the politics of ethnicity that evolve around issues of cultural and national identity (e.g., Gilroy, 1993).

Several of these approaches have addressed the issue of representation in regard to the location of the researcher. Different from arguments about subject position in feminist theories—where the scholar claims no more than to be able to speak from her or his own positionality—in postcolonial analyses researchers may first consider the position of privilege already occupied by the Third World scholar and, thus, his or her responsibility to use that space on behalf of others. Yet, she or he must also remember that in giving voice, she or he is silencing many other voices. Thus, a second representational move is on the question of silence. What other voices are there that the scholarly voice, no matter of what persuasion, cannot represent (e.g., Spivak, 1987)? Some experimental texts break the linear style with images, prose, poetry, and so on, which produce "interstices of silence" in the text (e.g., Trinh, 1989) in order to represent *the absence* of other voices.

As these paragraphs illustrate, poststructuralist concerns about meaning, representation, and subjectivity still surround postcolonial theorizations. Nonetheless, much of this work has been able to recover poststructuralist deconstructions with affirmative conceptualizations. Perhaps one of the most creative is "strategic essentialism" (Spivak, 1987), which promotes reclaiming the essential identity of a group as a temporary strategic gesture in the interest of agency for struggle, no matter how dispersed the identities of the members. Also, Haraway's (1985) concept of affinity has been invoked to signify the possibility of alliances among peoples who may not share a common heritage, ethnicity, gender, or so on, but who find themselves in agreement on certain critical issues that should be voiced. Who speaks for whom in this case is not the issue; the issue is that somebody has to be able to speak up for all in some cases. Further, by paying attention to popular culture, social movements, and testimonial writings, postcolonial theorists represent what other scholarly voices may be silencing, for, some argue, it is in these sites that particular configurations of identity, agency, and organization appear and transform under contemporary globalization processes (e.g., Alvarez, Dagnino, & Escobar, 1998).

What is the relevance of these analyses and conceptualizations for organizational studies? In our view, globalization processes, at their most conventional, belong in the province of our disciplines. Concerns with ethnocentrism in our "international" management theories have already been voiced (e.g., Boyacigiller & Adler, 1991). However, up to what point is scholarship in organization studies ready to accept "the other's" strange *knowledges*? For example, up to what point is the assumption of worldwide convergence in management knowledge an assumption that pays attention only to a cosmopolitan elite who is not that different? What differences are not represented in these assumptions? How many people in the world are left out of our theories? With what consequences?

Further, what is the complicity of Western organizational and international management theories with transnational institutions whose policies and practices impact the material conditions of millions of people in the world, both "at home" and "abroad" (e.g., Appadurai, 1990; Dirlik, 1994; Hall, 1996)? There is an increasing awareness that Western understandings of globalization, development, and the market are closely aligned with the interests of global capital—the same global capital to which organization theories attend and for which they speak. Yet, even "global capitalists" and such institutions as the International Monetary Fund are now ambivalent about policies they supported in the past and question their long-term impact on the survival of a reasonable capitalist world (e.g., Soros, 1998). How, then, could we think differently about these issues?

The stories we have written in much organization theory, our concepts and representations, no matter how global (or precisely because of this), represent the ways of thinking of certain peoples and not others. These theoretical representations have been profoundly implicated in blinding us to current global circumstances. Thus, if we are to really engage in a global conversation, postcolonial theories are an excellent place for us to start learning how to write in *theoretical voices* that allow spaces for "the other" to "speak back" (e.g., Alvarado, 1996; Calas, 1992; Mir, Calas, & Smircich, 1999; Radhakrishnan, 1994).

Actor-Network Theory and After

Better known now by its acronym, ANT, actor-network theory first appeared in the social studies of science and technology (e.g., Callon, 1980, 1986; Latour, 1987,

1988a, 1993; Law, 1994), yet it has been transformed over the years and continues today to be debated (e.g., Callon, 1997; Callon & Law, 1995; Latour, 1997). As discussed more recently by Law (1997a, b; see also Law & Hassard, 1999), ANT has become an assemblage of modest stories whose narratives have changed from great stories with a chronological ordering to many small stories that form a pattern with no possible chronology. However, in Law's view, such is precisely ANT's current theoretical value, for, despite much trying, actor-network "theory" has never been able to coalesce into a coherent theoretical perspective in the modernist sense.

ANT origins are mixed, including semiotics/structuralism, phenomenology, and ethnomethodology, to name a few, but one may find now in ANT some similarities with Foucault's notion of power/knowledge as power relations are produced through "actants" who perform the available discourses and practices. Even the notion of author-function may be invoked, except that in this case the "authors" are both human and nonhuman (e.g., Latour, 1988b). Concurrently, such notions as rhizomes, deterritorialization, nomadism, and the like in Deleuze and Guattari (1988) can be associated with the idea of "network" as a very dispersed and decentered chain of ongoing and mutant activities (e.g., Lee & Brown, 1994). Thus, "network" is approached as topography and as performance, rather than as a final or original state.

Early ANT comprised ideas of network as analytical structures, where the structure was actually constructed by the analyst. These structuralist and constructivist networks were materially heterogeneous and included social, technical, and natural actors. All elements of the network were actors, since they were capable of acting upon one another. Also, authors of early actor-network studies had more interest in understanding how things got centered, how they were drawn together, and how they were ordered as a network. More recently, scholars are paying attention to how things get both centered and decentered (e.g., Singleton, 1996) and to the movements and oscillations that occur. The concept of ontological choreography captures this latter idea (e.g., Cussins, 1988).

ANT highlights at least two issues. First, the actor and the network are not just things out there to be seen or apprehended by the researcher. Rather, actor-network is in itself the conceptual frame—a way of understanding social and technical processes. Second, *thinking* in networks requires conceiving of relationships among things in particular ways. Some actor-network studies are also explorations of ways to develop a vocabulary for conceptualizing those relationships (e.g., Akrich & Latour, 1992). The ANT scholar conceives of networks as constituted by scripts. For instance, machines have scripts prescribing *roles* that others in the network must play. Yet, the network is precarious, for it takes much effort to maintain the "enrolment." Thus, from this perspective, networks are processes or achievements, rather than stable relations or static structures. *Translation* represents the network's moves (Callon, 1980; Law, 1997b).

It is difficult to describe ANT as a theoretical tendency without also emphasizing its methodological aspects. ANT is reflexive, because it both constitutes and describes its object of interest. The studies may be conducted through ethnographic research in a laboratory, for instance, but both the way "things out there" are looked at and the way they are reported back contribute to the constitution of those same things "in here." There is irony behind this. Critics of positivism, many social constructionists, and all poststructuralists would say that such is exactly what any other empirical study does. Yet, ANT scholars do not hide that such is the case. Rather that is their point of departure, as well as their end. ANT, thus, provides a very good way of telling stories about "what happens out there" that defamiliarizes what we may otherwise take for granted. Latour's (1996) *Aramis*, in which he tells a heterogeneous story of a technological project that includes the technology's "voice," and Bowker and Star's (1996) analysis of classification and standardization as a political project of technoscience are good recent examples in this regard.

These approaches are not much seen (yet) in organizational journals in the United States. However, ANT's theoretical tendencies and methodological arguments have been represented in organizational sociology and organizational studies in Europe for several years (e.g., Brown, 1992; Kaghan & Phillips, 1998; Latour, 1986; Lee & Brown, 1994; Star, 1995).

If nothing else, ANT, with its focus on irreductionism and relationality, rather than facts and essences, may become a very useful exercise to counter conventional "theoretical tales" in organization studies. More immediately, as organizational studies face contemporary technologies in a reconfiguration of the time/space of organizations, as "the Web" and "virtuality" become part of our everyday mode of existence, and as our interactions with machines incrementally define our life experiences, ANT provides ways to navigate and represent these (dis)locations while displacing more conventional "organizational" thinking. In Law's words,

> How to deal with and fend off the simplicities implicit in a world in which: "Have theory, will travel" makes for easy intellectual and political progress. How to resist the singularities so commonly performed in the acts of naming and knowing. How to defy the overwhelming pressures on academic production to render knowing simple, transparent, singular, formulaic. . . . Well, the "after" in "actor-network and after" holds out promise. (1997a: 7)

Not Quite at the End (of Postmodernism)

Discussing these three theoretical tendencies—feminist poststructuralist theorizing, postcolonial analyses, and actor-network theory—returns us to the opening theme in our account of postmodernism—the incredulity toward meta or master narratives—and to a continuing question of how to *write* legitimate knowledge in postmodernity. For Lyotard, and for many of the scholars discussed in the above sections, legitimate knowledge can only be written in small stories or modest narratives (see also Haraway, 1997), mindful of their locality in space and time and capable of disappearing as needed. Legitimate knowledge would be in the form of temporary language games, recognized as such games that "assume" responsibility for their rules and effects as power. This leads to perhaps the most radical notion in all of this article. Should we not all start writing our theories differently? Should we not all explicitly recognize the textuality of knowledge making and become reflective narrators in/of our theoretical stories? Whereas we would not argue that every organizational researcher should stop what he or she is working on and begin to do poststructuralist feminist theorizing, postcolonial analysis, or actor-network theory, we *would* like each of us to follow the example of these theoretical tendencies and problematize the constitution of our theories at their most immediate: in the way we write and the language we use.

How would those writings look? They would surely look different. Whether we are involved in ethnography or statistics-heavy research, whether we are writing about institutional theory, population ecology, organizational justice, corporate mergers—whatever, no matter what topic or area or what methods we use—we are all producing orderliness in our writings, sequences of relationships (plots/story lines/models/cause maps), putting pieces together, picking and choosing to pay attention and ignore. No matter who "we" might be—men or women, from the Third World or not, trained in the sciences or the humanities or neither—in our writing we are fixing signification; excluding, including, concealing, favoring some people, some topics, some questions, some forms of representation, some values. Can we do our writing in a way that is "self-conscious" of our "choices," and, at the same time, can we recognize that we do not even exist as independent autonomous selves—that we are only products of multiple and competing discourses, and pretty lucky if we ever get to be author-functions? *And why ever would* we *want* to *write in such* a *different way?*

To someone, a reader who wishes to remain anonymous, it suggests an infinite regress—as *I think about myself thinking about my thinking . . . I'll be paralyzed.* In response, we can refer here to Karl Weick's suggestion in his "drop your tools" allegory for organization studies (Weick, 1996). As the story goes, some firemen in peril failed to drop their heavy tools in order to run unburdened. They perished in sight of safety. The message "drop your tools" ran counter to their practice and identity.

For us academics, one of our most important tools is writing—the key to success and identity. Dropping my (most favored way of) writing, the tools I spent so many years learning how to use . . . I might be rendered speechless. Maybe that wouldn't be so bad, take a time out. . . . Are you kidding, slow down my production? Now that's a truly dangerous suggestion. Gotta publish more not less, standards are tightening, tenure pressure's increasing, gotta make full professor some day, and now there's even post-tenure review!

Linda Putnam sets out the challenge of writing differently very well:

> Organizational researchers need ways to open up text for multiple readings; to decenter authors as authority figures; and to involve participants, readers, and audiences in the production of research. One venue for achieving these goals is to seek alternative ways of presenting research reports—ones that challenge conventional modalities, ground research in historical processes, promote reflexivity, and open up our text to an infinitude of meanings. (1996: 386)

In other words, can we write in a way that "fixes signification" tentatively, leaving room for others? Would it still be called research?

Writing while incorporating undecidability of meaning, the crisis of representation, and the problematization of subject and author locates the moral responsibility of the scholar, who cannot claim innocence from the representational force that she or he brings to the text (Czarniawka, 1995, 1997, 1998). It also means revamping our notions of authors—ourselves as agents, attending to the ways in which our theoretical narratives are embedded in institutions that write us as much as we write them. Along with Czarniawska, there have been others writing about narrative approaches to knowledge in organizational studies (e.g., Barry & Elmes, 1997; Deetz, 1996; Hatch, 1996; Polkinghorne, 1987; Putnam, 1996; Richardson, 1994; Van Maanen, 1996).

We know of some experimental writings that blur the boundaries between theory and method (e.g., Burrell, 1997; Calas, 1987; Goodall, 1989; Jacques, 1992; Richardson, 1998; St. Pierre, 1997) and some that present illusions of multivocality (Linstead, 1993; Linstead & Grafton-Small, 1992). Many of these draw an explicit thread between the exclusion of ethics and power relations in the language of our theories and the conventions of "writing theory," for it is behind these conventions that the ethics and values of our institutions hide. It is behind these conventions that the interests of a few are presented as the reality of many. One of our favorite attempts to bring the ethical closer to home is Denny Gioia's (1992) story of his employment as a recall manager for Ford Motor Co., in the era of Pinto fires. Shall a Pinto fire be represented in a sequestered photograph, or in the calculations of a cost-benefit analysis? Can we, should we, use our cherished theories to explain our own (in) action?

If we start writing and talking differently—what difference? If we start writing and talking differently—what else is there?

At the beginning of this text, we promised to present four contemporary approaches to organizational theorizing, the last being narrative approaches to knowledge. But as the reader may have gathered, this last approach—in this more or less self-exemplifying part of our text—as well as all the others, contains the message we most wanted to convey in this article, the approach we felt most compelled to write. How are the issues of representation and form implicated in sustaining the power relations behind our theories and our institutions? As we see it, finding ways to answer this question represents important work that we all can do past postmodernism.

We hope our many pages, written in friendship, have presented an optimistic and productive face for moving past postmodernism in organization studies. We have discussed the contributions of the postmodern turn as bringing reflexivity to our knowledge-making enterprise, as well as the contributions of poststructuralism through the analytics of Foucault's genealogies and Derrida's deconstructions. We have briefly discussed, as well, some contemporary theoretical perspectives that, influenced by postmodernism but also critical of some of its arguments, offer other positive conceptualizations and representational forms for organization studies.

One more general point, however, is that postmodernist, postfoundationalist perspectives have already touched many of us in organization studies. Perhaps some of us have been tourists in the land of postmodernism and may not wish to settle there permanently, but "we" have been "effected"—changed—by the meeting. We cannot erase the unsettling that has occurred because of these encounters. They have left traces in how we consider theory and ourselves. Connell and Nord (1996) say that what has happened is that practitioners of organization studies are now more ready to accept uncertainty and to recognize that interests or values have been and continue to be major factors in shaping what constitutes knowledge in the field. We hope they are right.

We are also aware that it is possible to write these words now, and in this location, because our institutions also have been changing. The "postmodern conversation" has affected our journals, the curricula of our programs, and even the way we think about ourselves as scholars and educators. Some colleagues may still debate how to preserve "the purity of our knowledge," but if they look around, they will notice that, in the university, the boundaries between disciplines are already fallen. We all are effects and producers of the postmodern, and it is showing (e.g., Aronowitz & Giroux, 1994; Readings, 1996).

In summary, our whole text concerns the questions "Can we do theory differently? How do we do that?" In that sense, our aim toward relevance has been focused on "doing theory" as the specific practice of our own community, without a direct interest in articulating the content of theories for some other constituency. However, given the type of argument on which we have been focusing, this exercise has also been our way to call attention to the absences of certain voices and issues in our theories. Ours has been an argument about the "power(s)" of theorizing. How do we address and deploy the powers of our community? Under whose ethics, and under whose values, will we continue the practices of our institutions? These are questions that, in our view, organizational theorists cannot avoid addressing any further. Thus, at the end, ours is not a theory (or a proposition) intended to be tested; it is the telling of a very small story that we hope resonates with others.

References

Academy of Management Review. (1989). Special issue on theory building, *14*(4).

Academy of Management Review. (1992). Special issue on new intellectual currents, *17*(3).

Adler, P. S., Forbes, L. C., & Willmott, H. (2007). Critical management studies. *Academy of Management Annals, 1.*

Administrative Science Quarterly. (1979). Special issue on qualitative research, *24*(4).

Administrative Science Quarterly. (1983). Special issue on organizational culture, *28*(3).

Adorno, T. W. (1973). *Negative dialectics.* New York: Seabury Press. (Original work published 1966)

Agger, B. (1991). Critical theory, poststructuralism, postmodernism: Their sociological relevance. *Annual Review of Sociology, 17,* 105–131.

Akrich, M., & Latour, B. (1992). A summary of a convenient vocabulary for the semiotics of human and nonhuman assemblies. In W. Bijker & J. Law (Eds.), *Shaping technology, building society: Studies in sociotechnical change* (pp. 259–264). Cambridge, MA: MIT Press.

Alchian, A. A., & Demsetz, H. (1972). Production, information costs, and economic organization. *American Economic Review, 62*(12), 777–795.

Alderfer, C. P. (1986). The invisible director on corporate boards. *Harvard Business Review, 64,* 38–52.

Aldrich, H. E. (1979). *Organizations and environments.* Englewood Cliffs, NJ: Prentice Hall.

Aldrich, H. E., & Pfeffer, J. (1976). Environments of organizations. *Annual Review of Sociology, 2,* 79–105.

Allaire, Y., & Firsirotu, M. E. (1984). Theories of organizational culture. *Organization Studies, 5,* 193–226.

Allen, M. P. (1981). Power and privilege in large corporations: Corporate control and managerial compensation. *American Journal of Sociology, 86*(5), 1112–1123.

Alvarado, F. (1996). Concerning postmodernity and organizations in the Third World: Opening a debate and suggestions for a research agenda. *Organization Science, 7,* 667–681.

Alvarez, S. E., Dagnino, E., & Escobar, A. (1998). *Cultures of politics/politics of culture.* Boulder, CO: Westview.

Alvesson, M., & Billing, Y. D. (1997). *Understanding gender and organizations.* London: Sage.

Alvesson, M., & Deetz, S. (1996). Critical theory and postmodernism approaches to organization studies. In S. R. Clegg, C. Hardy, & W. Nord (Eds.), *Handbook of organization studies* (pp. 191–217). London: Sage.

Amihud, Y., & Lev, B. (1981). Risk reduction as a managerial motive for conglomerate mergers. *Bell Journal of Economics, 12*(2), 605–617.

Anderson, E. (1985). The salesperson as outside agent of employee: A transaction cost analysis. *Marketing Science, 4,* 234–254.

Angelo, H., & Rice, E. M. (1983). Antitakeover amendments and stockholder wealth. *Journal of Financial Economics, 11,* 329–359.

Anzaldua, G. (1987). *Borderlands/Ia frontera: The new mestiza.* San Francisco: Aunt Lute Books.

Appadurai, A. (1990). Disjuncture and difference in the global cultural economy. *Public Culture, 2,* 1–24.

Argawal, A., & Mandelker, G. (1987). Managerial incentives and corporate investment and financing decisions. *Journal of Finance, 42,* 823–837.

Argyris, C. (1957). The individual and organization: Some problems of mutual adjustment. *Administrative Science Quarterly, 2,* 1–24.

Argyris, C. (1964). *Integrating the individual and the organization.* New York: John Wiley.

Armour, H. O., & Teece, D. J. (1978). Organization structure and economic performance: A test of the multidivisional hypothesis. *Bell Journal of Economics, 9,* 106–122.

Aron, R. (1968). *Main currents in sociological thoughts* (2nd ed). London: Weidenfeld and Nicolson.

Aronowitz, S., & Giroux. H. A. (1991). *Postmodern education.* Minneapolis: University of Minnesota Press.

Arrington, C. E., & Francis. J. R. (1989). Letting the chat out of the bag: Deconstruction, privilege and accounting research. *Accounting, Organizations and Society, 14,* 1–28.

Arrow, K. (1971). *Essays in the theory of risk bearing.* Chicago: Markham.

Arrow, K. J. (1969). *The organization of economic activity: The analysis and evaluation of public expenditure: The PPB system.* Joint Economic Committee, 91st Cong., lst Session, pp. 59–73.

Arrow, K. J. (1974). *Limits of organization.* New York: Norton.

Astley, W. G. (1985). Administrative science as socially constructed truth. *Administrative Science Quarterly, 30,* 497–513.

Astley, W. G., & van de Ven, A. (1983). Central perspectives and debates in organization theory. *Administrative Science Quarterly, 28,* 245–273.

Baack, D., & Prasch, T. (1997). The death of the subject and the life of the organization. *Journal of Management Inquiry, 6*(2), 131–141.

Barker, J. (1993). Tightening the iron cage: Concertive control in self-managing teams. *Administrative Science Quarterly, 38,* 408–437.

Barley, S. R., & Kunda, G. (1992). Design and devotion: Surges of rational and normative ideologies of control in managerial decision making. *Administrative Science Quarterly, 37,* 363–399.

Barnard, C. L. (1938). *The functions of the executive.* Cambridge, MA: Harvard University Press.

Barney, J. (1988). Agency theory, employee stock ownership and a firm's cost of equity capital. (Unpublished working paper), Texas A&M University, College Station.

Barney, J., & Ouchi, W. (Eds.). (1986). *Organizational economics.* San Francisco: Jossey-Bass.

Barry, D., & Elmes, M. (1997). Strategy retold: Toward a narrative view of strategic discourse. *Academy of Management Review, 22,* 429–452.

Bartlett, F. C. (1932). *Remembering.* Cambridge, UK: Cambridge University Press.

Basu, A., Lal, R., Srinivasan, V., & Staelin, R. (1985). Salesforce compensation plans: An agency theoretic perspective. *Marketing Science, 4,* 267–291.

Bauman, Z. (1992). *Intimations of postmodernity.* London: Routledge.

Baumol, W. (1967). *Business, behavior, value and growth.* New York: Harcourt Brace & World.

Beath, C. M., & Orlikowski, W. (1994). The contradictory structure of systems development methodologies: Deconstructing the IS–user relationship in information engineering. *Information Systems Research, 5,* 350–377.

Bell, D. (1970). *Work and its discontents.* New York: League for Industrial Democracy.

Bell, D. L., Denton, T., & Nkomo, S. (1993). Women of color: Toward an inclusive analysis. In E. A. Fagenson (Ed.), *Women in management: Trends, issues and challenges in managerial diversity* (pp. 105–130). Newbury Park, CA: Sage.

Bensimon, E. M. (1994). Total quality management in the academy: A rebellious reading. *Harvard Educational Review, 65,* 593–611.

Berger, P. L., & Luckmann, T. (1967). *The social construction of reality.* New York: Doubleday.

Berger, P. L., Berger, B., & Kellner, H. (1973). *The homeless mind: Modernization and consciousness.* New York: Random House, Vintage Books.

Berger, P., & Pullman, S. (1965). Reification and the sociological critique of consciousness. *History and Theory, 4,* 195–208.

Berger, S. (Ed.). (1981). Organizing interests in Western Europe: Pluralism, corporatism and the transformation of politics. New York: Cambridge University Press.

Berle, A., & Means, G. (1932). *The modern corporation and private property.* New York: Macmillan.

Bernstein, R. (1983). *Beyond objectivism and relativism.* Philadelphia: University of Pennsylvania Press.

Best, M. H., & Connolly, W. E. (1979). Politics and subjects: The limits of structural Marxism. *Socialist Review, 9,* 75–99.

Best, S., & Kellner, D. (1991). *Postmodern theory: Critical interrogations.* New York: Guilford Press.

Bhabha, H. K. (1988). The commitment to theory. *New Formations, 5,* 5–23.

Biddle, G. C. (1980). Accounting methods and management decisions: The case of inventory costing and inventory policy. *Journal of Accounting Research, 18*(Suppl.), 235–280.

Biddle, G. C., & Lindahl, F. W. (1982). Stock price reactions to LIFO adoptions: The association between excess returns and LIFO tax savings. *Journal of Accounting Research, 20,* 551–588.

Blau, P. M. (1972, April). Interdependence and hierarchy in organizations. *Social Science Research, I,* 1–24.

Blau, P. M., & Schoenherr, R. A. (1971). *The structure of organizations.* New York: Basic Books.

Blumer, H. (1969). *Symbolic interactionism: Perspective and method.* Englewood Cliffs, NJ: Prentice Hall.

Boje, D. M. (1995). Stories of the storytelling organization: A postmodern analysis of Disney as "Tamara-Land." *Academy of Management Journal, 38,* 997–1035.

Boje, D. M., Gephart, R. P., Jr., & Thatchenkery, T. J. (Eds.). (1996). *Postmodern management and organization theory.* Thousands Oaks, CA: Sage.

Bolton, M. (1988). *Organizational miming: When do late adopters of organizational innovations outperform pioneers?* Paper presented at the meeting of the Academy of Management, Anaheim, CA.

Bowen, R., Noreen, E. W., & Lacey, J. M. (1981). Determinants of the corporate decision to capitalize interest. *Journal of Accounting and Economics, 3,* 151–179.

Bowker, G., & Star, S. L. (1996). How things (actor-net)work: Classification, magic and the ubiquity of standards. *Philosophia, 25*(3–4), 195–220.

Boyacigiller, N., & Adler, N. (1991). The parochial dinosaur: Organization science in a global context. *Academy of Management Review, 16,* 262–290.

Bradley, M., & Wakeman, L. M. (1983). The wealth effects of targeted share repurchases. *Journal of Financial Economics, 11,* 301–328.

Bramel, D., & Friend, R. (1981). Hawthorne, the myth of the docile worker, and the class bias in psychology. *American Psychologist, 36,* 867–878.

Bramson, L. (1961). *The political content of sociology.* Princeton, NJ: Princeton University Press.

Braverman, H. (1974). *Labor and monopoly capital.* New York: Monthly Review Press.

Brown, C. A. (1992). Organization studies and scientific authority. In M. Reed & M. Hughes (Eds.), *Rethinking organization* (pp. 67–84). London: Sage.

Buckley, W. (1967). *Sociology and modern systems theory.* Englewood Cliffs, NJ: Prentice Hall.

Burawoy, M. (1979). *Manufacturing consent.* Chicago: University of Chicago Press.

Burawoy, M. (1985). The *politics of production.* London: Verso.

Burns, T., & Stalker, G. M. (1961). *The management of innovation.* London: Tavistock.

Burns, T. R. (1986). Actors, transactions and social structures. In U. Himmelstrand (Ed.), *Sociology: From crisis to science?* (2nd ed., pp. 8–37). London: Sage.

Burns, T. R., & Flam, H. (1986). *The shaping of social organization: Social rule system theory and its applications.* London: Sage.

Burrell, G. (1988). Modernism, postmodernism and organizational analysis 2: The contribution of Michel Foucault. *Organization Studies, 9,* 221–235.

Burrell, G. (1997). *Pandemonium: Towards a retro-organization theory.* London: Sage.

Burrell, G., & Morgan, G. (1979). *Sociological paradigms and organizational analysis.* London: Heinemann.

Burton, R., & Obel, B. (1980). Analysis of the m-form hypothesis for contracting technologies. *Administrative Science Quarterly, 25*(3), 457–466.

Butler, J. (1990). *Gender trouble: Feminism and the subversion of identity.* New York: Routledge.

Butler, J., & Scott, J. W. (1992). *Feminists theorize the political.* London: Routledge.

Calas, M. B. (1992). Another silent voice? Representing "Hispanic woman" in organizational texts. In A. J. Mills & P. Tancred (Eds.), *Gendering organizational analysis* (pp. 201–221). Newbury Park, CA: Sage.

Calas, M. B. (1993). Deconstructing charismatic leadership: Re-reading Weber from the darker side. *Leadership Quarterly, 4,* 305–328.

Calas, M. B., & Jacques, R. (1988). *Diversity* or *conformity?: Research by women on women in organizations.* Paper presented at the Seventh International Conference on Women and Organizations, Long Beach, CA.

Calas, M. B., & Smircich, L. (1991). Voicing seduction to silence leadership. *Organization Studies, 12,* 567–602.

Calas, M. B., & Smircich, L. (1992). Re-writing gender into organizational theorizing: Directions from feminist perspectives. In M. Reed & M. Hughes (Eds.), *Rethinking organization* (pp. 227–253). London: Sage.

Calas, M. B., & Smircich, L. (1993). Dangerous liaisons: The feminine-in-management meets globalization. *Business Horizons, 36*(2), 71–81.

Calas, M. B., & Smircich, L. (1996). From "the woman's" point of view: Feminist approaches to organization studies. In S. R. Clegg, C. Hardy, & W. Nord (Eds.), *Handbook of organization studies* (pp. 218–257). London: Sage.

Calas, M. B., & Smircich, L. (1997a). *Postmodem management theory.* Aldershot, UK: Ashgate/Dartmouth.

Calas, M. B., & Smircich, L. (1997b). Predicando la moral en calzoncillos: Feminist inquiries into business ethics. In A. Larson & R. E. Freeman (Eds.), *Business ethics and women's studies* (pp. 50–79). Oxford, UK: Oxford University Press.

Calas, M. B., & Smircich, L. (1999). Past postmodernism? Reflections and tentative directions. *Academy of Management Review, 24*(4), 649–671.

Calhoun, C. (1995). *Critical social theory.* Cambridge, MA: Blackwell.

Callon, M. (1980). Struggles and negotiations to define what is problematic and what is not: The sociology of translation. In K. D. Knorr, R. Krohn, & R. D. Whitley (Eds.), *The social process of scientific investigation* (Vol. 4, pp. 197–219). Dordrecht, the Netherlands: Reidel.

Callon, M. (1986). Some elements of a sociology of translation. In J. Law (Ed.), *Power, action and belief: A new sociology of knowledge?* (pp. 196–233). London: Routledge & Kegan Paul.

Callon, M. (1997). *Actor–network theory—The market test* [Keynote speech]. Centre for Social Theory and Technology, Keele University, Keele, England.

Callon, M., & Law, J. (1995). Agency and the hybrid collective. *South Atlantic Quarterly, 94,* 481–507.

Calvert, L., & Ramsey, J. V. (1992). Bringing women's voice to research on women in management: A feminist perspective. *Journal of Management Inquiry, 1,* 79–88.

Calvert, L., & Ramsey, J. V. (1995). Speaking as female and White: A non-dominant/dominant group standpoint. *Organization, 3,* 468–485.

Campbell, R. W. (1978). New concepts in the study of economic systems. Unpublished manuscript.

Cannella, A. A., & Paetzold, R. L. (1994). Pfeffer's barriers to the advance of organizational science: A rejoinder. *Academy of Management Review, 19,* 331–342.

Capitalism in the making. (1984, April 30). *Time,* 62.

Carman, J. M. (1979). Paradigms for marketing theory. In *Research in marketing.* Greenwich, CT: JAI Press.

Carter, P., & Jackson, N. (1987). Management, myth and meta theory—From scarcity to postscarcity. *International Studies of Management and Organization, 17*(3), 64–89.

Casey, C. (1999). Come, join our family: Discipline and integration in corporate organizational culture. *Human Relations, 52,* 155–178.

Chambers, I., & Curti, L. (1996). *The post-colonial question.* London: Routledge.

Chandler, A. (1962). *Strategy and structure.* New York: Doubleday.

Chandler, A. D., Jr. (1966). *Strategy and structure.* Cambridge, MA: MIT Press.

Chandler, A. D., Jr. (1977). *The visible hand: The managerial revolution in American business.* Cambridge, MA: Harvard University Press.

Chia, R. (1996). *Organizational analysis as deconstructive practice.* Berlin: de Gruyter.

Clawson, D. (1980). *Bureaucracy and the labor process.* New York: Monthly Review Press.

Clegg, S. (1979). *The theory of power and organization.* London: Routledge & Kegan Paul.

Clifford, G., & Marcus, G. (1986). *Writing culture.* Berkeley: University of California Press.

Coase, R. H. (1937). The nature of the firm. *Economica N. S., 4,* 386–405.

Coase, R. H. (1972). Industrial organization: A proposal for research. In V. R. Fuchs (Ed.), *Policy issues and research opportunities in industrial organization.* New York: Columbia University Press.

Coffee, J. C. (1988). Shareholders versus managers: The strain in the corporate web. In J. C. Coffee, L. Lowenstein, & S. Rose-Ackerman (Eds.), *Knights, raiders, and targets* (pp. 77–134). New York: Oxford University Press.

Cohen, S. F. (1968). *Modern social theory.* London: Heinemann.

Collinson, D. (1994). Strategies of resistance. In J. M. Jermier, D. Knights, & W. R. Nord (Eds.), *Resistance and power in organizations* (pp. 25–68). London: Routledge.

Collinson, D., & Hearn, J. (1994). Naming men as men: Implications for work organization and management. *Gender, Work & Organization, 1,* 2–22.

Commons, J. R. (1934). *Institutional economics.* Madison: University of Wisconsin Press.

Comparing public and private schools. H. M. Levin & T. James (Eds.), 128–160. New York: Faimer Press.

Conlon, E., & Parks, J. (1988). The effects of monitoring and tradition on compensation arrangements: An experiment on principal/agent dyads. In F. Hoy (Ed.), *Best papers proceedings of the Academy of Management* (pp. 191–195), Anaheim, CA.

Connell, A., & Nord, W. R. (1996). The bloodless coup: The infiltration of organization science by uncertainty and values. *Journal of Applied Behavioral Science, 32,* 407–427.

Connelly, W. E. (1993). *Political theory & modernity.* Ithaca, NY: Cornell University Press.

Cooper, C., & Puxty, A. (1994). Reading accounting writing. *Accounting, Organizations and Society, 19,* 127–146.

Cooper, R. (1986). Organization/disorganization. *Social Science Information, 25,* 299–335.

Cooper, R. (1989). Modernism, post modernism and organizational analysis: The contribution of Jacques Derrida. *Organization Studies, 10,* 479–502.

Cooper, R., & Burrell, G. (1988). Modernism. postmodernism and organizational analysis: An introduction. *Organization Studies, 9,* 91–112.

Coser, L. A. (1965). *The functions of social conflict.* London: Routledge & Kegan Paul.

Coughlan, A., & Schmidt, R. (1985). Executive compensation, management turnover, and firm performance. *Journal of Accounting and Economics, 7,* 43–66.

Cussins, C. (1988). Ontological choreography: Agency for women patients in an infertility clinic. In A. Mol & M. Berg (Eds.), *Differences in medicine: Unraveling practices, techniques* and *bodies.* Durham, NC: Duke University Press.

Cyert, R. M., & March, J. G. (1963). *A behavioral theory of the firm.* Englewood Cliffs, NJ: Prentice Hall.

Czarniawska, B. (1995). Narration or science? Collapsing the division in organization studies. *Organization, 2,* 11–34.

Czarniawska, B. (1997). *Narrating the organization.* Chicago: University of Chicago Press.

Czarniawska, B. (1998). A *narrative approach to organization studies.* Thousand Oaks. CA: Sage.

D'Aveni, R. (1996). A multiple-constituency, status-based approach to inter-organizational mobility of faculty and input–output competition among top business schools. *Organization Science, 7,* 167–189.

Daft, R. L., (2004). *Organization theory and design.* Mason, OH: Southwestern Publishing.

Dahrendorf, R. (1959). *Class and class conflict in industrial society.* London: Routledge & Kegan Paul.

Dann, L.Y., & DeAngelo, H. (1983). Corporate financial policy and corporate control: A study of defensive adjustments in asset and ownership structure. *Journal of Financial Economics, 20,* 87–127.

Davis, R. C. (1951). *The fundamentals of top management.* New York: Harper Brothers.

Dawe, A. (1970). The two sociologies. *British Journal of Sociology, 21,* 207–218.

Deci, E. L. (1971). Effects of externally mediated rewards on intrinsic motivation. *Journal of Personality and Social Psychology, 18,* 105–115.

Deetz, S. (1996). The positioning of the researcher in studies of organizations: De-hatching literary theory. *Journal of Management Inquiry, 5,* 387–391.

DeJong, D., Forsythe, R., & Uecker, W. (1985). Ripoffs, lemons and reputation formation in agency relationships: A laboratory market study. *Journal of Finance, 50,* 809–820.

Deleuze, G., & Guattari, F. (1988). A *thousand plateaus: Capitalism and schizophrenia.* London: Althone.

Demsetz, H. (1968). The cost of transacting. *Quarterly Journal of Economics, 82*(2), 33–53.

Demski, J. (1980). *A simple case of indeterminate financial reporting* (Working paper), Stanford University.

Demski, J., & Feltham, G. (1978). Economic incentives in budgetary control systems. *Accounting Review, 53,* 336–359.

Derrida, J. (1974). *Of grammatology*. Baltimore: Johns Hopkins University Press.

Derrida, J. (1982). *Margins of philosophy*. Chicago: University of Chicago Press.

DiMaggio, P. J. (1983). State expansion and organizational fields. In R. H. Hall & R. E. Quinn (Eds.), *Organizational theory and public policy* (pp. 147–161). Beverly Hills, CA: Sage.

DiMaggio, P. J. (1988). Interest and agency in institutional theory. In L. G. Zucker (Ed.), *Institutional patterns and organizations* (pp. 3–21). Cambridge, MA: Ballinger.

DiMaggio, P. J., & Powell, W. W. (1983). The iron cage revisited: Institutional isomorphism and collective rationality in organizational fields. *American Sociological Review, 48*, 147–160.

Dirlik, A. (1994). The postcolonial aura: Third World criticism in the age of global capitalism. *Critical Inquiry, 20*, 328–356.

Doeringer, P., & Piore, M. (1971). *Internal labor markets and manpower analysis*. Lexington, MA: D. C. Heath.

Donaldson, L. (1996). *For positivist organization theory: Proving the hard core*. London: Sage.

Donovan, F. R. (1929). *The saleslady*. Chicago: University of Chicago Press.

Dornbusch, S., & Scott, W. R. (1975). *Evaluation and the exercise of authority*. San Francisco: Jossey-Bass.

Douglas, J. D. (ed). (1970). *Understanding everyday life*. Chicago: Aldine.

Downs, A. (1967). *Inside bureaucracy*. Boston: Little, Brown.

Du Gay, P., & Salaman, G. (1992). The culture of the customer. *Journal of Management Studies, 29*, 615–633.

Durkheim, P. (1947). *The division of labor in society* (G. Simpson, Trans.). Glencoe, IL: Free Press.

Dyl, E. A. (1989). Agency, corporate control and accounting methods—The LIFO–FIFO choice. *Managerial and Decision Economics, 10*, 141–145.

Eccles, R. (1985). Transfer pricing as a problem of agency. In J. Pratt & R. Zeckhauser (Eds.), *Principals and agents: The structure of business* (pp. 151–186). Boston: Harvard Business School Press.

Eco, U. (1992). *Interpretation and overinterpretation*. Cambridge, UK: Cambridge University Press.

Edwards, R. C. (1979). *Contested terrain: The transformation of the workplace in the twentieth century*. New York: Basic Books.

Ehrenreich, J., & Ehrenreich, B. (1976). Work and consciousness. *Monthly Review, 28*, 10–18.

Eisenhardt, K. (1985). Control: Organizational and economic approaches. *Management Science, 31*, 134–149.

Eisenhardt, K. (1988). Agency and institutional explanations of compensation in retail sales. *Academy of Management Journal, 31*, 488–511.

Eisenhardt, K. (1989). Agency theory: An assessment and review. *Academy of Management Review, 14*, 57–74.

Elton, C. (1927). *Animal ecology*. London: Sidgwick & Jackson.

Etzioni, A. (1961). *A comparative analysis of complex organizations*. New York: Free Press.

Etzioni, A. (1964). *Modern Organization*. Upper Saddle River, NJ: Prentice Hall.

Evans, P. B., Rueschemeyer, D., & Skocpol, T. (Eds.). (1985). Bringing the state back in. Cambridge, UK: Cambridge University Press.

Evered, R., & Louis, M. R. (1981). Alternative perspectives in the organizational sciences: "Inquiry from the inside" and "inquiry from the outside." *Academy of Management Review, 6*, 385–395.

Ezzamel, M., & Willmott, H. (1998). Accounting for teamwork: A critical study of group based systems of organizational control. *Administrative Science Quarterly, 43*, 358–396.

Ezzy, D. (2001). A simulacrum of workplace community: Individualism and engineered culture. *Sociology, 55,* 631–650.

Fama, E. (1980). Agency problems and the theory of the firm. *Journal of Political Economy, 88,* 288–307.

Fama, E., & Jensen, M. (1983). Separation of ownership and control. *Journal of Law and Economics, 26,* 301–325.

Fayol, H. (1949). *General and industrial management in France* (C. Storrs, Trans.). London: Pitman.

Featherstone, M. (1988). In pursuit of the postmodern: An introduction. *Theory, Culture, and Society, 5,* 195–215.

Ferguson, K. (1994). On bringing more theory, more voices, and more politics to the study of organization. *Organization, I,* 81–99.

Fierman, J. (1990). The people who set the CEOs pay. *Fortune, 121*(6), 58–66.

Firat, A. F., & Venkatesh, A. (1993). Postmodernity: The age of marketing. *International Journal of Research in Marketing, 10,* 227–249.

Fischer, E., & Bristor, J. (1994). A feminist poststructuralist analysis of the rhetoric of marketing relationships. *International Journal of Research in Marketing, II,* 317–331.

Fitzroy, F. R., & Mueller, D. C. (1977). *Contract and the economics of organization* (Discussion paper, pp. 77–125.). Berlin: International Institute of Management.

Flax, J. (1987). Postmodern and gender relations in feminist theory. *Signs, 16,* 621–643.

Flax, J. (1992). The end of innocence. In J. Butler & J. W. Scott, *Feminists theorize the political.* London: Routledge.

Fleming, P. (2003). Working at a cynical distance: Implications·for power, subjectivity and resistance. *Organization, 10*(1), 157–179.

Fleming, P., & Sewell, G. (2002). Looking for the good soldier: Alternative modalities of resistance in the contemporary workplace. *Sociology, 36*(4), 857–872.

Fleming, P., & Spicer, A. (2003). Working at a cynical distance: Implications for power, subjectivity and resistance. *Organization, 10,* 157–179.

Fligstein, N. (1985). The spread of the multidivisional form among large firms, 1919–1979. *American Sociological Review, 50,* 377–391.

Fondas, N. (1997). Feminization unveiled: Management qualities in contemporary writings. *Academy of Management Review, 22,* 257–283.

Foster, H. (1983). Postmodernism: A preface. In H. Foster (Ed.), *The anti-aesthetic* (pp. ix–vi). Port Townsend, WA: Bay Press.

Foucault, M. (1977). What is an author? In D. F. Bouchard (Ed.), *Language, counter-memory, practice: Selected essays and interviews by Michel Foucault* (pp. 113–138). Ithaca, NY: Cornell University Press.

Foucault, M. (1979). *Discipline and punish.* New York: Vintage.

Foucault, M. (1980). *The history of sexuality: Vol. 1. An introduction.* New York: Vintage.

Fox, S. (1989). The panopticon: From Bentham's obsession to the revolution in management learning. *Human Relations, 42,* 717–739.

Franko, L. G. (1972). The growth, organizational efficiency of European multinational firms: Some emerging hypotheses. *Colloques International Aux C.N.RS, 549,* 335–366.

Freeman, J. (1975). *The unit problem in organizational research.* Paper presented at the annual meeting of the American Sociological Association, San Francisco.

Friedland, R., & Alford, R. R. (1987). *Bringing society back in: Symbols, structures and institutional contradiction.* Paper presented at the Conference on Institutional Change, Center for Advanced Study in the Behavioral Sciences, Stanford, CA, May 15–16.

Friedman, A. (1977). *Industry and Labour: Class Struggle at Work and Monopoly Capitalism.* London: McMillan.

Friedman, M. (1953). *Essays on positive economics.* Chicago: University of Chicago Press.

Friedson, E. (1986). *Professional powers: A study of the institutionalization of formal knowledge.* Chicago: University of Chicago Press.

Frost, P., Moore, L., Louis, M. R., Lundberg, C., & Martin, J. (Eds.). (1985). *Organizational culture.* Beverly Hills, CA: Sage.

Gabriel, Y. (1999). Beyond happy families: A critical reevaluation of the control–resistance–identity triangle. *Human Relations, 52,* 179–203.

Gadet, F. (1989). *Saussure and contemporary culture.* London: Hutchinson Radius.

Galbraith, J. (1973). *Designing complex organizations,* Reading, MA: Addison-Wesley.

Galbraith, J. K. (1967). *The new industrial state.* Boston: Houghton Mifflin.

Garcia-Canclini, N. (1990). *Culturas hibridas: Estrategias para entrar y salir de la modernidad.* Mexico, DF: Grijalbo.

Gergen, K. (1992). Organization theory in the postmodern era. In M. Reed & M. Hughes (Eds.), *Rethinking organization* (pp. 207–226). London: Sage.

Giddens, A. (1974). *Positivism and sociology.* London: Heinemann.

Gilroy, P. (1993). *The Black Atlantic: Modernity and double consciousness.* London: Verso.

Gioia, D. (1992). Pinto fires and personal ethics: A script analysis of missed opportunities. *Journal of Business Ethics, 11,* 43–53.

Golden-Biddle, K., & Locke, K. (1993). Appealing work: An investigation of how ethnographic texts convince. *Organization Science, 4,* 595–616.

Golden-Biddle, K., & Locke, K. (1997). *Composing qualitative research.* Thousand Oaks, CA: Sage.

Goldman, P. (1985). *Mainstream and critical perspectives on organizations: Shared and conflicting domains.* Unpublished paper, University of Oregon, Eugene.

Goldman, P., & Van Houten, D. R. (1977). Managerial strategies and the worker: A Marxist analysis of bureaucracy. *Sociological Quarterly, 18,* 108–115.

Goodall, H. L. (1989). *Casing a promised land.* Carbondale: Southern Illinois Press.

Gottfried, H. (1994). Learning the score: The duality of control and everyday resistance in the temporary-help service industry. In J. M. Jermier, D. Knights, & W. R. Nord (Eds.), *Resistance and power in organizations* (pp. 102–127). London: Routledge.

Gouldner, A. W. (1959). Reciprocity and autonomy in functional theory. In A. W. Gouldner, *For sociology,* op. cit.

Gouldner, A.W. (1954). *Patterns of industrial bureaucracy.* New York: Free Press.

Grabowski, H. G., & Mueller, D. C. (1972). Managerial and stockholder welfare models of firm expenditures. *Review of Economics and Statistics, 54,* 9–24.

Graham, J. K. (1996). Queer(y)ing capitalist organization. *Organization, 3,* 541–545.

Grandori, A. (1987). *Perspectives of organizational theory.* Cambridge, MA: Ballinger.

Granovetter, M. S. (1973, May). The strength of weak ties. *American Journal of Sociology 78,* 1360–1380.

Gray, B., Bougon, M., & Donnellon, A. (1985). Organizations as constructions and destructions of meaning. *Administrative Science Quarterly, 11,* 83–98.

Groff, J. E., & Wright, C. J. (1989). The market for corporate control and its implications for accounting policy choice. In B. N. Schwartz & Associates (Eds.), *Advances in accounting* (Vol. 7, pp. 13–21). Greenwich, CT: JAI Press.

Gross, B. (1980). *Friendly fascism: The new face of power in America.* Boston: South End Press.

Habermas, J. (1984). *The theory of communicative action, volume one. Reason and the rationalization of society.* Boston: Beacon Press.

Habermas, J. (1987). *The theory of communicative action, volume two. Lifeworld and system: A critique of functionalist reason.* Boston: Beacon Press.

Hagerman, R. L., & Zmijewski, M. E. (1979). Some economic determinants of accounting policy choice. *Journal of Accounting and Economics, 1,* 141–161.

Hall, R. H., & Tolbert, P. S. (2005). *Organizations: Structures, processes, and outcomes.* Upper Saddle River, NJ: Prentice Hall.

Hall, S. (1996). When was "the post-colonial"? Thinking at the limit. In I. Chambers & L. Curti (Eds.), *The post-colonial question: Common skies, divided horizons* (pp. 242–260). London: Routledge.

Halpern, P. (1973). Empirical estimates of the amount and distribution of gains to companies in mergers. *Journal of Business, 46,* 554–575.

Halpern, P. (1983). Corporate acquisitions: A theory of special cases? A review of event studies applied to acquisitions. *Journal of Finance, 38,* 297–317.

Hannan, M. T., & Freeman, J. (1974). *Environment and the structure of organizations.* Paper presented at the annual meeting of the American Sociological Association, Montreal.

Hannan, M., & Freeman, J. (1977). The population ecology of organizations. *American Journal of Sociology, 82*(3), 929–964.

Haraway, D. J. (1985). Manifesto for cyborgs: Science, technology and socialist feminism in the 1980s. *Socialist Review, 80,* 65–108.

Harris, M., & Raviv, A. (1978). Some results on incentive contracts with application to education and employment, health insurance, and law enforcement. *American Economic Review, 68,* 20–30.

Harris, M., & Raviv, A. (1979). Optimal incentive contracts with imperfect information. *Journal of Economic Theory, 20,* 231–259.

Hashimoto, M., & Yu, B. T. (1980). Specific capital, employment contracts and wage rigidity. *Bell Journal of Economics, 2,* 536–549.

Hassard, J. (1993). *Sociology and organization theory: Positivism, paradigms and postmodernity.* London: Sage.

Hassard, J., & Parker, M. (Eds.). (1993). *Postmodernism and organizations.* London: Sage.

Hastie, R. (1981). Schematic principles in human memory. In E. T. Higgins, C. F. Herman, & M. P. Zanna (Eds.), *Social cognition: The Ontario symposium* (pp. 39–88). Hillsdale, NJ: Lawrence Erlbaum.

Hatch, M. J. (1996). The role of the researcher: An analysis of narrative position in organization theory. *Journal of Management Inquiry, 5,* 359–374.

Hatch, M. J. (1997). *Organization theory: Modern, symbolic and postmodern perspectives.* Oxford, UK: Oxford University Press.

Haveman, H. A. (2000, May). The future of organizational sociology. *Contemporary Sociology, 29*(3), 476–486.

Hawley, A. H. (1944, May). Ecology and human ecology. *Social Forces, 22,* 398–405.

Hawley, A. H. (1950). *Human ecology: A theory of community structure.* New York: Ronald.

Hawley, A. H. (1968). Human ecology. In D. L. Sills (Ed.), *International encyclopedia of the social sciences* (pp. 328–337). New York: Macmillan.

Hearn, J., & Parkin, W. (1993). Organizations, multiple oppressions and postmodernism. In J. Hassard & M. Parker (Eds.), *Postmodernism and organizations* (pp. 148–162). London: Sage.

Herman, E. S., & Lowenstein, L. (1988). The efficiency effects of hostile takeovers. In J. C. Coffee, L. Lowenstein, & S. Rose-Ackerman (Eds.), *Knights, raiders, and targets* (pp. 211–240). New York: Oxford University Press.

Hertzler, J. O. (1961). *American social institutions.* Boston: Allyn & Bacon.

Hill, C. W., & Hansen, G. S. (1989). *Institutional holdings and corporate R&D intensity in research intensive industries* (pp. 17–21). Academy of Management Best Papers Proceedings, 49th Annual Meeting of the Academy of Management, Washington, DC.

Hill, C. W., Hitt, M., & Hoskinsson, R. E. (1988). Declining U.S. competitiveness: Reflections on a crisis. *Academy of Management Journal, 32,* 25–47.

Hindley, B. (1970). Separation of ownership and control in the modern corporation. *Journal of Law and Economics, 13,* 185–222.

Hinings, B., Clegg, S. R., Child, J., Aldrich, H., Karpik, L., & Donaldson, L. (1988). Offence and defence in organization studies: A symposium. *Organization Studies, 9,* 1–32.

Hirsch, P., & Friedman, R. (1986). Collaboration or paradigm shift? Economic VB. behavioral thinking about policy? In J. Pearce & R. Robinson (Eds.), *Best papers proceedings* (pp. 31–35). Chicago: Academy of Management.

Hirsch, P., Michaels, S., & Friedman, R. (1987). "Dirty hands" versus "clean models": Is sociology in danger of being seduced by economics? *Theory and Society,* 317–336.

Hirsch, P. M., Friedman, R., Koza, M. P. (1990). Collaboration or paradigm shift? Caveat emptor and the risk of romance with economic models for strategy and policy research. *Organization Science, 1,* 87–97.

Hofstede, G. (1980). *Culture's consequences: International differences in work-related values.* Beverly Hills, CA: Sage.

Hollander, E. O. (Ed.). (1967). *The future of small business.* New York: Praeger.

Hollway, W. (1991). *Work psychology and organizational behavior.* London: Sage.

Holmstrom, B. (1979). Moral hazard and observability. *Bell Journal of Economics, 10,* 74–91.

Holthausen, R. W., & Leftwich, R. W. (1983). The economic consequences of accounting choice. *Journal of Accounting and Economics, 5,* 77–117.

Horkheimer, M. (1933/1972). Materialism and metaphysics. In M. Horkheimer, *Critical theory: Selected essays* (pp. 10–46). New York: Seabury Press.

Horkheimer, M. (1937/1972). Traditional and critical theory. In M. Horkheimer, *Critical theory: Selected essays* (pp. 188–243). New York: Seabury Press.

Horkheimer, M. (1939/1972). The social function of philosophy. In M. Horkheimer, *Critical theory: Selected essays* (pp. 253–272). New York: Seabury Press.

Horkheimer, M. (1974). *Eclipse of reason.* New York: Continuum. (Original work published 1947)

Horkheimer, M., & Adorno, T. W. (1972). *Dialectic of enlightenment.* New York: Seabury Press. (Original work published 1944)

Hughes, E. C. (1939). Institutions. In R. E. Park (Ed.), *An outline of the principles of sociology* (pp. 283–346). New York: Barnes & Noble.

Hunt, H., III. (1986). The separation of corporate ownership and control: Theory, evidence, and implications. *Journal of Accounting Literature, 5,* 85–124.

Hunt, H. G., III. (1985). Potential determinants of corporate inventory accounting decisions. *Journal of Accounting Research, 23,* 448–467.

Hurtado, A. (1989). Relating to privilege: Seduction and rejection in the subordination of White women and women of color. *Signs, 14,* 833–855.

Hutchinson, G. E. (1957). Concluding remarks. Cold Spring Harbor Symposium on Quantitative Biology, *22,* 415–427.

Hutchinson, G. E. (1959). Homage to Santa Rosalia, or why are there so many kinds of animals?" *American Naturalist 93,* 145–59.

Huxley, A. (1969). *Brave new world.* New York: Harper & Row.

Huyssen, A. 1986. After the great divide. Bloomington: Indiana University Press. In M. W. Meyer (Ed.), *Environments and organizations* (pp. 78–109). San Francisco: Jossey-Bass.

Israel, J. (1975). Alienation and reification. *Social Praxis, 3,* 40–57.

Jackson, N., & Carter, P. (1992). Postmodern management: Past perfect or future imperfect? *International Studies of Management and Organization, 22*(3), 11–26.

Jacobson, S. W., & Jacques, R. (1997). Destabilizing the field: Poststructuralist knowledge-making strategies in a postmodern era. *Journal* of *Management Inquiry, 6,* 42–59.

Jacoby, R. (1975). *Social amnesia*. Boston: Beacon Press.

Jacques, R. (1992). Critique and theory building: Producing knowledge "from the kitchen." *Academy* of *Management Review. 17*, 582–606.

Jacques, R. (1996). *Manufacturing the employee: Management knowledge from the 19th to the 21st centuries*. London: Sage.

Jarrell, G. A., Brickley, J. A., & Netter, J. M. (1988). The market for corporate control: The empirical evidence since 1980. *Journal of Economic Perspectives, 2*, 49–68.

Jeffcutt, P. (1993). From interpretation to representation. In J. Hassard & M. Parker (Eds.), *Postmodernism and organizations* (pp. 25–48). London: Sage.

Jensen, M. (1983). Organization theory and methodology. *Accounting Review, 56*, 319–338.

Jensen, M. (1984). Takeovers: Folklore and science. *Harvard Business Review, 62*(6), 109–121.

Jensen, M., & Meckling, W. (1976). Theory of the firm: Managerial behavior, agency costs, and ownership structure. *Journal of Financial Economics, 3*, 305–360.

Jensen, M., & Roeback, R. (1983). The market for corporate control: Empirical evidence. *Journal of Financial Economics, 11, 5–50*.

Jepperson, R. L. (1987). *Conceptualizing institutions, institutionalization and institutional effects*. Paper presented at the Conference on Institutional Change, Center for Advanced Study in the Behavioral Sciences, Stanford, CA, May 15–16.

Jermier, J. M. *http://www.comp.lancs.ac.uk/sociology/ant.html#ear*

Jermier, J. M. (1982). Infusion of critical social theory into organizational analysis: Implications for studies of work adjustment. In D. Dunkerley & G. Salaman (Eds.), *The international yearbook of organization studies 1981* (pp. 195–211). London: Routlege & Kegan Paul.

Jermier, J. M. (Ed.). (1985a). *Journal* of *Management* (Special issue on organizational symbolism), *11*(2).

Jermier, J. M. (1985b). "When the sleeper wakes": A short story extending themes in radical organization theory. *Journal of Management, 11*, 67–80.

Jermier, J. M. (1988). Sabotage at work: The rational view. In S. Bacharach & N. DiTomaso (Eds.), *Research in the sociology of organizations* (pp. 103–134). Greenwich, CT: JAI Press.

Jermier, J. M. (1998). Critical perspectives on organizational control. *Administrative Science Quarterly, 43*, 235–256.

Journal of Management. (1985). Special issue on organizational symbolism, *11*(2).

Jung, C. G. (1970). *Psychological reflections: A new anthology of his writings, 1905–1961*. Princeton, NJ: Princeton University Press.

Kaghan, W., & Phillips, N. (1998). Building the Tower of Babel: Communities of practice and paradigmatic pluralism in organization studies. *Organization, 5*, 191–215.

Keat, R., & Urry, J. (1975). *Social theory as science*. London: Routledge & Kegan Paul.

Kellner, D. (1989). *Critical theory, Marxism and modernity*. Baltimore: Johns Hopkins University Press.

Kilduff, M. (1993). Deconstructing organizations. *Academy* of *Management Review, 18*, 13–31.

Kilduff, M., & Mehra, A. (1997). Postmodernism and organizational research. *Academy of Management Review, 22*, 453–481.

Kimberly, J. R. (1975). Environmental constraints and organizational structure: A comparative analysis of rehabilitation organizations. *Administrative Science Quarterly, 20*, 1–9.

Knights, D. (1992). Changing spaces: The disruptive impact of a new epistemological location for the study of management. *Academy of Management Review, 17*, 514–536.

Knights, D., & Collinson, D. (1985). Redesigning work on the shopfloor: A question of control or consent? In D. Knights, H. Willmott, & D. Collinson (Eds.), *Job redesign* (pp. 197–226). Aldershot, UK: Glower.

Knights, D., & Willmott, H. (1989). Power and subjectivity at work: From degradation to subjugation in social relations. *Sociology, 23*, 534–558.

Knorr-Cetina, K. (1981). *The manufacture of knowledge.* Oxford, UK: Pergamon.

Kolakowski, L. (1972). *Positivist philosophy.* Harmondsworth, UK: Penguin.

Kosnik, R. (1987). Greenmail: A study in board performance in corporate governance. *Administrative Science Quarterly, 32,* 163–185.

Kreiner, K. (1992). The postmodern epoch of organization theory. *International Studies of Management and Organization, 22*(2), 37–52.

Kroll, M., Simmons, S., & Wright, P. (1990). Determinants of CEO compensation following major acquisitions. *Journal of Business Research, 20,* 349–366.

Kuhn, T. (1962). *The structure of scientific revolutions.* Chicago: University of Chicago Press.

Laing, R. D. (1965). *The divided self.* Middlesex, UK: Penguin.

Lambert, R. (1983). Long-term contracts and moral hazard. *Bell Journal of Economics, 14,* 441–452.

Larson, M. S. (1977). *The rise of professionalism: A sociological analysis.* Berkeley: University of California Press.

Latour, B. (1986). The powers of association. In J. Law (Ed.), *Power, action and belief* (pp. 261–277). London: Routledge & Kegan Paul.

Latour, B. (1987). *Science in action.* Milton Keynes, UK: Open University Press.

Latour, B. (1988a). *The pasteurization of France.* Cambridge. MA: Harvard University Press.

Latour, B. (1993). *We have never been modern.* Cambridge, MA: Harvard University Press.

Latour, B. (1996). *Aramis, or the love for technology.* Cambridge, MA: Harvard University Press.

Latour, B. (1997). *On recalling ANT* (Keynote speech). Centre for Social Theory and Technology, Keele University, Keele, England.

Latour, B. (aka Jim Johnson). (1988b). Mixing humans and nonhumans together: The sociology of a door-closer. *Social Problems, 35,* 298–310.

Law, J. (1994). *Organizing modernity.* Oxford, UK: Blackwell.

Law, J. (1997a). *Topology and the naming of complexity.* Department of Sociology and Social Anthropology. Keele University, Keele, England.

Law, J. (1997b). *Traduction/trahison: Notes on ANT.* Department of Sociology and Social Anthropology, Keele University, Keele, England. Available online at http://www.keele.ac .uk/depts/so/staff/jl/pubs-IL2.htm

Law. J., & Hassard, J. (Eds.). (1999). *Actor network theory and after.* Oxford, UK: Blackwell.

Lawrence, D., & Lorsch, J. (1967). *Organization and environment.* Homewood, IL: R. D. Irwin.

Lee, N., & Brown, S. (1994). Otherness and the actor network: The undiscovered continent. *American Behavioral Scientist, 36,* 772–790.

Lefebvre, H. (1970). *The explosion.* New York: Monthly Review Press.

Leitch, V. (1996). *Postmodernism: Local effects, global flows.* Albany: State University of New York Press.

Letiche, H. (1992). Having taught postmodernists. *International Studies of Management and Organization, 22*(3), 46–70.

Levins, R. (1962 November–December). Theory of fitness in a heterogeneous environment I. The fitness set and adaptive function. *American Naturalist, 96,* 361–378.

Levins, R. (1968). *Evolution in changing environments.* Princeton, NJ: Princeton University Press.

Lewellen, W., Loderer, C., & Rosenfeld, A. (1985). Merger decisions and executive stock ownership in acquiring firms. *Journal of Accounting and Economics, 7,* 209–231.

Linstead, S. (1993). From postmodern anthropology to deconstructive ethnography. *Human Relations, 46,* 97–120.

Linstead, S., & Grafton-Small, R. (1992). On reading organizational culture. *Organization Studies, 13,* 331–355.

Lockwood, D. (1956). Some remarks on "The Social System." *British Journal of Sociology, 7,* 134–143.

Lukacs, G. (1971). *History and class consciousness.* Cambridge, MA: MIT Press. (Original work published 1923)

Lyotard, J.-F. (1984, Trans.). *The postmodern condition: A report on knowledge.* Minneapolis: University of Minnesota Press. (Original work published in 1979)

MacCrimmon, K., & Wehrung, D. (1986). *Taking risks: The management of uncertainty.* New York: Free Press.

Mackenzie, K. D. (1978). *Organizational structures.* Arlington Heights, IL: AHM Publishing.

Macneil, L. R. (1974). The many futures of contract. *Southern California Law Review, 47*(5), 691–816.

Macneil, L. R. (1978). Contracts: Adjustment of long-term economic relations under classical, neoclassical, and relational contract law. *Northwestern University Law Review, 72*(1), 854–905.

Magenheim, E. B., & Mueller, D. C. (1988). On measuring the effects of acquisitions on acquiring firm shareholders. In J. C. Coffee, L. Lowenstein, & S. Rose-Ackerman (Eds.), *Knights, raiders, and targets* (pp. 211–240). New York: Oxford University Press.

Malatesta, P. H., & Walking, R. A. (1988). Poison pill securities; stockholder wealth, profitability, and ownership structure. *Journal of Financial Economics, 20,* 347–376.

Malmgren, H. (1961). Information, expectations and the theory of the firm. *Quarterly Journal of Economics, 75,* 399–421.

Mann, M. (1973). *Consciousness and action among the Western working class.* London: Macmillan.

Maravelias, C. (2003). Post bureaucracy: Control through professional freedom. *Journal of Organizational Change Management, 19,* 22–37.

March, J. (1962). The business firm as a political coalition. *Journal of Politics, 24,* 662–678.

March, J. G., & Olsen, J. P. (1976). *Ambiguity and choice in organizations.* Bergen: Universitetsforlaget.

March, J. G., & Olsen, J. P. (1984). The new institutionalism: Organizational factors in political life. *American Political Science Review, 78,* 734–749.

March, J., & Simon, H. (1958). *Organizations.* New York: Wiley.

Marcuse, H. (1966). *One-dimensional man.* Boston: Beacon Press. (Original work published 1964)

Marcuse, H. (1969). *An essay on liberation.* Boston: Beacon Press.

Marglin, S. (1977). Catching flies with honey: An inquiry into management to humanize work. Unpublished manuscript, Harvard University.

Marris, R. (1964). *The economic theory of managerial capitalism.* New York: Free Press.

Martin, J. (1990). Deconstructing organizational taboos: The suppression of gender conflict in organizations. *Organization Science, 1,* 339–359.

Martin, J. (1992). *Cultures in organizations: Three perspectives.* New York: Oxford University Press.

Martin, J., & Frost, P. (1996). The organizational culture war games: A struggle for intellectual dominance. In S. Clegg, C. Hardy, & W. Nord (Eds.), *Handbook of organization studies* (pp. 599–621). London: Sage.

Martin, J., & Knopoff, K. (1997). The gendered implications of apparently gender-neutral theory: Re-reading Weber. In A. Larson & R. E. Freeman (Eds.), *Women's studies and business ethics* (pp. 30–49). New York: Oxford University Press.

Marx, K. (1867/ 1972). *Capital.* New York: Dutton.

Marx, K. (1964). *The economic and philosophical manuscripts of 1844.* New York: International Publishers. (Original work published 1932)

Maslow, A. H. (1965). *Eupsychian management.* Homewood, IL: Irwin.

Matza, D., & Wellman, D. (1980). The ordeal of consciousness. *Theory and Society, 9,* 1–28.

Mauws, M. K., & Phillips, N. (1995). Understanding language games. *Organization Science, 6,* 322–334.

Mayo, E. (1945). *The social problems of an industrial civilization.* Boston: Graduate School of Business Administration, Harvard University.

McCabe, Darren. (2007). Individualization at work? Subjectivity, teamworking and anti-unionism. *Organization, 14,* 243–266.

McCloskey, D. (1986). *The rhetoric of economics.* Madison: University of Wisconsin Press.

McEachern, W. A. (1975). *Managerial control and performance.* Lexington, MA: D.C. Heath & Co.

McGregor, D. (1960). *The human side of enterprise.* New York: McGraw-Hill.

McGuire, J. (1964). *Theories of business behavior.* New York: Prentice Hall.

McKinley, W., & Mone, M. A. (1998). The re-construction of organization studies: Wrestling with incommensurability. *Organization, 5,* 169–190.

McSweeney, B. (2006). Are we living in a post-bureaucratic epoch? *Journal of Organizational Change Management, 16,* 547–566.

Meade, J. E. (1971). *The controlled economy,* Albany: State University of New York Press.

"Meet Mike Jensen, the professor of merger mania." (1988, February 8). *Business Week,* pp. 66–67.

Merton, R. K. (1948). Manifest and latent functions. In R. K. Merton, *Social theory and social structure.* Glencoe, IL: The Free Press

Meyer, J. W. (1970). The charter: Conditions of diffuse socialization in schools. In W. R. Scott (Ed.), *Social processes and social structures* (pp. 564–578). New York: Holt, Rinehart & Winston.

Meyer, J. W. (1983). Centralization of funding and control in educational governance. In J. W. Meyer & W. R. Scott, *Organizational environments: Ritual and rationality* (pp. 179–198). Beverly Hills, CA: Sage.

Meyer, J. W., & Rowan, B. (1977). Institutional organizations: Formal structure as myth and ceremony. *American Journal of Sociology, 83,* 340–363.

Meyer, J. W., & Scott, W. R. (1983). (With the assistance of B. Rowan and T. E. Deal). *Organizational environments: Ritual and rationality.* Beverly Hills, CA: Sage.

Meyer, J. W., Scott, W. R., & Deal, T. E. (1981). Institutional and technical sources of organizational structure: Explaining the structure of educational organizations. In H. D. Stein (Ed.), *Organization and the human services: Cross-disciplinary reflections* (pp. 151–179). Philadelphia: Temple University Press.

Meyer, J. W., Scott, W. R., & Strang, D. (1987). Centralization, fragmentation and school district complexity. *Administrative Science Quarterly, 32,* 186–201.

Meyer, J. W., Scott, W. R., Strang, D., & Creighton, A. (1988). Bureaucratization without centralization: Changes in the organizational system of American public education, 1940–1980. In L. G. Zucker (Ed.), *Institutional patterns and organizations* (pp. 139–167). Cambridge, MA: Ballinger.

Meyer, M. W. (1999). Notes from a border discipline: Has the border become the center? *Contemporary Sociology, 28*(5), 507–510.

Miller, E. J., & Rice, A. K. (1967). *Systems of organization.* London: Tavistock.

Mills, C. W. (1959). *The sociological imagination.* London: Oxford University Press.

Mintzberg, H. (1973). *The nature of managerial work.* New York: Harper & Row.

Mintzberg, H. (1979). *The structuring of organizations.* Englewood Cliffs, NJ: Prentice Hall.

Mir, R. A., Calas, M. B., & Smircich, L. (1999). Global technoscapes and silent voices: Challenges to theorizing global cooperation. In D. Cooperrider & J. Dutton (Eds.), *Organizational dimensions of global change* (pp. 270–290). Thousand Oaks, CA: Sage.

Mirvis, P. H., & Louis, M. R. (1985). Self-full research: Working through the self as an instrument in organizational research. In D. N. Berg & K. K. Smith (Eds.), *Exploring clinical methods for social research* (pp. 229–246). Newbury Park, CA: Sage.

Mitnick, B. (1986). *The theory of agency and organizational analysis* (Unpublished working paper). University of Pittsburgh.

Mohanty, C. T. (1991). Under Western eyes: Feminist scholarship and colonial discourses. In C. T. Mohanty, A. Russo, & L. Torres (Eds.), *Third World women and the politics of feminism* (pp. 51–80). Bloomington: Indiana University Press.

Monod, J. (1971). *Chance and necessity*. New York: Vintage.

Morck, R., Schleifer, A., & Vishny R. W. (1989). Alternative mechanisms for corporate control. *American Economic Review, 79,* 842–853.

Morgan, G. (1984). Opportunities arising from paradigm diversity. *Administration and Society, 16,* 306–327.

Morgan, G., Frost, P. J., & Pondy, L. R. (1983). Organizational symbolism. In L. R. Pondy, P. J. Frost, G. Morgan, & T. C. Dondridge (Eds.), *Organizational symbolism*. Greenwich, CT: JAI Press.

Morgan, G., & Smircich, L. (1980). The case for qualitative research. *Academy of Management Review, 5,* 491–500.

Morse, D., & Richardson, G. (1983). The LIFO/FIFO decision. *Journal of Accounting Research, 21*(1), 106–127.

Mouzelis, N. (1967). *Organization and bureaucracy*. Chicago: Aldine.

Mumby, D. K., & Putnam, L. (1992). The politics of emotion: A feminist reading of bounded rationality. *Academy of Management Review, 17,* 465–486.

Nelson, J. S. (1993). Account and acknowledge, or represent and control? Post modern politics and economics of collective responsibility. *Accounting, Organizations and Society, 18,* 207–229.

Nicholson, L. J. (Ed.). (1990). *Feminism/postmodernism*. New York: Routledge.

Nisbet, R. A. (1967). *The sociological tradition*. London: Heinemann.

Nkomo, S. M. (1992). The emperor has no clothes: Rewriting "race in organizations." *Academy* of *Management Review, 17,* 487–513.

Nord, W. (1977). A Marxist critique of humanistic psychology. *Journal of Humanistic Psychology, 17,* 75–83.

Nord, W. R. (1974). The failure of current applied behavioral science—A Marxian perspective. *Journal of Applied Behavioral Science, 10,* 557–578.

North, D. C. (1978). Structures and performance: The task of economic history. *Journal of Economic Literature, 16,* 963–978.

Organization. (1996). Special issue on gender, race, class, and organization, *3*(4).

Organization. (1998). Special issue on pluralism and incommensurability in strategic management and organization theory, *5*(2).

Orwell, G. (1949/1981). *Nineteen eighty-four*. New York: Signet.

Ouchi, W. G. (1978). The transmission of control through organizational hierarchy. *Academy of Management Journal, 21,* 248–263.

Ouchi, W. G. (1979). A conceptual framework for the design of organizational control mechanisms. *Management Science, 29*(9), 833–845.

Ouchi, W. G., & van de Ven, A. H. (1980). Antitrust and organization theory. In. O. E. Williamson (Ed.), *Antitrust law and economics*. Houston: Dame Publications.

Parker, M. (1993). Life after Jean-Francois. In J. Hassard & M. Parker (Eds.), *Postmodernism and organizations* (pp. 204–212). London: Sage.

Parsons, T. (1949). *The structure of social action*. Glencoe, IL: Free Press.

Pearce, J., Stevenson, W., & Perry, J. (1985). Managerial compensation based on organizational performance: A time series analysis of the effects of merit pay. *Academy of Management Journal, 28,* 261–278.

Penrose, E. T. (1959). *The theory of the growth of the firm.* New York: Wiley.

Perrow, C. (1970). *Organizational analysis: A sociological overview.* Belmont, CA: Wadsworth.

Perrow, C. (1972). *Complex organizations: A critical essay.* Glenview, IL: Scott, Foresman.

Perrow, C. (1986). *Complex organizations.* New York: Random House.

Peshkin, A. (1985). Virtuous subjectivity: In the participant-observer's I's. In D. N. Berg & K. K. Smith (Eds.), *Exploring clinical methods for social research* (pp. 267–281). Newbury Park, CA: Sage.

Pettigrew, A. (1973). *The politics of organizational decision making.* London: Tavistock.

Pfeffer, J. (1978). *Organizational design.* Arlington Heights, IL: AHM Publishing.

Pfeffer, J. (1981). *Power in organizations.* Marshfield, MA: Pittman.

Pfeffer, J. (1993). Barriers to the advance of organizational science: Paradigm development as a dependent variable. *Academy of Management Review, 18,* 599–620.

Pfeffer, J. (1995). Mortality, reproducibility, and the persistence of styles of theory. *Organization Science, 6,* 681–686.

Pfeffer, J., & Salancik, G. (1978). *The external control of organization.* New York: Harper & Row.

Pichardo, N. A. (1997). New social movements: A critical review. *Annual Review of Sociology, 23,* 411–430.

Pieterse, J. N. (1994). Globalisation as hybridisation. *International Sociology, 9,* 161–184.

Polkinghorne, D. (1987). *Narrative knowing and the human sciences.* Albany: State University of New York Press.

Pondy, L., Frost, P., Morgan, G., & Dandridge, T. (Eds.). (1983). *Organizational symbolism.* Greenwich, CT: JAI Press.

Poole, R. (1972). *Towards deep subjectivity.* New York: Harper Torchbooks.

Popper, K. (1963). *Conjectures and refutations: The growth of scientific knowledge.* London: Routledge & Kegan Paul.

Posner, R. A. (1969). Natural monopoly and its regulation. *Stanford Law Review, 21,* 548–564.

Posner, R. A. (1972). The appropriate scope of regulation in the cable television industry. *Bell Journal of Economics, 3,* 98–129.

Putnam, L. (1996). Situating the author and text. *Journal of Management Inquiry, 5,* 382–386.

Pye, A. (1988). Management competence in the public sector. *Public Money & Management, 8*(4), 62–67.

Radhakrishnan, R. (1994). Postmodernism and the rest of the world. *Organization, 1,* 305–340.

Radhakrishnan, R. (1996). *Diasporic meditations: Between home and location.* Minneapolis: University of Minnesota Press.

Ramanujan, V., & Varadarajan, P. (1989). Research on corporate diversification: A synthesis. *Strategic Management Journal, 10*(6), 523–551.

Rao, M. V. H., & Pasmore, W. A. (1989). Knowledge and interests in organization studies: A conflict of interpretations. *Organization Studies, 10,* 225–240.

Ravenscraft, D. J., & Scherer, F. M. (1987). *Mergers, sell-offs, and economic efficiency.* Washington, DC: The Brookings Institution.

Readings, B. (1996). *The university in ruins.* Cambridge, MA: Harvard University Press.

Richardson, L. (1994). Writing: A method of inquiry. In N. K. Denzin & Y. S. Lincoln (Eds.), *Handbook of qualitative research* (pp. 516–529). Thousand Oaks. CA: Sage.

Richardson, L. (1998). The politics of location: Where am I now? *Qualitative Inquiry, 4,* 41–48.

Ritzer, G. (1975). *Sociology: A multiple paradigm science.* Boston: Allyn & Bacon.

Ritzer, G. (1981). *Toward an integrated sociological paradigm.* Boston: Allyn & Bacon.

Ritzer, G. (2004). *The McDonaldization of society.* Thousand Oaks, CA: Pine Forge Press.

Roethlisberger, F. J., & Dickson, W. J. (1939). *Management and the worker.* Cambridge, MA: Harvard University Press.

Roethlisberger. F. J. (1945). *The Foreman: Master and Victim of Doubletalk.* Cambridge: Harvard Business Review.

Roll, R. (1987). Empirical evidence on takeover activity and shareholder wealth. In T. E. Copeland (Ed.), *Modern finance and industrial economics* (pp. 287–325). New York: Basil Blackwell.

Rose, M. A. (1991). *The post-modem and the post-industrial.* Cambridge, UK: Cambridge University Press.

Rosenau, P. M. (1992). *Postmodernism and the social sciences.* Princeton, NJ: Princeton University Press.

Ross, S. (1973). The economic theory of agency: The principal's problem. *American Economic Review, 63,* 134–139.

Ryngaert, M. (1988). The effect of poison pill securities on shareholder wealth. *Journal of Financial Economics, 20,* 377–417.

Said, E. (1989). Representing the colonized: Anthropology's interlocutors. *Critical Inquiry, 15,* 205–225.

Sakolsky, R. (1992). Disciplinary power: The labor process and the constitution of the laboring subject. *Rethinking Marxism, 5*(4), 114–126.

Salaman, G. (1978). Towards a sociology of organizational structure. *Sociology, 26,* 519–554

Salancik, G. R., & Pfeffer, J. (1980). Effects of ownership and performance on executive tenure in U.S. corporations. *Academy of Management Journal, 23,* 653–664.

Saldivar, J. D. (1997). *Border matters: Remapping American cultural studies.* Berkeley: University of California Press.

Sartre, J-P. (1963). *Search for a method.* New York: Knopf. (Original work published 1960)

Salleh, A. (1997). *Ecofeminism as politics: Nature, Marx and the postmodern.* London: Zed Books.

Sartre, J-P. (1976). *Critique of dialectical reason.* London: NLB. (Original work published 1960)

Saussure, F. (1974). *Course in general linguistics.* London: Fontana. (Original work published in 1916)

Scherer, A. G. (1998). Pluralism and incommensurability in strategic management and organization theory: A problem in search of a solution. *Organization, 5,* 147–168.

Scherer, F. M., Beckenstein, A., Kaufer, E., & Murphy, R. (1975). *The economics of multiplant operation: An international comparison study.* Cambridge, MA: Harvard University Press.

Schleifer, A., & Vishny, R. W. (1988). *Managerial entrenchment.* Unpublished manuscript, University of Chicago.

Schultz, M. (1992). Postmodem pictures of culture. *International Studies of Management* and *Organization, 22*(2), 15–35.

Schutz, A. (1962). *Collected papers* (Vols. 1 and 2, M. Natanson, Ed). The Hague: Niihoff.

Schwab, D. P. (1999). *Research methods for organizational studies.* Mahnwah, NJ: Lawrence Erlbaum.

Scott, W. R. (1982). Health care organizations in the 1980s: The convergence of public and professional control systems. In A. W. Johnson, O. Grusky, & B. H. Raven (Eds.), *Contemporary health services: Social science perspectives.* (pp. 177–195). Boston: Auburn House.

Scott, W. R. (1985). Conflicting levels of rationality: Regulators, managers and professionals in the medical care sector. *Journal of Health Administration Education, 3,* part 2, 113–131.

Scott, W. R. (1987a). *Organizations: Rational, natural and open systems* (2nd ed.). Englewood Cliffs, NJ: Prentice Hall.

Scott, W. R. (1987b, December). The adolescence of institutional theory. *Administrative Science Quarterly, 32*(4), 493–511.

Scott, W. R. (2003). *Organizations: Rational, natural, and open systems,* Upper Saddle River, NJ: Prentice Hall.

Scott, W. R., & Meyer, J. W. (1983). The organization of societal sectors. In J. W. Meyer & W. R. Scott, *Organizational environments: Ritual and rationality* (pp. 129–153). Beverly Hills, CA: Sage.

Scott, W. R., & Meyer, J. W. (1987). Environmental linkages and organizational complexity: Public and private schools. In H. M. Levin & T. James (Eds.), *Comparing public and private schools* (pp. 128–160). New York: Falmer Press.

Selznick, P. (1949). *TVA and the grass roots.* Berkeley: University of California Press.

Selznick, P. (1957). *Leadership in administration.* New York: Harper & Row.

Sennett, R. (1998). The corrosion of character: The personal consequences of work in the new capitalism. New York: Norton.

Sewell, G., & Wilkinson, B. (1992). Someone to watch over me: Surveillance, discipline and the just-in-time labour process. *Sociology, 26,* 271–289.

Shallenberger, D. (1994). Professional and openly gay: A narrative study of the experience. *Journal of Management Inquiry, 3,* 119–142.

Shavell, S. (1979). Risk sharing and incentives in the principal and agent relationship. *Bell Journal* of *Economics, 10,* 53–73.

Shaw, M. (1975). *Marxism and social science.* London: Pluto.

Shotter, I., & Gergen, K. I. (1989). *Texts of identity.* London: Sage.

Silverman, D. (1970). *The theory of organisations.* London: Heinemann.

Simon, H. A. (1978). Rationality and process and product of thought. *American Economic Review, 68*(2), 1–16.

Simon, W. H. (1983). Legality, bureaucracy, and class in the welfare system. *Yale Law Journal, 92,* 1198–1269.

Singh, H., & Harianto, F. (1989). Management-board relationships, takeover risk and the adoption of golden parachutes: An empirical investigation. *Academy of Management Journal.*

Singh, J. V., Tucker, D. J., & House. R. J. (1986). Organizational legitimacy and the liability of newness. *Administrative Science Quarterly, 31,* 171–193.

Singleton, V. (1996). Feminism, sociology of scientific knowledge and postmodernism: Politics, theory and me. *Social Studies of Science, 26,* 445–468.

Soros, G. (1998). *The crisis of global capitalism: Open society endangered.* New York: BBS/ Public Affiars.

Spence, A. M. (1975). The economics of internal organization: An introduction. *Bell Journal of Economics, 6,* 163–172.

Spence, A. M., & Zeckhauser, R. (1971). Insurance, information, and individual action. *American Economic Review, 61,* 380–387.

Spender, I.-C. (1998). Pluralist epistemology and the knowledge-based theory of the firm. *Organization, 5,* 233–256.

Spivak, G. C. (1987). *In other worlds.* New York: Methuen.

Spivak, G. C. (1988). Can the subaltern speak? In C. Nelson & L. Grossberg (Eds.), *Marxism and the interpretation of culture* (pp. 271–313). Urbana: University of Illinois Press.

Sproull, L. S. (1981). Response to regulation: An organizational process framework. *Administration and Society, 12,* 447–470.

St. Pierre, E. A. (1997). Circling the text: Nomadic writing practices. *Qualitative Inquiry, 3,* 403–418.

Stablein, R., & Nord, W. (1985). Practical and emancipatory; interests in organizational symbolism: A review and evaluation. *Journal of Management, 11,* 13–28.

Star, S. L. (1995). The politics of formal representations: Wizards, gurus and organizational complexity. In S. L. Star (Ed.), *Ecologies of knowledge: Work and politics in science and technology* (pp. 88–118). Albany: State University of New York Press.

Starr, P. (1982). *The social transformation of American medicine.* New York: Basic Books.

Staw, B. M., Calder, B. J., Hess, R. K., & Sandelands, L. E. (1980). Intrinsic motivation and norms about payment. *Journal of Personality, 48,* 1–14.

Steer, F., & Cable, J. (1978). Internal organization and profit: An empirical analysis of large U.K. companies. *Journal of Industrial Economics, 27,* 13–30.

Stigler, G. J. (1968). *The organization of industry.* Homewood, IL: R. D. Irwin.

Stinchcombe, A. L. (1959, June). Bureaucratic and craft administration of production. *Administrative Science Quarterly, 4,* 168–187.

Stinchcombe, A. L. (1965). Social structure and organizations. In J. G. March (Ed.), *Handbook of organizations* (pp. 153–193). Chicago: Rand McNally.

Stogdill, R. M. (1966). Dimensions of organization theory. In J. D. Thompson (Ed.), *Approaches to organizational design.* Pittsburgh: University of Pittsburgh Press.

Strang, D., & Macy, M. W. (2001). In search of excellence: Fads, success, stories and adaptive emulation. *American Journal of Sociology, 107,* 147–182.

Streeck, W., & Schmitter, P. C. (1985). Community, market, state and associations? The prospective contribution of interest governance to social order. In W. Streeck and P. C. Schmitter (Eds.), *Private interest government: Beyond market and state* (pp. 1–29). London: Sage.

Sturdy, A., Knights, D., & Willmott, H. (Eds.). (1992). *Skill and consent.* London: Routledge.

Sunder, S. (1973). Relationship between accounting changes and stock prices: Problems of measurement and some empirical evidence. *Journal of Accounting Research, 11*(Suppl.), 1–45.

Sunder, S. (1975). Stock prices and risk related accounting changes in inventory valuation. *Accounting Review, 50,* 305–315.

Swidler, A. (1986). Culture in action: Symbols and strategies. *American Sociological Review, 51,* 273–286.

Teece, D. J. (1979). *Internal organization and economic performance.* Unpublished manuscript, Stanford University.

Thomas, R., & Davies, A. (2005). Theorizing the micro-politics of resistance: New public management and managerial identities in the UK public service. *Organization Studies, 26,* 683–706.

Thompson, J. (1967). *Organizations in action.* New York: McGraw-Hill.

Thompson, V. (1961). *Modern organizations.* New York: Knopf.

Tolbert, P. S., & Zucker, L. G. (1983). Institutional sources of change in the formal structure of organizations: The diffusion of civil service reforms, 1880–1935. *Administrative Science Quarterly, 23,* 22–39.

Townley, B. (1993). Foucault, power/knowledge, and its relevance for human resource management. *Academy of Management Review, 18,* 518–545.

Townley, B. (1994a). *Reframing human resource management: Power, ethics and the subject at work.* London: Sage.

Townley, B. (1994b). Writing in friendship. *Organization, 1,* 24–28.

Trinh, T. M. (1989). *Woman, native, other: Writing post-coloniality and feminism.* Bloomington: Indiana University Press.

Turner, B. (1986). Sociological aspects of organizational symbolism. *Organization Studies, 7,* 101–115.

Ungson, G., & Steers, R. (1984). Motivation and politics in executive compensation. *Academy of Management Review, 9,* 313–323.

Van de Ven, A., & Joyce, W. (1981). *Perspectives on organization design and behavior.* New York: Wiley.

Van Den Berghe, P. L. (1969). Dialectic and functionalism: Towards a theoretic synthesis. In W. L. Wallace (Ed.), *Sociological theory,* op. cit.

Van Maanen, J. (1988). *Tales of the field.* Chicago: University of Chicago Press.

Van Maanen, J. (1995a). Fear and loathing in organization studies. *Organization Science, 6,* 687–692.

Van Maanen, J. (1995b). Style as theory. *Organization Science, 6,* 133–143.

Van Maanen, J. (1996). On the matter of voice. *Journal of Management Inquiry, 5,* 375–381.

Wachter, M., & Williamson, O. E. (1978). Obligational markets and the mechanics of inflation. *Bell Journal of Economics, 9,* 549–571.

Walker, G., & Weber, D. (1984). A transaction cost approach to make-or-buy decisions. *Administrative Science Quarterly, 29,* 373–391.

Walking, R., & Long, M. (1984). Agency theory, managerial welfare, and takeover bid resistance. *Rand Journal of Economics, IS,* 54–68.

Walsh, D. (1972). Varieties of Positivism. In Filmer et al. (Eds.), *New directions of sociological theory,* op. cit.

Walsh, J. P., & Seward, J. K. (1990). On the efficiency of internal and external corporate control mechanisms. *Academy of Management Review, 15,* 421–458.

Weber, M. (1947). *The theory of social and economic organization* (T. Parsons, Trans.). New York: Free Press.

Weber, M. (1978). *Economy and society* (2 vols., G. Roth & C. Wittich, Eds.). Berkeley: University of California Press. (Originally published in 1922)

Weick, K. E. (1969). *The social psychology of organizing.* Reading, MA: Addison-Wesley.

Weick, K. E. (1979). Cognitive processes in organizations. In B. M. Staw (Ed.), *Research in organizational behavior* (Vol. 1, pp. 41–74). Greenwich, CT: JAI Press.

Weick, K. E. (1996). Drop your tools: An allegory for organizational studies. *Administrative Science Quarterly, 41,* 301–313.

Weisbrod, B. (1979). *Economics of institutional choice.* Unpublished manuscript.

Werner, S., & Tosi, H. L. (1995). Other people's money: The effects of ownership on compensation strategy and managerial pay. *Academy of Management Journal, 38,* 1672–1691.

White, H. (1985). Agency as control. In J. Pratt & R. Zeckhauser (Eds.), *Principals and agents: The structure of business* (pp. 187–214). Boston: Harvard Business School Press.

Whitley, R. D. (1984). *The intellectual and social organisation of the sciences.* Oxford, UK: Oxford University Press.

Whyte, W. F. (1959.) *Man and organization.* Homewood, IL: R. D. Irwin.

Wicks, A. C., & Freeman, R. E. (1998). Organization studies and the new pragmatism: Positivism, anti-positivism, and the search for ethics. *Organization Science, 9,* 123–140.

Wilkinson, A., & Willmott, H. (Eds.). (1995). *Making quality critical: New perspectives on organizational change.* London: Routledge.

Williams, M. J. (1985). Why chief executives pay keeps rising. *Fortune, 111*(7), 66–76.

Williamson, O. E. (1964). *The economics of discretionary behavior—Managerial objectives in a theory of the firm.* Englewood Cliffs, NJ: Prentice Hall.

Williamson, O. E. (1965, November). A dynamic theory of interfirm behavior. *Quarterly Journal of Economics.*

Williamson, O. E. (1967). Hierarchical control and optimum firm size. *Journal of Political Economy, 75,* 123–138.

Williamson, O. E. (1971). The vertical integration of production: Market failure considerations. *American Economic Review, 61,* 112–123.

Williamson, O. E. (1973). Markets and hierarchies: Some elementary considerations. *American Economic Review, 63,* 316–325.

Williamson, O. E. (1975). *Markets and hierarchies: Analysis and antitrust implications.* New York: Free Press.

Williamson, O. E. (1976). Franchise bidding for natural monopolies—In general and with respect to CATV. *Bell Journal of Economics, 7,* 73–104.

Williamson, O. E. (1979a). Assessing vertical market restrictions: Antitrust ramifications of the transaction cost approach. *University of Pennsylvania Law Review, 127,* 953–993.

Williamson, O. E. (1979b). *Public policy on saccharin: The decision process approach and its alternatives.* Unpublished manuscript.

Williamson, O. E. (1979c). Transaction-cost economics: The governance of contractual relations. *Journal of Law and Economics, 22,* 233–262.

Williamson, O. E. (1980). Emergence of the visible hand: Implications for industrial organization. In A. D. Chandler, Jr. (Ed.), *Managerial hierarchies* (pp. 183–202). Cambridge, MA: Harvard University Press.

Williamson, O. E. (1981). The economics of organizations: The transaction cost approach. *American Journal of Sociology, 87,* 548–577.

Williamson, O. E. (1985). *The economic institutions of capitalism.* New York: Free Press.

Williamson, O. E., & Ouchi, W. (1981). The markets and hierarchies and visible hand perspectives. In A. van de Ven & W. Joyce (Eds.), *Perspectives on organization design and behavior.* New York: Wiley.

Williamson, O. E., Wachter, M., & Harris, J. (1975). Understanding employment relations: The analysis of idiosyncratic change. *Bell Journal of Economics, 6,* 250–278.

Willmott, H. (1992). Postmodemism and excellence: The dedifferentiation of economy and culture. *Journal of Organizational Change Management, 5,* 58–68.

Willmott, H. (1993). Strength is ignorance, slavery is freedom: Managing culture in modern organizations. *Journal of Management Studies, 30,* 515–552.

Willmott, H. (2005). Theorizing contemporary control: Some post-structuralist responses to some critical realist questions. *Organization, 12,* 747–780.

Wilson, R. (1968). On the theory of syndicates. *Econometrica, 36,* 119–132.

Wolfson, M. (1985). Empirical evidence of incentive problems and their mitigation in oil and gas shelter programs. In J. Pratt & R. Zeckhauser (Eds.), *Principals and agents: The structure of business* (pp. 101–126). Boston: Harvard Business School Press.

Woodward, J. (1965). *Industrial organization: Theory and practice.* London: Oxford University Press.

Woolgar, S. (Ed.). (1988). *Knowledge & reflexivity.* London: Sage.

Wuthnow, R., Hunter, J. D., Bergesen, A., & Kurzweil, E. (1984). *Cultural analysis.* Boston: Routledge & Kegan Paul.

Zald, M. (1970). Political economy: A framework for analysis. In M. N. Zald (Ed.), *Power in organizations* (pp. 221–261). Nashville, TN: Vanderbilt University Press.

Zald, M. N. (1996). More fragmentation? Unfinished business in linking the social sciences and the humanities. *Administrative Science Quarterly, 41,* 251–261.

Zenger, T. (1988). *Agency sorting, agent solutions and diseconomies of scale: An empirical investigation of employment contracts in high technology R&D.* Paper presented at the meeting of the Academy of Management, Anaheim, CA.

Zimbalist, A. (1975). The limits of work humanization. *Review of Radical Political Economics, 7,* 50–60.

Zucker, L. G. (1977). The role of institutionalization in cultural persistence. *American Sociological Review, 42,* 726–743.

Zucker, L. G. (1983). Organizations as institutions. In S. B. Bacharach (Ed.), *Research in the sociology of organizations* (2nd ed., pp. 1–47). Greenwich, CT: JAI Press.

Zucker, L. G. (1987). Institutional theories of organizations. *Annual Review of Sociology, 13,* 443–464.

Name Index

Subject Index

paradox of, 200
positive *vs.* negative, 39
Learning, adaptive, 206, 213n2
Legitimacy, external, 203, 224–225
Levels, hierarchical, 6, 7, 91
Liaison devices, 138–139
Line functions, 41, 51
Line integration, 46
Line of command, 112–113
Line organization, devolution of, 44–45
Linguistic approach, 264
Linguistic play, 266
Linguistic symbol, 264
Linguistic turn, 274
Long-linked technologies, 81
Long-range planning, 40, 47, 119

Machine bureaucracy, 143–144 (figure),
150 (table)–151 (table)
Making-out, 245
Malintegration, 25
Management
administrative, 39, 40, 50–51
control, 37, 50–52
functions of, 13
humanistic, 246, 258
knowledge and, 38, 90, 109, 277
operative, 39–40, 50–51
organic functions of, 50
principles of, 13
science, 38
science of, 38, 40
theory, classical, 12, 13, 33, 37–53
theory, international, 277
Management-controlled firms, 170–171
Management learning, 269
The Management of Innovation (Burns &
Stalker), 103–107
Management system
mechanistic, 8, 103–105, 107–108
organic, 103, 104, 105–107, 108
Managerial capitalism, 91, 169–171, 170
Managerial discretion, 170
Managerialism model, 170–171
Managerial sociology, subjectivist, 244
Manifest functions, 28, 32n14
Manufacturing
routine, 129 (figure)–130
See also Production
"Margins" of organization studies,
260, 267, 274
Market
capital, 147, 153, 165, 179, 184, 189, 190
diversity of, 141, 146–147

efficient, 165
environment of, 9, 14, 90
external, 171
failure of, 175
free, 38
as governance mechanism, 156–157,
180, 183, 189
vertical restrictions on, 179
See also Markets and Hierarchies
(M&H) program
Market contracting, 92, 174
obligational, 177
relational, 185
Market discipline, effects on agency
relationship, 164
Marketing, routinized, 123
Markets and Hierarchies (M&H) program,
173–180
applications of, 178–180, 188–190
behavioral assumptions, 175–176
conceptual framework, 175
(figure)–176
contractual relations, 177–178
core methodological properties, 190
origins of, 174–175
See also Organizational design
Marxists, New Left, 257
Marxist theory, 26, 29, 32n12
worker as everyman in,
254 (table)–256 (table)
Masculinities, 275
Matrix organization, 139, 140
McDonaldization, 241
Means/ends relationship, 161–162
Measurability of outcome, 160, 166
Mechanism, adaptive, 228
Mechanistic structure, 7, 8, 103–105,
106, 107–108, 111, 113, 128
Mediating technology, 81
Memetic mechanism, 220, 226, 227
Merger, 146, 164, 170, 280
Metanarrative, 279
incredulity toward, 261
Metatheory, 262
Methodological debate, 20–21, 23
M-form organization, 179, 189
Middle line, 135 (figure), 136
Miniorganization, 136
Mintzberg, Henry, 133–151
Mission, 50, 217
Mixed model, 123–124
Modernist logic, 267
Modernist theory of, 263–264
Modernization, societal, 219

Poststructuralism
  analytics, 267, 270–271
  antiessentialism and, 273
  as theory, 235, 264
  as theory of modernism, 263–264
  authorship notion in, 265
  feminist, 273–275
  genealogies and, 269
  knowledge and, 264–265, 271–272
  language in, 265–266
  perspectives in, 260
  postcolonial analyses and, 275–277
  postmodernism and, 263
  relationship with postmodernism, 263–264
  signification and, 264
Power
  coercive, 73, 224
  defined, 72
  dynamics of, 253, 257
  involvement and, 73
  knowledge relation to, 260, 266, 268,
      271, 272, 274, 276, 278
  moral, 72–73
  remunerative, 72
  social, 72–73, 197
  type of organization and, 72, 73–75,
      187–188
Pragmatism, 235, 263
Pressure, peer, 268
Price mechanism, 161
Primary compliance structure, 73
Primary objective, of business
    organization, 38
Principle-agent theory, 156–160, 165–166
Principle of the primacy of the service
    objective, 48
Principles, of management, 13
Private property, right of, 4, 38, 44
Privilege, studies on, 275
Problem, analyzable, 128–129
Problematization
  of foundational theorizing, 270–271
  of subject/author, 261, 266, 280–281
Problem-solving process, 100, 101
Procedural safeguards, 186
Procedure, business, 52–53
Process
  administrative, 87–88, 115
  analytic, 99
Process specialization, 101, 138
Process technology, 114–115
Production
  batch, and technological change, 120
  continuous process, 113, 119, 181

cost of, 181
  large batch, 113, 117
  mass, 117, 143–144, 183
  routinized, 123
  small batch, 114, 117
  social relations of, 257
  stable environment for, 124
  system of, 112 (table), 113, 115, 131
  system of, mixed, 115–116
  technical, 139
  unit, 113, 117
Professional body, 231
Professional bureaucracy, 144–146, 145
    (figure), 150 (table)–151 (table)
Professionalization, and coordination, 208
Professional organization, 74–75, 146
Profit, 38, 39, 53, 169, 177
Profitability, maximizing, 9–10, 69,
    178, 179
Program coherence, 228
Programmability, of behavior/tasks,
    159–160
Programs, 100–101
  development/elaboration of new, 102
  innovative, 101–102
Promotion ladder, 186
Property-based knowledge, 257
Property-based power, 257
Propositions, 8, 13
Psychic process, 246, 258
Psychological factors, in behavior, 57
Psychology, 91, 263
  managerial, 246
  organizational, 233
Purpose, of organization
  formulating and defining, 61–62
  vs. individual motive, 62

Quality of life, 241
Queer theory, 275

Race, 252, 274, 275, 276
Racial harassment, 241
Racialization of theory, 275
Radical change, sociology of, 30–31
Radical organization theory, 246–253
Rational decision maker *vs.* mindless
    mechanical worker, 270
Rational form of organization, 212
Rationality
  cognitive limits of, 99–101
  collective, 203
  economic, 94–95
  enlightenment, 261, 264

About the Author

Henry L. Tosi is currently the McGriff Professor of Management Emeritus at the University of Florida. He received his PhD from the Ohio State University in 1964. Before coming to Gainesville, he was on the faculty at Michigan State University and at the University of Maryland. In the United States, he has been a visiting faculty member at the University of California, Irvine, Emory University, and Cornell University. He also has held visiting appointments in Italy at Luigi Bocconi University (Milan), LUISS (Rome), the University of Catania in Sicily, and the University of Modena. He has been the president of the Midwest Division of the Academy of Management and is a founding member of the Organizational Behavior Division and the Research Methods Division of the Academy of Management, where he has also served on the board of governors. In addition, he has served on the editorial review boards of *Administrative Science Quarterly,* the *Journal of Business Research,* and the *Academy of Management Review.* Along with Bernard Bass and Robert House, he is a founding editor of *Leadership Quarterly.*

His research has covered a range of diverse topics. His work on Management by Objectives was among the first serious research studies on the role of goals and goal setting in organizations. His most recent work has been on CEO compensation issues and organizational control. His scholarly papers have appeared in the *Academy of Management Journal,* the *Academy of Management Review, Administrative Science Quarterly, Personnel Psychology,* the *Journal of Applied Psychology,* the *Journal of Business, Organization Science,* and the *Strategic Management Journal.*

25353667R00181

Made in the USA
Lexington, KY
21 August 2013